Econometrics of Qualitative Dependent Variables

This text aims to introduce students progressively to various aspects of qualitative models and assumes a knowledge of basic principles of statistics and econometrics. Inferring qualitative characteristics of data on socioeconomic class, education, employment status, and the like, given their discrete nature, requires an entirely different set of tools from those applied to purely quantitative data. Written in accessible language and offering cogent examples, the text offers students valuable means to gauge real-world economic phenomena. After the introduction, Chapters 2 through 6 present models with endogenous qualitative variables, examining dichotomous models, model specification, estimation methods, descriptive usage, and qualitative panel data. Tobit models, in which the exogenous variable is sometimes qualitative and sometimes quantitative, are the subject of Chapter 7. Changing-regime models, in which the dependent variable is qualitative but expressed in quantitative terms, follow in Chapters 8–10. The final two chapters describe models that explain variables assumed by discrete or continuous positive variables.

Christian Gourieroux is Professor of Mathematics and Head of the Finance and Insurance Laboratory at CREST-INSEE, Paris. He is the author of numerous articles in international journals and several books on statistics, econometrics, and finance, including *Statistics and Econometric Models* (2 volumes, 1995, coauthored with Alain Monfort) and *Time Series and Dynamic Models* (1996, coauthored with Alain Monfort) in the Themes in Modern Econometrics series published by Cambridge University Press. Professor Gourieroux is a Fellow of the Econometric Society and is regularly invited to give courses at universities around the world. In 1990 he was awarded (with Alain Monfort and Alain Trognon) the Koopmans Prize for the best paper published in *Econometric Theory*.

Themes in Modern Econometrics

Managing editor
PETER C.B. PHILLIPS, *Yale University*

Series editors
ADRIAN PAGAN, *Australian National University*
CHRISTIAN GOURIEROUX, *CREST and CEPREMAP, Paris*
MICHAEL WICKENS, *University of York*

Themes in Modern Econometrics is designed to service the large and growing need for explicit teaching tools in econometrics. It will provide an organised sequence of textbooks in econometrics aimed squarely at the student population, and will be the first series in the discipline to have this as its express aim. Written at a level accessible to students with an introductory course in econometrics behind them, each book will address topics or themes that students and researchers encounter daily. While each book will be designed to stand alone as an authoritative survey in its own right, the distinct emphasis throughout will be on pedagogic excellence.

Titles in the series

Statistics and Econometric Models: Volumes 1 and 2
CHRISTIAN GOURIEROUX and ALAIN MONFORT
Translated by QUANG VUONG

Time Series and Dynamic Models
CHRISTIAN GOURIEROUX and ALAIN MONFORT
Translated and edited by GIAMPIERO GALLO

Unit Roots, Cointegration, and Structural Change
G.S. MADDALA and IN-MOO KIM

Generalized Method of Moments Estimation
Edited by LÁSZLÓ MÁTYÁS

Nonparametric Econometrics
ADRIAN PAGAN and AMAN ULLAH

ECONOMETRICS OF QUALITATIVE DEPENDENT VARIABLES

CHRISTIAN GOURIEROUX
CREST-INSEE, Paris

Translated by Paul B. Klassen

CAMBRIDGE
UNIVERSITY PRESS

CAMBRIDGE
UNIVERSITY PRESS

32 Avenue of the Americas, New York NY 10013-2473, USA

Cambridge University Press is part of the University of Cambridge.

It furthers the University's mission by disseminating knowledge in the pursuit of education, learning and research at the highest international levels of excellence.

www.cambridge.org
Information on this title: www.cambridge.org/9780521589857

Originally published in French as *Econométrie des Variables Qualitatives* by Economica 1991
Published in English as Econometrics of Qualitative Dependent Variables by Cambridge University Press 2000

First published 2000

A catalogue record for this publication is available from the British Library

Library of Congress Cataloguing in Publication data

Gourieroux, Christian, 1949–

[Econométrie des variables qualitatives. English]
Econometrics of qualitative dependent variables / Christian Gourieroux; translated by Paul B. Klassen.

p. cm. – (Themes in modern econometrics)
Includes bibliographical references and index.
ISBN 0-521-33149-8
1. Econometrics. 2. Economics, Mathematical. I. Title. II. Series.
HB139 .G6813 2000
330'.01'5195 – dc21 00-029263

ISBN 978-0-521-33149-4 Hardback
ISBN 978-0-521-58985-7 Paperback

Contents

1 Introduction

1.1 Background

The study of models describing qualitative variables dates from the 1940s and 1950s (Berkson [Ber44], [Ber51]). Their initial applications were in the field of biology, followed by psychology and sociology. Only recently have these models been applied to economic data, where the development of qualitative models has taken two principal directions.

- It has often been possible to construct models of individual behaviour based directly on the underlying economic theory. This approach has led to a better understanding of the significance of certain common models, e.g. the logit model (McFadden [McF74]). Furthermore, the modelling of certain economic phenomena (consumption of durable goods, disequilibrium analysis, etc.), though strictly speaking not of a qualitative nature, draws heavily on these models (cf. Tobin [Tob58], Fair-Jaffee [FJ72] and Heckman [Hec76]).
- The second development has been the introduction of exogenous variables to explain the values assumed by the qualitative variable. The primary role of these models is explanatory. It is natural to compare these explanatory models to the traditional linear formulation.

1.2 Review of Qualitative Variables

1.2.1 Generalities

Statistical data available to the researcher often reflect qualitative characteristics of the study subjects, such as: socio-economic class, field of education, employment status, whether or not they have purchased a certain good, etc. Inference from this data requires an entirely different set of tools from those applied to the more typical quantitative data, as the former is characterized by its discrete nature and, frequently, the absence of a natural order.

In the text, we will formulate this problem as follows: let a variable y assume $K+1$ disjoint values denoted $k = 0, \ldots, K$. If $K+1 = 2\,(3)$, the variable y is called dichotomous (trichotomous). In the general case with K being some positive integer, y is called polychotomous (or polytomous).

When y is stochastic, its distribution is defined by the probabilities associated with k, these probabilities are denoted P_k, $k = 0, \ldots, K$.

1.2.2 Quantitative Representation of a Qualitative Variable

It is always possible to represent a qualitative variable quantitatively without losing any information: this process is known as *coding*. For example, let the variable y represent "socio-economic class" assuming $K+1 = 3$ possible values, defined:

0 — labourer,
1 — salaried employee,
2 — executive.

Example 1: Define the quantitative variable $\tilde{y}$ as:

$$\tilde{y} = \begin{cases} 1, & \text{if } y = \text{labourer}, \\ 2, & \text{if } y = \text{salaried employee}, \\ 3, & \text{if } y = \text{executive}. \end{cases}$$

From a given value of $\tilde{y}$ we can immediately derive the corresponding value of y, and vice versa.

Example 2: Consider the vector ε with three elements $\varepsilon = (\varepsilon_1, \varepsilon_2, \varepsilon_3)'$, defined:

$$\varepsilon_1 = \begin{cases} 1, & \text{if } y = \text{labourer}, \\ 0, & \text{otherwise}, \end{cases}$$

$$\varepsilon_2 = \begin{cases} 1, & \text{if } y = \text{salaried employee}, \\ 0, & \text{otherwise}, \end{cases}$$

$$\varepsilon_3 = \begin{cases} 1, & \text{if } y = \text{management}, \\ 0, & \text{otherwise}. \end{cases}$$

This is a different quantitative representation of y, now assuming values in $\{0, 1\}^3$. Notice that $\varepsilon_1 + \varepsilon_2 + \varepsilon_3 = 1$.

Example 3: A general formulation of all the quantitative representations of y can be written $\psi(y)$, where ψ is a one-to-one mapping of $\{0, 1, 2\}$ into $\mathbb{R}^p$.

We now generalize these results to the case of a qualitative variable y assuming $K+1$ values. The coding of example 1 now becomes $\tilde{y} = k+1$ if $y = k$. From example 2 we have $\varepsilon = (\varepsilon_1 \ldots, \varepsilon_{K+1})'$ with:

$$\varepsilon_k = \begin{cases} 1, & \text{if } y = k-1, \\ 0, & \text{otherwise.} \end{cases}$$

We still observe that:

$$\sum_{k=1}^{K+1} \varepsilon_k = 1.$$

The primary advantage of using a quantitative representation of the data is that it allows us to work with discrete distributions on $\mathbb{R}$, or on $\mathbb{R}^p$. The distribution of ε is seen to be multinomial, since ε_k is a Bernoulli variable. We must, however, exercise care associating distributions with these representations, the only information truly representative of the quantitative variable y is that which is independent of the function ψ. It is comprised in the values assumed by $P_0, \ldots, P_K$.

Example 4: We cannot accord much significance to the moments (mean, variance, etc.) of the function $\psi(y)$. Notice, though, that in the case of the coding ε the mathematical expectation may be used to recover the vector of probabilities $\mathbf{P} = (P_0, \ldots P_K)'$.

Example 5: Consider a second quantitative variable, x. A traditional method of testing for dependence between x and y is to calculate the correlation coefficient. In the case of qualitative variables both the sign and the value of this statistic $\rho[x, \psi(y)]$ depend upon the coding, ψ.

Example 6: We may, however, still test for independence. If ψ and ψ^* are two different codings, and if x and $\psi(y)$ are independent, then x and $\psi^*(y)$ will also be independent.

Example 7: Most importantly (as it constitutes the raison-d'être for this book), linear regression methods are not generally applicable to these coded variables. We cannot simultaneously have:

$$\mathrm{E}[\psi(y)|x] = \mathbf{xb}$$

and

$$\mathrm{E}\left[\psi^*(y)\middle|x\right] = \mathbf{xc}.$$

1.2.3 Vectors of Qualitative Variables

Consider Q qualitative variables $y_q, q = 1, \ldots, Q$ assuming $K_q + 1$ values $k_q, k_q = 0, \ldots, K_q$ respectively. The vector $\mathbf{y} = \left(y_1, \ldots, y_Q\right)'$ can be viewed as a qualitative variable whose domain is restricted to the $\sum_{q=1}^{Q}\left(K_q + 1\right)$ values $\left(k_1, \ldots, k_Q\right)$. The corresponding probabilities are denoted $P_{k_1}, \ldots, P_{k_Q}$.

Conversely, any given polychotomous qualitative variable can be expressed as a vector of dichotomous qualitative variables. We have seen that a variable y assuming $K + 1$ values can be represented by $\varepsilon = (\varepsilon_1, \ldots, \varepsilon_{K+1})'$, where $\varepsilon_k = \{0, 1\}$ indicates whether or not y assumes the value $k - 1$.

Consequently, there is no fundamental difference between the study of one qualitative variable and that of a series of such variables. Nonetheless, the vector representation shall prove practical when we turn our attention to the issues of dependence between several variables and calculation of marginal and conditional distributions.

1.3 Overview of the Book

The chapters are organized so as to introduce the various aspects of qualitative models progressively. Chapters 2 through 6 present models with endogenous qualitative variables. In chapter 7 we look at models within which the exogenous variable is sometimes quantitative and sometimes qualitative. Chapters 8 through 10 are devoted to changing-regime models, where the dependent variable is quantitative, but is expressed in terms of a qualitative variable. The final two chapters describe models which explain values assumed by discrete or continuous positive variables.

The simplest models arise when the qualitative endogenous variable is dichotomous (cf. chapter 2). Our examination of this case shall provide an opportunity to clearly establish the difference between quantitative and qualitative dependent variable models, and to explore in some detail the principal estimation methods.

The process of model building itself assumes more importance when we move into the domain of quantitative variables taking more than two values. In contrast to what we shall encounter in the dichotomous case, polychotomous qualitative dependent variables can be modelled using significantly different functional forms. In these cases specification must be based upon economic reasoning. Examples of this are explored in chapter 3. Estimation methods, and the properties of the corresponding estimators, are discussed in chapter 4.

Chapter 5 is devoted to the descriptive use of qualitative models. In this chapter we introduce the log-linear model, which is of particular use for analysing independence between variables.

The introduction of panel data poses a further problem: we now must account for possible correlations between the observations. In chapter 6 we examine a partial solution to this problem using Markov chains.

In chapter 7 we turn our attention to models in which the dependent variable is quantitative, but is constrained by a threshold (floor or ceiling). This cut-off point may be fixed (the simple Tobit model), or random (the generalized Tobit model). These models combine a qualitative aspect (reflecting whether or not the threshold has been reached) and a quantitative aspect (for the unconstrained range of the data). This structure is very important in economics, where it is used to analyse the consumption of durable goods and the behaviour of disequilibrium markets, for example. This latter application is examined in detail in chapter 8.

It is possible to find a general formulation incorporating all of the above-mentioned models, qualitative and Tobit, as special cases, and this is the subject of chapters 9 and 10. The purpose of this exercise is not only to create a unified theory of the econometrics of limited dependent variables, but also to expand our analysis to include more than one endogenous variable, limited or not, and in particular to account for the existence of simultaneity. Furthermore, this exercise focuses our attention on some of the problems occurring in the construction of such models, especially the issue of identification.

The Tobit model may be viewed as an intermediate form between qualitative and linear models. Other intermediate forms are obtained from models of variables with integer dependent values (chapter 11).

Finally, the modelling of discrete variables is closely tied to the issue of modelling durations. This is the topic of chapter 12.

This book presupposes knowledge of the basic principles of statistics and econometrics. Suggested references are Johnston [Joh84] and Theil [The71].

2 The Simple Dichotomy

In this chapter we shall study the modelling of dichotomous endogenous variables. These variables may assume two values, usually denoted zero (0) and one (1). The models presented here are a subset of those introduced in chapters 3 and 4, yet they merit separate treatment because their very simplicity allows us to highlight some of the issues with which this book will deal. We shall illustrate the basic differences between qualitative and quantitative models and introduce some of the estimation methods which shall be generalized subsequently.

2.1 Why not Use a Linear Model?

A specific treatment of models with qualitative endogenous variables is worthy of interest only insofar as the issues with which they deal with cannot be adequately handled by the classical linear model with its associated least-squares estimators, ordinary or generalized.

Assume we have n observations on an endogenous variable y_i, $i = 1, \ldots, n$ with corresponding vectors of K exogenous variables denoted $\mathbf{x}_i = (x_{1i}, \ldots, x_{Ki})^\dagger$, $i = 1, \ldots, n$. The linear model is written:

$$y_i = \mathbf{x}_i \mathbf{b} + u_i, \quad i = 1, \ldots, n, \tag{2.1}$$

where $\mathbf{b}$ is a K-dimensional vector of unknown parameters and u_i is the disturbance (error) term associated with the i-th observation. When y is dichotomous, this formulation is clearly inadequate. Following are some reasons, which draw on both intuition and mathematical reasoning.

† The vector $\mathbf{x}_i$ is often represented $\mathbf{x}_{i.}$ to reflect the fact that we are referring to all columns of the i-th row of the $n \times k$ matrix X. In what follows there is no ambiguity, so we shorten the notation.

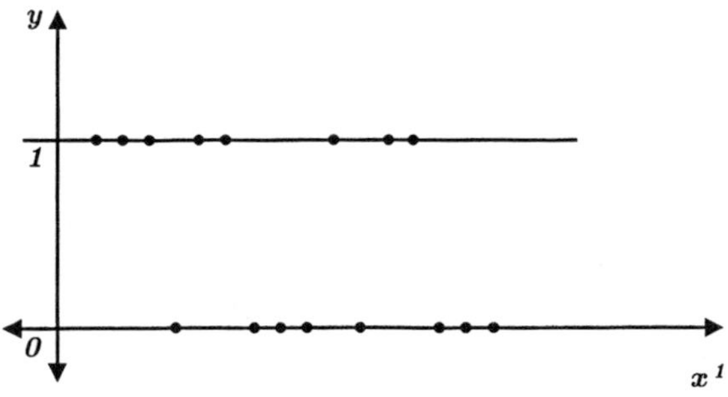

Fig. 2.1. Scatter of $y = \{0, 1\}$

(i) The two sides of equation (2.1) are different types of mathematical entity: y_i is a discrete variable, while $\mathbf{x}_i\mathbf{b} + u_i$ is continuous. There is obviously something wrong here.

(ii) The coding on the left hand side of equation (2.1) is fundamentally arbitrary. A given estimate of $\mathbf{b}$, say $\mathbf{b}_0$, generated by one coding will differ from that obtained from another. For example, if the coding $y = (0, 1)$ yields an estimator $\mathbf{b}_0$, then letting $y = (0, 2)$ will generate $2\mathbf{b}_0$. Consequently, the value of the parameter $\mathbf{b}$ is meaningless.

(iii) The inadequacy of the linear formulation can also be illustrated graphically. Consider the special case of equation (2.1) corresponding to a simple regression:

$$y_i = b_0 + x_i b_1 + u_i, \quad i = 1, \ldots, n.$$

If we plot the observations (x_i, y_i) in the usual Cartesian plane, the data points will be strung out along the two parallel lines $y = 0$ and $y = 1$, making it difficult to fit them with a single straight line! This is depicted in figure 2.1.

These intuitive arguments are sufficient grounds for rejecting the linear model in equation (2.1), but they are reinforced by considerations of a more mathematical nature.

(iv) For fixed values of the vector $\mathbf{x}_i$ the disturbance term u_i can only assume one of the following values: $1 - \mathbf{x}_i\mathbf{b}$, or $-\mathbf{x}_i\mathbf{b}$. Thus the distribution of the error term is discrete. It is not, in particular, normal.

(v) Turning our attention now to the probability distribution associated with y, we see that requiring the disturbance to have zero mean implies that P_i is uniquely determined, because:

$$\mathrm{E}(u_i) = P_i(1 - \mathbf{x}_i\mathbf{b}) - (1 - P_i)\mathbf{x}_i\mathbf{b} = 0 \Rightarrow P_i = \mathbf{x}_i\mathbf{b}.$$

Notice that this imposes the following constraints on the parameters:

$$0 \leq \mathbf{x}_i \mathbf{b} \leq 1, \quad i = 1, \ldots, n.$$

These constraints may be incompatible with the data.

(vi) If the constraints are not incompatible, we encounter at least two more difficulties. First, the parameter vector **b** must be estimated subject to inequality constraints. Second, it is possible to forecast the value y_{n+1} only if $0 \leq \mathbf{x}_n \mathbf{b} \leq 1$ implies $0 \leq \mathbf{x}_{n+1} \mathbf{b} \leq 1$.

(vii) Finally, turning to the error variance, we have:

$$\begin{aligned} \operatorname{var}(u_i) &= (1 - \mathbf{x}_i \mathbf{b})^2 P_i + (-\mathbf{x}_i \mathbf{b})^2 (1 - P_i), \\ &= (1 - \mathbf{x}_i \mathbf{b})^2 \mathbf{x}_i \mathbf{b} + (\mathbf{x}_i \mathbf{b})^2 (1 - \mathbf{x}_i \mathbf{b}), \\ &= \mathbf{x}_i \mathbf{b} (1 - \mathbf{x}_i \mathbf{b}). \end{aligned}$$

Notice that this variance is heteroscedastic. However, the method of weighted least squares is not applicable here, since the covariance matrix of the errors depends on the same unknown parameter **b** which appears on the right hand side of equation (2.1).

2.2 Modelling the Simple Dichotomy

The models in this chapter were first developed in the biological sciences, but are now widely applied. They are most frequently used to investigate the level of tolerance which individuals (be they insects, weeds, or people) have to some product (insecticide, herbicide, or drug). To this end numerous experiments are performed in which individuals with different characteristics are placed under differing environmental conditions and given varying dosages of the product. For each trial the individuals' reactions to the test are observed and the values:

$$y_i = \begin{cases} 0, & \text{if the individual withstands the dosage,} \\ 1, & \text{if the individual succumbs (or reacts) to the dosage,} \end{cases}$$

are assigned to the dichotomous endogenous variable.

The outcome y_i depends on the vector of conditions $\mathbf{x}_i$ associated with trial i and on the dose ℓ_i to which the individual was subjected. It is usual to complete the model by introducing an auxiliary variable y_i^* (known as the *latent* variable) representing the maximum dose the subject of the i-th trial can withstand. This variable is a function of the vector $\mathbf{x}_i$ and can be considered random, since two individuals with the same characteristics, placed under the same conditions, will not necessarily react identically.

The observed qualitative variable is defined in terms of this auxiliary variable by:

$$y_i = \begin{cases} 0, & \text{if } y_i^* > \ell_i, \\ 1, & \text{otherwise.} \end{cases} \tag{2.2}$$

It remains to specify how the threshold tolerance, as represented by the latent variable, depends on the conditions of the experiment. The usual form adopted is the linear model

$$y_i^* = \mathbf{x}_i \mathbf{b} + u_i, \quad i = 1, \ldots, n. \tag{2.3}$$

In equation (2.3) the disturbance terms u_i are assumed independent and identically distributed, with zero mean and a shared cumulative density function (c.d.f.) which is known up to a scaling parameter. In other words, we assume that the random variable $\frac{u_i}{\sigma}$ has c.d.f. F, where σ is an unknown positive parameter.

Notice that the assumption of independent disturbances is not innocuous. In our experimental example, this assumption requires that the trials be performed on different groups of individuals, otherwise the result of one trial may incorporate the impact of previous participation by the same subject.

Notice also that equation (2.3) is logically consistent, in that both sides of the equation are continuous.

The distribution of y follows easily from equations (2.2) and (2.3):

$$\begin{aligned} \Pr(y_i = 1) &= \Pr\left(y_i^* < \ell_i\right), \\ &= \Pr(\mathbf{x}_i \mathbf{b} + u_i < \ell_i), \\ &= \Pr\left(\frac{u_i}{\sigma} < \frac{\ell_i}{\sigma} - \frac{\mathbf{x}_i \mathbf{b}}{\sigma}\right), \\ &= F\left(\frac{\ell_i}{\sigma} - \frac{\mathbf{x}_i \mathbf{b}}{\sigma}\right), \\ &= P_i \text{ (by construction).} \end{aligned}$$

Appealing to the assumption of independence, we obtain the likelihood:

$$\begin{aligned} L(\mathbf{y}; \mathbf{b}, \sigma) &= \prod_{i=1}^{n} \left[P_i^{y_i} (1 - P_i)^{1-y_i}\right], \\ &= \prod_{i=1}^{n} \left\{F\left(\frac{\ell_i}{\sigma} - \frac{\mathbf{x}_i \mathbf{b}}{\sigma}\right)^{y_i} \left[1 - F\left(\frac{\ell_i}{\sigma} - \frac{\mathbf{x}_i \mathbf{b}}{\sigma}\right)\right]^{1-y_i}\right\}. \end{aligned}$$

To simplify notation, let $\mathbf{z}_i$ denote the row vector of exogenous variables

$$\mathbf{z}_i = (\ell_i, -\mathbf{x}_i),$$

and define the vector of parameters:

$$\mathbf{c} = \frac{1}{\sigma}\begin{bmatrix} 1 \\ \mathbf{b} \end{bmatrix}.$$

The model may then be written:

$$L(\mathbf{y}; \mathbf{c}) = \prod_{i=1}^{n} \left\{ F(\mathbf{z}_i \mathbf{c})^{y_i} \left[1 - F(\mathbf{z}_i \mathbf{c})\right]^{1-y_i} \right\}, \tag{2.4}$$

where F is a c.d.f. with zero mean.

Henceforth, we shall call this model the *simple dichotomy*. Expression (2.4) follows from the formulation of $P_i = \Pr(y_i = 1)$ and the hypothesis of independence of the y_i^*-s. As we shall see in section 3.4.2, relaxing these assumptions yields different models with dichotomous dependent variables.

2.3 Examples

The models in section 2.2 have numerous applications, of which we give two examples.

2.3.1 Choice of University

Several of the earliest economic studies using qualitative response models focused on the behaviour of students, in particular on what motivates them to choose a particular institute of higher education. Studies of this kind were developed mainly in the United States, as a result of the organizational structure of university education in that country (cf. Kohn-Manski-Mundel [KMM76] and Miller-Radner [MR70]).

We begin by dividing the universities into two groups: residential and non-residential. Students choose which type to attend based on a vector of characteristics, including: income, gender, distance of the university from home, and personal preference vis-à-vis living on or off campus.

The probability that a student chooses to study at a residential institution can be written:

$$\Pr(y_i = 1) = F(\mathbf{x}_i \mathbf{b})$$

where $\mathbf{x}_i$ is student i's vector of characteristics.

Estimation of this model using survey data shows that, *ceteris paribus*, the probability increases with distance and with income, as in figure 2.2.

We also observe that the probability of choosing a residential institution is positively correlated with an expressed preference for living on campus. The fact that students' choices reflect their preferences is hardly surprising, but it is interesting to note that preference appears less important than income and distance.

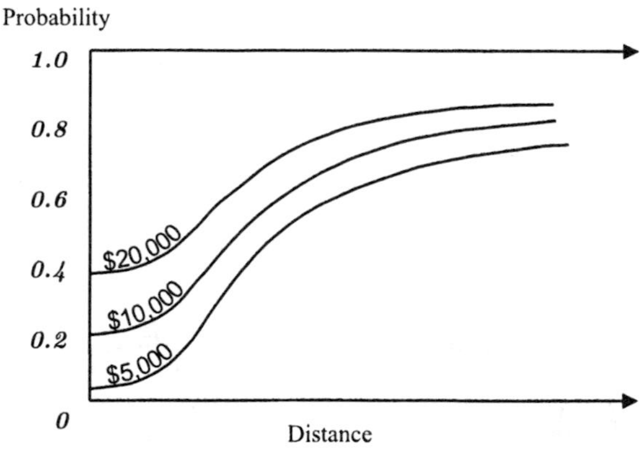

Fig. 2.2. Probability of living on campus (men who prefer living on campus)

A further result is that men are more likely that women to live in residence.

2.3.2 Non-Response

In any survey, there is always a certain proportion of non-respondents. This may be due to: refusal to participate, failure to understand the questions, or absence from home when the interviewer calls. The non-response rate depends on the method of data collection as well as on the personal characteristics (age, education, gender) of both respondents and interviewers. Clearly, it is important to understand how non-response depends on these factors in order to find ways of diminishing its incidence.

This problem reduces to describing the dichotomous variable "does/does not respond" as a function of other variables, which can be dealt with using a model of the form (2.4).

2.4 Estimation by the Maximum-Likelihood Method

2.4.1 The Likelihood Equation

We have seen that, once the identifiable parameters are established, the likelihood function of the simple dichotomy is written:

$$L(\mathbf{y}; \mathbf{b}) = \prod_{i=1}^{n} \left\{ F(\mathbf{x}_i \mathbf{b})^{y_i} \left[1 - F(\mathbf{x}_i \mathbf{b})\right]^{1-y_i} \right\}, \tag{2.5}$$

where F is a cumulative density function with zero mean.

To complete the model we need to specify F. It is common to select either a standard normal distribution, in which case the model is known as the *probit model*, or a logistic distribution, yielding the *logit model*.

Specifically, we have:

$$F(x) = \Phi(x) = \int_{-\infty}^{x} \frac{1}{\sqrt{2x}} e^{-\frac{t^2}{2}} dt$$

in the probit model, and:

$$F(x) = \frac{1}{1+e^{-x}}$$

in the logit model†. Both these distributions are symmetric with $F(-x) = 1 - F(x)$, so their means are zero.

2.4.2 *Uniqueness of the Maximum-Likelihood Estimator*

From equation (2.5) we obtain an expression for the log-likelihood:

$$\begin{aligned} \log(L) &= \sum_{i=1}^{n} \{y_i \log[F(\mathbf{x}_i\mathbf{b})] + (1-y_i)\log[1-F(\mathbf{x}_i\mathbf{b})]\}, \\ &= \sum_{i:y_i=1} \log[F(\mathbf{x}_i\mathbf{b})] + \sum_{i:y_i=0} \log[1-F(\mathbf{x}_i\mathbf{b})], \end{aligned} \tag{2.6}$$

A sufficient condition for uniqueness of the global maximum of $\log(L)$ (assuming it exists) is that this function be strictly concave or, equivalently, that $\log(F)$ and $\log(1-F)$ be strictly concave.

This condition holds in the case of both the probit and the logit models. We shall verify this for the logit model.

We have:

$$\begin{aligned} \frac{d}{dx}\left[\log F(x)\right] &= \frac{1}{F(x)}\frac{d}{dx}F(x), \\ &= \frac{e^{-x}}{1+e^{-x}}, \\ &= 1 - F(x). \end{aligned}$$

Furthermore:

$$\begin{aligned} \frac{d^2}{dx^2}\left[\log F(x)\right] &= \frac{-e^{-x}}{(1+e^{-x})^2}, \\ &= -F(x)[1-F(x)] < 0, \end{aligned}$$

† In keeping with convention, throughout this book Φ represents the cumulative densify function of the normal distribution.

so log (F) is strictly concave. And:

$$\log[1 - F(x)] = \log \frac{e^{-x}}{1 + e^{-x}},$$
$$= -x + \log[F(x)],$$

which is also strictly concave.

The demonstration for the probit case, where $F = \Phi$, is left to the reader (cf. exercise 4 at the end of the chapter).

Thus, in the two standard cases, the maximum-likelihood (ML) estimator may be obtained from the first-order conditions for a maximum.

2.4.3 Solving the Likelihood Equation

Let us differentiate the log-likelihood function (2.6) with respect to the parameter vector **b** and set the vector of derivatives equal to zero:

$$\frac{\partial \log L}{\partial \mathbf{b}} = \sum_{i:y_i=1} \frac{f(\mathbf{x}_i\mathbf{b})}{F(\mathbf{x}_i\mathbf{b})}\mathbf{x}_i' - \sum_{i:y_i=0} \frac{f(\mathbf{x}_i)}{1 - F(\mathbf{x}_i\mathbf{b})}\mathbf{x}_i' = 0, \tag{2.7}$$

where f is the density function associated with F and $\mathbf{x}_i'$ denotes the transpose of $\mathbf{x}_i$.

$$0 = \sum_{i=1}^{n} \left[\frac{y_i}{F(\mathbf{x}_i\mathbf{b})} - \frac{1 - y_i}{1 - F(\mathbf{x}_i\mathbf{b})}\right] f(\mathbf{x}_i\mathbf{b})\,\mathbf{x}_i',$$
$$= \sum_{i=1}^{n} \frac{y_i - F(\mathbf{x}_i\mathbf{b})}{F(\mathbf{x}_i\mathbf{b})\,[1 - F(\mathbf{x}_i\mathbf{b})]} f(\mathbf{x}_i\mathbf{b})\,x_i'.$$

In the logit model we can simplify this last equation using the fact that:

$$f(x) = F(x)\,[1 - F(x)] = \frac{e^{-x}}{(1 + e^{-x})^2},$$

yielding:

$$0 = \sum_{i=1}^{n} [y_i - F(\mathbf{x}_i\mathbf{b})]\,\mathbf{x}_i',$$
$$\sum_{i=1}^{n} y_i\mathbf{x}_i' = \sum_{i=1}^{n} F(\mathbf{x}_i\mathbf{b})\,\mathbf{x}_i'. \tag{2.8}$$

The likelihood equations associated with the probit and logit models are non-linear in the parameters. Simple closed-form expressions for the ML estimators are not available, so they must be solved using numerical algorithms (section 2.5 below).

2.4.4 Maximum-Likelihood Estimators: Existence and Asymptotic Properties

We have just seen that in the case of the probit and logit models the solution of the likelihood equation, assuming it exists, is unique and maximizes the function $\log(L)$. Existence of a solution, however, is not always assured. Consider, for example, the case of the logit model with a single, positive, explanatory variable x. Equation (2.8) then becomes:

$$\sum_{i=1}^{n} y_i x_i = \sum_{i=1}^{n} F(x_i b)\, x_i .$$

Now, both sides of this equation are bounded by zero and $(x_1 + \ldots + x_n)$. The left hand side equals zero when $y_i = 0, \forall i$, and equals $\sum x_i$ when $y_i = 1, \forall i$. The value assumed by the right hand side, however, is constrained to lie in the open interval $\left(0, \sum x\right)$. Thus the likelihood has a solution if, and only if, y assumes each of the values zero and one at least once in the sample.

The solution to the likelihood equation, even when it exists, does not necessarily have nice asymptotic properties. Consistency and asymptotic normality are assured only when certain conditions are imposed on the large-sample behaviour of the explanatory variables. There are two ways of dealing with this:

(i) Assume that the explanatory variables are stochastic. The conditions are then of the form "the $\mathbf{x}_i$-s are independent, identically distributed random variables admitting moments of sufficiently high order" (cf. Amemiya [Ame76] and McFadden [McF74]).

(ii) Assume that the explanatory variables are fixed, in which case the relevant conditions are that:

 (1) the asymptotic variance-covariance matrix of the y_i-s exists; or

 (2) the $\mathbf{x}_i$-s are bounded, i.e. for some fixed constants m, M; $m > -\infty$, $M < \infty$ we have:

$$m < x_i^k < M, \quad \forall i, k.$$

 (Gourieroux-Monfort [GM81]).

We shall assume from now on that one or the other of these conditions is satisfied. It follows that the maximum-likelihood estimator β_{ML} exists for all sufficiently large n, converges to the true value $\mathbf{b}$, and is asymptotically normally distributed with mean $\mathbf{b}$ and covariance matrix equal to the inverse of the Fisher information matrix:

$$I^{-1} = \left\{ -\mathrm{E}\left[\frac{\partial^2 \log(L)}{\partial \mathbf{b} \partial \mathbf{b}'} \right] \right\}^{-1} .$$

The expectation here is understood to be conditional on $\mathbf{x}$.

Summarizing our results, we have:

$$\beta_{ML} \sim \mathrm{N}\left(\mathbf{b}, \left\{-\mathrm{E}\left[\frac{\partial^2 \log(L)}{\partial\mathbf{b}\partial\mathbf{b}'}\right]\right\}^{-1}\right).$$

Notice, though, that we are indulging in a common and convenient abuse of mathematical language. The correct statement of the result is that:

$$\left\{-\mathrm{E}\left[\frac{\partial^2 \log(L)}{\partial\mathbf{b}\partial\mathbf{b}'}\right]\right\}^{\frac{1}{2}} (\beta_{ML} - \mathbf{b})$$

converges in distribution to $\mathrm{N}(0, I)$.

In practice, the asymptotic covariance matrix of β_{ML}, which depends on the unknown parameter $\mathbf{b}$, must be estimated. We do this by replacing $\mathbf{b}$ by β_{ML} in the expression:

$$\mathrm{var}_{asy}(\beta_{ML}) = \left\{-\mathrm{E}\left[\frac{\partial^2 \log(L)}{\partial\mathbf{b}\partial\mathbf{b}'}\right]\right\}^{-1}_{\mathbf{b}=\beta_{ML}}. \tag{2.9}$$

2.4.5 *Calculation of the Asymptotic Covariance Matrix*

The matrix of second derivatives [the Hessian matrix in equation (2.9)] is derived from expression (2.7):

$$\begin{aligned}
\frac{\partial^2 \log(L)}{\partial\mathbf{b}\partial\mathbf{b}'} &= \frac{\partial}{\partial\mathbf{b}}\left[\frac{\partial \log(L)}{\partial\mathbf{b}}\right]', \\
&= \sum_{i:y_i=1} \frac{f'F - f^2}{F^2}\mathbf{x}_i'\mathbf{x}_i - \sum_{i:y_i=0} \frac{f'(1-F) + f^2}{(1-F)^2}\mathbf{x}_i'\mathbf{x}_i, \\
&= \sum_{i=1}^{n} \left[\frac{f'F - f^2}{F^2}\mathbf{x}_i'\mathbf{x}_i y_i - \frac{f'(1-F) + f^2}{(1-F)^2}\mathbf{x}_i'\mathbf{x}_i(1-y_i)\right],
\end{aligned}$$

where $F = F(\mathbf{x}_i\mathbf{b})$ and $f = f(\mathbf{x}_i\mathbf{b})$.

The Fisher information matrix is obtained when we multiply through by minus one and take expectations. Using the fact that $\mathrm{E}(y_i) = F(\mathbf{x}_i\mathbf{b})$, we have:

$$I = \mathrm{E}\left[\frac{-\partial^2 \log(L)}{\partial\mathbf{b}\partial\mathbf{b}'}\right] = \sum_{i=1}^{n} \frac{[f(\mathbf{x}_i\mathbf{b})]^2}{F(\mathbf{x}_i\mathbf{b})[1 - F(\mathbf{x}_i\mathbf{b})]}\mathbf{x}_i'\mathbf{x}_i.$$

The asymptotic variance-covariance matrix of β_{ML} is therefore:

$$\mathrm{var}_{asy}(\beta_{ML}) = I^{-1} = \left\{\sum_{i=1}^{n} \frac{[f(\mathbf{x}_i\mathbf{b})]^2}{F(\mathbf{x}_i\mathbf{b})[1 - F(\mathbf{x}_i\mathbf{b})]}\mathbf{x}_i'\mathbf{x}_i\right\}^{-1},$$

and is estimated with:

$$\text{var}_{asy}(\mathbf{b}) = I^{-1} = \left\{ \sum_{i=1}^{n} \frac{[f(\mathbf{x}_i \boldsymbol{\beta}_{ML})]^2}{F(\mathbf{x}_i \boldsymbol{\beta}_{ML})[1 - F(\mathbf{x}_i \boldsymbol{\beta}_{ML})]} \mathbf{x}_i' \mathbf{x}_i \right\}^{-1}.$$

Remark 1: In the special case of the logit model:

$$f = F(1 - F),$$

and so:

$$\mathrm{E}\left[\frac{-\partial^2 \log(L)}{\partial \mathbf{b} \partial \mathbf{b}'}\right] = \sum_{i=1}^{n} F(\mathbf{x}_i \mathbf{b})[1 - F(\mathbf{x}_i \mathbf{b})]\, \mathbf{x}_i' \mathbf{x}_i.$$

Remark 2: It is possible to express the Hessian matrix in a more compact form. Let X be the $n \times k$ dimensional matrix of observations on the exogenous variables, and let $\mathbf{x}_i$ continue to represent the i-th row of this matrix. Denote Λ the diagonal matrix of order n whose i-th diagonal entry is:

$$\frac{[f(\mathbf{x}_i \mathbf{b})]^2}{F(\mathbf{x}_i \mathbf{b})[1 - F(\mathbf{x}_i \mathbf{b})]}.$$

Then:

$$\mathrm{E}\left[\frac{-\partial^2 \log(L)}{\partial \mathbf{b} \partial \mathbf{b}'}\right] = X' \Lambda X,$$

and:

$$\text{var}_{asy}(\boldsymbol{\beta}_{ML}) = \left(X' \Lambda X\right)^{-1}.$$

This form of the covariance matrix is reminiscent of the generalized least squares estimator.

2.5 Numerical Solution of the Likelihood Function

All of the commonly used approaches to the numerical solution of likelihood equations derive from Newton's method. Its direct application leads to the Newton-Raphson algorithm.

2.5.1 Newton-Raphson Method

The goal of this algorithm is to find a root of the equation:

$$\frac{\partial \log(L)}{\partial \mathbf{b}} = 0.$$

To this end, we choose an initial value $\mathbf{b}_0$ and consider the mapping of $\mathbf{b}$ onto the tangent plane:

$$\delta(\mathbf{b}) : \mathbf{b} \to d = \frac{\partial \log(L)}{\partial \mathbf{b}}.$$

The first-order Taylor expansion around an initial value $\mathbf{b}_0$ is†:

$$d = \frac{\partial \log[L(\mathbf{b})]}{\partial \boldsymbol{\beta}_0} + \frac{\partial^2 \log[L(\mathbf{b})]}{\partial \boldsymbol{\beta}_0 \partial \boldsymbol{\beta}_0'} (\mathbf{b} - \boldsymbol{\beta}_0),$$

which constitutes a linear approximation to the original map. We can therefore approach the desired solution with:

$$\frac{\partial \log[L(\mathbf{b})]}{\partial \boldsymbol{\beta}_0} + \frac{\partial^2 \log[L(\mathbf{b})]}{\partial \boldsymbol{\beta}_0 \partial \boldsymbol{\beta}_0'} (\boldsymbol{\beta}_1 - \boldsymbol{\beta}_0) = 0,$$

yielding:

$$\boldsymbol{\beta}_1 = \boldsymbol{\beta}_0 - \left\{ \frac{\partial^2 \log[L(\mathbf{b})]}{\partial \boldsymbol{\beta}_0 \partial \boldsymbol{\beta}_0'} \right\}^{-1} \frac{\partial \log[L(\mathbf{b})]}{\partial \boldsymbol{\beta}_0},$$

where $\boldsymbol{\beta}_1$ constitutes our first estimate of $\mathbf{b}$. We take this value as our starting point for the next iteration. The algorithm thus yields a sequence of approximate solutions $\{\boldsymbol{\beta}_h\}$ given by the recurrence formula:

$$\boldsymbol{\beta}_{h+1} = \boldsymbol{\beta}_h - \left\{ \frac{\partial^2 \log[L(\mathbf{b})]}{\partial \boldsymbol{\beta}_h \partial \boldsymbol{\beta}_h'} \right\}^{-1} \frac{\partial \log[L(\mathbf{b})]}{\partial \boldsymbol{\beta}_h}. \tag{2.10}$$

If the sequence $\{\boldsymbol{\beta}_h\}$ converges to a limit $\{\boldsymbol{\beta}\}$, then this limit must be a root of the likelihood equation, because:

$$\boldsymbol{\beta} = \lim_{h \to \infty} \boldsymbol{\beta}_{h+1} = \boldsymbol{\beta} - \left\{ \frac{\partial^2 \log[L(\mathbf{b})]}{\partial \boldsymbol{\beta} \partial \boldsymbol{\beta}'} \right\}^{-1} \frac{\partial \log[L(\mathbf{b})]}{\partial \boldsymbol{\beta}},$$

$$0 = \frac{\partial \log[L(\mathbf{b})]}{\partial \boldsymbol{\beta}}.$$

2.5.2 *The Method of Scoring*

This method consists of replacing the term:

$$\frac{\partial^2 \log[L(\mathbf{b})]}{\partial \boldsymbol{\beta} \partial \boldsymbol{\beta}'}$$

in equation (2.10) by its expectation conditional on $\mathbf{x}$. This can be justified

† $\frac{\partial \cdots}{\partial \boldsymbol{\beta}}$ represents the derivative of $\cdots$ with respect to b evaluated at $b = \boldsymbol{\beta}$.

when the model has good asymptotic properties, in particular in the case of random sampling from a "well-behaved" population. The recurrence formula then becomes:

$$\beta_{h+1} = \beta_h + \mathrm{E}\left\{-\frac{\partial^2 \log [L(\mathbf{b})]}{\partial\beta\partial\beta'}\right\}^{-1} \frac{\partial \log [L(\mathbf{b})]}{\partial\beta}. \tag{2.11}$$

In the special case of the simple dichotomy we can derive this formula in another way. Since $\mathrm{E}(y_i) = F(\mathbf{x}_i\mathbf{b})$ and $\mathrm{var}(y_i) = F(\mathbf{x}_i\mathbf{b})[1 - F(\mathbf{x}_i\mathbf{b})]$, we may write:

$$y_i = F(\mathbf{x}_i\mathbf{b}) + v_i,$$

where $\mathrm{E}(v_i) = 0$ and $\mathrm{var}(v_i) = F \cdot (1 - F)$.

If we know, *à priori,* that the true value of $\mathbf{b}$ is close to some known vector $\mathbf{b}_0$, it is reasonable to expand $F(\mathbf{x}_i\mathbf{b})$ linearly around $\mathbf{b}_0$. This yields:

$$y_i \approx F(\mathbf{x}_i\mathbf{b}_0) + f(\mathbf{x}_i\mathbf{b}_0)\,\mathbf{x}_i(\mathbf{b} - \mathbf{b}_0) + v_i$$

and:

$$y_i - F(\mathbf{x}_i\mathbf{b}_0) + f(\mathbf{x}_i\mathbf{b}_0)\,\mathbf{x}_i\mathbf{b}_0 \approx f(\mathbf{x}_i\mathbf{b}_0)\,\mathbf{x}_i\mathbf{b} + v_i.$$

The i-th observation on the endogenous variable is: $y_i - F(\mathbf{x}_i\mathbf{b}_0) + f(\mathbf{x}_i\mathbf{b}_0)\,\mathbf{x}_i\mathbf{b}_0$, and on the exogenous variable – $f(\mathbf{x}_i\mathbf{b}_0)\,\mathbf{x}_i$. The covariance matrix of $\mathbf{v}$ is approximated using the same matrix with β replacing $\mathbf{b}$. The weighted least-squares estimator of $\mathbf{b}$ is then:

$$\begin{aligned}
&\left\{\sum_{i=1}^{n} \frac{\mathbf{x}_i'[f(\mathbf{x}_i\beta_h)]^2\,\mathbf{x}_i}{F(\mathbf{x}_i\beta_h)[1 - F(\mathbf{x}_i\beta_h)]}\right\}^{-1} \\
&\quad\times \left\{\sum_{i=1}^{n} \frac{[y_i - F(\mathbf{x}_i\beta_h) + f(\mathbf{x}_i\beta_h)\,\mathbf{x}_i\beta_h]\,f(\mathbf{x}_i\beta_h)\,\mathbf{x}_i'}{F(\mathbf{x}_i\beta_h)[1 - F(\mathbf{x}_i\beta_h)]}\right\} \\
&= \mathrm{E}\left\{-\frac{\partial^2 \log [L(\beta_h)]}{\partial\mathbf{b}\partial\mathbf{b}'}\right\}^{-1} \\
&\quad\times \left(\frac{\partial \log [L(\beta_h)]}{\partial\mathbf{b}} + \mathrm{E}\left\{-\frac{\partial^2 \log [L(\beta_h)]}{\partial\mathbf{b}\partial\mathbf{b}'}\beta_h\right\}\right), \\
&= \beta_h + \mathrm{E}\left\{-\frac{\partial^2 \log [L(\beta_h)]}{\partial\mathbf{b}\partial\mathbf{b}'}\right\}^{-1} \frac{\partial \log [L(\beta_h)]}{\partial\mathbf{b}}, \\
&= \beta_{h+1}.
\end{aligned}$$

Thus, the recurrence formula obtained by successive application of linearization and weighted least-squares estimation is identical to that from the method of scoring.

2.5.3 *The Berndt-Hall-Hall-Hausman Method*

Moving from the Newton-Raphson algorithm to the method of scoring is a matter of replacing:

$$-\frac{\partial^2 \log(L)}{\partial \mathbf{b} \partial \mathbf{b}'} \text{ with } \mathrm{E}\left[-\frac{\partial^2 \log(L)}{\partial \mathbf{b} \partial \mathbf{b}'}\right].$$

From the right-hand side, we may write:

$$\mathrm{E}\left\{\sum_{i=1}^{n}\left[-\frac{\partial^2 \log(L_i)}{\partial \mathbf{b} \partial \mathbf{b}'}\right]\right\} = \sum_{i=1}^{n} \mathrm{E}\left[\frac{\partial \log(L_i)}{\partial \mathbf{b}} \frac{\partial \log(L_i)}{\partial \mathbf{b}'}\right],$$

where L_i denotes the likelihood of the i-th observation.

Removing the expectations operator we obtain a new algorithm involving only first-order derivatives. The recurrence formula is now:

$$\beta_{h+1} = \beta_h + \left\{\sum_{i=1}^{n} \frac{\partial \log[L_i(\beta_h)]}{\partial \mathbf{b}} \frac{\partial \log[L_i(\beta_h)]}{\partial \mathbf{b}'}\right\}^{-1} \frac{\partial \log[L(\beta_h)]}{\partial \mathbf{b}}. \tag{2.12}$$

2.5.4 *Convergence*

To ensure that these algorithms converge, and do so in a reasonable time, we should choose an initial value, β_0, which is likely to be close to the true value $\mathbf{b}$. Thus the statistical problem of estimating $\mathbf{b}$ in a manner which is simpler than maximum likelihood is not only interesting in its own right, but also yields useful results for ML estimation.

Even given a good start, convergence of these algorithms can still be rather slow when the recurrence formulas above are applied directly. It is possible to improve on each of the algorithms by using a variable step-length. In this vein, the Berndt-Hall-Hall-Hausman algorithm expands on the recurrence formula (2.12) by the introduction of a coefficient λ; $0 \leq \lambda \leq 1$, yielding:

$$\beta_{h+1} = \beta_h + \lambda_h \left\{\sum_{i=1}^{n} \frac{\partial \log[L_i(\beta_h)]}{\partial \mathbf{b}} \frac{\partial \log[L_i(\beta_h)]}{\partial \mathbf{b}'}\right\}^{-1} \times \frac{\partial \log[L(\beta_h)]}{\partial \mathbf{b}},$$

where λ_h is chosen by a search procedure to maximize the increase in the log-likelihood.

2.6 Grouped Data

2.6.1 Description

When applying qualitative models to data, we often encounter repetition in the values assumed by the exogenous variables such that these repeated values correspond to different values of the endogenous variable. This is often built into controlled experiments, but can also occur in samples of non-experimental data. The latter case may involve, for example, households grouped by characteristics (size, location, age of members, income class of household head, etc.) in cross-section studies.

Let $\mathbf{x}^j$, $j = 1, \ldots, J$, represent the J possible values of the vector of K explanatory variables, and call a "trial of type j" a run of the experiment performed under the conditions $\mathbf{x} = \mathbf{x}^j$. Let there be n_j such trials, the values of the dichotomous endogenous variable are denoted by y_i^j, $i = 1, \ldots, n_j$, $j = 1, \ldots, J$.

In this case the likelihood function (2.5) becomes:

$$L(\mathbf{y}; \mathbf{b}) = \prod_{j=1}^{J} \prod_{i=1}^{n_j} \left\{ F\left(\mathbf{x}^j \mathbf{b}\right)^{y_i^j} \left[1 - F\left(\mathbf{x}^j \mathbf{b}\right)\right]^{1-y_i^j} \right\},$$

$$= \prod_{j=1}^{J} \left\{ F\left(\mathbf{x}^j \mathbf{b}\right)^{\sum_{i=1}^{n_j} y_i^j} \left[1 - F\left(\mathbf{x}^j \mathbf{b}\right)^{n_j - \sum_{i=1}^{n_j} y_i^j}\right] \right\}.$$

Letting $\hat{p}_j$ denote the proportion of trials of type j for which $y = 1$:

$$\hat{p}_j = \frac{1}{n_j} \sum_{i=1}^{n_j} y_i^j,$$

we may write the likelihood in the form:

$$L(\mathbf{y}; \mathbf{b}) = \prod_{j=1}^{J} \left\{ F\left(\mathbf{x}^j \mathbf{b}\right)^{n_j \hat{p}_j} \left[1 - F\left(\mathbf{x}^j \mathbf{b}\right)\right]^{n_j(1-\hat{p}_j)} \right\}.$$

Notice that the observed frequencies $\hat{p}_j$, $j = 1, \ldots, J$, constitute sufficient statistics, so we can focus on their distributions. In fact, the products $n_j p_j$, $j = 1, \ldots, J$ are independent binomial variates with distributions parameterized by n_j and $P_j = F\left(\mathbf{x}_j \mathbf{b}\right)$. The likelihood is:

$$L(\hat{p}; \mathbf{b}) =$$

$$\prod_{j=1}^{J} \left\{ \frac{n_j!}{n_j \hat{p}_j! \left(n_j - n_j \hat{p}_j\right)!} F\left(\mathbf{x}^j \mathbf{b}\right)^{n_j \hat{p}_j} \left[1 - F\left(\mathbf{x}^j \mathbf{b}\right)\right]^{n_j(1-\hat{p}_j)} \right\}.$$

2.6.2 *Berkson's Method*

Assume that we are analysing data from an experiment which is repeated a large number of times under each of several sets of conditions. We shall see that the model can be approximated linearly.

Let J be given and assume that each of the integers $n_1, \ldots, n_J$ is large (notice that this assumption is stronger than that encountered in section 2.4.4, which merely stated that the sum $n = n_1 + \ldots + n_J$ be large). For each j, $\hat{p}_j$ is the sample mean of the large random sample $\left\{ y_i^j, i = 1, \ldots, n_j \right\}$. Since n_j is large, $\hat{p}_j$ is close to $\mathrm{E}\left(y_i^j\right) = F\left(\mathbf{x}^j \mathbf{b}\right) = p_j$ by the law of large numbers. Also, by the central limit theorem, the random variable $\sqrt{n_j}\left(\hat{p}_j - p_j\right)$ is approximately normally distributed with mean zero and variance equal to:

$$\operatorname{var}\left(y_i^j\right) = F\left(\mathbf{x}_i^j \mathbf{b}\right)\left[1 - F\left(\mathbf{x}_i^j \mathbf{b}\right)\right] = p_j\left(1 - p_j\right).$$

We can therefore write:

$$\hat{p}_j = F\left(\mathbf{x}_i^j \mathbf{b}\right) + v_i^j, \quad j = 1 \ldots J,$$

where the errors are independent and normally distributed with mean zero and variance:

$$\operatorname{var}\left(u_i^j\right) = \frac{p_j\left(1 - p_j\right)}{n_j}.$$

We still do not have a model which is linear in the parameter **b**, however. To move in that direction, we use Slutsky's well-known theorem on convergence in probability (cf. Cramer [Cra46]). Since n_j is large:

$$F^{-1}\left(\hat{p}_j\right) \approx F^{-1}\left(p_j\right) = F^{-1}\left[F\left(\mathbf{x}^j \mathbf{b}\right)\right] = \mathbf{x}^j \mathbf{b},$$

and the random variable:

$$\sqrt{n}_j\left[F^{-1}\left(\hat{p}_j\right) - F^{-1}\left(p_j\right)\right] = \sqrt{n_j}\left[F^{-1}\left(\hat{p}_j\right) - \mathbf{x}^j \mathbf{b}\right]$$

is approximately normally distributed with mean zero and variance:

$$p_j\left(1 - p_j\right)\left[\left(\frac{dF^{-1}(t)}{dt}\right)_{t=p_j}\right]^2 = \frac{p_j\left(1 - p_j\right)}{\left\{f\left[F^{-1}\left(p_j\right)\right]\right\}^2},$$

$$= \frac{p_j\left(1 - p_j\right)}{\left[f\left(\mathbf{x}^j \mathbf{b}\right)\right]^2}.$$

This brings us finally to the approximating model:

$$F^{-1}\left(\hat{p}_j\right) = \mathbf{x}^j \mathbf{b} + w_j, \quad j = 1, \ldots, J,$$

where the w_j-s are independent and normally distributed, with mean zero and variance:

$$\operatorname{var}\left(w_j\right) = \frac{p_j\left(1 - p_j\right)}{n_j\left[f\left(\mathbf{x}^j\mathbf{b}\right)\right]^2} = \frac{F\left(\mathbf{x}^j\mathbf{b}\right)\left[1 - F\left(\mathbf{x}^j\mathbf{b}\right)\right]}{n_j\left[f\left(\mathbf{x}^j\mathbf{b}\right)\right]^2}.$$

This approximation can be regarded as a model in which the deterministic part is linear in **b**. Notice that **b** enters into the expression for $\operatorname{var}\left(w_j\right)$, so the error term is heteroscedastic, though not serially correlated. The parameter **b** can therefore be estimated by weighted least squares, with weights obtained, for example, by replacing $\operatorname{var}\left(w_j\right)$ with:

$$\frac{\hat{p}_j\left(1 - \hat{p}_j\right)}{n_j\left\{f\left[F^{-1}\left(\hat{p}_j\right)\right]\right\}^2}.$$

In the case of the logit model, the variance of the disturbance term becomes:

$$\operatorname{var}\left(w_j\right) = \frac{F\left(\mathbf{x}^j\mathbf{b}\right)\left[1 - F\left(\mathbf{x}^j\mathbf{b}\right)\right]}{n_j\left[f\left(\mathbf{x}^j\mathbf{b}\right)\right]^2} = \frac{1}{n_j F\left(\mathbf{x}^j\mathbf{b}\right)\left[1 - F\left(\mathbf{x}^j\mathbf{b}\right)\right]}.$$

2.6.3 The Minimum Chi-Square Method

This method consists of finding parameter values minimizing a measure of the distance between the observed frequencies $\hat{p}_j$ and the theoretical frequencies $F\left(\mathbf{x}^j\mathbf{b}\right)$. Generally, the measure chosen is of the type used in classical χ^2 tests of goodness of fit. The distance for trials of type j is therefore:

$$\begin{aligned}
&\varphi_i^j\left(\mathbf{b}\right)\\
&= n_j\left(\frac{\left[\hat{p}_j - F\left(\mathbf{x}_i^j\mathbf{b}\right)\right]^2}{F\left(\mathbf{x}_i^j\mathbf{b}\right)} + \frac{\left\{\left(1 - \hat{p}_j\right) - \left[1 - F\left(\mathbf{x}_i^j\mathbf{b}\right)\right]\right\}^2}{1 - F\left(\mathbf{x}_i^j\mathbf{b}\right)}\right),\\
&= n_j\frac{\left[\hat{p}_j - F\left(\mathbf{x}_i^j\mathbf{b}\right)\right]^2}{F\left(\mathbf{x}_i^j\mathbf{b}\right)\left[1 - F\left(\mathbf{x}_i^j\mathbf{b}\right)\right]}.
\end{aligned}$$

The minimand over the entire set of observations is given by:

$$\begin{aligned}
\varphi_1\left(\mathbf{b}\right) &= \sum_{j=1}^{J}\varphi_i^j\left(\mathbf{b}\right),\\
&= \sum_{j=1}^{J} n_j\frac{\left[\hat{p}_j - F\left(\mathbf{x}_i^j\mathbf{b}\right)\right]^2}{F\left(\mathbf{x}_i^j\mathbf{b}\right)\left[1 - F\left(\mathbf{x}_i^j\mathbf{b}\right)\right]}.
\end{aligned}$$

Alternatively, we can minimize:

$$\varphi_2(\mathbf{b}) = \sum_{j=1}^{J} n_j \frac{\left[\hat{p}_j - F\left(\mathbf{x}_i^j \mathbf{b}\right)\right]^2}{\hat{p}_j\left(1-\hat{p}_j\right)}.$$

The estimator obtained by minimizing φ_2 is the same as that obtained by writing the model in the form $\hat{p}_j = F\left(\mathbf{x}_j b\right) + v_j$ (as in Berkson's method) and applying nonlinear least squares, with the obvious correction for heteroscedasticity.

Given that n_j is large, it is intuitively clear that there is little to choose between minimizing either φ_1 or φ_2. Unfortunately, neither set of first order conditions can be appreciably simplified, even if we specify the form of F (cf. section 4.4 below). Consequently, parameter estimation must be performed using numerical methods.

2.7 Example: Pass Rates of First-Year Medical Students in France

This study, described in Lassibile [1979], utilizes a logit model to explain a single dichotomous variable. The observed endogenous variable, y, reflects the grade received on the final examination by first-year medical students: $y_i = 0$ indicates a failing grade, $y_i = 1$—passing.

The probability of success is assigned the logistic form:

$$\Pr(y_i = 1) = \frac{1}{1 + \exp(-\mathbf{x}_i \mathbf{b})}.$$

The explanatory variables and their estimated coefficients are shown in table 2.1. Notice that the last four explanatory variables, excluding the constant, are dichotomous (dummy) variables. "Previous studies" is set to one if the student was enrolled in higher education the previous year, zero otherwise. "Type of high school" is assigned the value one if the student attended a public high school (in the French or American sense), zero otherwise. The last two dummy variables correspond to a three-way division of subject areas in the matriculation exam. The "omitted category", with both dummies taking the value zero, occurs when the student specialized in natural sciences.

Notice that the numerical value of an estimated coefficient has no direct interpretation, whereas its sign and significance have. The sign of a coefficient tells us whether the probability of passing the examination is an increasing or decreasing function, *ceteris paribus*, of the variable. Thus, for example, the negative coefficient on age implies that older students have less chance of passing, and significantly so, at the one percent level. Conversely, the insignificance at the five percent level of the coefficient of "type of high school" shows this to be a variable with little explanatory power with respect to success or failure in the exam.

Table 2.1. *Estimated coefficients of factors affecting pass rates*

Variable	Estimated coefficient	Significance
Size of home community	−0.31	+++
Parents' wealth	1.16	+++
Age	−3.65	+++
Grade obtained on a test of logical ability	0.18	+++
Average grade at undergraduate level	5.27	+++
Previous studies	1.85	++
Type of high school	0.37	+
Bachelors degree in math or physics	1.39	+++
Bachelors degree in humanities	−15.13	+
Constant	−0.53	+++

+ : 10% ++ : 5% +++ : 1%

The "quality" of the model was evaluated using the likelihood-ratio test (cf. section 4.8.2), which involves comparing the model with the estimated coefficients to that obtained by setting all coefficients other than the constant to zero. The χ^2-statistic of 86 with nine degrees of freedom is very significant.

Lassibile used this model to predict the probability of students with given characteristics passing the exam. Other possible applications may include, for example, determining an admissions policy to ensure in a given pass rate.

2.8 Specification Error

The estimation methods which we have introduced – maximum likelihood, Berkson's method, minimum-χ^2 – have nice asymptotic properties when applied to the correct model, i.e. when equation (2.5) represents the "true" likelihood function for the observations. It is obviously important to see how well these estimators perform in the presence of specification errors.

Errors which may occur include: incorrect specification of the functional form F, violation of the assumption of independence of the observations, improper selection of explanatory variables, and the introduction of biases via the sampling methodology (cf. exercises 6 and 7).

2.8.1 Misspecification of F

2.8.1.1 The Choice between Logit and Probit

The logit model was originally introduced as a computationally simpler approximation to the probit model. What are the consequences of

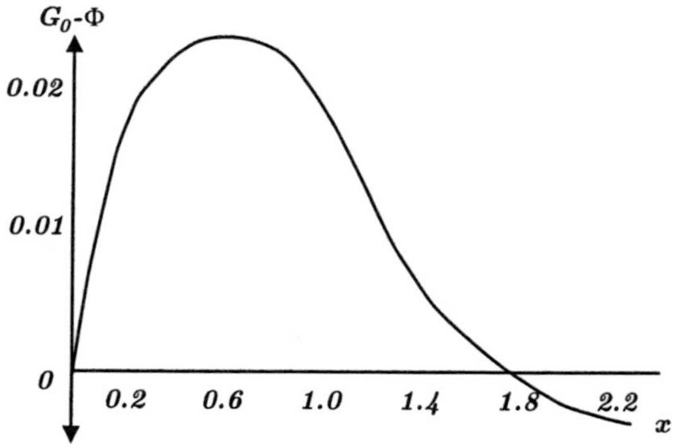

Fig. 2.3. $|G_0(x) - \phi(x)|$

assuming a logistic form for F when the true distribution is normal? Using Monte Carlo studies, Morimune [Mor79] demonstrated that there is generally little difference in parameter estimates obtained by the two methods – apart from a scale factor, which we shall discuss presently – or in the precision of the estimates.

This is explained by the fact that the shape of the normal and logistic distributions are very similar. The usual form of the logistic function, namely:

$$F(x) = \frac{1}{1+e^{-x}},$$

has mean zero and variance $\frac{\pi^2}{3}$. Thus, to compare the normal and logistic distributions we should use the standard normal and a variant of the logistic cumulative density function given by:

$$G_0(x) = \frac{1}{(1+e^{cx})},$$

where $c = \frac{\pi}{\sqrt{3}}$.

As figure 2.2 shows, $|G_0(x) - \Phi(x)|$ is small for all real x.

2.8.1.2 Misspecification of F when X Normally Distributed

We consider here the consistency of estimators for **b** obtained by maximizing a likelihood function which incorporates an incorrect choice of F. Suppose that the true model, conditional on **x**, is that $y_1, \ldots, y_n$ are independent, with:

$$\Pr(y_i = 1) = G(\mathbf{x}_i\mathbf{b}),$$
$$\Pr(y_i = 0) = 1 - G(\mathbf{x}_i\mathbf{b}), \quad \forall i,$$

where G is a cumulative density function. Suppose further that we estimate **b** by maximizing:

$$\log(L) = \sum_{i=1}^{n} \left\{ y_i \log\left[F\left(\mathbf{x}_i \tilde{\mathbf{b}}^*\right)\right] + (1 - y_i) \log\left[1 - F\left(\mathbf{x}_i \tilde{\mathbf{b}}^*\right)\right]\right\}, \tag{2.13}$$

where F is some c.d.f. which differs from G.

Proposition 1: Let the model contain a constant term, so that:

$$\mathbf{x}_i \mathbf{b} \equiv b_0 + x_{i1} b_1 + \ldots + x_{iK} b_K,$$

Assume that $(x_{i1}, \ldots, x_{iK}), i = 1, \ldots, n$ are n independent random vectors with the same multivariate normal distribution, then the estimators $\tilde{\beta}$ obtained by maximizing the incorrect likelihood function (2.13) are such that $\frac{\tilde{\beta}_k}{\tilde{\beta}_\ell}$ converges to $\frac{\mathbf{b}_k}{\mathbf{b}_\ell}$, $\forall j, \ell$, where $\tilde{\beta}^*_j$ is the estimate for $\mathbf{b}_j$ derived from the improperly specified model.

Thus the coefficients of the explanatory variables in the true model are consistently estimated to within a scaling factor. We now sketch a proof, referring the reader to the article by Ruud [Ruu83] for a more rigorous demonstration.

Proof: Asymptotically, the maximum-likelihood estimators obtained by maximizing $\frac{\log(L)}{n}$ tend in probability to the solution of the limit-problem:

$$\max_{\mathbf{b}^*} \text{plim}_n \frac{1}{n} \log\left[L\left(\mathbf{b}^*\right)\right],$$

with:

$$\text{plim}_n \frac{1}{n} \log\left[L\left(\mathbf{b}^*\right)\right] = \text{E}_\mathbf{x}\left(\text{E}_{y|\mathbf{x}}\left\{y \log\left[F\left(\mathbf{x}\mathbf{b}^*\right)\right] + (1-y)\log\left[1 - F\left(\mathbf{x}\mathbf{b}^*\right)\right]\right\}\right),$$

where plim means probability limit as usual, E_x denotes taking expectations with respect to the marginal distribution of x, and $\text{E}_{y|\mathbf{x}}$ – expectations with respect to the conditional expectation of y given $\mathbf{x}^\dagger$.

Since $\text{E}(y) = G(xb)$, where $\mathbf{b}$ is the true parameter value, we have:

$$\text{plim}_n \frac{1}{n} \log\left[L\left(\mathbf{b}^*\right)\right] = \text{E}_\mathbf{x}\left\{G(\mathbf{x}\mathbf{b}) \log\left[F\left(\mathbf{x}\mathbf{b}^*\right)\right] + \left[1 - G(\mathbf{x}\mathbf{b})\right]\log\left[1 - F\left(\mathbf{x}\mathbf{b}^*\right)\right]\right\}.$$

† for a discussion of the application of the expectations operator to bivariate distributions, cf. Johnston [Joh84], appendix A-8.

To focus our attention on the ratios of the coefficients we perform the following transformations:

$$c_1^* = \frac{b_1^*}{b_1},$$
$$c_k^* = b_k^* - c_1^* b_k, \quad k \geq 2,$$
$$c_0^* = b_0^* - c_1^* b_0.$$

Let:

$$\tilde{\mathbf{c}}^* = \left(c_2^*, \ldots, c_K^*\right)',$$
$$\tilde{\mathbf{x}}^* = \left(x_2, \ldots, x_K\right),$$
$$x_1^* = \mathbf{xb},$$

then:

$$\begin{aligned}
\mathbf{xb}^* &= \mathbf{b}_0^* + x_{1i} b_1^* + x_{2i} b_2^* + \ldots + x_{Ki} b_K^*, \\
&= c_0^* + c_1^* b_0 + x_{i1} b_1 c_1^* + x_{2i} \left(b_2 c_1^* + c_2^*\right) \\
&\quad + \ldots + x_{Ki} \left(b_K c_1^* + c_K^*\right) *, \\
&= c_0^* + \mathbf{x}_{1i}^* \mathbf{c}_1^* + \tilde{x}^* \tilde{c}^* = x^* c^*.
\end{aligned}$$

In terms of the new parameters, the maximization problem becomes:

$$\max_{\mathbf{c}^*} \operatorname{plim}_n \frac{1}{n} \log \left[L^* \left(\mathbf{c}^*\right)\right],$$

with:

$$\begin{aligned}
\operatorname{plim}_n \frac{1}{n} \log \left[L^* \left(\mathbf{c}^*\right)\right] = \mathrm{E}_x \Big\{ & G\left(\mathbf{xb}\right) \log \left[F\left(\mathbf{x}^* \mathbf{c}^*\right)\right] \\
& + \left[1 - G\left(\mathbf{xb}\right)\right] \log \left[1 - F\left(\mathbf{x}^* \mathbf{c}^*\right)\right] \Big\}.
\end{aligned}$$

The asymptotic first-order conditions may be written:

$$\mathrm{E}_{\mathbf{x}} \left\{ \frac{f\left(\mathbf{x}^* \mathbf{c}^*\right)}{F\left(\mathbf{x}^* \mathbf{c}^*\right)\left[1 - F\left(\mathbf{x}^* \mathbf{c}^*\right)\right]} \left[G\left(\mathbf{xb}\right) - F\left(\mathbf{x}^* \mathbf{c}^*\right)\right] \mathbf{x}^{*\prime} \right\} = 0.$$

We must now see whether these equations have a unique solution $\mathbf{c}^*$, such that $\tilde{\mathbf{c}}^* = 0$. Equivalently, we can verify whether the system of $K+1$ equations:

$$\mathrm{E}_{\mathbf{x}} \frac{f\left(c_0^* + \mathbf{x}_1^* \mathbf{c}_1^*\right)\left[G\left(x_1^*\right) - F\left(c_0^* + \mathbf{x}_1^* \mathbf{c}_1^*\right)\right]}{F\left(c_0^* + \mathbf{x}_1^* \mathbf{c}_1^*\right)\left[1 - F\left(c_0^* + \mathbf{x}_1^* \mathbf{c}_1^*\right)\right]} \begin{pmatrix} 1 \\ x_1^* \\ \tilde{\mathbf{x}}^{*\prime} \end{pmatrix} = 0,$$

solves uniquely for c_0^* and c_1^*. By our assumption of normality, we have:

$$\mathrm{E}_{\mathbf{x}} \left(\tilde{\mathbf{x}}^* \middle| \mathbf{x}_1^*\right) = \mathbf{z} + \mathbf{w}\mathbf{x}_1^*,$$

where z and w are vectors of constants. Writing the last $K-1$ equations of the system in the form:

$$\mathrm{E}_{\mathbf{x}}\left\{\frac{f\left(c_0^*+\mathbf{x}_1^*\mathbf{c}_1^*\right)\left[G\left(x_1^*\right)-F\left(c_0^*+\mathbf{x}_1^*\mathbf{c}_1^*\right)\right]}{F\left(c_0^*+\mathbf{x}_1^*\mathbf{c}_1^*\right)\left[1-F\left(c_0^*+\mathbf{x}_1^*\mathbf{c}_1^*\right)\right]}\mathrm{E}_x\left[x^{*\prime}|1,x_1^*\right]\right\}=0,$$

we see that they are linear combinations of the first two equations, so the result holds as required. □

2.8.2 Non-Parametric Methods

As we have just seen, the maximum-likelihood method, applied to a misspecified distribution function F, does not yield consistent estimates of all the parameters.

It may therefore be of interest to introduce non-parametric methods of estimation, i.e. methods which make no assumptions about the form of F. Such methods are more robust than those just described, but are less precise in cases where a fairly good approximation to F can be chosen.

2.8.2.1 The Maximum-Score Method

This method (which should not be confused with the method of scoring described in section 2.5.2) was proposed by Manski [Man75]. It yields consistent parameter estimates provided that the distribution F has median zero.

The model is as follows. Suppose that, conditional on $\mathbf{x}$, the observations $y_1, \ldots, y_n$ on the endogenous variable are independent with:

$$\Pr(y_i=1)=F(\mathbf{x}_i\mathbf{b}),$$
$$\Pr(y_i=0)=1-F(\mathbf{x}_i\mathbf{b}).$$

for all i. Here F is an *unknown* c.d.f. whose median is assumed to be zero.

To estimate $\mathbf{b}$ by the maximum-score method we count, for an arbitrary $\mathbf{b}$, the number of sample points i for which *either* $\mathbf{x}_i\mathbf{b}>0$ and $y_i=1$ *or* $\mathbf{x}_i\mathbf{b}\leq 0$ and $y_i=0$. The maximum-score (MS) estimator of $\mathbf{b}$ is given by the value which maximizes this count.

Proposition 2: Maximum-score estimation yields strongly consistent estimators†.

Proof: A common method of estimation consists of maximizing (or minimizing), with respect to a parameter $\mathbf{b}$, some objective function of the

† An estimate is said to be strongly consistent if it converges to the true value of the parameter with probability one as n tends to infinity.

form:

$$\sum_{i=1}^{n} g\left(y_i, \mathbf{x}_i; \mathbf{b}\right),$$

where g is known.

We shall examine whether such an estimator exists and is strongly consistent. We assume throughout that $\mathbf{x}$ is stochastic. As in the proof of proposition (1), $\mathrm{E}_{\mathbf{x}}$ denotes the expectation with respect to the marginal distribution of $\mathbf{x}$, and $\mathrm{E}_{y|\mathbf{x}}$ the conditional expectation of y given $\mathbf{x}$. The general proceedure is as follows.

(i) We investigate whether:

$$\frac{1}{n}\sum_{i=1}^{n} g\left(y_i, \mathbf{x}_i; \mathbf{b}\right) \tag{2.14}$$

tends to a limit as n tends to infinity. Under assumptions such as "conditional on the $\mathbf{x}_i$-s, the random variables $y_1, \ldots, y_n$ are independent", and "the $\mathbf{x}_i$-s are obtained by random sampling from a well-behaved continuous distribution," it can be shown that:

$$\frac{1}{n}\sum_{i=1}^{n} g\left(y_i, \mathbf{x}_i; \mathbf{b}\right) \to^{a.s.} \mathrm{E}_{\mathbf{x}}\left\{\mathrm{E}_{y|\mathbf{x}}\left[g\left(y_i, \mathbf{x}_i; \mathbf{b}\right)\right]\right\}.$$

(See Jennrich [Jen69] for details of conditions and proofs).

(ii) As to the maximization problem:

$$\max_b \mathrm{E}_{\mathbf{x}}\left[\mathrm{E}_{y|\mathbf{x}} g\left(y_i, \mathbf{x}_i; \mathbf{b}\right)\right],$$

if this equation has the true value of the parameter, $\mathbf{b}_0$, as its unique solution, then the value of $\mathbf{b}$ which maximizes equation (2.14) exists almost surely for sufficiently large n, and is a strongly consistent estimator for $\mathbf{b}_0$.

We now follow this approach to study the asymptotic properties of the maximum-score estimator in our model.

Define a function $\sigma(t) : \mathbb{R} \to \{0, 1\}$, such that:

$$\sigma(t) = \begin{cases} 1, & \text{if } t > 0, \\ 0, & \text{otherwise.} \end{cases}$$

Maximum likelihood estimation is then a matter of choosing $\mathbf{b}$ to maximize:

$$\sum_{i=1}^{n} g\left(y_i, \mathbf{x}_i; \mathbf{b}\right).$$

where:

$$g(y_i, \mathbf{x}_i; \mathbf{b}) = \begin{cases} \sigma(\mathbf{x}_i\mathbf{b}), & \text{if } y_i = 1, \\ 1 - \sigma(\mathbf{x}_i\mathbf{b}), & \text{if } y_i = 0. \end{cases}$$

The associated limit-problem is to maximize $\mathrm{E}_{\mathbf{x}}[G(\mathbf{x}; \mathbf{b})]$, where:

$$\begin{aligned} G(\mathbf{x}_i; \mathbf{b}) &= \mathrm{E}[g(y_i, \mathbf{x}_i; \mathbf{b})], \\ &= \sigma(\mathbf{x}_i\mathbf{b}) \Pr(y = 1 | x) + [1 - \sigma(\mathbf{x}_i\mathbf{b})] \Pr(y = 0 | x), \\ &= \sigma(\mathbf{x}_i\mathbf{b}) F(\mathbf{x}_i\mathbf{b}_0) + [1 - \sigma(\mathbf{x}_i\mathbf{b})][1 - F(\mathbf{x}_i\mathbf{b}_0)], \\ &= \begin{cases} F(\mathbf{x}_i\mathbf{b}_0), & \text{if } \mathbf{x}_i\mathbf{b} > 0, \\ 1 - F(\mathbf{x}_i\mathbf{b}_0), & \text{otherwise.} \end{cases} \end{aligned}$$

Now observe that $G(\mathbf{x}, \mathbf{b})$ differs from $G(\mathbf{x}, \mathbf{b}_0)$ only if *either* **i)** $\mathbf{x}_i\mathbf{b} \leq 0 < \mathbf{x}_i\mathbf{b}_0$ *or* **ii)** $\mathbf{x}_i\mathbf{b}_0 \leq 0 < \mathbf{x}_i\mathbf{b}$. By our assumption about the median, F is an increasing function such that $F(0) = \frac{1}{2}$. Thus $G(\mathbf{x}, \mathbf{b}) < \frac{1}{2} < G(\mathbf{x}, \mathbf{b}_0)$ in case **i**, while $G(\mathbf{x}, \mathbf{b}_0) \leq \frac{1}{2} \leq G(\mathbf{x}_i\mathbf{b})$ in case **ii**, with strict inequalitites if $\mathbf{x}_i\mathbf{b} < 0$. It follows that $G(\mathbf{x}_i\mathbf{b}) \leq G(\mathbf{x}_i\mathbf{b}_0)$ for all $\mathbf{x}$, $\mathbf{b}$, with strict inequality if $(\mathbf{x}_i\mathbf{b})(\mathbf{x}_i\mathbf{b}_0) < 0$.

Let $\mathbf{b}$ be any vector which is not a scalar multiple of $\mathbf{b}_0$. Then the set of $\mathbf{x}$ for which $(\mathbf{x}_i\mathbf{b})(\mathbf{x}_i\mathbf{b}_0) < 0$ is non-empty, and under weak assumptions about the distribution of $\mathbf{x}$ will have positive probability, and thus $\mathrm{E}[G(\mathbf{x}_i\mathbf{b})] < \mathrm{E}[G(\mathbf{x}_i\mathbf{b}_0)]$. We now have shown that $\mathbf{b}_0$ is the unique solution of the limit problem; the existence and strong consistency of the MS estimator follow from this. □

Notice that the procedure just described does not involve estimating the unknown c.d.f. F. This can, however, be done using non-parametric methods – (cf. Cosslett [Cos81] and Manski [Man85]).

2.8.2.2 "Semi-Parametric Discriminant Analysis"

Klein and Spady [KS86] introduced a procedure which differs from that proposed by Manski and Cosslett. It is founded upon the following two observations.

First Observation There are a variety of non-parametric methods for estimating densities, many are based on approaches of the "kernel" type. These can, in principle, be used to estimate the form of the conditional probability:

$$\Pr(y = 1 | x).$$

Unfortunately, these methods require a very large number of observations when there are several exogenous variables. Thus, for a given degree of precision in estimation, the required number of observations increases by a factor of about

17 when the number of explanatory variables increases from one to three, and 210,000 times when the number of explanatory variables increases from one to ten.

We can revert to the case of a single conditioning variable by using Bayes' Theorem. Let the variables $\mathbf{x}_i$ and y_i be independent and identically distributed. Suppose further that $\mathbf{x}$ is continuous with $g(\mathbf{x})$ and $g(\mathbf{x}|\, y = 1)$ denoting the marginal and conditional joint densities respectively, then:

$$\Pr(y = 1|\,\mathbf{x}) = \Pr(y = 1)\,\frac{g(\mathbf{x}|\, y = 1)}{g(\mathbf{x})}.$$

Second Observation This application of Bayes' Theorem makes the conditioned rather than the conditioning variable a vector. The problem can be further simplified in our model, where $\mathbf{x}$ affects y only via the scalar quantity $\mathbf{xb}$, if we write:

$$\Pr(y = 1|\,\mathbf{x}) = \Pr(y = 1)\,\frac{\tilde{g}(\mathbf{xb}|\, y = 1)}{\tilde{g}(\mathbf{xb})}. \tag{2.15}$$

Denote the right hand side of equation (2.15) $\Pr(\mathbf{xb})$. If $\mathbf{b}$ were known, we could estimate $\Pr(\mathbf{xb})$ by:

$$\widehat{\Pr}(\mathbf{xb}) = \bar{y}\,\frac{\hat{g}(\mathbf{xb}|\, y = 1)}{\hat{g}(\mathbf{xb})}, \tag{2.16}$$

where $\hat{g}(\mathbf{xb})$ and $\hat{g}(\mathbf{xb}|y = 1)$ are non-parametric estimates of the densities $g(\mathbf{xb})$ and $g(\mathbf{xb}|y = 1)$, and $\bar{y}$ the observed mean of y. For example, adopting the Gaussian kernel $\phi(z) = \frac{1}{\sqrt{2\pi}}\exp\left(-\frac{z^2}{2}\right)$ yields:

$$\hat{g}(\mathbf{xb}\,|y = 1) = \frac{\sum_{j=1}^{n}\frac{y_j}{h}\phi\left[\frac{\mathbf{xb}-\mathbf{x}_j\mathbf{b}}{h}\right]}{\sum_{j=1}^{n} y_j},$$

$$\hat{g}(\mathbf{xb}) = \frac{\sum_{j=1}^{n}\frac{1-y_j}{h}\phi\left[\frac{\mathbf{xb}-\mathbf{x}_j\mathbf{b}}{h}\right]}{n - \sum_{j=1}^{n} y_j}. \tag{2.17}$$

In fact, $\mathbf{b}$ is unknown, so the expression $\hat{p}(\mathbf{xb})$ in equations (2.15) and (2.17) is not a feasible estimate of $\Pr(y = 1|\mathbf{x})$. We therefore adopt the following two-step procedure:

(i) We solve:

$$\max_b \sum_{i=1}^{n} \left\{ y_i \log[\widehat{\Pr}(\mathbf{x}_i\mathbf{b})] + (1 - y_i) \log\left[1 - \widehat{\Pr}(\mathbf{x}_i\mathbf{b})\right]\right\}$$

to find an "approximate maximum-likelihood" estimator, $\tilde{\beta}_{ML}$, for **b**.

(ii) We then use $\widehat{\Pr}\left(\mathbf{x}\tilde{\beta}_{ML}\right)$ as an estimator for the response function $\Pr(y = 1|\mathbf{x})$.

Klein and Spady [KS86] demonstrated that $\tilde{\beta}_{ML}$ is a consistent estimator for **b**. It is probably asymptotically normal, though this has yet to be demonstrated.

The interest of this approach is that it provides estimates, not only of the vector **b**, but also of the response function $\Pr(y = 1|\mathbf{x})$, without making any à priori assumptions about the form of the density function.

2.8.3 Omitted Variables

2.8.3.1 Errors in the List of Explanatory Variables

It is well known that we can estimate the standard linear regression model by ordinary least squares whenever relevant variables which have been omitted from the model are orthogonal to the included regressors. Unfortunately, this property of the linear model does not generalize to maximum-likelihood estimation of qualitative response models.

We shall verify this using a logit model with two explanatory variables x^1 and x^2:

$$\Pr(y_i = 1) = F\left(x_i^1 b_1 + x_i^2 b_2\right),$$

with:

$$F(\mathbf{x}) = \frac{1}{1 - \exp(-\mathbf{x})}.$$

Suppose we estimate b_1 by applying maximum likelihood to the misspecified model:

$$\overset{*}{\Pr}(y_i = 1) = F\left(x_i^1 b_1^*\right).$$

We solve:

$$\sum_{i=1}^{n} \left[y_i - F\left(x_i^1 b_i^*\right)\right] x_i^1 = 0,$$

which converges in probability to the solution of:

$$0 = \mathrm{E}_{\mathbf{x}}\left\{\mathrm{E}_{y|\mathbf{x}}\left[y - F\left(x^1 b_1^*\right)\right] x^1\right\},$$

Substituting for y, we have:

$$0 = \mathrm{E}_{\mathbf{x}}\left\{\left[F\left(x^1 b_1 + x^2 b_2\right) - F\left(x^1 b_1^*\right)\right] x^1\right\}.$$

This yields a consistent estimator of b_1 if, and only if, the last equation is solved by $b_1 = b_1^*$, and this happens if and only if x^1 is orthogonal to:

$$F\left(x^1 b_1 + x^2 b_2\right) - F\left(x^1 b_1\right).$$

This orthogonality condition is very different from the corresponding one for the linear model: $\mathrm{E}_{\mathbf{x}}\left(x^1 x^2\right) = 0$. As it depends on the unknown parameters $\mathbf{b}_1$ and $\mathbf{b}_2$, it is of no practical use.

2.8.3.2 Correction for Omitted-Variable Bias

Consider again the system with repeated observations from section 2.6. As in that section, let $n = n_1 + \ldots + n_J$, where n_j denotes the number of trials of type j, and let $\hat{p}_j$ denote the proportion of trials of type j for which $y = 1$. Then:

$$\hat{p}_j = F\left(\mathbf{x}^j \mathbf{b}\right) + v_j, \quad j = 1, \ldots, J,$$

where v_j is a random disturbance term with mean zero and variance:

$$\frac{F\left(\mathbf{x}^j \mathbf{b}\right)\left[1 - F\left(\mathbf{x}^j \mathbf{b}\right)\right]}{n_j}.$$

It often happens in practice that the number of observations (n_j) for each trial of type j is sufficiently large that the foregoing expression for the variance evaluates to a negligible amount. However, a deterministic model of the form $\hat{p} = F\left(\mathbf{x}^j \mathbf{b}\right)$ will not fit the data exactly.

This difficulty arises because the error structure of the model takes into account only the random component of individual behaviour and ignores other sources of error: for example, errors in measurement and voluntary or involuntary omission of variables. We shall examine the latter source of error.

Let the observed qualitative variable $y_i^j, i = 1, \ldots, n_j, j = 1, \ldots, J$ be related to a latent quantitative variable y_i^{j*} as follows:

$$y_i^j = \begin{cases} 1, & \text{if } y_i^{j*} \geq 0, \\ 0, & \text{otherwise,} \end{cases}$$

and let the latent variable be determined by the model:

$$y_i^{j*} = \mathbf{x}_i^{j*} \mathbf{b}^* + u_i^j, \quad j = 1, \ldots, J, \quad i = 1, \ldots n_j.$$

Assume further that only the exogenous variables $\left\{\mathbf{x}^j\right\} \subset \left\{\mathbf{x}^{j*}\right\}$ are observed. We can then write:

$$y_i^{j*} = \mathbf{x}^j \mathbf{b} + \epsilon_i^j + u_i^j,$$

where ϵ_i^j represents the joint effect of the omitted variables. This additional error is independent of the structural disturbance u_i^j. Furthermore, it is reasonable to suppose that some of the omitted variables depend only on the trial type j, while others depend on the individual i. We therefore decompose ϵ_i^j as follows:

$$\epsilon_i^j = \alpha^j + \beta_i^j,$$

where α^j and β_i^j are random variables with mean zero, and which are independent of each other and of the $\mathbf{x}^j$-s.

Pulling all this together, we have:

$$y_i^{j*} = \mathbf{x}^j \mathbf{b} + \alpha_i^j + u_i^{j*},$$

where:

$$u_i^{j*} = \beta_i^j + \epsilon_i^j.$$

The essential difference between this model and the usual one comes from the term α^j – different trials of the same type are no longer independent.

Turning our attention to the observed qualitative variables y_i^j, recall that $\hat{p}_j$ denotes the proportion of trials of type j for which $y = 1$:

$$\hat{p}_j = \frac{1}{n_j} \sum_{i=1}^{n_j} y_i^j.$$

Conditional on α^j, the random variable $n_j \hat{p}_j$ follows a binomial distribution with parameters n_j and $F\left(\mathbf{x}_j \mathbf{b} + \alpha_j\right)$, where F denotes the c.d.f. of $-u_i^{j*}$. Again, we see that the usual model is complicated by the introduction of the random variable α^j. What we do about this complication depends on the available number of observations n_j. There are three cases to consider:

(i) $n_j = 1$ for all j. Here the type effect cannot be separated from the individual effect, and there is nothing we can do.

(ii) n_j is large for all j. Here we have, approximately:

$$\hat{p}_j = F\left(\mathbf{x}_j \mathbf{b} + \alpha_j\right) \Leftrightarrow F^{-1}\left(\hat{p}_j\right) = \mathbf{x}_j \mathbf{b} + \alpha_j,$$

and we revert to a linear model. Since the variance of the error term α^j does not depend on the parameter $\mathbf{b}$, we can estimate $\mathbf{b}$ by ordinary least squares, regressing $F^{-1}\left(\hat{p}_j\right)$ on $\mathbf{x}_j$.

(iii) For all j, $n_j \neq 1$ but n_j is not very large. In this case we must take into account the distribution of the random variable α^j. Assuming that this random variable is continuous with density function ψ, the unconditional likelihood function is given by:

$$\prod_{j=1}^{J} \int \frac{n_j!}{n_j \hat{p}_j! \left(n_j - n_j \hat{p}_j\right)!} F\left(\mathbf{x}_i \mathbf{b} + \alpha\right)^{n_j \hat{p}_j}$$
$$\times \left[1 - F\left(\mathbf{x}_j b + \alpha\right)\right]^{n_j (1-\hat{p}_j)} \psi(\alpha)\, d\alpha.$$

Assuming for simplicity that ψ is known up to a scale parameter, we may maximize the likelihood with respect to **b** and that parameter. The awkward aspect of this procedure is that the ML estimator of **b** depends strongly on the hypothesized form for ψ.

2.8.4 Correlated Errors

In the linear model, some of the nice properties of OLS estimation carry over to the case of correlated errors – unbiasedness and consistency, for example. A similar result holds for ML estimation in the simple dichotomy.

Suppose that the observed dichotomous variable y is related in the usual way to an unobserved latent variable y^*, generated by a linear model, and suppose that the errors in this linear model follow a first-order autoregressive process. Specifically, let:

$$y_t = \begin{cases} 1, & \text{if } y_t^* \geq 0, \\ 0, & \text{otherwise;} \end{cases} \qquad t = 1, \ldots, T, \tag{2.18}$$

and:

$$y_t^* = \mathbf{x}_t \mathbf{b} + u_t,$$
$$u_t = \rho u_{t-1} + \epsilon_t,$$

where $\{\epsilon_t\}$ is a series of independent N (0, 1) variates and $|\rho| < 1$. In this case, the vector of latent variables $\left(y_1^*, \ldots, y_T^*\right)$ has a T-dimensional normal distribution depending on **b** and ρ. Denote the corresponding density function by $\phi\left(y_1^*, \ldots, y_T^*; \mathbf{b}, \rho\right)$.

In terms of the latent variables y^*, we see that the likelihood function is:

$$L\left(y_1, \ldots, y_T; \mathbf{b}, \phi\right) = \int \cdots \int \phi\left(y_1^*, \ldots, y_T^*; \mathbf{b}, \phi\right) dy_1^* \ldots dy_T^*,$$

where the region of integration is dictated by equation (2.18).

Thus, the correctly specified likelihood function is a T-dimensional integral. Attempting to maximize such a function leads to insuperable computational problems.

Under these conditions it is often practical to simply ignore the existence of correlation, i.e. to proceed as if ρ were zero. The estimator of **b** is then the solution of the system:

$$\max_{\mathbf{b}} \sum_{t=1}^{T} \{y_t \log [\Phi (\mathbf{x}_t \mathbf{b})] + (1 - y) \log [1 - \Phi (\mathbf{x}_t \mathbf{b})]\}.$$

It has been shown by Robinson [Rob82] and by Gourieroux, Monfort and Trognon [GMT80] that this estimator of b is consistent, but that the usual formulas for standard errors have to be modified.

Exercises

2.1 Can the use of a linear formulation [as in equation (2.1)] be justified if we possess à priori information of the type: the value of the parameter **b** is close to some known value $\mathbf{b}_0$?

2.2 Consider a logit model with a constant term. From equation (2.8), show that the maximum-likelihood estimator β_{ML} satisifies:

$$\sum_{i=1}^{n} [y_i - F (\mathbf{x}_i \beta_{ML})] = 0.$$

How can this result be used to verify the precision of numerical calculations of β_{ML}?

2.3 An argument which may be made against using the model:

$$\Pr (y_i = 1) = F (\mathbf{x}_i \mathbf{b}),$$

where F is a distribution function, is that this formulation only allows for a monotonic relationship between the explanatory variables and the probability of observing 1. Do you agree or disagree with this argument?

2.4 Let Φ represent the standard normal distribution. Show that $\log (\Phi)$ and $\log (1 - \Phi)$ are concave functions.

2.5 Consider a population in which each individual will become ill with probability P. n individuals are drawn at random from this population, what is the distribution of this sample?

Now we continue drawing until the number of sick people is equal to some value n_1. What is the distribution of the observations now? Verify that if the number of individuals who are well, n_0, and the number of sick individuals, n_1, are the same in the two samples, the likelihoods only differ by a constant.

2.6 Endogenous sampling

An individual with characteristics $\mathbf{x}_i$ prefers taking the subway ($y_i = 1$) with probability $F (\mathbf{x}_i \mathbf{b})$ and taking the bus ($y_i = 0$) with probability $1 - F (\mathbf{x}_i \mathbf{b})$.

In order to estimate **b**, we draw a random sample of ten individuals in the subway and twenty individuals in the bus and observe their characteristics. Why is this sampling technique called endogenous sampling? What is the distribution of the observations?

2.7 (Continuation of 6).

Show that estimates of the parameters obtained from the standard dichotomous model will be biased.

2.8 Using the logistic model:

$$p_t = \frac{1}{1 + \exp(at + b)}.$$

we wish to describe how the proportion of the population owning a certain good, p_t, evolves over time. Show that:

$$\frac{dp_1}{1 - p_t} = -ap_t dt,$$

and that this relationship implies that the rate of change of the population proportion possessing the good is a function of the number of people who already own it. How can we modify this model so that the share of owners does not exceed $c \leq 1$?

2.9 Verify that the maximum-score method is equivalent to minimizing:

$$\sum_{i=1}^{n} \left| z_{\mathbf{x}_i \mathbf{b} > 0} - z_{y_i} = 1 \right|.$$

where:

$$z_{\mathbf{x}_i \mathbf{b}} = \begin{cases} 1 & \text{if } \mathbf{x}_i \mathbf{b} > 1 \\ 0 & \text{otherwise} \end{cases},$$

and

$$z_{y_i} = \begin{cases} 1 & \text{if } y_i > 1 \\ 0 & \text{otherwise} \end{cases}.$$

3 Modelling

We have seen several cases involving a single dichotomous variable (cf. section 2.3), and have discovered that they can all be described by the same model (cf. sections 2.2 and 2.3).

When dependent variables can take more than two values, or when we have more than one dependent variable, qualitative models assume a variety of forms. The search for the appropriate form is thus a crucial element of the study of qualitative response models.

In this chapter, we describe several representative models and look at some of their applications.

3.1 Grouping

3.1.1 The Case of a Single Variable

Assume that we want to examine how household i's income, y_i^*, depends on a vector $\mathbf{x}_i$ of explanatory characteristics. While income is, in principle, a continuous variable, we often only dispose of data on income brackets. Let the breakdown be as in table 3.1.

The observed value, income bracket, is in fact a qualitative variable taking $K + 1$ values. Letting $k = 0, 1, \ldots, K$ represent the values in their natural order, and y_i the qualitative variable, we have:

$$y_i = k \Leftrightarrow r_k \leq y_i^* < r_{k+1},$$

where $r_0 = -\infty, r_{K+1} = +\infty$.

To complete the model we note that it is reasonable to use a linear formulation to describe the relationship between the unobserved actual salary (the latent variable) y_i^* and the household's characteristics:

$$y_i^* = \mathbf{x}_i \mathbf{b} + u_i, \tag{3.1}$$

where $\mathbf{b}$ is a vector of unknown parameters and where the distribution of the

Table 3.1. *Breakdown by salary group*

salary less than r_1
salary greater than r_1 and less than r_2, where $(r_1 < r_2)$
⋮
salary greater than r_{K-1} and less than r_K, where $(r_{K-1} < r_K)$
salary greater than r_K.

disturbance term, u_i, is such that $\frac{u_i}{\sigma}$ follows a cumulative density function F. Assume that the error terms corresponding to different individuals are uncorrelated. From equation (3.1) we derive the distribution of the qualitative variable y_i:

$$
\begin{aligned}
P_{0i}(\mathbf{b}) &= \Pr(y_i = 0) = \Pr\left(y_i^* < r_1\right), \\
&= F\left(\frac{r_1}{\sigma} - \frac{\mathbf{x}_i \mathbf{b}}{\sigma}\right), \\
P_{1i}(\mathbf{b}) &= \Pr(y_i = 1) = \Pr\left(r_1 \le y_i^* < r_2\right), \\
&= F\left(\frac{r_2}{\sigma} - \frac{\mathbf{x}_i \mathbf{b}}{\sigma}\right) - F\left(\frac{r_1}{\sigma} - \frac{\mathbf{x}_i \mathbf{b}}{\sigma}\right), \\
&\vdots \\
P_{Ki}(\mathbf{b}) &= \Pr(y_i = K) = \Pr\left(r_K \le y_i^*\right), \\
&= 1 - F\left(\frac{r_K}{\sigma} - \frac{\mathbf{x}_i \mathbf{b}}{\sigma}\right).
\end{aligned}
$$

This type of model is sometimes called *ordered polychotomous univariate* (a natural order to the values assumed by y, several values, one variable).

When the distribution function F is normal with mean zero the model is called *probit* and when F is the logistic function we speak of the *logit* model.

From a practical point of view, methods appropriate for grouped data are only of interest when the number of groups is sufficiently small. Otherwise, a linear regression will yield an acceptable continuous approximation to the variable y_i.

3.1.2 The Case of Two Variables

Assume that we want to explain salary y_i^{1*} and savings y_i^{2*} as a function of a household's characteristics, and that we have grouped data on these two endogenous variables. To simplify, we'll assume that each of y_i^1 and y_i^2 can take two values, and that these are determined by the threshold values w and s

respectively. This is the case of two dichotomous variables:

$$y_i^1 = \begin{cases} 1, & \text{if } y_i^{1*} \geq w, \\ 0, & \text{otherwise,} \end{cases}$$

$$y_i^2 = \begin{cases} 1, & \text{if } y_i^{2*} \geq s, \\ 0, & \text{otherwise.} \end{cases}$$

The relationship between the latent variables y_i^{1*}, y_i^{2*} and the exogenous variables $\mathbf{x}$ can be made explicit through use of a linear model:

$$y_i^{1*} = x_i^1 b^1 + u_i^1,$$
$$y_i^{2*} = x_i^2 b^2 + u_i^2,$$

where $\mathbf{b} = \begin{bmatrix} b^1 \\ b^2 \end{bmatrix}$ is a vector of parameters and where the error terms $\left(u_i^1, u_i^2\right)$ have a joint density function $F\left(u^1, u^2\right)$. We assume that disturbances for different individuals are independent:

$$\begin{aligned}
P_{00i}(b) &= \Pr\left(y_i^1 = 0, y_i^2 = 0\right), \\
&= \Pr\left(y_i^{1*} < w, y_i^{2*} < s\right), \\
P_{01i}(b) &= \Pr\left(y_i^1 = 0, y_i^2 = 1\right), \\
&= \Pr\left(y_i^{1*} < w, y_i^{2*} \geq s\right), \\
&= \Pr\left(y_i^{1*} < w\right) - \Pr\left(y_i^{1*} < w, y_i^{2*} < s\right), \\
P_{10i}(b) &= \Pr\left(y_i^1 = 1, y_i^2 = 0\right), \\
&= \Pr\left(y_i^{1*} \geq w, y_i^{2*} < s\right), \\
&= \Pr\left(y_i^{2*} < s\right) - \Pr\left(y_i^{1*} < w, y_i^{2*} < s\right), \\
P_{11i}(b) &= \Pr\left(y_i^1 = 1, y_i^2 = 1\right), \\
&= \Pr\left(y_i^{1*} \geq w, y_i^{2*} \geq s\right).
\end{aligned}$$

These probabilities can be expressed in terms of F, yielding:

$$\begin{aligned}
P_{00i}(b) &= F\left(w - \mathbf{x}_i^1\mathbf{b}^1, s - \mathbf{x}_i^2\mathbf{b}^2\right), \\
P_{01i}(b) &= F\left(w - \mathbf{x}_i^1\mathbf{b}^1, +\infty\right) - F\left(w - \mathbf{x}_i^1\mathbf{b}^1, s - \mathbf{x}_i^2\mathbf{b}^2\right), \\
P_{10i}(b) &= F\left(+\infty, s - \mathbf{x}_i^2\mathbf{b}^2\right) - F\left(w - \mathbf{x}_i^1\mathbf{b}^1, s - \mathbf{x}_i^2\mathbf{b}^2\right), \qquad (3.2) \\
P_{11i}(b) &= 1 - F\left(+\infty, s - \mathbf{x}_i^2\mathbf{b}^2\right) - F\left(w - \mathbf{x}_i^1\mathbf{b}^1, +\infty\right) \\
&\quad + F\left(w - \mathbf{x}_i^1\mathbf{b}^1, s - \mathbf{x}_i^2\mathbf{b}^2\right)
\end{aligned}$$

This model is called *ordered bivariate dichotomous.*

But what distribution should we postulate for F? It is usual in these cases to assume that the disturbance terms u_{1i} and u_{2i} are correlated. We obtain a *probit* if we let the distribution function be normal two-dimensional with mean zero and a variance-covariance matrix given by:

$$\begin{bmatrix} \sigma_1^2 & \rho\sigma_1\sigma_2 \\ \rho\sigma_1\sigma_2 & \sigma_2^2 \end{bmatrix}.$$

Even though this formulation reflects a simple model we see that the probabilities involve double integrals, rendering their calculation difficult. Derivation of a *logit* model for this case would require a straightforward generalization of the logistic distribution to the two-dimensional case. This generalization, if it exists, is not yet known.

3.2 Models with Interpretable Quantitative Variables

The models we shall examine in this section differ from those in the previous section in that the qualitative variables do not have the same intuitive interpretation as the underlying latent variables.

3.2.1 Reactions in Physiological Systems

In a 1970 study of respiratory ailments in coal miners, Ashford and Sowden [AS70] sought to explain shortness of breath and wheezing as a function of age.

For each symptom we define a resistance function depending on the miner's age:

$$\begin{aligned} y^{1*} &= a^1 + b^1x + u^1 \text{ (shortness of breath)}, \\ y^{2*} &= a^2 + b^2x + u^2 \text{ (wheezing)}, \end{aligned}$$

where a^1, a^2, b^1, and b^2 are unknown coefficients, x represents the miner's age, and u^1 and u^2 are random variables whose distribution is bivariate normal with mean zero and covariance matrix:

$$\begin{bmatrix} 1 & \rho \\ \rho & 1 \end{bmatrix}.$$

As in section 2.2, y^1 and y^2 can be interpreted as the difference between the applied dosage and the highest dose the organism is capable of withstanding. However, neither the dosage nor the tolerance are observable. Since the only explanatory variable we have is age, only the sign of this difference is identifiable.

Table 3.2. *Number of miners showing symptoms, as a function of age*

Shortness of breath		Yes		No		
Wheezing		Yes	No	Yes	No	Total
Age Group	20–24	9	7	95	1841	1952
	25–29	23	9	105	1654	1791
	30–34	54	19	177	1863	2113
	35–39	121	48	257	2357	2783
	40–44	169	54	273	1778	2274
	45–49	269	88	324	1712	2393
	50–54	404	117	245	1324	2090
	55–59	406	152	225	967	1750
	60–64	372	106	132	526	1136
Total		1827	600	1833	14022	18282

The miner shows symptom j, where $j = \{1, 2\}$, when $y^{j*} \geq 0$, and does not when $y^{j*} < 0$. The observed qualitative variables are the two dichotomous variables:

$$y^1 = \begin{cases} 1, & \text{if } y^{1*} \geq 0, \\ 0, & \text{otherwise,} \end{cases}$$

$$y^2 = \begin{cases} 1, & \text{if } y^{2*} \geq 0, \\ 0, & \text{otherwise.} \end{cases}$$

For each observation this couplet can take one of four values: $(1, 1)$, $(1, 0)$, $(0, 1)$, $(0, 0)$, which are observed with probabilities analogous in form to equation (3.2).

Note that the goodness of fit of the model can be inspected visually. Let $p_{1\cdot}(x)$ represent the proportion of miners of age x showing the first symptom; if the model is true, we have approximately (cf. section 2.6.2):

$$\Phi^{-1}[p_{1\cdot}(x)] \approx a^1 + b^1 x.$$

The points defined by $\Phi^{-1}[p_{1\cdot}(x)]$ should, more or less, fall on a straight line. Furthermore, the values α^1 for a^1, and β^1 for b^1 obtained by visual examination of their graph provide useful initial values for numeric estimation procedures.

3.2.2 Success in University Studies

We can easily generalize the example in section 2.7 to a case in which we simultaneously consider the probability of success or failure in several successive years of university studies.

Consider, for example, the case of a two-year program. Each year ends with an examination, if the student receives a grade greater than or equal to fifty percent he passes, otherwise he fails. A passing grade at the end of the first year allows the student to move on to the second year, while a pass after the second year results in a diploma being awarded. Failure in any year results in expulsion from the program.

Three scenarios are possible:

Results of a Two-year Program

Case 1: The student fails his first year,
Case 2: The student passes his first year and fails his second year,
Case 3: The student receives his diploma.

These cases, y_j, $j = \{1, 2, 3\}$ obviously follow directly from the students' grades, which constitute the natural focus of our model building.

Let V_i^1 represent the grade received by student i after the first year. This grade depends upon the student's characteristics: $V_i^1 = \mathbf{x}_{1i}\mathbf{b}_1 + v_i^1$. In the same manner we model the student's grade on the second exam: $V_i^2 = aV_i^1 + \mathbf{x}_{2i}\mathbf{b}_2 + v_i^2$. The presence of V_i^1 in the second equation indicates that the second year's results are influenced by those of the first year. The distribution of the observed qualitative variable is seen to be:

$$
\begin{aligned}
P_{1i} &= \Pr(y_i = 1), \\
&= \Pr\left(V_i^1 < 50\right), \\
P_{2i} &= \Pr(y_i = 2), \\
&= \Pr\left(V_i^1 \geq 50,\, V_i^2 < 50\right), \\
P_{3i} &= \Pr(y_i = 3), \\
&= \Pr\left(V_i^1 \geq 50,\, V_i^2 \geq 50\right).
\end{aligned}
$$

This type of model is called *trichotomous sequential.* To complete the model it remains to specify the distribution of the disturbance terms $\left(v_i^1, v_i^2\right)$ (cf. exercise 1).

3.2.3 Choices Based on Cost Comparisons

A manufacturer considering replacing some machines, a firm looking to site a new plant, a household evaluating which type of energy to use for heating: all these represent situations in which cost comparisons are appropriate.

Let us denote the individuals $i, i = 1, \ldots, N$, and the options they face $k, k = 1, \ldots, K$. Option k chosen by individual i entails a cost of V_i^k. This cost depends upon the characteristics of the individual (for example, the size of the house), as well as on the characteristics of the selection (i.e. electricity, gas, etc.). To model these dependencies we use a linear formulation:

$$V_i^k = x_i^k b^k + u_i^k,$$

where u_i^k represents the error term.

Individual i chooses the least cost option. The probability that he will choose option zero is thus:

$$\begin{aligned}\Pr(y_i = 0) &= \Pr\left(V_i^0 < V_i^1, V_i^0 < V_i^2, \ldots, V_i^0 < V_i^K\right), \\ &= \Pr\left(u_i^0 - u_i^k \leq x_i^k b_k - x_i^0 - b_0\right), \quad k = 1, \ldots K.\end{aligned}$$

The exact form of these probabilities depends upon the specification of the error term u_i^k (cf. section 3.3 and exercise 2).

3.3 Individual Preferences: One Decision-Maker†

In the cases we have examined thus far the values assumed by the latent variables were directly interpretable; that will not be the case for the models introduced in this section. While the models we are about to consider are mathematically close to those in section 3.2.3, the interpretation of the results, especially the coefficient estimates, is very different.

The purpose of these models is to analyse individuals' preferences based on observations of their behaviour when confronted with certain choices. These models are usually constructed on the basis of the theory of stochastic preferences, which derives from the application of statistics to the principles of revealed preference. They can be used, for example, to describe how people select vacation destinations, the mode of transportation they use to commute, how they vote, under what conditions firms may opt to delay investments, etc. The difference with our analysis in section 3.2.3 is that now the criteria on which decisions are based are fundamentally subjective.

3.3.1 Choice Sets

In order to conceptualize how an individual makes choices, the best place to start may be simply to imagine her faced with certain options, and then to watch her.

Suppose she has to select one option m from a set of possibilities M, called the feasible set, and that the choice depends on a vector ω representing the state of the world (or state of nature). Her behaviour would be perfectly defined (deterministic) if we knew how she would react in every possible state of the

† The material in this section, as well as in appendix 3.1 owes a lot to previous work conducted with Eric Renault.

world $\omega \in \Omega$, i.e. for each $m \in M$ and $\omega \in \Omega$ we have an unambiguous relationship from ω to m.

$A_{m|M}$ is called the *choice set* of m and represents the set of all ω for which m is chosen. The family of choice sets generated when m varies in M constitutes a partition of Ω, and, conversely, every partition of Ω defines a possible course of action.

In this scenario, in which a person's choices are observed and analysed, the individual conducting an experiment can sometimes dictate which options are available. Thus, for example, he may ask: do you prefer going to the theatre, to the cinema, or to a museum? Or he may simply ask: do you prefer going to the theatre or to the cinema?

Let us formulate a model to describe the individual's behaviour for each possible outcome. If we denote $\mathcal{M}$ the universe of all choice sets, we have:

$$\left\{A_{m|M}, \quad M \subset \mathcal{M}, \quad \text{card}\,(M) \geq 2, \quad m \in \mathcal{M}\right\}.$$

For example, if M includes three options $\{1, 2, 3\}$, the family of choice sets contains nine members:

$$\begin{array}{ccc} A_{1|123} & A_{2|123} & A_{3|123} \\ & A_{1|12} & A_{2|12} \\ & A_{1|13} & A_{3|13} \\ & A_{2|23} & A_{3|23} \end{array} \tag{3.3}$$

Definition 1: We call an individual's choices rational if:

$$\forall m \in M' \subset M, \quad A_{m|M} \subset A_{m|M'}$$

As the number of choices increases, the number of states of the world which results in each one being chosen decreases. In other words, a rational individual who prefers m when given a choice from the set M will also prefer m when choosing from a smaller set which contains m.

Remark 3: A traditional representation of the individual's behaviour assumes that preferences can be represented by a utility function V. Let $V_m(\omega)$ represent the level of utility associated with m when the state of nature is ω. If the consumer makes choices in order to maximize utility, his choice set $A_{m|M}$ is given by:

$$A_{m|M} = \{\omega : V_m(\omega) > V_{m'}(\omega), \quad \forall m' \neq m, \quad m' \in M\},$$

[we exclude the possibility that $V_m(\omega) = V_{m'}(\omega)$]. It can easily be verified that, given the form of the choice set, this represents a rational choice by the individual.

A more interesting case is provided by the inverse situation.

Proposition 3: Rational choices can be represented by a utility function.

For a proof see appendix 3.1.

From here on we will make use of the notion of a utility function. This function has all the usual properties, such as being unique up to a monotonic transformation, i.e. if $V(\omega)$ is a utility function, then $h[V(\omega), \omega]$, where h is strictly increasing with respect to its first argument, is also a utility function and represents the same preference ordering.

Using the notion of utility function, we write the choice sets as follows:

$$\begin{aligned}
A_{1|123} &= (V_1 > V_2, V_1 > V_3),\\
A_{2|123} &= (V_2 > V_1, V_2 > V_3),\\
A_{3|123} &= (V_3 > V_1, V_3 > V_2),\\
A_{1|12} &= (V_1 > V_2),\\
A_{2|12} &= (V_2 > V_1),\\
A_{1|13} &= (V_1 > V_3),\\
A_{3|13} &= (V_3 > V_1),\\
A_{2|23} &= (V_2 > V_3),\\
A_{3|23} &= (V_3 > V_2).
\end{aligned}$$

These can all be expressed as the union of the six following elementary sets:

$$\begin{aligned}
A_{1>2>3} &= (V_1 > V_2 > V_3),\\
A_{1>3>2} &= (V_1 > V_3 > V_2),\\
A_{2>1>3} &= (V_2 > V_1 > V_3),\\
A_{2>3>1} &= (V_2 > V_3 > V_1),\\
A_{3>2>1} &= (V_3 > V_2 > V_1),\\
A_{3>1>2} &= (V_3 > V_1 > V_2).
\end{aligned} \tag{3.4}$$

Where, for example, the first line should be read "the set of ω for which one is preferred to two, and two preferred to three," and so on. Thus we have:

$$\begin{aligned}
A_{1|123} &= A_{1>2>3} \cup A_{1>3>2},\\
A_{1|12} &= A_{1>2>3} \cup A_{1>3>2} \cup A_{3>1>2},
\end{aligned}$$

etc.

3.3.2 *Introduction to Probabilistic Choice Models*

At this point it may be useful to take a more formal look at what constitutes the state of the world at the point in time in which the choice is made. Among the elements of ω which impact on the decision, some may be known: traits of the individual and variables controllable by the researcher, to mention a few. We will denote these $\mathbf{x}$. Other factors, which we will call α, may be unknown or known and unobservable. These are generally considered random. Since we only know a subset $\mathbf{x}$ of the environment we cannot foresee the individual's choices with certainty. We can however, form a reasonable prediction of how he will act in any given state of the world by calculating the probability of each choice from the conditional distribution of α given $\mathbf{x}$.

The *selection probability* associated with $A_{m|M}$ is denoted $P_{m|M}$ (This probability is conditional on $\mathbf{x}$, but for simplicity this dependence is suppressed in the notation).

The decomposition of the choice sets into elementary sets translates directly into the selection probabilities. Consider the three-value case:

$$\begin{aligned}
q_1 &= \Pr(A_{1>2>3}),\\
q_2 &= \Pr(A_{1>3>2}),\\
q_3 &= \Pr(A_{2>1>3}),\\
q_4 &= \Pr(A_{2>3>1}),\\
q_5 &= \Pr(A_{3>2>1}),\\
q_6 &= \Pr(A_{3>1>2}),
\end{aligned}$$

which yields:

$$\begin{aligned}
P_{1|123} &= q_1 + q_2,\\
P_{2|123} &= q_3 + q_4,\\
P_{3|123} &= q_5 + q_6,\\
P_{1|12} &= q_1 + q_2 + q_6,\\
P_{2|12} &= q_3 + q_4 + q_5,\\
P_{1|13} &= q_1 + q_2 + q_3,\\
P_{3|13} &= q_4 + q_5 + q_6,\\
P_{2|23} &= q_3 + q_4 + q_1,\\
P_{3|23} &= q_5 + q_6 + q_2.
\end{aligned} \tag{3.5}$$

3.3.3 *Specifying the Model*

Here we have a classical model of qualitative choice. For each experiment conducted under conditions $\mathbf{x}$ we have defined the probability of observing a given result $m : P_{m|M}$, where M is the choice set. To complete the model we now have to specify the relationship between these probabilities and $\mathbf{x}$. We will look at three suggested formulations for the case of three values:

3.3.3.1 First Approach

The probabilities $q_1 \ldots q_6$ are formulated in terms of **x**, from which the selection probabilities are derived. We could, for example, let:

$$q_i = \frac{\exp(\mathbf{x}_i \mathbf{b}_i)}{\sum_{i=1}^{6} \exp(\mathbf{x}_i \mathbf{b}_i)}.$$

The disadvantage of this method is that the selection probabilities tend to have complicated forms and are hence difficult to estimate.

3.3.3.2 Second Approach

The selection probabilities are directly expressed as functions of **x**. When using this approach we must ensure that the axioms of rational behaviour are satisfied.

3.3.3.3 Third Approach

Postulating the distribution of the utility function a priori, we derive the expressions for the selection probabilities. This is the usual approach. We write $V_m = \mathbf{x}_m \mathbf{b}_m + v_m$, where v_m is a disturbance term. When we specify the distribution of this term we have the analytical form of the selection probabilities.

This methodology is very similar to the one we used in sections 3.1 and 3.2 because it is based on latent variables V_m. However, estimation of the utility function, which is defined up to a monotonic transformation, yields non-interpretable values. We can, furthermore, question the usefulness of the formulation $V_m = \mathbf{x}_m \mathbf{b}_m + v_m$, as it is not invariant with respect to a monotonic transformation of V_m.

Example 8: Consider a three-value case and assume that the error terms v_1, v_2, v_3 are independent and identically distributed according to the Weibull distribution, given by $F(v) = \exp\left[-\exp(-v)\right]$.

We have:

$$\begin{aligned}
P_{1|123} &= \Pr(V_1 > V_2, V_1 > V_3), \\
P_{1|123} &= \Pr(\mathbf{x}_1\mathbf{b}_1 + v_1 > \mathbf{x}_2\mathbf{b}_2 + v_2, \mathbf{x}_1\mathbf{b}_1 + v_1 > \mathbf{x}_3\mathbf{b}_3 + v_3), \\
&= \Pr(v_2 < v_1 + \mathbf{x}_1\mathbf{b}_1 - \mathbf{x}_2\mathbf{b}_2, v_3 < v_1 + \mathbf{x}_1\mathbf{b}_1 - \mathbf{x}_3\mathbf{b}_3), \\
&= \int_{-\infty}^{+\infty} \exp\{-\exp[-(v + \mathbf{x}_1\mathbf{b}_1 - \mathbf{x}_2\mathbf{b}_2)]\} \\
&\quad \exp\{-\exp[-(v + \mathbf{x}_1\mathbf{b}_1 - \mathbf{x}_3\mathbf{b}_3)]\}\, d\left\{\exp\left[-\exp(-v)\right]\right\},
\end{aligned}$$

$$= \int_{-\infty}^{+\infty} \exp\left\{-\exp(-v)\left[\exp(\mathbf{x}_2\mathbf{b}_2 - \mathbf{x}_1\mathbf{b}_1) + \exp(\mathbf{x}_3\mathbf{b}_3 - \mathbf{x}_1\mathbf{b}_1) + 1\right]\right\} d\left[\exp(-v)\right],$$

$$= \frac{1}{\exp(\mathbf{x}_2\mathbf{b}_2 - \mathbf{x}_1\mathbf{b}_1) + \exp(\mathbf{x}_3\mathbf{b}_3 - \mathbf{x}_1\mathbf{b}_1) + 1},$$

$$= \frac{\exp(\mathbf{x}_1\mathbf{b}_1)}{\sum_{i=1}^{3}\exp(\mathbf{x}_i\mathbf{b}_i)}.$$

The other selection probabilities have similar forms:

$$P_{2|123} = \frac{\exp(\mathbf{x}_2\mathbf{b}_2)}{\sum_{i=1}^{3}\exp(\mathbf{x}_i\mathbf{b}_i)},$$

$$P_{3|123} = \frac{\exp(\mathbf{x}_3\mathbf{b}_3)}{\sum_{i=1}^{3}\exp(\mathbf{x}_i\mathbf{b}_i)},$$

$$P_{1|12} = \frac{\exp(\mathbf{x}_1\mathbf{b}_1)}{\sum_{i=1}^{2}\exp(\mathbf{x}_i\mathbf{b}_i)},$$

$$P_{2|12} = \frac{\exp(\mathbf{x}_2\mathbf{b}_2)}{\sum_{i=1}^{2}\exp(\mathbf{x}_i\mathbf{b}_i)},$$

etc.

These forms generalize the dichotomous logit model to the *polychotomous logit model.*

Notice that we had to choose a rather unusual distribution function in order to obtain tractable forms for the selection probabilities. However, as it is generally true that any monotonically increasing transformation h of a utility function f will yield the same choices as f, we have some flexibility in our choice. Notice also that under the formulation given above the parameters cannot be recovered, since the probabilities depend only on the differences $\mathbf{x}_1\mathbf{b}_1 - \mathbf{x}_2\mathbf{b}_2$, $\mathbf{x}_1\mathbf{b}_1 - \mathbf{x}_3\mathbf{b}_3$, and $\mathbf{x}_2\mathbf{b}_2 - \mathbf{x}_3\mathbf{b}_3$. In order to obtain identifiability, we must impose exclusion conditions on the parameters, such as $\mathbf{b}_1 = 0$ if $\mathbf{x}_1 = \mathbf{x}_2 = \mathbf{x}_3 = \mathbf{x}$, which corresponds to performing a translation of $\mathbf{x}\mathbf{b}_1$ onto utility V.

3.3.4 *Independence of an Irrelevant Alternative*

A fundamental principle which applies to these models is known as the independence of irrelevent alternatives. If a new option is added to an individual's choice set, and if it is similar to a option which already exists, then the probability of any other option being chosen should not be affected.

Examination of the polychotomous logit model obtained in example 8 reveals that:

$$\frac{P_{1|123}}{P_{2|123}} = \frac{P_{1|12}}{P_{2|12}} = \frac{\exp(\mathbf{x}_1\mathbf{b}_1)}{\exp(\mathbf{x}_2\mathbf{b}_2)}.$$

The choice between one and two is unaffected by the availability of option three. We say that the choice between one and two is independent of the irrelevant alternative three. Given the symmetry of the polychotomous logit model, this holds for choices one and two as well.

Consider a set of selection probabilities between three options and assume that the independence of irrelevant alternatives (i.i.a.) holds:

$$\frac{P_{1|123}}{P_{2|123}} = \frac{P_{1|12}}{P_{2|12}},$$
$$\frac{P_{1|123}}{P_{3|123}} = \frac{P_{1|13}}{P_{3|13}},$$
$$\frac{P_{2|123}}{P_{3|123}} = \frac{P_{2|23}}{P_{3|23}}.$$

The first equality yields:

$$\frac{P_{1|12}}{P_{1|123}} = \frac{P_{2|12}}{P_{2|123}} = \frac{1}{P_{1|123} + P_{2|123}} \Rightarrow P_{1|12} = \frac{P_{1|123}}{P_{1|123} + P_{2|123}}.$$

Repeating this exercise for each equality, we see that the choice probabilities have the form:

$$P_{1|123} = \frac{\alpha_1}{\alpha_1 + \alpha_2 + \alpha_3},$$
$$P_{2|123} = \frac{\alpha_2}{\alpha_1 + \alpha_2 + \alpha_3},$$
$$P_{3|123} = \frac{\alpha_3}{\alpha_1 + \alpha_2 + \alpha_3},$$
$$P_{1|12} = \frac{\alpha_1}{\alpha_1 + \alpha_2},$$
$$P_{2|12} = \frac{\alpha_2}{\alpha_1 + \alpha_2},$$
$$P_{1|13} = \frac{\alpha_1}{\alpha_1 + \alpha_3},$$
$$P_{3|13} = \frac{\alpha_3}{\alpha_1 + \alpha_2},$$
$$P_{1|23} = \frac{\alpha_2}{\alpha_2 + \alpha_3},$$
$$P_{3|23} = \frac{\alpha_3}{\alpha_2 + \alpha_3},$$

where $\alpha_1, \alpha_2, \alpha_3 \geq 0$.

This is similar to what we saw in example 8, except that α_i is not explicitly formulated in terms of the conditions $\mathbf{x}$. Thus we see that choosing the polychotomous logit model is tantamount to making the hypothesis of the independence of irrelevant alternatives.

We now wish to see under what conditions this hypothesis is satisfied in practice. The best illustration can be found in an example where it manifestly does not hold, commonly referred to as the "blue bus, red bus" problem.

Assume you ask an individual which means he prefers for his commute to work: **i)** the subway, **ii)** a blue bus, or **iii)** a red bus. We can reasonably assume that the colour of the bus is not a significant factor in a typical individual's choice of which form of transportation to use, so we would expect that $P_{2|123} = P_{3|123}$. If you now ask him whether he prefers taking the subway or a bus, the choice probabilities should be:

$$P_{1|12} = P_{1|123},$$
$$P_{2|12} = P_{2|123} + P_{3|123}.$$

This gives us:

$$\frac{P_{1|12}}{P_{2|12}} = \frac{P_{1|123}}{P_{2|123} + P_{3|123}},$$
$$= \frac{1}{2}\frac{P_{1|123}}{P_{2|123}},$$

so the hypothesis that the choice between options one and two does not depend on three is not borne out.

Due to the i.i.a., this form of the polychotomous logit model is not suitable to explain all types of behaviour. In light of this problem, we have several choices:

(i) We can select a distribution for the utility function for which the independence of irrelevant alternatives does not hold. We can, for example, postulate that the errors (v_1, v_2, v_3) are distributed:

$$N\left[\begin{pmatrix} 0 \\ 0 \\ 0 \end{pmatrix} \begin{pmatrix} 1 & \rho_{12} & \rho_{13} \\ \rho_{12} & 1 & \rho_{23} \\ \rho_{13} & \rho_{23} & 1 \end{pmatrix}\right].$$

(ii) We can reformulate the model, while retaining use of the logistic function, to create a structure in which the i.i.a. is no longer an issue. For example, in the blue bus, red bus scenario we can break the decision down into two stages: first the individual chooses between the subway and the bus, which we analyse using a dichotomous logit model, then chooses between the blue and red buses with probability $\frac{1}{2}$, $\frac{1}{2}$ (cf. section 3.4.1).

Finally, notice that observations will generally correspond to selections from one solution set, for example $\{1, 2, 3\}$. In this case, only the expressions for $P_{1|123}$, $P_{2|123}$, and $P_{3|123}$ can be recovered, and they may be identical to those yielded by the polychotomous logit model. This will not hold true for the other probabilities (cf. exercise 4).

3.4 Individual Preferences: Several Decision-Makers

The theory derived in the previous section incorporates the implicit assumption that there is only one decision maker. Clearly, situations exist in which that is not realistic. For example, when individual choices result from a sequence of successive decisions, behaviour should not be modelled as a single maximization of a utility function, but rather as a series of maximizations, each one conditional on previous decisions. This situation is best represented by a model of several decision makers, even though it pertains to a single individual's behaviour. This approach is suitable, for example, for modelling how an individual chooses his vacation destination and what means of transportation he will use to get there. It seems reasonable that the decision of where to go precedes, and determines, the choice of how to get there.

In the same vein, the theory discussed in the previous section is not applicable to modelling situations in which several different agents make decisions simultaneously. This problem is examined more closely in section 3.4.2 where we look at some examples.

3.4.1 Sequential Decisions†

At the end of the previous section we observed that the "blue bus, red bus" problem can intuitively be handled by a two-stage process: first the individual chooses between the subway and the bus, then decides on the colour of the bus. We thus distinguish between the "means of transportation" aspect and the "colour" aspect. This process can be illustrated by a *decision tree*, each node represents a stage of the decision making process with branches for the available choices at that level. This approach can easily be generalized as follows:

Define a partition of the consumption set into K elements, $k = 1, \ldots, K$ (first aspect), and subsequently partition each of the ensuing K subsets into L_k elements $\ell = 1, \ldots, L_k$ (second aspect), and so on until we have reached the most detailed level, corresponding to the original choices. The resulting H-order sequential model of the various aspects gives rise to H nested choices. The ordering of the aspects obviously plays a key role in this model.

† cf. Tversky [Tve72a], [Tve72b], [Tve77].

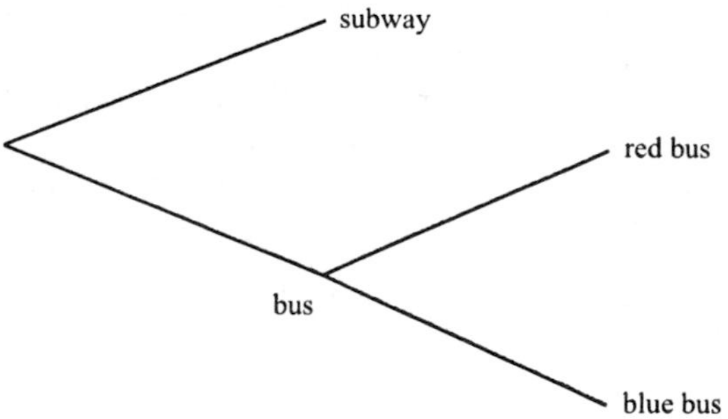

Fig. 3.1. A decision tree

Use of the polychotomous logit model to formulate the decision at each branch of the tree allows us to derive the selection probabilities. Consider, for example, the case of two successive aspects. Each choice m is characterized by two elements: k – denoting the primary aspect, and ℓ – the secondary aspect. We can write $m = (k, \ell)$. The values $k = 1, \ldots, K$ of the primary aspect are formulated using a logit model, yielding the probability:

$$\frac{\alpha_k}{\alpha_1 + \ldots + \alpha_K},$$

for aspect k. If k is chosen at the first stage, it remains to select $\ell = 1, \ldots, L_k$ among the secondary aspects. If we model this choice with the logit polychotomous model as well, the probability of selecting ℓ at this second stage is given by:

$$\frac{\beta_{k\ell}}{\beta_{k1} + \ldots + \beta_{kL_k}}.$$

The selection probability of $m = (k, \ell)$ has the form:

$$P_{m|M} = P_{(k,\ell)|M} = \frac{\alpha_k}{\alpha_1 + \ldots + \alpha_K} \frac{\beta_{k\ell}}{\beta_{k1} + \ldots + \beta_{kL_k}}. \tag{3.6}$$

If the parameters α_k, β_{kl} are written as exponentiations of linear functions of the explanatory variables, this model is called *sequential logit*.

Postulating that each stage of the decision making process fits a polychotomous logit model is tantamount to assuming that at each level the independence of irrelevant alternatives obtains. This suggests that the placement of the options in the decision tree is important. Notice, though, that even if the i.i.a. hypothesis must hold for each level of the decision tree, it does not need to hold globally.

To illustrate, assume that we have a model of choice with two primary aspects $\{1, 2\}$. Option one leads to a further choice between two options $\{1, 2\}$ while primary aspect two presents only one possibility at the second stage, {3}. In other words, the decision maker must first choose between two options, and only if the first is selected is a further choice necessary. The selection probabilities are:

$$P_{1|123} = \frac{\alpha_1}{\alpha_1 + \alpha_2} \frac{\beta_1}{\beta_1 + \beta_2},$$
$$P_{2|123} = \frac{\alpha_1}{\alpha_1 + \alpha_2} \frac{\beta_2}{\beta_1 + \beta_2},$$
$$P_{3|123} = \frac{\alpha_2}{\alpha_1 + \alpha_2}.$$

If we restrict the consumption set and apply the conditional logit model at each stage, we can calculate new selection probabilities:

$$P_{1|12} = \frac{\beta_1}{\beta_1 + \beta_2},$$
$$P_{2|12} = \frac{\beta_2}{\beta_1 + \beta_2},$$
$$P_{1|13} = P_{2|23} = \frac{\alpha_1}{\alpha_1 + \alpha_2},$$
$$P_{3|13} = P_{3|23} = \frac{\alpha_2}{\alpha_1 + \alpha_2}.$$

We see that:

$$\frac{P_{1|12}}{P_{2|12}} = \frac{P_{1|123}}{P_{2|123}},$$

so the choice between alternatives one and two is independent of alternative three. On the other hand,

$$\frac{P_{1|13}}{P_{3|13}} = \frac{\alpha_1}{\alpha_2}$$

is not, generally, the same as:

$$\frac{P_{1|123}}{P_{3|123}} = \frac{\alpha_1}{\alpha_2} \frac{\beta_1}{\beta_1 + \beta_2}.$$

3.4.2 *Simultaneous Decisions Involving More than One Agent*

3.4.2.1 *Unanimous Decisions*

A model of this type was proposed by Poirier [Poi80] to examine factors which affect the level of difficulty which an unemployed person experiences finding a job.

A job-seeker will fill a given position if the following two conditions are satisfied: He must deem the job suitable:

$$y^1 = \begin{cases} 1, & \text{if the job is suitable,} \\ 0, & \text{otherwise,} \end{cases}$$

and the prospective employer must feel that he has the necessary abilities:

$$y^2 = \begin{cases} 1, & \text{if the candidate is qualified,} \\ 0, & \text{otherwise.} \end{cases}$$

Assume that y^1, y^2 are independent and that:

$$\Pr\left(y^1 = 1\right) = F\left(\mathbf{x}^1\mathbf{b}^1\right),$$
$$\Pr\left(y^2 = 1\right) = F\left(\mathbf{x}^2\mathbf{b}^2\right).$$

The observed variable y is:

$$y = \begin{cases} 1, & \text{if the applicant occupies the position,} \\ 0, & \text{otherwise,} \end{cases}$$

For $y = 1$, both agents, job-seeker and employer, must agree:

$$\begin{aligned} \Pr(y = 1) &= \Pr\left(y^1 = 1, y^2 = 1\right), \\ &= F\left(\mathbf{x}^1\mathbf{b}^1\right) F\left(\mathbf{x}^2\mathbf{b}^2\right), \\ \Pr(y = 0) &= 1 - F\left(\mathbf{x}^1\mathbf{b}^1\right) F\left(\mathbf{x}^2\mathbf{b}^2\right). \end{aligned}$$

We obtain a dichotomous model of a different form from that studied in chapter 2.

3.4.2.2 Behaviour Conditional on that of Another Agent

Assume we want to study the question of why, in some households, only one spouse works, while in others both have a job. We need to explain the values taken by two dichotomous variables:

$$y^1 = \begin{cases} 1, & \text{if the man works,} \\ 0, & \text{otherwise,} \end{cases}$$
$$y^2 = \begin{cases} 1, & \text{if the woman works,} \\ 0, & \text{otherwise.} \end{cases}$$

Several models have been proposed, each reflecting different assumptions concerning the couple's behaviour.

Case One Assume first that the husband (wife) makes the decision for the household. In this case there is only one decision maker and we can apply the polychotomous logit model from section 3.3, giving us:

$$\begin{aligned}
P_{11} &= \Pr\left(y^1 = 1, y^2 = 1\right), \\
&= \frac{\exp\left(\mathbf{x}^1\mathbf{b}^1\right)}{\sum_{h=1}^{4} \exp\left(\mathbf{x}^h\mathbf{b}^h\right)}, \\
P_{10} &= \Pr\left(y^1 = 1, y^2 = 0\right), \\
&= \frac{\exp\left(\mathbf{x}^2\mathbf{b}^2\right)}{\sum_{h=1}^{4} \exp\left(\mathbf{x}^h\mathbf{b}^h\right)}, \\
P_{01} &= \Pr\left(y^1 = 0, y^2 = 1\right), \\
&= \frac{\exp\left(\mathbf{x}^3\mathbf{b}^3\right)}{\sum_{h=1}^{4} \exp\left(\mathbf{x}^h\mathbf{b}^h\right)}, \\
P_{11} &= \Pr\left(y^1 = 0, y^2 = 0\right), \\
&= \frac{\exp\left(\mathbf{x}^4\mathbf{b}^4\right)}{\sum_{h=1}^{4} \exp\left(\mathbf{x}^h\mathbf{b}^h\right)}.
\end{aligned}$$

Case Two Another possible way of modelling the couple's behaviour is as follows. The man decides first whether or not he'll work.

$$\begin{aligned}
\Pr\left(y^1 = 1\right) &= \frac{1}{1 + \exp\left(\mathbf{x}^1\mathbf{b}^1\right)}, \\
\Pr\left(y^1 = 0\right) &= \frac{\exp\left(\mathbf{x}^1\mathbf{b}^1\right)}{1 + \exp\left(\mathbf{x}^1\mathbf{b}^1\right)}.
\end{aligned}$$

Subsequently, the woman bases her decision on his choice:

$$\begin{aligned}
\Pr\left(y^2 = 1 \middle| y^1 = 1\right) &= \frac{1}{1 + \exp\left(\mathbf{x}^2\mathbf{b}^2\right)}, \\
\Pr\left(y^2 = 0 \middle| y^1 = 1\right) &= \frac{\exp\left(\mathbf{x}^2\mathbf{b}^2\right)}{1 + \exp\left(\mathbf{x}^2\mathbf{b}^2\right)}, \\
\Pr\left(y^2 = 1 \middle| y^1 = 0\right) &= \frac{1}{1 + \exp\left(\mathbf{x}^3\mathbf{b}^3\right)}, \\
\Pr\left(y^2 = 0 \middle| y^1 = 0\right) &= \frac{\exp\left(\mathbf{x}^3\mathbf{b}^3\right)}{1 + \exp\left(\mathbf{x}^3\mathbf{b}^3\right)}.
\end{aligned}$$

We can now derive the probabilities of the joint distribution. For example:

$$\begin{aligned}
P_{11} &= \Pr\left(y^1 = 1\right) \Pr\left(y^2 = 1 \middle| y^1 = 1\right), \\
&= \frac{1}{1 + \exp\left(\mathbf{x}^1\mathbf{b}^1\right)} \frac{1}{1 + \exp\left(\mathbf{x}^2\mathbf{b}^2\right)}.
\end{aligned}$$

These probabilities are *marginal-conditional.*

Case Three If each individual selects his own course of action on the principle that the other's behaviour is given, we come up with yet another model. This model is defined by the following four conditional distributions:

$$\begin{aligned}
\Pr\left(y^1 = 1 \middle| y^2 = 0\right) &= \frac{1}{1 + \exp\left(\mathbf{x}^1\mathbf{b}^1\right)}, \\
\Pr\left(y^1 = 1 \middle| y^2 = 1\right) &= \frac{1}{1 + \exp\left(\mathbf{x}^2\mathbf{b}^2\right)}, \\
\Pr\left(y^2 = 1 \middle| y^1 = 0\right) &= \frac{1}{1 + \exp\left(\mathbf{x}^3\mathbf{b}^3\right)}, \\
\Pr\left(y^2 = 1 \middle| y^1 = 1\right) &= \frac{1}{1 + \exp\left(\mathbf{x}^4\mathbf{b}^4\right)}.
\end{aligned} \tag{3.7}$$

Intuitively, we can easily see that this type of conditional behaviour is not necessarily compatible. Assume, for example, that the man decides to work if his wife works, and not to work if she doesn't. The wife, on the other hand, decides not to work if her husband works and to work if he doesn't. This is obviously incompatible behaviour.

In order for the postulated conditional distributions to unambiguously define a course of action for the couple, they clearly have to be compatible. Mathematically, this means that $\mathbf{x}^1\mathbf{b}^1 + \mathbf{x}^3\mathbf{b}^3 = \mathbf{x}^2\mathbf{b}^2 + \mathbf{x}^4\mathbf{b}^4$ must be satisfied. In this case the couple's behaviour is perfectly defined (cf. appendix 3.2). This model is called *conditional-conditional.*

3.4.2.3 *Behaviour Conditional on that of a Group of Agents*

In the preceding section we looked at ways to model how an agent adjusts his behaviour to account for that of another individual. The model is different, however, when we divide all the agents into two groups, assumed very large, and make the behaviour of a given member of one group dependent on the collective behaviour of all the members of the other group. Consider, for example, ownership of a certain durable good by two different categories of people. If imitation plays a role, members of the first group, when making their purchasing decision, will take into consideration the proportion of the second group who own the good. If p_1 (p_2) is the proportion of members of the first (second) group who own the good, then p_1 (p_2) represents the probability of a member of group one (two) owning the good (if the groups are large), and this probability depends on p_2 (p_1). Using the logistic form, we write:

$$\begin{aligned}
p_1 &= \frac{1}{1 + \exp\left(a_1 p_2 + b_1\right)}, \\
p_2 &= \frac{1}{1 + \exp\left(a_2 p_1 + b_2\right)}.
\end{aligned} \tag{3.8}$$

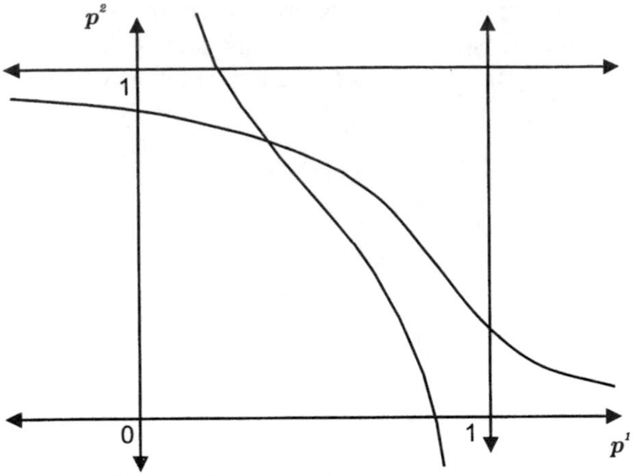

Fig. 3.2. Behaviour conditional on a group of agents

Obviously, we have to verify that this system yields a unique solution in p_1 and p_2. Assume, for example, that a_1 and a_2 are strictly positive. The mapping of $p_2 \in \mathbb{R}$ to:

$$\frac{1}{1 + \exp(a_1 p_2 + b_1)}$$

is decreasing, approaching one as p_2 approaches $-\infty$ and zero as p_2 approaches $+\infty$. The function which maps $p_1 \in \mathbb{R}$ to:

$$\frac{1}{1 + \exp(a_2 p_1 + b_2)}$$

has similar properties.

Graphing these functions together, with p_1 on the abscissa and p_2 on the ordinate, we see that they have a unique point of intersection such that values of p_1 and p_2 are contained in the open interval $(1, 0)$.

In this case, the behaviour of an individual in the first group is independent of the behaviour of any one individual in the second group. Or, more precisely, the latter's influence is negligible as it only works through his impact on p_2.

3.5 Importance of the Sampling Method

Models of qualitative choice contain two sources of randomness. So far we have examined the first, originating in the behaviour of individuals. We now turn our attention to the second, which results from the sampling procedure itself.

Models of individual behaviour attempt to describe the actions of a clearly defined population. Usually, however, the entire population cannot be observed. Denote the population Π, each individual has a vector of exogenous characteristics $\mathbf{x}$ and a vector of endogenous characteristics $\mathbf{y}$. These latter, qualitative variables, take values j conditional on $\mathbf{x} = \mathbf{x}_i$ with probability p_{ij}. p_{ij} depends on $\mathbf{x}_i$ and on the parameters $\mathbf{b}$: $p_{ij} = p_j(\mathbf{x}_i; \mathbf{b})$, which are to be estimated. Furthermore, the exogenous characteristics $\mathbf{x}$ are distributed over the population by $\mu(\mathbf{x})$.

3.5.1 *Equi-Probable Sampling with Replacement*

Let the sample s comprising n individuals be drawn equi-probably with replacement from the population Π. The distribution of the observations $(\mathbf{x}_i, \mathbf{y}_i)$, $i \in s$ is proportional to:

$$\prod_{i \in s} \left\{ \mu(\mathbf{x}_i) \prod_{j=0}^{J} \left[P_j(\mathbf{x}_i; \mathbf{b})\right]^{z_i} \right\} = \prod_{i \in s} [\mu(\mathbf{x}_i)] \prod_{i \in s} \prod_{j=0}^{J} \left[P_j(\mathbf{x}_i; \mathbf{b})^{z_i}\right],$$

hence it is also proportional to:

$$\prod_{i \in s} \prod_{j=0}^{J} \left[P_j(\mathbf{x}_i; \mathbf{b})^{z_i}\right]. \tag{3.9}$$

Since only this part of the distribution depends upon the parameter $\mathbf{b}$, it is all we need to obtain our estimates, using, for example, maximum-likelihood estimators. This simply means that it is possible for us to reason conditional on $\{\mathbf{x}_i; i \in s\}$. When a sampling method leads to an expression of the form (3.9) we have a *multinomial distribution*.

3.5.2 *Exogenous Stratification*

Assume that the exogenous variables can only assume a finite number of values $\mathbf{x}^k, k = 1, \ldots, K$, and that we stratify our sample using $\mathbf{x}$. We need to establish the optimal size of each sample n_k drawn independently from the sub-populations Π_k.

If n_{kj} indicates the number of individuals from the k-th sample for whom y_i assumes the value j, the distribution of the observations is proportional to:

$$\prod_{k=1}^{K} \prod_{j=0}^{J} P_j(\mathbf{x}_k; \mathbf{b})^{n_{kj}} = \prod_{i \in s} \prod_{j=0}^{J} \left[P_j(\mathbf{x}_j; \mathbf{b})\right]^{z_i}.$$

Again, this is multinomial.

3.5.3 Endogenous Stratification

When studying the means of transportation used by individuals commuting to work it is standard procedure to question them where they get off the bus, exit the subway, etc. This is stratification by an endogenous characteristic y, also called choice-based sampling.

Let n_j represent the size of a sample drawn independently from the sub-population Π_j of individuals for whom $y_i = j$, and n_{kj} the number of individuals from the j-th sample for whom $\mathbf{x}_i$ assumes the value $\mathbf{x}_k$. The distribution of the observations is proportional to:

$$\prod_{j=0}^{J} \prod_{k=1}^{K} \left[\Pr \left(\mathbf{x}_k \,|\, y_i = j; \mathbf{b} \right)^{n_{kj}} \right],$$

where $\Pr(\mathbf{x}_k | \mathbf{y}_i = j; \mathbf{b})$ is the probability that $\mathbf{x}_i$ has the value $\mathbf{x}_k$, given that $y_i = j$. This conditional probability can also be written:

$$\Pr(\mathbf{x}_k \,|\, y_i = j; \mathbf{b}) = \frac{P_j(\mathbf{x}_k; \mathbf{b})\, \mu(\mathbf{x}_k)}{\sum_{k=1}^{K} P_j(\mathbf{x}_k, \mathbf{b})\, \mu(\mathbf{x}_k)} \quad \text{(Bayes' formula)}.$$

This equation is no longer multinomial, and has a more complicated distribution for the behavioural parameters $\mathbf{b}$. The distribution is proportional to:

$$\prod_{j=0}^{J} \prod_{k=1}^{K} \left[\frac{P_j(\mathbf{x}_k, \mathbf{b})}{\sum_{k=1}^{K} P_j(\mathbf{x}_k, \mathbf{b})\, \mu(\mathbf{x}_k)} \right]^{n_{kj}}.$$

Henceforth we will always assume that the multinomial distribution obtains, but it is important to bear in mind that this formulation is inappropriate for certain types of sampling procedures. Its use in these cases yields non-convergent estimators (cf. exercises 6 and 7).

3.6 Variations on the Basic Models

The various models considered in the preceding sections must be considered archetypes requiring modification before being applied to practical cases. The original model is generally expanded by the addition of supplementary parameters so as to obtain a more tractable form of the response function. We will present two such modifications for the ordered univariate model (cf. section 3.1.1).

These modified models are sometimes used to evaluate responses to questionnaires on trend data. The study group is asked to conjecture on the evolution of a given variable, and given a choice among the following three possibilities:

↗	→	↘
increase	no change	decrease.

If we denote Δr the change in value of a variable r, and α_0 and α_1 ($\alpha_0 < \alpha_1$), the threshold values used by the respondents to evaluate the change in r, we have:

$$\begin{aligned}
&\nearrow \text{ if } \Delta r < \alpha_0,\\
&\rightarrow \text{ if } \alpha_0 \leq \Delta r < \alpha_1,\\
&\searrow \text{ if } \Delta r \geq \alpha_1.
\end{aligned}$$

The probabilities associated with each value assumed by the variables are then given by:

$$\begin{aligned}
P_0 &= \Pr(\Delta r < \alpha_0),\\
P_1 &= \Pr(\alpha_0 \leq \Delta r < \alpha_1),\\
P_2 &= \Pr(\alpha_1 \leq \Delta r).
\end{aligned}$$

3.6.1 *Modification by a Scaling Factor*

The procedure used in section 3.1.1 consisted of describing the latent variable Δr with a linear model: $\Delta r = \mathbf{xb} + u$, where u is distributed according to a density function F. This gave us:

$$\begin{aligned}
P_0 &= F(\alpha_0 - \mathbf{xb}),\\
P_0 + P_1 &= F(\alpha_1 - \mathbf{xb}).
\end{aligned}$$

Anderson [And84] proposed a modification of this model entailing the addition of a scaling factor in front of the explanatory variables, yielding:

$$\begin{aligned}
P_0 &= F(\alpha_0 - \beta_0\mathbf{xb}),\\
P_0 + P_1 &= F(\alpha_1 - \beta_1\mathbf{xb}).
\end{aligned}$$

Obviously, the auxiliary parameters must be constrained:

(i) to ensure the identifiability of the parameters (set $\beta_0 = 1$).

(ii) to ensure the inequality $p_1 \geq 0$ (set $\beta_1 \leq \beta_0 = 1$, if $\mathbf{xb}$ is always positive).

This expanded model includes the original as the special case $\beta_0 = \beta_1 = 1$.

3.6.2 *The Stochastic Indifference Interval*

Sometimes it is possible to augment the qualitative results of trend surveys with quantitative results from other surveys. Thus, in some cases, we simultaneously have available responses to qualitative questions about $\nearrow$, $\rightarrow$, $\searrow$ and data on Δr. We can then attempt to understand how the respondents formed their responses to the qualitative questions – that is, how they establish the cut-off points α_0 and α_1. If we retain the same formulas for the probabilities of

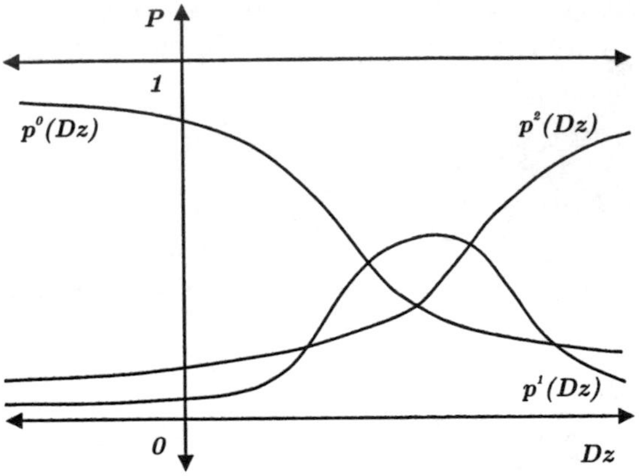

Fig. 3.3. Response functions for the stochastic indifference interval

the responses:

$$P_0(\Delta r) = \Pr(\Delta r < \alpha_0),$$
$$P_1(\Delta r) = \Pr(\alpha_0 \leq \Delta r < \alpha_1),$$
$$P_2(\Delta r) = \Pr(\alpha_1 \leq \Delta r),$$

Δr can now be considered an exogenous variable and the values α_0 and α_1, which vary among respondents, as random.

Under the hypothesis that the distribution of the threshold values no longer depends upon Δr, we see that:

(i) $P_0(\Delta r)$ is decreasing in Δr,
(ii) $P_2(\Delta r)$ is increasing in Δr,
(iii) $P_1(\Delta r)$ tends toward 0 as Δr tends toward $\pm\infty$, and, if this function is reasonably regular, it is likely to be increasing at first and then decreasing.

In summary, the response functions have the shapes given in figure 3.3.

We see that we can define a model by first stipulating the distribution function of the threshold values α_0 and α_1. This procedure is not, however, necessarily straightforward, as the variables must be selected such that $\alpha_0 < \alpha_1$. Another possible solution involves directly postulating the functional forms for P_0, P_1, and P_2 so as to satisfy the above mentioned limits and conditions of monotonicity.

Thus, starting from a logit polychotomous formulation:

$$P_j(\Delta r) = \frac{\exp(\alpha_j + \beta_j \Delta r)}{\sum_{j=0}^{2} \exp(\alpha_j + \beta_j \Delta r)}, \quad j = \{0, 1, 2\}$$

we can easily show the following result (Ronning [Ron86]).

Proposition 4: In the polychotomous logit case:

(i) P_0 is decreasing with $P_0(-\infty) = 1$, $P_0(+\infty) = 0$.
(ii) P_1 has a unique maximum and $P_1(-\infty) = P_1(+\infty) = 0$.
(iii) P_2 is increasing with $P_2(-\infty) = 0$, $P_0(+\infty) = 1$,
iff $\beta_0 < \beta_1 < \beta_2$.

This example shows how the polychotomous logit model can be adapted to describe some ordered variables.

Exercises

3.1 Consider the example in section 3.2.1 and assume that the observations are as in table 3.2.
Represent this data in a graph. Does the model in the example explain the data? Use the graph to estimate the parameters a^1, b^1, a^2, and b^2. Is the correlation between the symptoms, ρ, positive?

3.2 Find the probabilities P_{1i}, P_{2i}, P_{3i} corresponding to the sequential trichotomous model in section 3.2.2 when (v_{1i}, v_{2i}) are normally distributed:

$$N\left[\begin{pmatrix}0\\0\end{pmatrix}\begin{pmatrix}1 & \rho\\ \rho & 1\end{pmatrix}\right].$$

3.3 Consider the model in section 3.2.3 with $K = 2$. Let:

$$(v_{1i}, v_{2i}, v_{3i}) \sim N\left[\begin{pmatrix}0\\0\\0\end{pmatrix}\begin{pmatrix}\sigma_1^2 & 0 & 0\\ 0 & \sigma_2^2 & 0\\ 0 & 0 & \sigma_3^2\end{pmatrix}\right].$$

Discuss the identification of the parameters: $b_1, b_2, b_3, \sigma_1^2, \sigma_2^2, \sigma_3^2$.

3.4 From the model in example 8, determine the distribution of $\exp(V)$ and find the other assumptions which need to be imposed on the random utility function in order to derive the polychotomous logit model.

3.5 Consider the following set of selection probabilities:

$$P_{1|123} = \frac{\exp\left(\mathbf{x}^1\mathbf{b}^1\right)}{\sum_{i=1}^{3}\exp\left(\mathbf{x}^i\mathbf{b}^i\right)},$$

$$P_{2|123} = \frac{\exp\left(\mathbf{x}^2\mathbf{b}^2\right)}{\sum_{i=1}^{3}\exp\left(\mathbf{x}^i\mathbf{b}^i\right)},$$

$$P_{3|123} = \frac{\exp\left(\mathbf{x}^3\mathbf{b}^3\right)}{\sum_{i=1}^{3}\exp\left(\mathbf{x}^i\mathbf{b}^i\right)},$$

$$P_{1|12} = P_{1|13} = P_{1|23}$$

$$P_{2|23} = P_{3|23} = \frac{1}{2}$$

$$P_{2|12} = P_{3|13} = 2P_{3|123}.$$

Show that these correspond to rational behaviour. Does the independence of independent alternatives apply?

3.6 Consider $n + m$ individuals having the same characteristics. The first n are given a choice between three options $1, 2, 3$ (with selection probabilities $P_1 = P_{1|123}$, $P_2 = P_{2|123}$, and $P_3 = P_{3|123}$). n_1 (n_2, n_3) choose option $1, (2, 3)$. The second group of m individuals are then made to choose between options 1 and 2 (with probabilities $R_1 = P_{1|12}$ and $R_2 = P_{2|12}$. m_1 choose 1, while $m_2 = m - m_1$ choose 2.

Find the maximum-likelihood estimators of P_1, P_2, P_3, R_1 and R_2. What are the maximum-likelihood estimators if the assumption of the i.i.a. applies to option 3. Test this assumption using the Lagrange multiplier method.

3.7 Verify that:

$$\frac{P_{1|123}}{P_{2|123}} = \frac{P_{1|12}}{P_{2|12}}$$

if and only if z_1 and z_2 are independent, where:

$$z_1 = \begin{cases} 1, & \text{if } V_1 > V_2, \\ 0, & \text{otherwise,} \end{cases}$$

and:

$$z_2 = \begin{cases} 1, & \text{if } V_3 > \max(V_1, V_2), \\ 0, & \text{otherwise.} \end{cases}$$

3.8 Show that if V_1, V_2, V_3 are independent random variables, it is possible to find an increasing transformation ϕ such that $\phi[V_1(\omega), \omega]$, $\phi[V_2(\omega), \omega]$ and $\phi[V_3(\omega), \omega]$ are as highly correlated as desired.

3.9 The quantities of goods consumed by an individual may be considered the result of a series of sequential decisions. Consider a person having income, R, and assume that he splits his income between consumption goods in a fixed proportion, such that $R = K \cdot R_0$, $K \in N$. The first amount, R_0, is allocated to the consumption of one of the goods $\ell = 1, \dots, L$, with probability P_ℓ, such that:

$$P_\ell > 0, \quad \sum_{\ell=1}^{L} P_\ell = 1.$$

The second amount, R_1, is independently allocated to the consumption of another good, using the same probability structure. This continues until all K sums are spent. Let n_ℓ represent the number of sums allocated to the consumption of good $\ell \left(\sum_{\ell=1}^{L} n_\ell = K \right)$. Find the distribution of $(n_1, \dots n_L)$. Express the expenditure on each good, D_t, as a function of n_t and derive the mean and the covariance matrix of $(D_t, \dots, D_\ell)$. Compare this mean with those which are traditionally used to describe completed demand systems.

Appendix 3.1 Existence of a Utility Function

Assume that the individual makes rational choices. Consequently, the choice sets are such that:

$$\forall m \in M' \subset M : A_{m|M} \subset A_{m|M'}.$$

We shall show that:

(i) all rational choices reduce to choices from among two options (binary choices),
(ii) rational choices are transitive,
(iii) making rational choices is equivalent to maximizing a utility function.

Lemma 1: We have:

$$A_{m|M} = \bigcap_{\substack{m' \in M \\ m' \neq m}} A_{m|M-\{m'\}}.$$

Proof:

(i) The hypothesis of rationality implies:

$$\forall m' \in M - \{m\} : A_{m|M} \subset A_{m|M-\{m'\}},$$

so:

$$A_{m|M} \subset \bigcap_{\substack{m' \in M \\ m' \neq m}} A_{m|M-\{m'\}}$$

(ii) To complete the proof we need to demonstrate that:

$$A_{m|M} \supset \bigcap_{\substack{m' \in M \\ m' \neq m}} A_{m|M-\{m'\}}.$$

For:

$$\forall m' \in M - \{m\}, \quad \forall m'' \in M - \{m, m'\},$$

we have:

$$A_{m''|M} \subset A_{m''|M-\{m'\}}.$$

Specifically:

$$A_{m''|M} \cap A_{m|M-\{m'\}} = \emptyset.$$

From which we derive that:

$$\forall m'' \in M - \{m\} : A_{m''|M} \cap \left[\bigcap_{\substack{m' \in M \\ m' \neq m}} A_{m|M-\{m'\}} \right] = \emptyset,$$

and so:

$$\cup_{\substack{m'' \in M \\ m'' \neq m}} A_{m''|M} \cap \left[\bigcap_{\substack{m' \in M \\ m' \neq m}} A_{m|M-\{m'\}} \right] = \emptyset.$$

Since the choice sets constitute a partition of Ω, we see that:

$$\bigcap_{\substack{m' \in M \\ m' \neq m}} A_{m|M-\{m'\}} \subset A_{m|M}.$$

□

Lemma 2: We know that:

$$A_{m|M} = \bigcap_{\substack{m' \in M \\ m' \neq m}} A_{m|m,m'}.$$

Proof: This result follows directly from lemma 1. Applying it to $A_{m|M-\{m',m''\}}$, we see that:

$$A_{m|M} = \bigcap_{\substack{m' \in M \\ m' \neq m}} \left[\bigcap_{\substack{m'' \in M \\ m'' \neq m}} A_{m|M-\{m',m''\}} \right].$$

Continuing in this vein leads to a decomposition consisting only of binary choices. □

Lemma 3:

$$A_{m|m,m'} \cap A_{m'|m',m''} \subset A_{m|m,m''}.$$

This reflects the transitive nature of binary choices, if m is prefered to m', and m' is prefered to m'', then m is prefered to m''.

Proof: From lemma 2 we know that:

$$A_{m|m,m',m''} = A_{m|m,m'} \cap A_{m|m,m''},$$
$$A_{m'|m,m',m''} = A_{m'|m,m'} \cap A_{m'|m',m''},$$
$$A_{m''|m,m',m''} = A_{m''|m,m''} \cap A_{m''|m',m''}.$$

Binary choices partition the set of states-of-the-world, Ω, as follows:

$$\Omega = A_{m|m,m'} \cup A_{m'|m,m'},$$
$$\Omega = A_{m|m,m''} \cup A_{m''|m,m''},$$
$$\Omega = A_{m'|m',m''} \cup A_{m''|m',m''}.$$

These three sets generate eight partitions of Ω. For example, $A_{m|m,m',m''}$, is composed of:

$$A_{m|m,m',m''} = \left(A_{m|m,m'} \cap A_{m|m,m''} \cap A_{m'|m',m''}\right)$$
$$\cup \left(A_{m|m,m'} \cap A_{m|m,m''} \cap A_{m''|m',m''}\right).$$

which we recognize as the union of two composites. $A_{m'|m,m',m''}$ and $A_{m''|m,m',m''}$ can be constructed similarly. Only six of the eight partitions of Ω come into play, however, since:

$$\Omega = A_{m|m,m',m''} \cup A_{m'|m,m',m''} \cup A_{m''|m,m',m''},$$

the following two set intersections are empty:

$$A_{m|m,m'} \cap A_{m'|m',m''} = \emptyset,$$
$$A_{m'|m,m'} \cap A_{m''|m',m''} = \emptyset.$$

In particular, the first equation allows us to write:

$$A_{m|m,m'} \cap A_{m'|m',m''} \subset^{c} A_{m''|m',m''} = A_{m|m,m''}$$

□

Theorem 1: Choice sets can be derived from utility maximization if and only if choices are rational.

Proof: The necessary condition is easy to verify, we discussed it in remark 3. To demonstrate the sufficient condition, we assume that choices are rational and define the function V as:

$$V_m(\omega) = \sum_{\substack{m' \in \mathcal{M} \\ m' \neq m}} Z_{m|m,m'}(\omega),$$

where $\mathcal{M}$ is the set of all possible options and $Z_{m|m,m'}(\omega)$ is defined:

$$Z_{m|m,m'}(\omega) = \begin{cases} 1, & \text{if } \omega \in A_{m|m,m'} \\ 0, & \text{otherwise.} \end{cases}$$

This utility function represents choices if:

$$\omega \in A_{m|M} \Leftrightarrow \forall m' \in M, \quad m' \neq m, \quad V_m(\omega) > V_{m'}(\omega).$$

According to lemma 2:

$$A_{m|M} = \bigcap_{\substack{m' \in M \\ m' \neq m}} A_{m|m,m'}.$$

To show the equivalence, it is sufficient to demonstrate that:

$$\forall m \in \mathcal{M}, \quad \forall m \in \mathcal{M} - \{m\} : \omega \in A_{m|m,m'} \Leftrightarrow V_m(\omega) > V_{m'}(\omega).$$

We shall do this in two steps.

A1.0.3 Necessary Condition

$$\omega \in A_{m|m,m'} \Rightarrow V_m(\omega) > V_{m'}(\omega).$$

We have:

$$\begin{aligned} V_m(\omega) - V_{m'}(\omega) &= \sum_{\substack{m'' \in \mathcal{M} \\ m'' \notin \{m,m'\}}} \left[Z_{m|m,m''}(\omega) - Z_{m|m',m''}(\omega) \right] \\ &\quad + \left[Z_{m|m,m'}(\omega) - Z_{m'|m,m''}(\omega) \right], \\ &= \sum_{\substack{m'' \in \mathcal{M} \\ m'' \notin \{m,m'\}}} \left[Z_{m|m,m''}(\omega) - Z_{m|m',m''}(\omega) \right] + 1, \end{aligned}$$

since $\omega \in A_{m|m,m'}$ by assumption, and thus $\omega \notin A_{m'|m,m'}$.

It is sufficient to show that each term on the RHS is non-negative. We shall procede by contradiction. Assume that one of these terms is negative:

$$Z_{m|m,m''}(\omega) - Z_{m|m',m''}(\omega) < 0.$$

In this case we must have:

$$\omega \notin A_{m|m,m''} \quad \text{and} \quad \omega \in A_{m'|m',m''}.$$

But according to lemma 3, this implies that $\omega \in A_{m'|m,m'}$, which contradicts our assumption. So all of the terms must be positive or null.

A1.0.4 Sufficient Condition

$$V_m(\omega) > V_{m'}(\omega) \Rightarrow \omega \in A_{m|m,m'}$$

It is sufficient to show the inverse:

$$\omega \notin A_{m|m,m'} \Rightarrow V_m(\omega) < V_{m'}(\omega),$$

or:

$$\omega \in A_{m'|m,m'} \Rightarrow V_{m'}(\omega) > V_m(\omega),$$

which follows directly from the necessary condition. □

Appendix 3.2 Compatibility Conditions

A2.1 Necessary Condition

Lemma 4:

$$\frac{\Pr\left(y^1 = 0 \mid y^2 = 0\right) \Pr\left(y^2 = 0 \mid y^1 = 1\right)}{\Pr\left(y^1 = 1 \mid y^2 = 0\right) \Pr\left(y^2 = 1 \mid y^1 = 1\right)} = \frac{\Pr\left(y^1 = 0 \mid y^2 = 1\right) \Pr\left(y^2 = 0 \mid y^1 = 0\right)}{\Pr\left(y^1 = 1 \mid y^2 = 1\right) \Pr\left(y^2 = 1 \mid y^1 = 0\right)}.$$

Proof: To demonstrate this equality it is sufficient to express the conditional probabilities in terms of the joint and marginal probabilities. We see that each member is equal to:

$$\frac{\Pr\left(y^1 = 0, y^2 = 0\right)}{\Pr\left(y^1 = 1, y^2 = 1\right)}$$

□

Replacing the conditional probabilities by their expression as functions of the explanatory variables, we obtain:

$$\exp\left(x^1 b^1\right) \exp\left(x^4 b^4\right) = \exp\left(x^2 b^2\right) \exp\left(x^3 b^3\right)$$
$$x^1 b^1 + x^4 b^4 = x^2 b^2 + x^3 b^3$$

A2.2 Sufficient Condition

Assume that the compatibility condition holds:

$$x^1 b^1 + x^4 b^4 = x^2 b^2 + x^3 b^3.$$

Define the joint distribution $(P_{00}, P_{01}, P_{10}, P_{11})$ by the relations:

$$P_{00} = \exp\left(x^1 b^1 + x^4 b^4\right) P_{11},$$
$$P_{10} = \exp\left(x^4 b^4\right) P_{11},$$
$$P_{01} = \exp\left(x^2 b^2\right) P_{11},$$
$$P_{11} = 1 - P_{00} + P_{10} + P_{01}.$$

We can easily confirm that the conditional distributions associated with this distribution are given by (3.7)

$$\Pr\left(y^1 = 1 \middle| y^2 = 0\right) = \frac{P_{10}}{P_{00} + P_{10}},$$
$$= \frac{1}{1 + \exp\left(x^1 b^1\right)},$$
$$\Pr\left(y^1 = 1 \middle| y^2 = 1\right) = \frac{P_{11}}{P_{01} + P_{11}},$$
$$= \frac{1}{1 + \exp\left(x^2 b^2\right)},$$
$$\Pr\left(y^2 = 1 \middle| y^1 = 0\right) = \frac{P_{01}}{P_{00} + P_{01}},$$
$$= \frac{\exp\left(x^2 b^2\right)}{\exp\left(x^1 b^1 + x^4 b^4\right) + \exp\left(x^2 b^2\right)},$$
$$= \frac{1}{1 + \exp\left(x^3 b^3\right)} \quad \text{because of the compatibility condition,}$$
$$\Pr\left(y^2 = 1 \middle| y^1 = 0\right) = \frac{P_{11}}{P_{10} + P_{11}},$$
$$= \frac{1}{1 + \exp\left(x^4 b^4\right)},$$

4 Estimation Methods and Tests

4.1 The General Model

The qualitative response models which we introduced in the previous chapters, be they univariate or multivariate, based on normal distributions (probit) or logistic distributions (logit), can all be described by means of a general mathematical model. This formulation, which was introduced by Amemiya [Ame76], is very useful for the study of various estimation methods.

Consider a series of observable independent random variables $y_{ij}, j = 1, \ldots, J, i = 1, \ldots, n_j$, assuming $K + 1$ values with probabilities given by:

$$P_{kj}(\mathbf{b}) = F^k\left(\mathbf{x}_{1j}\mathbf{b}_1, \mathbf{x}_{2j}\mathbf{b}_2, \ldots, \mathbf{x}_{Hj}\mathbf{b}_H\right), \quad k = 0, \ldots, K, \tag{4.1}$$

where the $\mathbf{b}_h, h = 1, \ldots, H$ are vectors of unknown parameters with q_h elements and the $\mathbf{x}_{hj}$ are q_h-dimensional row vectors with observations of type j on the exogenous variables.

The functions F^k, assumed known, are constrained by:

$$F^k > 0, \quad \forall k,$$

$$\sum_{k=0}^{K} F^k = 1.$$

The likelihood of the observations $y_{ij}, j = 1, \ldots, J, i = 1, \ldots, n_j$, is given by:

$$L(\mathbf{y}; \mathbf{b}) = \prod_{j=1}^{J}\prod_{k=0}^{K}\left[P_{kj}(\mathbf{b})\right]^{n_{kj}},$$

where n_{kj} indicates the number of times $\mathbf{y}$ takes the value k from among the observations of type j.

This likelihood only depends on the observations over the intermediary of the values $n_{kj}, k = 0, \ldots, K, j = 1, \ldots, J$, so these are exhaustive statistics for estimation of the parameters. Similarly, if we denote π_{kj} the proportion of observations for which the variable $\mathbf{y}$ takes the value k during an experiment of type j, we have $\pi_{kj} = \frac{n_{kj}}{n_j}$, which implies that the quantities $\pi_{kj}, k = 0, \ldots, K, j = 1, \ldots, J$ are exhaustive statistics (cf. section 2.6.1).

The log of the likelihood function is:

$$\log\left[L\left(\mathbf{y};\mathbf{b}\right)\right] = \sum_{j=1}^{J}\sum_{k=0}^{K} n_{kj} \log\left[P_{kj}\left(\mathbf{b}\right)\right], \tag{4.2}$$

or:

$$\log\left[L\left(\mathbf{y};\mathbf{b}\right)\right] = \sum_{j=1}^{J}\left\{n_j \sum_{k=0}^{K} \pi_{kj} \log\left[P_{kj}\left(\mathbf{b}\right)\right]\right\}. \tag{4.3}$$

Equation (4.1) describes a univariate (one variable) model where the dependent variable assumes several values. Models with several variables, each assuming a number of values, can always be reduced to a univariate model with more outcomes. Frequently, however, we will prefer keeping the distinction between the different qualitative variables, as this allows us to investigate the concepts of marginal and conditional probabilities.

To simplify matters, we begin our examination with a bivariate model. The observations are on the pair:

$$\mathbf{y}_{ij} = \left\{y_{ij}^1, y_{ij}^2\right\}, \quad j = 1, \ldots, J, \quad i = 1, \ldots, n_j,$$

which assumes the values $\{k_1, k_2\}, k_1 = 0, \ldots, K_1, k_2 = 0, \ldots, K_2$, with probabilities:

$$P_{k_1k_2j}\left(\mathbf{b}\right) = F^{k_1k_2}\left(\mathbf{x}_{1j}\mathbf{b}_1, \mathbf{x}_{2j}\mathbf{b}_2, \ldots, \mathbf{x}_{Hj}\mathbf{b}_H\right), \quad j = \{1, 2\}. \tag{4.4}$$

This is structurally equivalent to a univariate model assuming the values $\{k_1, k_2\}$.

The log of the likelihood function is given by:

$$\log\left(L\right) = \sum_{j=1}^{J}\sum_{k_1=0}^{K_1}\sum_{k_2=0}^{K_2} n_{k_1k_2j} \log\left[P_{k_1k_2j}\left(\mathbf{b}\right)\right]. \tag{4.5}$$

Denote $P_{k_1j}\left(\mathbf{b}\right) = \sum_{k_2=0}^{K_2} P_{k_1k_2j}\left(\mathbf{b}\right)$ the marginal distribution of y_{ij}^1 and $n_{k_1j} = \sum_{k_2=0}^{K_2} n_{k_1k_2j}$ the number of times we observe $y_{ij}^1 = k_1$ among trials of type j. The conditional distributions are written:

$$P_{k_2|k_1j}\left(\mathbf{b}\right) = \frac{P_{k_1k_2j}\left(\mathbf{b}\right)}{P_{k_1j}\left(\mathbf{b}\right)},$$

and we define:

$$n_{k_2|k_1j} = \frac{n_{k_1k_2j}}{n_{k_1j}}.$$

Substituting, equation (4.5) becomes:

$$\log(L) = \sum_{j=1}^{J}\sum_{k_1=0}^{K_1}\sum_{k_2=0}^{K_2} n_{k_1k_2j}\left\{\log\left[P_{k_1j}(\mathbf{b})\right] + \log\left[P_{k_2|k_1j}(\mathbf{b})\right]\right\},$$

$$= \sum_{j=1}^{J}\sum_{k_1=0}^{K_1} n_{k_1j}\log\left[P_{k_2j}(\mathbf{b})\right]$$

$$+ \sum_{j=1}^{J}\sum_{k_1=0}^{K_1} n_{k_1j}\left\{\sum_{k_2=0}^{K_2} n_{k_2|k_1j}\log\left[P_{k_2|k_1j}(\mathbf{b})\right]\right\},$$

that is:

$$\log(L) = \log(L_1) + \log\left(L_{2|1}\right), \tag{4.6}$$

where $\log(L_1)$ is the logarithm of the marginal likelihood of the observations n_{k_1j} and $\log\left(L_{2|1}\right)$ can be interpreted as the conditional likelihood of the observations $n_{k_1k_2j}$ given the values n_{k_1j}.

By symmetry, we also have:

$$\log(L) = \log(L_2) + \log\left(L_{1|2}\right). \tag{4.7}$$

4.2 Estimation Methods

4.2.1 Maximum Likelihood

This method consists of choosing as estimator the value of **b** which maximizes the logarithm of the likelihood function [equation (4.2)]:

$$\log(L) = \max_{\mathbf{b}} \sum_{j=1}^{J}\sum_{k=0}^{K} n_{kj}\log\left[P_{kj}(\mathbf{b})\right].$$

As we shall see, the log likelihood formulation results in nonlinear systems. It will generally be necessary to solve them using iterative processes, such as the method of scoring.

4.2.2 Minimum Chi-square

Observations corresponding to an index j, $n_{0j}, \ldots, n_{Kj}$, follow a multinomial distribution with parameters n_j, $P_{0j}(\mathbf{b}), \ldots, P_{Kj}(\mathbf{b})$. For this index j, the distance between the fitted values and the actual values can be measured by the χ^2 distance:

$$\chi_j^2 = \sum_{k=0}^{K} \frac{\left[n_{kj} - n_j P_{kj}(\mathbf{b})\right]^2}{n_j P_{kj}(\mathbf{b})}.$$

For the set of all indices j, this distance can be measured by:

$$\varphi_1(\mathbf{b}) = \sum_{j=1}^{J} \chi_j^2 = \sum_{j=1}^{J}\sum_{k=0}^{K} \frac{\left[n_{kj} - n_j P_{kj}(\mathbf{b})\right]^2}{n_j P_{kj}(\mathbf{b})}. \tag{4.8}$$

We call the value obtained from minimizing $\varphi_1(\mathbf{b})$ the *minimum chi-square estimator*.

Asymptotically, i.e. when J is fixed and all the n_j-s tend to infinity, the function φ_1 can be replaced by a function simpler to minimize:

$$\varphi_2(\mathbf{b}) = \sum_{j=1}^{J}\sum_{k=0}^{K} \frac{\left[n_{kj} - n_j P_{kj}(\mathbf{b})\right]^2}{n_{kj}}. \tag{4.9}$$

Again, the first order conditions lead to nonlinear equation systems which must be solved using iterative procedures.

4.2.3 The Generalized Berkson Method

This estimation procedure, which we presented for the dichotomous case in section 2.6.2, was partially generalized by Amemiya [Ame77]. We will give a unified presentation here. Asymptotically $\left(J \text{ fixed}, n_j \to \infty, \forall j\right)$, the observed frequencies π_{kj} converge to the true probabilities $P_{kj}(\mathbf{b})$ and are such that $\left\{\sqrt{n_j}\left[\pi_{kj} - P_{kj}(\mathbf{b})\right]\right\}$ is distributed normally. For the principal models used in qualitative analysis, it is generally possible to find a function $G : \mathbb{R}^K \to \mathbb{R}^K$, such that G has an inverse and $G\left[P_{1j}(\mathbf{b}), \ldots, P_{Kj}(\mathbf{b})\right]$ is linear in $\left(\mathbf{x}_{1j}\mathbf{b}_1, \mathbf{x}_{2j}\mathbf{b}_2, \ldots, \mathbf{x}_{Hj}\mathbf{b}_H\right)$:

$$G\left[P_{1j}(\mathbf{b}), \ldots, P_{Kj}(\mathbf{b})\right] = A \begin{bmatrix} \mathbf{x}_{1j}\mathbf{b}_1 \\ \vdots \\ \mathbf{x}_{Hj}\mathbf{b}_H \end{bmatrix} = AX_j\mathbf{b},$$

where:

$$X_j = \begin{pmatrix} \mathbf{x}_{1j} & 0 & \cdots & 0 \\ 0 & \mathbf{x}_{2j} & & \vdots \\ \vdots & & & 0 \\ 0 & 0 & & \mathbf{x}_{Hj} \end{pmatrix} \qquad \mathbf{b} = \begin{bmatrix} \mathbf{b}_1 \\ \vdots \\ \mathbf{b}_H \end{bmatrix}.$$

The mapping G is defined up to an isomorphic transformation. $P_{0j}(\mathbf{b})$ is not explicitly represented in G because of the constraint $\sum_{k=0}^{K} P_{kj}(\mathbf{b}) = 1$ on the probabilities.

Let us replace the true probabilities in the function G with the observed frequencies and write a first-order Taylor expansion. Asymptotically, we have:

$$\begin{aligned}\hat{G}_j &= G\left(\pi_{1j}, \ldots, \pi_{Kj}\right), \\ &\approx G\left[P_{1j}(\mathbf{b}), \ldots, P_{Kj}(\mathbf{b})\right] \\ &\quad + \sum_{k=1}^{K} \frac{\partial G\left(P_{1j}, \ldots, P_{Kj}\right)}{\partial P_{kj}} \left[\pi_{kj} - P_{kj}(\mathbf{b})\right],\end{aligned}$$

where $\frac{\partial G(P_{1j},\ldots,P_{Kj})}{\partial P_{kj}}$ is an K-dimensional vector comprising the derivatives of G with respect to P_{kj}.

This structure is equivalent to:

$$\hat{G}_j \approx A X_j \mathbf{b} + u_j, \tag{4.10}$$

with:

$$u_j = \sum_{k=1}^{K} \frac{\partial G\left(P_{1j}, \ldots, P_{Kj}\right)}{\partial P_{kj}} \left[\pi_{kj} - P_{kj}(\mathbf{b})\right].$$

The formulation in equation (4.10) appears asymptotically equivalent to a model which is linear in **b**, but with the covariances of the normally distributed disturbance terms depending on the parameters.

The Berkson method consists of either:

- estimating **b** by the maximum-likelihood method applied to the almost normal model in (4.10), or, more simply,
- estimating the model using weighted least squares.

4.2.4 Limited Information Maximum Likelihood Estimation (LIML)

Application of the maximum-likelihood method can prove forbidding when the number of parameters is very large, or when the functional form F^k is too complex. Instead we can reduce our scope and estimate either:

- the marginal likelihoods L_1 and L_2, or
- the conditional likelihoods $L_{1|2}$ and $L_{2|1}$, or
- first the marginal likelihood L_1, and then the conditional likelihood $L_{2|1}$.

In the remainder of this chapter we shall study in detail these various methods of estimation. We shall assume that the functions F^k are twice continuously differentiable, which is always true for the probit and logit models. Furthermore, we shall assume that the parameters $\mathbf{b}_1, \ldots, \mathbf{b}_H$ are identified – the identification problem is generally resolved at the stage of model building (cf. chapter 3) – and that they are not correlated. This last assumption is not always satisfied in practice (cf. section 3.4.2.2), but the estimation techniques we shall examine can easily be generalized to account for this problem. We simply incorporate the relationships between the parameters as constraints on the maximizations or minimizations.

4.3 The Maximum-Likelihood Method

4.3.1 The Estimator and its Properties

The maximum-likelihood estimator is obtained by writing the first-order conditions

$$0 = \frac{\partial \log (L)}{\partial \mathbf{b}_h},$$

$$0 = \sum_{j=1}^{J} \sum_{k=0}^{K} n_{kj} \frac{F_h^k (j)}{F^k (j)} \mathbf{x}_{hj}, \tag{4.11}$$

where $h = 1, \ldots, H$, $F^k (j) = P_{kj} (\mathbf{b}) = F^k \left(\mathbf{x}_{1j} \mathbf{b}_1, \ldots, \mathbf{x}_{Hj} \mathbf{b}_H\right)$, and where $F_h^k (j)$ indicates the partial derivative of $F^k (j)$ with respect to the h-th coordinate:

$$F_h^k (j) = \frac{\partial F^k \left(\mathbf{x}_{1j} \mathbf{b}_1, \ldots, \mathbf{x}_{Hj} \mathbf{b}_H\right)}{\partial \mathbf{b}_h}.$$

The likelihood equations can be written in matrix form. Denote:

$$D [F (j)] = \underset{(K+1) \times (K+1)}{\begin{pmatrix} F^0 (j) & \cdots & 0 \\ \vdots & \ddots & \vdots \\ 0 & \cdots & F^K (j) \end{pmatrix}},$$

$$\Delta [F (j)] = \underset{(K+1) \times H}{\begin{pmatrix} F_1^0 (j) & \cdots & F_H^0 (j) \\ \vdots & \ddots & \vdots \\ F_1^K (j) & \cdots & F_H^K (j) \end{pmatrix}},$$

$$N (j) = \underset{(K+1) \times 1}{\begin{pmatrix} n_{0j} \\ \vdots \\ n_{Kj} \end{pmatrix}},$$

$$X_j = \begin{pmatrix} \mathbf{x}_{1j} & 0 & \cdots & 0 \\ 0 & \mathbf{x}_{2j} & & \vdots \\ \vdots & & \ddots & 0 \\ 0 & \cdots & 0 & \mathbf{x}_{Hj} \end{pmatrix},$$

$$H \times \left(q = \textstyle\sum_{h=1}^{H} q_h\right)$$

$$\mathbf{b} = \underset{q \times H}{\begin{pmatrix} \mathbf{b}_1 \\ \vdots \\ \mathbf{b}_H \end{pmatrix}}.$$

Using this notation, we have:

$$\frac{\partial \log(L)}{\partial \mathbf{b}} = \sum_{j=1}^{J} X_j' \Delta [F(j)]' D [F(j)]^{-1} N(j) = 0 \tag{4.12}$$

The maximum-likelihood estimator β_{ML} which solves equation system, (4.12) asymptotically $\left(J \text{ fixed}, n_j \to \infty, \forall j\right)$ converges to $\mathbf{b}$. Furthermore, it is asymptotically normally distributed:

$$\beta_{ML} \overset{asy}{\rightsquigarrow} \left\{ \mathbf{b}; \mathrm{E}\left[-\frac{\partial^2 \log(L)}{\partial \mathbf{b} \partial \mathbf{b}'}\right]^{-1} \right\}. \tag{4.13}$$

(In section 4.6 we shall examine the existence, convergence, and asymptotic normality of the estimators).

It remains to find the asymptotic covariance matrix of β_{ML}. For this we require the matrix of second derivatives:

$$\frac{\partial^2 \log(L)}{\partial \mathbf{b}_h \partial \mathbf{b}_\ell'}, \quad \forall h, \ell.$$

Denoting $F_{h\ell}^k$ the second order derivative of $F^k(j)$ with respect to the elements indexed by h and ℓ, we have:

$$\frac{\partial^2 \log(L)}{\partial \mathbf{b}_h \partial \mathbf{b}_\ell'} = \sum_{j=1}^{J} \sum_{k=0}^{K} n_{kj} \frac{\partial}{\partial \mathbf{b}_\ell'} \left[\frac{F_h^k(j)}{F^k(j)}\right] \mathbf{x}_{hj}',$$

$$= \sum_{j=1}^{J} \sum_{k=0}^{K} n_{kj} \left[\frac{-F_h^k(j) F_\ell^k(j)}{\left(F^k\right)^2(j)} + \frac{F_{h\ell}^k(j)}{F^k(j)}\right] \mathbf{x}_{hj}' \mathbf{x}_{\ell j},$$

$$= -\sum_{j=1}^{J}\sum_{k=0}^{K} n_{kj} \frac{F_h^k(j)\, F_\ell^k(j)}{\left(F^k\right)^2(j)} \mathbf{x}_{hj}' \mathbf{x}_{\ell j}$$

$$+ \sum_{j=1}^{J}\sum_{k=0}^{K} n_{kj} \frac{F_{h\ell}^k(j)}{F^k(j)} \mathbf{x}_{hj}' \mathbf{x}_{\ell j}.$$

Taking expectations of the negative of this amount:

$$\mathrm{E}\left[-\frac{\partial^2 \log(L)}{\partial \mathbf{b}_h \partial \mathbf{b}_\ell'}\right] = \sum_{j=1}^{J}\sum_{k=0}^{K} n_j \frac{F_h^k(j)\, F_\ell^k(j)}{F^k(j)} \mathbf{x}_{hj}' \mathbf{x}_{\ell j}$$

$$- \sum_{j=1}^{J}\sum_{k=0}^{K} n_j F_{h\ell}^k(j)\, \mathbf{x}_{hj}' \mathbf{x}_{\ell j},$$

$$= \sum_{j=1}^{J}\sum_{k=0}^{K} n_j \frac{F_h^k(j)\, F_\ell^k(j)}{F^k(j)} \mathbf{x}_{hj}' \mathbf{x}_{\ell j},$$

since the derivative of $\sum_{k=0}^{K} F^k(j) = 1$ is zero everywhere.

Finally, we have the derivatives in matrix form:

$$\mathrm{E}\left[-\frac{\partial^2 \log(L)}{\partial \mathbf{b} \partial \mathbf{b}'}\right]$$

$$= \sum_{j=i}^{J} n_j X_j' \left[\Delta F(j)\right]' \left[DF(j)\right]^{-1} \Delta F(j)\, X_j. \tag{4.14}$$

In practice, when we evaluate the precision of the estimator β_{ML} we replace the unknown parameters in $\mathrm{E}\left[-\frac{\partial^2 \log(L)}{\partial \mathbf{b} \partial \mathbf{b}'}\right]$ by their estimates.

4.3.2 *Examples using Probit and Logit*

Application of the maximum-likelihood method to dichotomous models has already been discussed in chapter 2. We will now present several more examples.

4.3.2.1 *Univariate Polychotomous, or Multinomial, Logit Model*

This model is written:

$$P_{kj}(\mathbf{b}) = \frac{\exp\left(\mathbf{x}_{kj} \mathbf{b}_k\right)}{\sum_{\ell=0}^{K} \exp\left(\mathbf{x}_{\ell j} \mathbf{b}_\ell\right)},$$

where, by convention, $\mathbf{x}_{0j}\mathbf{b}_0$ is set equal to zero to avoid problems of identification.

Assuming that there is no linear dependence between the parameters $\mathbf{b}_k$, we have:

$$F_h^k(j) = \begin{cases} -F^k(j)\,F^h(j), & \text{if } k \neq h, \\ \left[1 - F^k(j)\right] F^k(j), & \text{if } k = h. \end{cases}$$

Accounting for these equalities we substitute into the likelihood equation (4.11), yielding:

$$0 = \sum_{j=1}^{J}\left[-\sum_{k=0}^{K} n_{kj} F^h(j)\,\mathbf{x}'_{hj} + n_{hj}\mathbf{x}'_{hj}\right],$$

$$0 = \sum_{j=1}^{J} n_j \left[\pi_{hj} - F^h(j)\right] \mathbf{x}'_{hj},$$

where $h = 1, \ldots, H$.

Hence, as in the dichotomous case, we find an orthogonality condition relating the explanatory variables and the residuals $\pi_{hj} - F^h(j)$.

4.3.2.2 Bivariate Dichotomous Conditional Logit Model

Consider the pair of dichotomous variables $\left(y_j^1, y_j^2\right)$ fitting a conditional logit distribution:

$$\Pr\left(y_j^1 = 1 \middle| y_j^2 = 0\right) = \frac{1}{1 + \exp\left(\mathbf{x}_{1j}\mathbf{b}_1\right)},$$

$$\Pr\left(y_j^1 = 1 \middle| y_j^2 = 1\right) = \frac{1}{1 + \exp\left(\mathbf{x}_{2j}\mathbf{b}_2\right)},$$

$$\Pr\left(y_j^2 = 1 \middle| y_j^1 = 0\right) = \frac{1}{1 + \exp\left(\mathbf{x}_{3j}\mathbf{b}_3\right)},$$

$$\Pr\left(y_j^2 = 1 \middle| y_j^1 = 1\right) = \frac{1}{1 + \exp\left(\mathbf{x}_{4j}\mathbf{b}_4\right)}.$$

As we saw in section 3.4.2, these conditional distributions are compatible (i.e. determine a unique solution) if and only if:

$$\mathbf{x}_{1j}\mathbf{b}_1 + \mathbf{x}_{4j}\mathbf{b}_4 = \mathbf{x}_{2j}\mathbf{b}_2 + \mathbf{x}_{3j}\mathbf{b}_3, \quad \forall j.$$

In this case we can derive the joint distribution from the conditional probabilities, for example:

$$P_{11j}(\mathbf{b}) = \Pr\left(y_j^1 = 1, y_j^2 = 1\right),$$

and similarly for $P_{10j}(\mathbf{b})$, $P_{01j}(\mathbf{b})$, and $P_{00j}(\mathbf{b})$. This in turn yields the likelihood equation. Maximization of the likelihood must respect the compatibility constraint, however.

4.3.2.3 *Bivariate Dichotomous Probit Model*

Consider two choice functions of the form:

$$V_j^1 = -x_{1j}b_1 + v_{1j},$$
$$V_j^2 = -x_{2j}b_2 + v_{2j},$$

where the v_{1j} and v_{2j} are identically distributed with correlation coefficient ρ:

$$N\left[\begin{pmatrix}0\\0\end{pmatrix}, \begin{pmatrix}1 & \rho\\ \rho & 1\end{pmatrix}\right].$$

The dependent variables are defined by:

$$y_j^k = \begin{cases}1, & \text{if } V_j^k < 0,\\ 0, & \text{otherwise}\end{cases}, \quad k = \{1, 2\}$$

For each index j, there are four choice probabilities given by:

$$P_{1j} = \Pr\left(y_j^1 = 1, y_j^2 = 1\right) = F^1\left(\mathbf{x}_{1j}\mathbf{b}_1, \mathbf{x}_{2j}\mathbf{b}_2, \rho\right),$$
$$= \int_{-\infty}^{x_{1j}b_1}\int_{-\infty}^{x_{2j}b_2} f\left(\rho, u_1, u_2\right) du_1 du_2,$$

where $f\left(\rho, u_1, u_2\right)$ describes the density function:

$$N\left[\begin{pmatrix}0\\0\end{pmatrix}, \begin{pmatrix}1 & \rho\\ \rho & 1\end{pmatrix}\right],$$

and F^1 the corresponding (normal bivariate) distribution.

Further:

$$P_{2j} = \Pr\left(y_j^1 = 1, y_j^2 = 0\right) = \Pr\left(y_j^1 = 1\right) - \Pr\left(y_j^1 = 1, y_j^2 = 1\right),$$
$$= \Phi\left(\mathbf{x}_{1j}\mathbf{b}_1\right) - F_1\left(\mathbf{x}_{1j}\mathbf{b}_1, \mathbf{x}_{2j}\mathbf{b}_2, \rho\right),$$
$$P_{3j} = \Pr\left(y_j^1 = 0, y_j^2 = 1\right) = \Phi\left(\mathbf{x}_{2j}\mathbf{b}_2\right) - F_1\left(\mathbf{x}_{1j}\mathbf{b}_1, \mathbf{x}_{2j}\mathbf{b}_2, \rho\right),$$

and:

$$P_{4j} = 1 - P_{1j} - P_{2j} - P_{3j}.$$

These probabilities contain double integrals which must be evaluated using numeric techniques. Because these techniques are computationally very demanding, the logit formulation has a clear advantage over probit.

4.3.2.4 *Sequential Trichotomous Model*

The probabilities are given by:

$$P_{1j} = F\left(\mathbf{x}_{ij}\mathbf{b}_1\right),$$
$$P_{2j} = \left[1 - F\left(\mathbf{x}_{1j}\mathbf{b}_1\right)\right] F\left(\mathbf{x}_{2j}\mathbf{b}_2\right),$$
$$P_{3j} = \left[1 - F\left(\mathbf{x}_{1j}\mathbf{b}_1\right)\right]\left[1 - F\left(\mathbf{x}_{2j}\mathbf{b}_2\right)\right].$$

Notice that the logarithm of each of these probabilities is the sum of a function of $\mathbf{b}_1$ plus a function of $\mathbf{b}_2$. Maximizing $\log(L)$ reduces to the separate maximization of two functions, one on $\mathbf{b}_1$ and one on $\mathbf{b}_2$. It is, in fact, equivalent to estimating two dichotomous models.

The preceding observation generalizes directly to the maximization of sequential models in which the dependent variable assumes more than three values.

4.3.3 *The Method of Scoring*

This method is an iterative procedure used to calculate the maximum-likelihood estimator. It has the same properties in the general qualitative response model as it does in the special case of the dichotomous model we discussed in section 2.5.2.

Starting from an original value β_0 obtained, for example, as an estimate generated by the Berkson generalized method (cf. section 4.2.3), we apply the algorithm:

$$\beta_{m+1} = \beta_m + \mathrm{E}\left[-\frac{\partial^2 \log(L)}{\partial \beta_m \partial \beta_m'}\right]^{-1} \frac{\partial \log(L)}{\partial \beta_m}, \tag{4.15}$$

where the $\frac{\partial(-)}{\partial \beta_m}$ notation indicates that the derivative is evaluated at $\mathbf{b} = \beta_m$.

If this procedure converges to $\mathbf{b}$ as $m \to \infty$, the limit is characterized by:

$$\frac{\partial \log(L)}{\partial \beta_\infty} = 0.$$

When the model is well behaved, this solution to the likelihood equation is identical to β_{ML}.

Amemiya [Ame76] has shown that this iterative procedure can be interpreted as a generalized least-squares type approach applied to a well chosen linear model.

Consider the observed frequencies: $\pi_{kj} = \frac{n_{kj}}{n_j}$, we have:

$$\pi_{kj} = F^k(j) + u_{kj},$$

where u_{kj} has mean zero and variance:

$$\operatorname{var}(u_{kj}) = \frac{1}{n_j} F^k(j)\,[1 - F_k(j)].$$

For a given index value j, the u_{kj}-s are correlated:

$$\operatorname{cov}(u_{kj}, u_{\ell j}) = -\frac{1}{n_j} F^k(j)\, F^\ell(j), \quad k \neq \ell.$$

Letting $F^*(j)$ be a K-dimensional vector with elements $F^k(j)$, $k = 1, \ldots, K$, and $DF^*(j)$ a diagonal matrix with the elements of $F^*(j)$ on the diagonal, the covariance matrix of $(u_{1j}, \ldots, u_{Kj})$ is given by:

$$\Lambda_j = \frac{1}{n_j}\left[DF^*(j) - F^*(j)\,F^*(j)'\right].$$

Notice that this matrix is non-singular since we did not incorporate the disturbance corresponding to $k = 0$. Given an initial value of the parameter β_0, we can expand the functions $F^k(j) = P_{kj}(\mathbf{b})$ around this value, yielding:

$$F^k(j) \approx F^k(j)\big|_{\mathbf{b}=\beta} + \sum_{h=1}^{K}\left[F_h^k(j)\right]_{\mathbf{b}=\beta}\left[x_{hj}\mathbf{b}_h - x_{hj}\beta_h\right],$$

and thus:

$$\pi_{kj} - F^k(j)\big|_{\mathbf{b}=\beta} + \sum_{h=1}^{K} F_h^k(j)\big|_{\mathbf{b}=\beta}\mathbf{x}_{hj}\boldsymbol{\beta}_h$$

$$\approx \sum_{h=1}^{K} F_h^k(j)\big|_{\mathbf{b}=\beta}\mathbf{x}_{hj}\mathbf{b}_h + u_{kj}.$$

Using $\overline{p_{kj}}$ to denote the LHS, for which the value is known, we obtain a linear formulation:

$$\overline{p_{kj}} \approx \sum_{h=1}^{K}\left[F_h^k(j)\right]_{\mathbf{b}=\beta}\mathbf{x}_{hj}\mathbf{b}_h + u_{kj}, \quad k = 1, \ldots, K, \quad j = 1, \ldots, J.$$

The variance-covariance matrix Λ_j is a function of $\mathbf{b}$. If we use this model to calculate the weighted least-squares estimator for $\mathbf{b}$ using the covariance matrix $\Lambda_j\big|_{\mathbf{b}=\beta}$, the value obtained is identical to that given by the method of scoring [cf. equation (4.15)]. In consequence, we can interpret this latter method as a succession of estimates using the method of weighted least squares.

Finally, recall that there exist other procedures, such as the Berndt-Hall-Hall-Hausman method, for solving the maximum-likelihood equations.

4.4 The Minimum Chi-Squared Method

4.4.1 The Estimator Associated with φ_1

To derive this estimator we begin by writing the first-order conditions from equation (4.8):

$$0 = \frac{\partial \varphi_1}{\partial \mathbf{b}_h}, \quad h = 1, \ldots, H,$$

$$= \sum_{j=1}^{J}\sum_{k=0}^{K}\left[-2\frac{n_{kj} - n_j F_k(j)}{F_k(j)} - \frac{\left[n_{kj} - n_j F_k(j)\right]^2}{n_j F_k(j)^2}\right] F_h^k(j)\,\mathbf{x}_{hj}',$$

$$0 = -\sum_{j=1}^{J}\sum_{k=0}^{K} 2\frac{n_{kj} - n_j F_k(j)}{F_k(j)} F_h^k(j)\,\mathbf{x}'_{hj}$$

$$-\sum_{j=1}^{J}\sum_{k=0}^{K} \frac{\left[n_{kj} - n_j F_k(j)\right]^2}{n_j F_k(j)^2} F_h^k(j)\,\mathbf{x}'_{hj}. \tag{4.16}$$

In expression (4.16) the second term becomes vanishingly small relative to the first term as the value of n_j tends to infinity. Furthermore, $\sum_{k=0}^{K} F_h^k(j) = 0$.

The likelihood equations can be rewritten:

$$0 = \sum_{j=1}^{J}\sum_{k=0}^{K} n_{kj} \frac{F_h^k(j)}{F^k(j)} \mathbf{x}'_{hj} + \delta_h,$$

where δ_h is vanishingly small compared to the first term. In matrix form we have:

$$0 = \sum_{j=1}^{J} X'_j \Delta \left[F(j)\right]' \left[DF(j)\right]^{-1} N(j) + \delta. \tag{4.17}$$

If we compare this result to the likelihood equations (4.12) we find that the minimum chi-square estimator, $\boldsymbol{\beta}_1$, obtained by minimizing φ_1 is asymptotically equivalent to the maximum-likelihood estimator.

4.4.2 *The Estimator Associated with φ_2*

The first-order conditions are :

$$0 = \frac{\partial \varphi_2}{\partial \mathbf{b}_h}, \quad h = 1, \ldots, H,$$

$$= \sum_{j=1}^{J}\sum_{k=0}^{K} 2\frac{\left[n_{kj} - n_j F_h^k(j)\right]}{n_{kj}} n_j F_h^k(j)\,\mathbf{x}'_{hj}, \tag{4.18}$$

$$= \sum_{j=1}^{J}\sum_{k=0}^{K} \frac{n_j^2}{n_{kj}} F^k(j)\, F_h^k(j)\,\mathbf{x}'_{kh},$$

since $\sum_{k=0}^{K} F_h^k(j) = 0$.

In matrix form, condition (4.18) is:

$$\sum_{j=1}^{J} X'_j \Delta \left[F(j)\right]' \left[D\pi(j)\right]^{-2} D(j)\, N(j) = 0 \tag{4.19}$$

Asymptotically, as $n_j \to \infty$, $\pi(j)$ is equivalent to $F(j)$ and equation (4.19) is equivalent to (4.12). β_2, the solution to the current equation system, is asymptotically equal to β_{ML}, the solution to the maximum-likelihood equation (Morimune [Mor79]).

4.5 The Generalized Berkson Method

4.5.1 Finding the Function G for Various Models

We shall present this method for several of the models introduced in chapter 3. The material in this section remains valid regardless of whether a linear dependence exists between the parameters $\mathbf{b}_h$.

4.5.1.1 Bivariate Dichotomous Probit Model

As we saw in section 4.3.2.3, this model is defined by:

$$\begin{aligned} P_{1j} &= F_1\left(\mathbf{x}_{1j}\mathbf{b}_1, \mathbf{x}_{2j}\mathbf{b}_2, \rho\right), \\ P_{2j} &= \Phi\left(\mathbf{x}_{1j}\mathbf{b}_1\right) - F_1\left(\mathbf{x}_{1j}\mathbf{b}_1, \mathbf{x}_{2j}\mathbf{b}_2, \rho\right), \\ P_{3j} &= \Phi\left(\mathbf{x}_{2j}\mathbf{b}_2\right) - F_1\left(\mathbf{x}_{1j}\mathbf{b}_1, \mathbf{x}_{2j}\mathbf{b}_2, \rho\right), \\ P_{4j} &= 1 - P_{1j} - P_{2j} - P_{3j}, \end{aligned}$$

where Φ, as usual, is the standard normal density and F_1 the bivariate normal:

$$N\left[\begin{pmatrix} 0 \\ 0 \end{pmatrix} \begin{pmatrix} 1 & \rho \\ \rho & 1 \end{pmatrix}\right].$$

We have:

$$\begin{aligned} \mathbf{x}_{1j}\mathbf{b}_1 &= \Phi^{-1}\left(P_{1j} + P_{2j}\right), \\ \mathbf{x}_{2j}\mathbf{b}_2 &= \Phi^{-1}\left(P_{1j} + P_{3j}\right), \\ \rho &= G_3\left(P_{1j}, P_{2j}, P_{3j}\right), \end{aligned}$$

where G_3 is determined by:

$$P_{1j} = F_1\left[\Phi^{-1}\left(P_{1j} + P_{2j}\right), \Phi^{-1}\left(P_{1j} + P_{3j}\right), G_3\left(P_{1j}, P_{2j}, P_{3j}\right)\right].$$

4.5.1.2 Polychotomous Logit Model

In this model the existence of a linear relationship between the parameters is also immaterial. The formulation includes the standard univariate and multivariate models as special cases.

The model is defined by:

$$P_{kj} = \frac{\exp\left(\mathbf{x}_{kj}\mathbf{b}_k\right)}{\sum_{\ell=0}^{K} \exp\left(\mathbf{x}_{\ell j}\mathbf{b}_\ell\right)}, \quad k = 0, \ldots, K,$$

where, by convention, $\mathbf{x}_{0j}\mathbf{b}_0 = 0$. We derive:

$$\log\left(\frac{P_{kj}}{P_{0j}}\right) = \mathbf{x}_{kj}\mathbf{b}_k, \quad k = 1, \ldots, K.$$

4.5.1.3 Univariate Ordered Trichotomous Model

The probabilities are:

$$\begin{aligned}
P_{1j} &= F\left(\mathbf{x}_j\mathbf{b} + a_1\right),\\
P_{2j} &= F\left(\mathbf{x}_j\mathbf{b} + a_2\right) - F\left(\mathbf{x}_j\mathbf{b} + a_1\right), \quad a_2 > a_1,\\
P_{3j} &= 1 - P_{1j} - P_{2j},
\end{aligned}$$

yielding:

$$\begin{aligned}
F^{-1}\left(P_{1j}\right) &= \mathbf{x}_j\mathbf{b} + a_1,\\
F^{-1}\left(P_{1j} + P_{2j}\right) &= \mathbf{x}_j\mathbf{b} + a_2.
\end{aligned}$$

4.5.1.4 Sequential Trichotomous Model

The formulation is (as in section 4.3.2.4):

$$\begin{aligned}
P_{1j} &= F\left(\mathbf{x}_{1j}\mathbf{b}_1\right),\\
P_{2j} &= \left[1 - F\left(\mathbf{x}_{1j}\mathbf{b}_1\right)\right] F\left(\mathbf{x}_{2j}\mathbf{b}_2\right),\\
P_{3j} &= \left[1 - F\left(\mathbf{x}_{1j}\mathbf{b}_1\right)\right]\left[1 - F\left(\mathbf{x}_{2j}\mathbf{b}_2\right)\right].
\end{aligned}$$

yielding:

$$\begin{aligned}
\mathbf{x}_{1j}\mathbf{b}_1 &= F^{-1}\left(P_{1j}\right),\\
\mathbf{x}_{2j}\mathbf{b}_1 &= F^{-1}\left(\frac{P_{2j}}{1 - P_{1j}}\right).
\end{aligned}$$

4.5.2 The Estimator and its Properties

Recalling the notation introduced in section 4.2.3, the linear approximation is written:

$$\hat{G}_j = G\left(\pi_{1j}, \ldots, \pi_{Kj}\right) \approx AX_j\mathbf{b} + u_j, \tag{4.20}$$

with:

$$u_j = \sum_{k=1}^{K} \frac{\partial G\left(P_{1j}, \ldots, P_{Kj}\right)}{\partial P_{kj}}\left(\pi_{kj} - P_{kj}\right).$$

We write $\Delta G\,(j)$ for the matrix of partial derivatives of G evaluated at the point

$(P_{1j}, \ldots, P_{Kj})$. The covariance matrix of $\pi_{kj} - P_{kj}, k = 1, \ldots, K$ is given by:

$$\Lambda_j = \frac{1}{n_j}\left[DF^*(j) - F^*(j)\,F^*(j)'\right],$$

and we derive the variance-covariance matrix of the error terms:

$$\Omega_j = \mathrm{cov}\left(u_j\right) = \Delta G(j)\,\Lambda_j \Delta G(j)'.$$

The generalized Berkson estimator is obtained by applying generalized least squares to this model with the observed frequencies π_{kj} replacing the unknown true probabilities P_{kj} in Ω_j (the ensuing matrix is denoted $\hat{\Omega}_j$).

The Berkson estimator is:

$$\beta_B = \left(\sum_{j=1}^{J} X_j' A' \hat{\Omega}_j^{-1} A X_j\right)^{-1} \sum_{j=1}^{J} X_j' A' \hat{\Omega}_j^{-1} \hat{G}_j, \tag{4.21}$$

and a consistent estimator of its variance is given by:

$$\widehat{\mathrm{var}}\left(\beta_B\right) = \left[\sum_{j=1}^{J} X_j' A' \Omega_j^{-1} A X_j\right]^{-1}. \tag{4.22}$$

G being non-singular, we can substitute the expression for Ω^{-1}, yielding:

$$\mathrm{var}\left(\beta_B\right) = \left\{\sum_{j=1}^{J} X_j' A' \left[\Delta G(j)'\right]^{-1} \Lambda_j^{-1} \left[\Delta G(j)\right]^{-1} A X_j\right\}^{-1}.$$

Since $G(j)^{-1} A = F^*(j)$, we differentiate to obtain:

$$\left[\Delta G(j)\right]^{-1} A = \Delta F^*(j).$$

Yielding a consistent estimate of the variance of the estimator β_B:

$$\mathrm{cov}\left(\beta_B\right) = \left[\sum_{j=1}^{J} X_j' \Delta F^*(j)' \Lambda_j^{-1} \Delta F^*(j)\, X_j\right]^{-1}.$$

Now, the inverse of Λ_j is known to be:

$$\Lambda_j^{-1} = n_j \left\{\left[DF^*(j)\right]^{-1} - \frac{1}{P_{0j}} \mathbf{e}\mathbf{e}'\right\},$$

where $\mathbf{e}$ is a K-dimensional column vector of ones. Substituting into the equation for var (β_B), we have:

$$\operatorname{var}(\beta_B) = \left\{ \sum_{j=1}^{J} n_j X'_j \Delta F^*(j)' DF^*(j)^{-1} \Delta F^*(j) X_j - \frac{n_j}{P_{0j}} X'_j \left[e' \Delta F^*(j)\right]' e' \Delta F^*(j) X_j \right\}^{-1},$$

$$= \left[\sum_{j=1}^{J} n_j X'_j \Delta F(j)' DF(j)^{-1} \Delta F(j) X_j \right]^{-1}.$$

Comparing this expression with equation (4.14) we see that the generalized Berkson estimator is asymptotically efficient.

4.6 Asymptotic Properties of the Estimators

In the preceding sections we used rather intuitive arguments to derive some asymptotic results. Rigorous proofs of these results are generally founded on a methodology proposed by Jennrich [Jen69]. We shall follow this procedure, assuming that J is fixed and that $n_j = \theta_j n$, where the θ_j are fixed and where n tends to infinity. This type of asymptote corresponds to the notion of repeated experiments.

4.6.1 Strong Convergence of the Estimators

The estimators which we have examined are all based on the optimization of a given set of criteria expressed as functions of the parameters **b** and variables $Z_n = \pi_{kj}, k = 0, \ldots, K, j = 1, \ldots, J$. The functions are:

- for the maximum-likelihood estimator:

$$g_1(Z_n, \mathbf{b}) = \log(L) - \log(n) = \sum_{j=1}^{J} \theta_j \sum_{k=0}^{K} \pi_{kj} \left\{ \log\left(P_{kj}(\mathbf{b})\right)\right\},$$

- for the minimum chi-square estimator:

$$g_2(Z_n, \mathbf{b}) = \frac{1}{n}\varphi_1(\mathbf{b}) = \sum_{j=1}^{J} \theta_j \sum_{k=0}^{K} \frac{\left[\pi_{kj} - P_{kj}(\mathbf{b})\right]^2}{P_{kj}(\mathbf{b})},$$

- for the Generalized Berkson method:

$$g_3(Z_n, \mathbf{b}) = \sum_{j=1}^{J} \left(\hat{G}_j - AX_j\mathbf{b}\right)' \hat{\Omega}_j^{-1} \left(\hat{G}_j - AX_j\mathbf{b}\right).$$

These estimators are well behaved when applied to the usual logit and probit models. In particular, they are continuous and possess indefinitely high-order derivatives with respect to the parameters. Furthermore, the values assumed by Z_n are elements of a compact set, $\pi_{kj} \in [0, 1], \forall k, j$.

In what follows we assume that the value of the estimator is contained within a compact set B, and that the value of the unknown true parameter $\mathbf{b}_0$ is also in the interior of B.

Theorem 2: Consider two compact sets $\mathbb{Z}$ and B in Euclidean space and let g be a continuous real function defined on $\mathbb{Z} \otimes B$:

$$g : \{\mathbf{z}, \mathbf{b}\} \to \{\mathbf{z}, \mathbf{b}\}$$

(i) For each $\mathbf{z} \in \mathbb{Z}$, there exists at least one value $\boldsymbol{\beta}(\mathbf{z}) \in B$ such that $g[\mathbf{z}, \boldsymbol{\beta}(\mathbf{z})] = \max_{\mathbf{b} \in B} [g(\mathbf{z}, \mathbf{b})]$.

(ii) If Z_n converges to a limit $\mathbf{z}_0$ such that the set of solutions $\boldsymbol{\beta}(\mathbf{z})$ converges to a point $\mathbf{b}_0$, then $\boldsymbol{\beta}(Z_n)$ tends to $\mathbf{b}_0$.

The last property is a result of the continuity of the mapping $\boldsymbol{\beta}$ with respect to $\mathbf{z}$.

Proof:

(i) The partial mapping $\mathbf{b} \to g(\mathbf{z}, \mathbf{b})$ is continuous on the compact set B and hence has a minimum $\boldsymbol{\beta}(\mathbf{z})$ for at least one value of $\mathbf{z}$.

(ii) Consider a sequence of solutions $\boldsymbol{\beta}(Z_n)$. As this sequence has values in B, there exists a subsequence $\boldsymbol{\beta}\left(Z_{n_j}\right)$ which converges to a limit $\mathbf{b}_\infty$. For this subsequence we have:

$$g\left[Z_{n_j}, \boldsymbol{\beta}\left(Z_{n_j}\right)\right] \geq g\left(Z_{n_j}, \mathbf{b}_0\right).$$

so:

$$\lim_{n_j \to \infty} g\left[Z_{n_j}, \boldsymbol{\beta}\left(Z_{n_j}\right)\right] \geq g\left(Z_{n_j}, \mathbf{b}_0\right).$$

Using the continuity of the mapping g, we see that:

$$g(\mathbf{z}_0, \mathbf{b}_\infty) \geq g(\mathbf{z}_0, \mathbf{b}_0).$$

As $\boldsymbol{\beta}(z_0)$ converges to $\mathbf{b}_0$, we see that $\mathbf{b}_\infty = \mathbf{b}_0$. In consequence, every convergent subsequence converges to the same limit $\mathbf{b}_0$. Since B is compact, this implies that the sequence converges to $\mathbf{b}_0$. □

Proposition 5: The estimators obtained by optimizing g_1, g_2, or g_3 converge almost surely to the value of the true parameter $\mathbf{b}_0$.

Proof: We will demonstrate this for the case of the maximum-likelihood estimator. We have already seen that the function g_1 satisfies the assumptions of theorem 2.

Let $\mathbf{z}_0 = P_{kj}(\mathbf{b}_0)$, then:

$$g_1 \left\{ \left[P_{kj}(\mathbf{b}_0) \right], \mathbf{b} \right\} = \sum_{j=1}^{J} \theta_j \sum_{k=0}^{K} P_{kj}(\mathbf{b}_0) \log \left[P_{kj}(\mathbf{b}) \right],$$

is maximized over $\mathbf{b}$ such that:

$$P_{kj}(\mathbf{b}) = P_{kj}(\mathbf{b}_0), \quad \forall k, j$$

(cf. exercise 25).

Once the model is identified, this condition is equivalent to $\mathbf{b} = \mathbf{b}_0$, and:

$$\boldsymbol{\beta} \left[P_{kj}(\mathbf{b}_0) \right] = \mathbf{b}_0.$$

We define the sequence Z_n as comprising the empirical frequencies π_{kj}. According to the law of large numbers, as Z_n converges almost surely to $\mathbf{z}_0 = \Pr(\mathbf{b}_0)$, the maximum-likelihood estimator $\boldsymbol{\beta}(Z_n)$ converges almost surely to $\boldsymbol{\beta}\left[P_{kj}(\mathbf{b}_0)\right] = \mathbf{b}_0$. □

Remark 4: From a purely mathematical perspective, we must point out the a step has been omitted from the foregoing demonstration. We would need to show that, when Z_n is stochastic, it is possible to select a point in $\boldsymbol{\beta}(Z_n)$ such that for each value assumed by Z_n, $\boldsymbol{\beta}(Z_n)$ is an estimator, i.e. a measurable function (cf. Jennrich [Jen69]).

4.6.2 Asymptotic Normality

We shall demonstrate that the maximum-likelihood and minimum chi-square estimators are asymptotically normally distributed. First we need to make an additional assumption concerning the functions g_1 and g_2. In particular, we postulate that they are three times continuously differentiable.

Given one of these functions, g, and a value which maximizes it, $\boldsymbol{\beta}(Z_n)$, we have seen that $g(Z_n, \mathbf{b})$ converges almost surely to $\mathbf{b}_0$. In other words, for all ϵ, there exists a value of N and a neighbourhood Ω_N such that:

$$\|\boldsymbol{\beta}[Z_n(\omega)] - \mathbf{b}_0\| < \epsilon, \quad \forall \omega \in \Omega_N, \quad \forall n \geq N,$$

with probability greater that $1 - \epsilon$.

Since $\mathbf{b}_0$ is in the interior of B, we can, by taking a sufficiently small ϵ, ensure that $\forall \omega \in \Omega_N, \forall n \geq N, \boldsymbol{\beta}[Z_n(\omega)]$ is also in the interior of B. Since g is differentiable, $\boldsymbol{\beta}[Z_n(\omega)]$ satisfies the first-order conditions:

$$\frac{\partial g\{Z_n(\omega); \boldsymbol{\beta}[Z_n(\omega)]\}}{\partial \mathbf{b}} = 0, \quad \forall \omega \in \Omega_N, \quad \forall n \geq N.$$

This f.o.c. can be written in a more tractable form. Since g is three times continuously differentiable, we can perform the following expansion of the first-order derivative:

$$\frac{\partial g}{\partial b}(\mathbf{z},\mathbf{b}) = \frac{\partial g(\mathbf{z},\mathbf{b}_0)}{\partial \mathbf{b}} + \frac{\partial^2 g(\mathbf{z},\mathbf{b}_0)}{\partial \mathbf{b}\partial \mathbf{b}'}\left(^2\right)$$
$$+\,O\left(\|\mathbf{b}-\mathbf{b}_0\|^2\right),$$
$$= \frac{\partial g(\mathbf{z},\mathbf{b}_0)}{\partial \mathbf{b}} + \frac{\partial^2 g(\mathbf{z}_0,\mathbf{b}_0)}{\partial \mathbf{b}\partial \mathbf{b}'}(\mathbf{b}-\mathbf{b}_0) + O\left(\|\mathbf{b}-\mathbf{b}_0\|^2\right)$$
$$+\,O\left(\|\mathbf{b}-\mathbf{b}_0\|\cdot\|\mathbf{z}-\mathbf{z}_0\|\right).$$

Substituting Z_n for $\mathbf{z}$ and $\beta(Z_n)$ for $\mathbf{b}$, and setting $\mathbf{z}_0 = \Pr(\mathbf{b}_0)$, we obtain:

$$\frac{\partial g(Z_n,\mathbf{b}_0)}{\partial \mathbf{b}} + \frac{\partial^2 g[P_0(\mathbf{b}_0),\mathbf{b}_0]}{\partial \mathbf{b}\partial \mathbf{b}'}[\beta(Z_0)-\mathbf{b}_0]$$
$$= o_p\left(\|\beta(Z_n)-\mathbf{b}_0\|\right),$$

where o_p is infinitesimal in probability.

We can now apply the central limit theorem to the functions g, permitting us to conclude that:

$$-\sqrt{n}\frac{\partial g}{\partial \mathbf{b}}(Z_n,\mathbf{b}_0)$$

converges in distribution to the normal distribution.

In consequence:

$$\frac{\partial^2}{\partial b\partial b'}g[\Pr(\mathbf{b}_0),\mathbf{b}_0]\sqrt{n}[\beta(Z_n)-\mathbf{b}_0], \text{ and } \sqrt{n}[\beta(Z_n)-\mathbf{b}_0]$$

converge in distribution to normal, since the matrix $\frac{\partial^2 g[\Pr(\mathbf{b}_0),\mathbf{b}_0]}{\partial \mathbf{b}\partial \mathbf{b}'}$ is non-singular when the model is identified.

4.7 Limited Information Maximum Likelihood (LIML)

This method involves a loss of efficiency compared to the full information maximum-likelihood method discussed in section 4.3. On the other hand it is simpler to calculate and justifies to some extent the introduction of marginal-conditional, conditional-conditional, etc. models.

4.7.1 Information Derived from the Marginal Distributions

This method, introduced by Ashford-Sowden [AS70], is of particular interest for evaluating probit models with more than three choice functions. It avoids the computationally very demanding evaluation of multiple integrals.

Consider three latent variables:

$$V_j^1 = \mathbf{x}_{1j}\mathbf{b}_1 + v_{1j},$$
$$V_j^2 = \mathbf{x}_{2j}\mathbf{b}_2 + v_{2j},$$
$$V_j^3 = \mathbf{x}_{3j}\mathbf{b}_3 + v_{3j},$$

which define three dichotomous variables:

$$y_j^k = \begin{cases} 1, & \text{if } V_j^k > 0, \\ 0, & \text{otherwise,} \end{cases} \qquad k = \{1, 2, 3\}.$$

Let (v_1, v_2, v_3) be characterized by the following normal distribution:

$$N\left[\begin{pmatrix} 0 \\ 0 \\ 0 \end{pmatrix} \begin{pmatrix} 1 & \rho_{12} & \rho_{13} \\ \rho_{12} & 1 & \rho_{23} \\ \rho_{13} & \rho_{23} & 1 \end{pmatrix}\right].$$

The estimation proceeds as follows:

- Estimate b_1 (respectively b_2, b_3) by maximizing the marginal likelihood of y_j^1 (y_j^2, y_j^3). This yields the estimators $\beta_1, \beta_2, \beta_3$,
- Estimate the correlation coefficients using the marginal distributions of the ordered pairs. For example, to estimate ρ_{12} we calculate the density of (y_j^1, y_j^2), $j = 1 \dots J$, by substituting β_1, β_2, derived in the first step, for b_1 and b_2 in the likelihood function. We then maximize the new function over ρ_{12}. This procedure is consistent, but not asymptotically efficient.

4.7.2 Two-stage Estimation using the Marginal and Conditional Distributions

This procedure, described by Amemiya [Ame78], was applied to a bivariate logit model defined on two classes of parameters $\mathbf{b}_1$ and $\mathbf{b}_2$ by Domenich-McFadden. The marginal distribution of the first group, L_1, only depends on $\mathbf{b}_1$, while the conditional distribution of the second, $L_{2|1}$, given the first, is a function of both $\mathbf{b}_1$ and $\mathbf{b}_2$. The procedure is:

- Estimate $\mathbf{b}_1$ by maximizing $\log(L_1)$, yielding the estimator $\boldsymbol{\beta}_1$,
- Maximize $\log\left[L_{2|1}(\mathbf{b}_2, \boldsymbol{\beta}_1)\right]$ with respect to $\mathbf{b}_2$ to generate the estimate $\boldsymbol{\beta}_2$.

These estimators are consistent, but they are not asymptotically efficient (except in the special case of the sequential model where $L_{2|1}$ does not depend on $\mathbf{b}_1$). The appeal of this approach is that it facilitates computation of the estimates since it reduces the number of parameters to be estimated in each maximization. At each stage we can replace the maximum-likelihood method with the generalized Berkson method.

4.7.3 *Estimation of Conditional Logit Models*

In these models (cf. section 3.4.2) the parameters are derived from the conditional distributions. In consequence, we limit our analysis to these more tractable computations and ignore the joint distributions.

We begin by examining the case of a conditional dichotomous bivariate logit model:

$$\begin{aligned}
\Pr\left(y_j^1 = 1 \middle| y_j^2 = 0\right) &= \frac{1}{1+\exp\left(\mathbf{x}_{1j}\mathbf{b}_1\right)},\\
\Pr\left(y_j^1 = 1 \middle| y_j^2 = 1\right) &= \frac{1}{1+\exp\left(\mathbf{x}_{2j}\mathbf{b}_2\right)},\\
\Pr\left(y_j^2 = 0 \middle| y_j^1 = 0\right) &= \frac{1}{1+\exp\left(\mathbf{x}_{3j}\mathbf{b}_3\right)},\\
\Pr\left(y_j^2 = 1 \middle| y_j^1 = 1\right) &= \frac{1}{1+\exp\left(\mathbf{x}_{4j}\mathbf{b}_4\right)}.
\end{aligned} \tag{4.23}$$

Under the compatibility condition:

$$\mathbf{x}_{1j}\mathbf{b}_1 + \mathbf{x}_{4j}\mathbf{b}_4 = \mathbf{x}_{2j}\mathbf{b}_2 + \mathbf{x}_{3j}\mathbf{b}_3.$$

Denote the observed frequencies $\pi_{00j}, \pi_{01j}, \pi_{10j}, \pi_{11j}$ for each trial of type j. To estimate $\mathbf{b}_1$ we simply calculate the conditional frequency:

$$\frac{\pi_{10j}}{\pi_{10j}+\pi_{00j}},$$

and apply Berkson's method.

Consider the *logit transformation* defined by:

$$\text{logit}\,(y) = \log\left(\frac{y}{1-y}\right),$$

we have:

$$\text{logit}\left(\frac{\pi_{10j}}{\pi_{10j}+\pi_{00j}}\right) \approx x_{1j}b_1 + u_{1j},$$

and can apply generalized least squares to this equation.

Notice that this method can be improved by simultaneously performing the logit transformation on the first three equations of (4.23) and then applying least squares. The residuals u_{1j}, u_{2j}, u_{3j} are, of course, correlated.

Finally, observe that separate estimation of the parameters from the equations in (4.23) can serve to verify whether the specification of the model as a conditional distribution is appropriate. We simply test the compatibility conditions *à posteriori*.

4.8 Principal Test Procedures

The aforementioned techniques yield estimators which are asymptotically normal as the sample size tends to infinity. Furthermore, we have seen that in the case of grouped data several of these methods yield estimators which are asymptotically equivalent.

It is relatively simple to use these estimators to generate test procedures, several of which will, again, be asymptotically equivalent.

We shall present the primary test procedures using, as our starting point, the maximum-likelihood method. This estimator is consistent even in the absence of grouped data (which is not the case for Berkson's method). Furthermore, this is the most widely used estimation method.

Denote:

$$\log\left[L\left(\mathbf{y};\mathbf{b}\right)\right] = \sum_{j=1}^{J}\sum_{k=0}^{K} n_{kj}\log\left[P_{kj}\left(\mathbf{b}\right)\right]$$

the log-likelihood under the general hypothesis H.

Now we partition the parameter vector $\mathbf{b}$ into two groups $\mathbf{b} = \begin{pmatrix}\mathbf{b}_1\\ \mathbf{b}_2\end{pmatrix}$, where $\mathbf{b}_1$ is r-dimensional and $\mathbf{b}_2$ comprises $(q-r)$ elements. The null hypothesis is:

$$H_0 : \{\mathbf{b}_1 = \mathbf{0}\}.$$

We consider two different maximum-likelihood estimators for $\mathbf{b}$.

The unconstrained estimator $\beta^u = \begin{pmatrix}\beta_1\\ \beta_2\end{pmatrix}$ solves the problem $\max\{\log[L(\mathbf{y};\mathbf{b})]\}$. As we have seen, this estimator is consistent and asymptotically normal with a covariance matrix given by the inverse of the Fisher information matrix. Performing a decomposition corresponding to the sub-vectors, we have:

$$\beta = \begin{pmatrix}\beta_1\\ \beta_2\end{pmatrix} \overset{asy}{\rightsquigarrow} N\left[\begin{pmatrix}\mathbf{b}_1\\ \mathbf{b}_2\end{pmatrix}\begin{pmatrix}I_{11} & I_{12}\\ I_{21} & I_{22}\end{pmatrix}^{-1}\right].$$

Inverting the Fisher information matrix by partition yields:

$$\mathrm{var}\left(\beta_1\right) \approx \left[I_{11} - I_{12}I_{22}^{-1}I_{21}\right]^{-1}.$$

(i) The constrained estimator is calculated under the null hypothesis. It is of the form:

$$\beta^c = \begin{pmatrix} \mathbf{0} \\ \beta_2^c \end{pmatrix},$$

where β_2^c solves the maximization of $\log\left[L\left(\mathbf{y}; \mathbf{0}, \beta_2\right)\right]$ over $\mathbf{b}_2$.

Under the null hypothesis, β_2^c is consistent and asymptotically normal:

$$\beta_2^c \overset{asy}{\rightsquigarrow} N\left(\mathbf{b}, I_{22}^{-1}\right).$$

We see that there are various asymptotically equivalent ways to test the hypothesis $H_0 : \mathbf{b}_1 = 0$.

4.8.1 *The Wald Test*

The idea underlying this test is to accept the null hypothesis if the unconstrained estimate of $\mathbf{b}_1$ is close to zero. The statistic is a measure of $\mathbf{b}_1$-s proximity to zero, given by:

$$\begin{aligned} \xi_w &= \beta_1' \left[\operatorname{var}\left(\beta_1\right)\right]^{-1} \beta_1, \\ &= \beta_1' \left[\hat{I}_{11} - \hat{I}_{12}\hat{I}_{22}^{-1}\hat{I}_{21}\right] \beta_1, \end{aligned} \tag{4.24}$$

where $\hat{I}$ denotes a consistent estimator of the information matrix.

If the null hypothesis H_0 obtains, this statistic is asymptotically chi-square distributed with r degrees of freedom. Denote $\chi^2_{95\%}(r)$ the 95 percent critical point of this distribution, the Wald test of the null hypothesis with five percent significance is:

$$\begin{cases} \text{accept } H_0, \text{ if } \xi_w < \chi^2_{95\%}(r), \\ \text{reject } H_0, \text{ if } \xi_w > \chi^2_{95\%}(r). \end{cases} \tag{4.25}$$

4.8.2 *The Likelihood-Ratio Test*

This test is based on a comparison of two maximum-likelihood estimators, generated by maximizing the constrained and unconstrained likelihood function. The statistic is:

$$\xi_{LR} = -2\left\{\log\left[L\left(\mathbf{y}; \beta^c\right)\right] - \log\left[L\left(\mathbf{y}; \beta^u\right)\right]\right\}, \tag{4.26}$$

which is also asymptotically $\chi^2(r)$. The test consists of:

$$\begin{cases} \text{accept } H_0, \text{ if } \xi_{LR} < \chi^2_{95\%}(r), \\ \text{reject } H_0, \text{ if } \xi_{LR} > \chi^2_{95\%}(r). \end{cases} \tag{4.27}$$

This procedure is asymptotically equivalent to the Wald test.

4.8.3 The Maximum Score Test (Lagrange Multiplier Test)

When the null hypothesis is true, the two estimators β and β^c should be very close to each other. The same is true for the vectors of scores:

$$\frac{\partial \log [L(\mathbf{y}; \mathbf{b}^u)]}{\partial \beta} = \begin{bmatrix} \frac{\partial \log(L)}{\partial \beta_1}(\mathbf{y}; \mathbf{b}^u) \\ \frac{\partial \log(L)}{\partial \beta_2}(\mathbf{y}; \mathbf{b}^u) \end{bmatrix} = \mathbf{0},$$

and:

$$\frac{\partial \log \left[L\left(\mathbf{y}; \mathbf{0}; \mathbf{b}_2^c\right)\right]}{\partial \beta} = \begin{bmatrix} \frac{\partial \log(L)}{\partial \beta_1}\left(y; \mathbf{0}; \mathbf{b}_2^c\right) \\ \frac{\partial \log(L)}{\partial \beta_2}\left(y; \mathbf{0}; \mathbf{b}_2^c\right) \end{bmatrix} = \begin{bmatrix} \frac{\partial \log(L)}{\partial \beta_1}\left(\mathbf{y}; \mathbf{0}; \mathbf{b}_2^c\right) \\ \mathbf{0} \end{bmatrix}.$$

The score statistic is defined by:

$$\xi_{LM} = \frac{\partial \log \left[L\left(\mathbf{y}; \mathbf{b}^u\right)\right]}{\partial \beta_1} \left(\hat{I}_{11} - \hat{I}_{12}\hat{I}_{22}^{-1}\hat{I}_{21}\right)^{-1} \frac{\partial \log \left[L\left(\mathbf{y}; \mathbf{b}^c\right)\right]}{\partial \beta_1}, \tag{4.28}$$

and is asymptotically equivalent (under H_0) to the Wald statistic, ξ_w, and to the likelihood-ratio statistic, ξ_{LR}.

The test is:

$$\begin{cases} \text{accept } H_0, \text{ if } \xi_{LM} < \chi^2_{95\%}(r), \\ \text{reject } H_0, \text{ if } \xi_{LM} > \chi^2_{95\%}(r). \end{cases} \tag{4.29}$$

Due to their asymptotic equivalence, the criteria for choosing between these procedures reduces in large measure to their ease of use. In practice the Lagrange multiplier is the most popular, as it is calculated by a simple regression.

Since $\left[\hat{I}_{11} - \hat{I}_{12}\hat{I}_{22}^{-1}\hat{I}_{21}\right]^{-1}$ is a part of the inverse of the Fisher information matrix, we see that:

$$\xi_{LM} = \frac{\partial \log [L(\mathbf{y}; \mathbf{b})]}{\partial (\beta^c)'} \hat{I}^{-1} \frac{\partial \log [L(\mathbf{y}; \mathbf{b})]}{\partial \beta^c}. \tag{4.30}$$

We now insert the individual observations into the likelihood equation, which we indicate with:

$$\log [L(\mathbf{y}; \mathbf{b})] = \sum_{i=1}^{n} \log [l(y_i; \mathbf{b})].$$

If the observations are not correlated between each other, we have:

$$\frac{\partial \log [L(\mathbf{y}; \mathbf{b})]}{\partial (\beta^u)'} = \sum_{i=1}^{n} \frac{\partial \log [l_i(y_i; \mathbf{b})]}{\partial (\beta^u)'}.$$

Furthermore, a consistent estimator of the Fisher information matrix is given by:

$$\hat{I} = \sum_{i=1}^{n} \frac{\partial \log [l_i (y_i; \mathbf{b})]}{\partial \beta^u} \frac{\partial \log [l_i (y_i; \mathbf{b})]}{\partial (\beta^u)'}.$$

We can now write the statistic ξ_{LM}:

$$\xi_{LM} = \sum_{i=1}^{n} \frac{\partial \log [l_i (y_i; \mathbf{b})]}{\partial (\beta^u)'} \times \left[\sum_{i=1}^{n} \frac{\partial \log [l_i (y_i; \mathbf{b}_0)]}{\partial \beta^u} \frac{\partial \log [l_i (y_i; \mathbf{b}_0)]}{\partial (\beta^u)'} \right]^{-1} \times \sum_{i=1}^{n} \frac{\partial \log [l_i (y_i; \mathbf{b}_0)]}{\partial \beta^u}. \tag{4.31}$$

Denote $\breve{I}$ the $n \times q$ matrix defined:

$$\breve{I} = \frac{\partial \log [l_i (y_i; \mathbf{b}_0)]}{\partial \beta'},$$

and $\mathbf{e}$ the n-dimensional vector comprised of ones. Expression (4.31) shows that the statistic ξ_{LM} is exactly the sum of squares of the predictions in the artificial linear regression:

$$\mathbf{e} = \breve{I} \cdot \mathbf{a} + errors, \tag{4.32}$$

where $\mathbf{a}$ is a vector of q parameters.

4.8.4 *Hausman's Specification Test*

A final notion we will touch on involves comparing the two estimates of the nuisance parameter $\mathbf{b}$. The statistic is of the form:

$$\xi_H = \left(\beta - \beta^c\right)' \left[\widehat{\text{var}} (\beta) - \widehat{\text{var}} \left(\beta^c\right)\right]^- \left(\beta - \beta^c\right), \tag{4.33}$$

where $[\cdots]^-$ denotes a generalized inverse.

Under H_0, when $\left[\widehat{\text{var}} (\beta) - \widehat{\text{var}} (\beta^c)\right]^-$ converges to a generalized inverse of $\widehat{\text{var}} (\beta) - \widehat{\text{var}} (\beta^c) = \text{var} (\beta - \beta^c)$, we can show that ξ_H is asymptotically chi-square with r^* $\{= \text{rank} [\text{var} (\beta) - \text{var} (\beta^c)]\}$ degrees of freedom. The variances are evaluated under the null hypothesis.

The rank r^* is always less than or equal to the number of constraints, r. In the special case $r^* = r$, the statistic ξ_H is equivalent to ξ_w, ξ_{LR} and ξ_{LM} which we have already seen.

A particular advantage of Hausman's procedure is that it can easily be extended to the case of two estimators: $\tilde{\beta}$ and β^c, where the former is consistent under H_0 and the latter is consistent and efficient under H_0. The test consists of:

$$\begin{cases} \text{accept } H_0, \text{ if } \xi_H < \chi^2_{95\%}(r), \\ \text{reject } H_0, \text{ if } \xi_H > \chi^2_{95\%}(r), \end{cases} \tag{4.34}$$

with:

$$\xi_H = \left(\tilde{\beta} - \beta^c\right)' \left[\widehat{\text{var}}\left(\tilde{\beta}\right) - \widehat{\text{var}}\left(\beta^c\right)\right]^- \left(\tilde{\beta} - \beta^c\right),$$
$$r^* = \text{rank}\left[\widehat{\text{var}}\left(\tilde{\beta}\right) - \widehat{\text{var}}\left(\beta^c\right)\right] = \text{rank}\left[\text{var}\left(\tilde{\beta} - \beta^c\right)\right].$$

For this test to be consistent it is clearly essential that $\tilde{\beta} - \beta^c$ does not tend to zero if H_0 is not true.

Finally, notice that the value of the rank r^*must be derived from *à priori* theoretical knowledge. There is no way to estimate it from the equation $r^* = \text{rank}\left[\text{var}\left(\tilde{\beta}\right) - \text{var}\left(\beta^c\right)\right]$, since rank is not a continuous mapping.

4.9 Goodness of Fit

Just as in the linear case, we can introduce measures of goodness of fit. These are analogous to the familiar R^2 coefficient of determination. The underlying idea is to compare the chosen model as represented by the estimated likelihood function $L(\mathbf{y}; \mathbf{b})$ with a more general model which can be written:

$$P_{kj} = \gamma_{kj},$$

where the γ_{kj}, $k = 1, \ldots, K$, $j = 1, \ldots, K$ are independent parameters (γ_{0j} is constrained by $\sum_{k=0}^{K} \gamma_{kj} = 1$). This is the formulation which defines the null hypothesis H_0.

4.9.1 Measures Associated with the Likelihood-Ratio Test

For the unconstrained maximization of the log-likelihood the theoretical probabilities P_{kj} are replaced by the observed frequencies π_{kj} in the expression for $\log(L)$, yielding:

$$\log\left(\hat{L}\right) = \sum_{j=1}^{J} \sum_{k=0}^{K} n_{kj} \log\left(\pi_{kj}\right).$$

The likelihood-ratio statistic is given by:

$$\xi_{LR} = -2\left\{\log\left[L(\mathbf{y}, \beta) - \log\left(\hat{L}\right)\right]\right\},$$
$$= -2 \sum_{j=1}^{J} \sum_{k=0}^{K} n_{kj} \log\left[\frac{P_{kj}(\beta)}{\pi_{kj}}\right]. \tag{4.35}$$

The dimension of the null hypothesis is equal to the number of elements in **b**, that is, $q = \sum_{h=1}^{H} q_h$. The alternative hypothesis is characterized by $K \cdot J$ independent parameters.

When the initial model obtains, ξ_{LR} will be distributed $\chi^2 (K \cdot J - q)$.

4.9.2 *Chi-square Goodness of Fit Measures*

If the chosen statistic is not maximum likelihood, but rather chi-square, it seems reasonable to use the following measure of goodness-of-fit:

$$\varphi_1 (\boldsymbol{\beta}_1) = \sum_{j=1}^{J} \sum_{k=0}^{K} \frac{\left[n_{kj} - n_j P_{kj} (\boldsymbol{\beta}_1)\right]^2}{n_j P_{kj} (\boldsymbol{\beta}_1)},$$

or

$$\varphi_2 (\boldsymbol{\beta}_2) = \sum_{j=1}^{J} \sum_{k=0}^{K} \frac{\left[n_{kj} - n_j P_{kj} (\boldsymbol{\beta}_2)\right]^2}{n_{kj}}. \tag{4.36}$$

Under the null hypothesis, these statistics are asymptotically equivalent to the ML expression:

$$-2 \left\{\log [L (\boldsymbol{\beta})] - \log \left(\hat{L}\right)\right\},$$

as all the n_j-s tend to infinity. In fact:

$$-2 \left\{\log [L (\boldsymbol{\beta})] - \log \left(\hat{L}\right)\right\} = -2 \sum_{j=1}^{J} \sum_{k=0}^{K} n_{kj} \log \left[\frac{P_{kj} (\boldsymbol{\beta})}{\pi_{kj}}\right].$$

If the null hypothesis is true, both π_{kj} and $P_{kj} (\boldsymbol{\beta})$ converge towards $P_{kj} (\boldsymbol{\beta}^c)$ asymptotically. Rewriting the expression as a second order expansion we have:

$$\begin{aligned}
&-2 \left\{\log [L (\boldsymbol{\beta})] - \log \left(\hat{L}\right)\right\} \\
&\approx -2 \sum_{j=1}^{J} \sum_{k=0}^{K} n_{kj} \left\{\frac{P_{kj} (\boldsymbol{\beta}) - \pi_{kj}}{\pi_{kj}} - \frac{1}{2} \frac{\left[P_{kj} (\boldsymbol{\beta}) - \pi_{kj}\right]^2}{\pi_{kj}^2}\right\}, \\
&\approx -2 \sum_{j=1}^{J} \sum_{k=0}^{K} n_{kj} \left[\frac{P_{kj} (\boldsymbol{\beta}) - \pi_{kj}}{\pi_{kj}} - \frac{1}{2} \frac{\left(P_{kj} (\boldsymbol{\beta}) - \pi_{kj}\right)^2}{\pi_{kj}^2}\right].
\end{aligned}$$

The first term on the right-hand side is nil, since it is equal to:

$$-2\sum_{j=1}^{J} n_j \left\{ \sum_{k=0}^{K} \left[P_{kj}(\boldsymbol{\beta}) - \pi_{kj} \right] \right\} = 0,$$

and hence:

$$-2\left\{\log\left[L(\boldsymbol{\beta})\right] - \log\left(\hat{L}\right)\right\} \approx \sum_{j=1}^{J}\sum_{k=0}^{K} n_j \frac{\left[\pi_{kj} - P_{kj}(\boldsymbol{\beta})\right]^2}{\pi_{kj}},$$
$$= \varphi_2(\boldsymbol{\beta})$$

In particular, $\varphi_1(\boldsymbol{\beta})$ and $\varphi_2(\boldsymbol{\beta})$ are asymptotically chi-square with $(K \cdot J - Q)$ degrees of freedom.

4.10 Omitted and Irrelevant Variables

Given a qualitative model, for example a polychotomous logit model defined by the probabilities:

$$P_k(\mathbf{b}) = \frac{\exp(\mathbf{x}_k \mathbf{b}_k)}{\sum_{\ell=0}^{K} \exp(\mathbf{x}_\ell \mathbf{b}_\ell)}, \quad b_0 = 0, \tag{4.37}$$

wemay wonder whether some important explanatory variables have not been forgotten. On the other hand, some of the included variables may not belong in the equation, having no real power to explain the qualitative endogenous variable. In the former case equation (4.37) will constitute the null hypothesis, while in the latter case it will be the alternative hypothesis. If we dispose of maximum-likelihood estimators, $\boldsymbol{\beta}_k$, of the true parameters, $\mathbf{b}_k$, $k = 1, \ldots, K$, it seems reasonable to use a maximum-score test for the case of omitted variables and a Wald test for the case of irrelevant variables.

4.10.1 Omitted Variables

Let's look at the case of an explanatory variable, z, which has not been incorporated into the probability $\frac{P_{k_0}(\mathbf{b})}{P_0(\mathbf{b})}$. The general model corresponds to the polychotomous logit model defined by:

$$\overset{\approx}{P}_k(a, \mathbf{b}) = \begin{cases} \dfrac{\exp(\mathbf{x}_k \mathbf{b}_k)}{\sum_{k \neq k_0} \exp(\mathbf{x}_k \mathbf{b}_k) + \exp\left(\mathbf{x}_{k_0} \mathbf{b}_{k_0} + za\right)}, & \text{if } k \neq k_0, \\[2ex] \dfrac{\exp(x_k b_k + za)}{\sum_{k \neq k_0} \exp(\mathbf{x}_k \mathbf{b}_k) + \exp\left(\mathbf{x}_{k_0} \mathbf{b}_{k_0} + za\right)}, & \text{otherwise.} \end{cases}$$

The null hypothesis, that is the original model, obtains when $\alpha = 0$.

The log-likelihood of the general model is:

$$\log\left[\overset{\approx}{L}(\mathbf{y}; a, \mathbf{b})\right] = \sum_{j=1}^{J}\sum_{k=0}^{K} n_{kj}\log\left[\overset{\approx}{P}_{kj}(a, \mathbf{b})\right],$$

$$= \sum_{j=1}^{J} n_j \log\left[\overset{\approx}{P}_{0j}(a, \mathbf{b})\right]$$

$$+ \sum_{j=1}^{J}\sum_{k=1}^{K} n_{kj}\log\left[\frac{\overset{\approx}{P}_{kj}(a, \mathbf{b})}{\overset{\approx}{P}_{0j}(a, \mathbf{b})}\right].$$

This form of the log-likelihood equation is particularly interesting, as the expression $\log\left[\frac{\overset{\approx}{P}_{kj}(a,\mathbf{b})}{\overset{\approx}{P}_{0j}(a,\mathbf{b})}\right]$ is linear in the parameters.

The score for the parameter a is:

$$\frac{\partial \log\left[\overset{\approx}{L}(\mathbf{y}; a, \mathbf{b})\right]}{\partial a} = \sum_{j=1}^{J}(-n_j)\,\overset{\approx}{P}_{k_0,j}(a, \mathbf{b})\, z_j + \sum_{j=1}^{J} n_{k_0 j}\cdot z_j,$$

$$= \sum_{j=1}^{J} n_j \left[\pi_{k_0,j} - \overset{\approx}{P}_{k_0,j}(a, \mathbf{b})\right] z_j.$$

Replacing the parameters by their estimates under the null hypothesis, we have:

$$\frac{\partial \log\left[\overset{\approx}{L}(\mathbf{y}; 0, \boldsymbol{\beta})\right]}{\partial a} = \sum_{j=1}^{J} n_j \left[\pi_{k_0,j} - \overset{\approx}{P}_{k_0,j}(0, \boldsymbol{\beta})\right] z_j.$$

Notice that $\pi_{k_0,j} - \overset{\approx}{P}_{k_0,j}(0, \boldsymbol{\beta}) = \frac{n_{k_0,j}}{n_j} - \overset{\approx}{P}_{k_0,j}(0, \boldsymbol{\beta})$ can be interpreted as the difference between $\frac{n_{k_0,j}}{n_j}$ and a natural estimator of its mean, and hence viewed as a residual of the estimation. The estimated score is the scalar product of this residual and the omitted variable. When this variable is "almost orthogonal" to the residuals, the score will be close to zero and the original model must be deemed the "true" model. Obviously, to complete the test we still have to examine the variance of the score $I_{\alpha\alpha} - I_{\alpha b} I_{bb}^{-1} I_{b\alpha}$. This is left as an exercise for the reader.

4.10.2 Irrelevant Variables

Assume now that among the variables $\mathbf{x}_{k_0}$, some do not contribute to explaining the endogenous variables. We can decompose $\mathbf{x}_{k_0} = \left(\mathbf{x}_{k_0}^{*}, \mathbf{x}_{k_0}^{**}\right)$ and $\mathbf{b}_{k_0} = \left(\mathbf{b}_{k_0}^{*}, \mathbf{b}_{k_0}^{**}\right)'$, and test the null hypothesis, $H_0 : \mathbf{b}_{k_0}^{*} = 0$, (i.e. the $\mathbf{x}_{k_0}$ are irrelevant). The simplest way to verify this is given by the Wald test.

For example, if $\mathbf{x}_{k_0}$ consists of a single variable, the Wald statistic is $\xi_w = \left|\frac{\beta^*_{k_0}}{\hat{\sigma}_{\beta^*_{k_0}}}\right|$ and, under the null hypothesis, it is asymptotically distributed χ^2 with one degree of freedom. Setting the Type I error cut-off level at five percent, this test consists of accepting the null hypothesis H_0 if the student's t-statistic associated with the coefficient $\beta^*_{k_0}$ is less than two, and rejecting it otherwise:

$$\begin{cases} \text{accept } H_0, & \text{if } \left|\frac{\beta^*_{k_0}}{\hat{\sigma}_{\beta^*_{k_0}}}\right| < 2, \\ \text{reject } H_0, & \text{if } \left|\frac{\beta_{k_0}}{\hat{\sigma}_{\beta^*_{k_0}}}\right| > 2. \end{cases}$$

The two test procedures we have just seen for omitted and irrelevant variables are similar to the tests typically applied to the linear model.

4.11 A Test for the Polychotomous Logit Formulation

4.11.1 Characterization of the Logit Polychotomous Model

Before developing test procedures for the polychotomous logit model, it may be of some interest to characterize this formulation in terms of the conditional probabilities of a restricted number of alternatives.

Let us consider a polychotomous logit model corresponding to the alternatives $k = \{0, \ldots, K\}$. We have:

$$P_k(\mathbf{b}) = \frac{\exp(\mathbf{x}_k \mathbf{b}_k)}{\sum_{h=0}^{K} \exp(\mathbf{x}_h \mathbf{b}_h)}, \quad k = 0, \ldots, K, \quad b_0 = 0.$$

If A is a subset of $\{0, \ldots, K\}$, we can calculate the probability of an alternative k, knowing that it belongs to A. We have:

$$P_{k|A}(\mathbf{b}) = \frac{P_k(\mathbf{b})}{\sum_{h \in A} P_h(\mathbf{b})} = \frac{\exp(\mathbf{x}_k \mathbf{b}_k)}{\sum_{h \in A} \exp(\mathbf{x}_h \mathbf{b}_h)}, \quad k \in A.$$

Hence this restricted conditional model is also polychotomous logit. This property can be related to the *preservation property of log-linear models upon conditioning* (cf. chapter 5).

We can even derive the following, more precise result:

Proposition 6: A model is polychotomous logit if all its conditional probabilities:

$$\left[P_{k|(k,\ell)}(\mathbf{b}), P_{\ell|(k,\ell)}(\mathbf{b})\right], \quad \forall k, \ell$$

define a dichotomous logit model.

Proof: Essentially, we need to demonstrate the sufficiency condition. Consider the conditional probabilities $P_{k|(k,0)}(\mathbf{b})$, $k = 1, \ldots, K$. Since the conditional models are polychotomous logit, we can write:

$$P_{k|(k,0)}(\mathbf{b}) = \frac{\exp(\mathbf{x}_k \mathbf{b}_k)}{1 + \exp(\mathbf{x}_k \mathbf{b}_k)},$$

or, equivalently:

$$\frac{P_{k|(k,0)}(\mathbf{b})}{P_{0|(k,0)}(\mathbf{b})} = \frac{P_k(\mathbf{b})}{P_0(\mathbf{b})} = \exp(\mathbf{x}_k \mathbf{b}_k), \quad \forall k = 1, \ldots, K.$$

We conclude that:

$$\frac{1}{P_0(\mathbf{b})} = \sum_{k=0}^{K} \frac{P_k(\mathbf{b})}{P_0(\mathbf{b})} = 1 + \sum_{k=1}^{K} \exp(\mathbf{x}_k \mathbf{b}_k),$$

and so that:

$$P_k(\mathbf{b}) = \frac{\exp(\mathbf{x}_k \mathbf{b}_k)}{1 + \sum_{k=1}^{K} \exp(\mathbf{x}_k \mathbf{b}_k)}.$$

□

In the case of some other models, such as the sequential logit, this property works for finding some conditional probabilities, but not for all.

Remark 5: Be careful not to confuse the property we just discussed with the property of the irrelevance of independent alternatives. Conditional probabilities are calculated for the whole set of choice probabilities {0, 1,..., K}.

4.11.2 Hausman Test for Polychotomous Logit Formulation

The aforementioned property of the logit model constitutes the basis for a variant on the Hausman test which is very simple to apply. If the model is true, there exist several consistent estimators of the parameters.

To simplify the analysis, let's focus our attention on the parameters $\mathbf{b}_k$, $k \in A$, where A contains the alternative o.

We can estimate the $\mathbf{b}_k$-s by applying the maximum-likelihood method to the logit model. The estimator, β_k, $k \in A$ is asymptotically efficient.

We can also consider the log-likelihood conditional on A, that is:

$$\log[L|A(\mathbf{y}; \mathbf{b})] = \sum_{j=1}^{J} \sum_{k \in A} n_k \log\left[P_{k|A}(\mathbf{b})\right],$$

and derive the estimator $\left(\tilde{\beta}_k, k \in A\right)$ which maximizes this function. This estimator is consistent but not, generally, asymptotically efficient.

If the null hypothesis is true (i.e. the model is polychotomous logit) the statistic given by:

$$\xi_H = \left(\tilde{\beta}_A - \beta_A\right)' \left[\widehat{\text{var}}\left(\tilde{\beta}_A\right) - \widehat{\text{var}}\left(\beta_A\right)\right]^- \left(\tilde{\beta}_A - \beta_A\right),$$

where β_A denotes the vector $(\beta_k, k \in A)$ and where $[\cdots]^-$ indicates a generalized inverse, is asymptotically chi-square with degrees of freedom equal to the rank of $\widehat{\text{var}}\left(\tilde{\beta}_A\right) - \widehat{\text{var}}\left(\beta_A\right)$. Note that this rank depends on the dimension of the subset A comprising the alternatives under consideration.

According to this specification test we accept the polychotomous logit model if $\xi_H < \chi^2_{95\%}\left\{\text{rank}\left[\text{var}\left(\tilde{\beta}_A\right) - \text{var}\left(\beta_A\right)\right]\right\}$, and reject it otherwise.

Observe that we did not specify the alternative hypothesis H_1. To ensure convergence we could define H_1 as the set of distributions for which ξ_H tends to $+\infty$ under H_1.

4.11.3 The Multinomial Logit Model as a Special Case

A traditional approach to specification testing has been to introduce a general model of which the model in question is a special case. To simplify, we shall examine an example with three alternatives. Hausman-McFadden [HM84] propose the following probability structure:

$$P_1(\mathbf{b}, \lambda) = \frac{\exp\left(\frac{\mathbf{x}_1\mathbf{b}_1}{\lambda}\right)\exp(\lambda a)}{\exp\left\{a\left[\exp(\mathbf{x}_3\mathbf{b}_3) + \exp(\lambda a)\right]\right\}},$$

$$P_2(\mathbf{b}, \lambda) = \frac{\exp\left(\frac{\mathbf{x}_2\mathbf{b}_2}{\lambda}\right)\exp(\lambda a)}{\exp\left\{a\left[\exp(\mathbf{x}_3\mathbf{b}_3) + \exp(\lambda a)\right]\right\}},$$

$$P_3(\mathbf{b}, \lambda) = \frac{\exp(\mathbf{x}_3\mathbf{b}_3)}{\exp(\mathbf{x}_3\mathbf{b}_3) + \exp(\lambda a)},$$

where λ is a scalar parameter and where the constant a is defined:

$$a = \log\left[\exp\left(\frac{x_1 b_1}{\lambda}\right) + \exp\left(\frac{x_2 b_2}{\lambda}\right)\right],$$

so that the three probabilities sum to one.

This model includes the multinomial logit as a special case corresponding to $\lambda = 1$, and we can test the hypothesis $H_0 : (\lambda = 1)$ using one of the procedures introduced in section 4.8.

Similar "super-models" can be applied in a number of circumstances (cf. Ben-Akiva [Aki74], McFadden [McF76]).

Exercises

4.1 Consider the model in section 3.2.2 and assume that the errors $\left(v_i^1, v_i^2\right)$ are independent and distributed:

$$N\left[\begin{pmatrix} 0 \\ 0 \end{pmatrix}, \begin{pmatrix} \sigma_1^2 & \rho\sigma_{12} \\ \rho\sigma_{12} & \sigma_2^2 \end{pmatrix}\right],$$

Write the probability of each value in terms of the parameters. Can these probabilities we written in the form of equation (4.1)?

4.2 (Difficult) We have data on independent dichotomous variables $y_{ij}, i = 1, \ldots, n,$ $j = 1, 2$. These variables are such that:

$$\Pr\left(y_{i1} = 1\right) = F\left(\alpha_i\right),$$
$$\Pr\left(y_{i2} = 1\right) = F\left(\beta + \alpha_i\right)$$

where the function F is the logististic distribution. Show that the maximum-likelihood estimator for β converges to 2β as $n \to \infty$. Calculate $\Pr\left(y_{i1} = 1 \middle| y_{i1} + y_{i2} = 1\right)$ and use this to find another estimaor for β. Is this estimator consistent as $n \to \infty$?

4.3 Consider the bivariate dichotomous conditional logit model in section 4.3.2 and assume that the compatibility condition is satisfied. Show that:

$$\frac{\Pr\left(y^1 = 0 \middle| y^2 = 0\right)}{\Pr\left(y^2 = 0 \middle| y^1 = 0\right)} + \frac{\Pr\left(y^1 = 1 \middle| y^2 = 0\right)}{\Pr\left(y^2 = 0 \middle| y^1 = 1\right)} = \frac{1}{\Pr\left(y^2 = 0\right)}.$$

Derive the probabilities and the distribution of $P_{11}, P_{10}, P_{01}, P_{00}$.

4.4 (Continuation of exercise 3) Derive the forms of the probabilities of the joint distribution and the likelihood equations. Don't forget that the maximization must respect the compatitibility constraint.

4.5 (Continuation of exercise 3) For the model which you just derived, find the function G permitting it to be expressed as a linear approximation. Is this different than the one which would have been obtained directly from the conditional probabilities? Apply generalized least squares to this model, don't forget to account for the compatibility constraint.

4.6 Berkson's method allows us to approximate any qualitative response model with a linear model. Show that in this correspondence:

(a) The simple dichotomy corresponds to a single-equation linear model.
(b) The polychotomous logit model corresponds to a nested regression with serial correlation.
(c) The sequential logit model corresponds to a recursive model.

Find the analogies with: ANOVA, analysis of lagged variable models, simultaneous equation models.

4.7 Recall that if $u(x)$ is a strictly convex function, we have $\mathrm{E}\left[u(x)\right] \geq u\left[\mathrm{E}(x)\right]$, where the equality only holds when x is almost surely constant (the Jenson, or convexity, inequality).

(a) Let $P_k, k = 1, \ldots, K$ and $P_{0k}, k = 0, \ldots, K$ be two discrete probabilities. Define:

$$d_u(P, P_0) = \sum_{k-0}^{K} P_{0k}\left[u\left(\frac{P_k}{P_{0k}}\right) - u(1)\right],$$

where u is a strictly convex function.

1. Verify that $d_u(P, P_0)$ is always positive.
2. Show that $d_u(P, P_0)$ is nil if and only if $P = P_0$.

(b) Provide an interpretation of the function d_u when: $u(x) = \log(x), u(x) = (x-1)^2$.

Assume that we have n independent observations from the distribution of the elementary probabilities $P_k(b)$, and denote π_k the observed frequencies associated with each alternative. Define the estimator $\beta(u)$ as the solution to the problem:

$$\min_b \sum_{k=0}^{K}\left[u\left(\frac{P_k}{\pi_k}\right) - u(1)\right].$$

Show that the estimators $\beta(u)$ are asymptotically equivalent to the maximum-likelihood estimator.

5 The Log-Linear Model and its Applications

5.1 Introduction

In chapter 3 we presented procedures useful for analysing models of one or more dependent variables assuming several discrete values. These models must be constructed on a case by case basis, reflecting our intuition of the dynamics underlying the phenomena under investigation. The formulation may be that of a continuous latent variable with a threshold determining the value of the qualitative variable, or it may involve assumptions about the number of decision-makers and their behaviour. This intuitive understanding of the behaviour we are modelling is essential, but it must be complemented with rigorous statistical methods.

In the first sections of this chapter we shall introduce a series of techniques suitable for studying relationships between qualitative variables – testing for independence and conditional independence, for example. This *descriptive* approach is useful for specifying the model.

To begin, we assume that our observations correspond to a single setting of the exogenous variable, i.e. the probability associated with each value of the endogenous variable is independent of the observation. The various probabilities are summarized in a *contingency table,* the number of entries of which being determined by the number of variables.

Let us examine a few specific cases to illustrate how the tests are applied.

(i) The joint distribution of two dichotomous variables can be summarized in a two by two (2 × 2) contingency table.

$y_1 \backslash y_2$	0	1
0	P_{00}	P_{01}
1	P_{10}	P_{11}

The two variables are independent if the conditional distribution of y_1 given y_2 does not depend on y_2. This condition can be written:

$$\frac{P_{00}}{P_{00}+P_{01}} = \frac{P_{10}}{P_{10}+P_{11}},$$

$$P_{11}P_{00} = P_{01}P_{10}.$$

(ii) In the case of two variables, with y_1 dichotomous and y_2 trichotomous, we have a two by three (2×3) contingency table:

y_1 \ y_2	0	1	2
0	P_{00}	P_{01}	P_{02}
1	P_{10}	P_{11}	P_{12}

The variables are independent when:

$$P_{11}P_{00} = P_{10}P_{01},$$

$$P_{02}P_{10} = P_{00}P_{12}.$$

In the preceding examples the assumption of independence translates into linear constraints on the vector of the logarithms of the joint probabilities, log (**P**). This concept is fundamental to the construction of the log-linear model, it is equivalent to postulating that: **i)** log (**P**) belongs to a given subspace of $\mathbb{R}^n$, $\mathcal{M}$, and **ii)** the probabilities sum to one.

$$\begin{aligned} \log(\mathbf{P}) &\in \mathcal{M}, \\ \mathbf{e}'\mathbf{P} &= 1 \end{aligned} \tag{5.1}$$

where **e** is a vector of ones. Thus, assuming independence between the variables is equivalent to postulating that log (**P**) is linear.

From a practical point of view, log (**P**) must be expressed relative to a given base. We shall see that the base usually applied to the analysis of variance is particularly suited to problems of independence or conditional independence (though it is clearly not applicable to all problems of this nature).

In the following sections we will examine several specific cases, two (section 5.2) and three (section 5.3) dichotomous variables, and two polychotomous variables (section 5.4). A general examination of contingency tables is presented in section 5.5, while section 5.6 is devoted to the simultaneous analysis of several contingency tables and to the relationship between the log-linear model and certain logistic models. Finally, section 5.7 provides an application to the question of how business executives form expectations.

5.2 The Case of Two Dichotomous Variables

5.2.1 *The Saturated Model*

The distribution of a pair of dichotomous variables (y_1, y_2) is represented by the two by two (2×2) contingency table:

$y_1 \backslash y_2$	0	1
0	P_{00}	P_{01}
1	P_{10}	P_{11}

where the probabilities satisfy:

$$P_{00} + P_{01} + P_{10} + P_{11} = 1, \quad P_{ij} \geq 0, \quad i = \{0, 1\}, \quad j = \{0, 1\}. \tag{5.2}$$

We say that the model is *saturated* if the probabilities are not subject to further constraints. This saturated model is a special case of the log-linear model in equation (5.1), because:

$$\log(P) = \begin{pmatrix} \log(P_{00}) \\ \log(P_{01}) \\ \log(P_{10}) \\ \log(P_{11}) \end{pmatrix} \in \mathcal{M} = \mathbb{R}^4,$$

$$1 = P_{00} + P_{01} + P_{10} + P_{11}.$$

These joint probabilities are easily estimated if we have n independent observations on the variables $\left(y^1, y^2\right)$. They can be represented in a frequency table:

$y_1 \backslash y_2$	0	1	
0	n_{00}	n_{01}	
1	n_{10}	n_{11}	
			n

The distribution of these observations is polynomial with parameters n, P_{00}, P_{01}, P_{10}, P_{11}. We have:

$$\Pr(n_{00}, n_{01}, n_{10}, n_{11}) = \frac{1}{n_{00}!n_{01}!n_{10}!n_{11}!} P_{00}^{n_{00}} P_{01}^{n_{01}} P_{10}^{n_{10}} P_{11}^{n_{11}}.$$

Application of the maximum-likelihood method leads us to maximize $\log[\Pr(n_{00}, n_{01}, n_{10}, n_{11})]$ under the constraints in equation (5.2). The solution is simply the observed frequencies:

$$\hat{p}_{i_1 i_2} = \frac{n_{i_1 i_2}}{n}, \quad i_1 = \{0, 1\}, \quad i_2 = \{0, 1\}.$$

The calculations above were performed in $\mathbb{R}^4$ defined by the standard base: $(1, 0, 0, 0)'$, $(0, 1, 0, 0)'$, $(0, 0, 1, 0)'$, $(0, 0, 0, 1)'$. Other bases for the n-space can be chosen. In particular, we shall look at one corresponding to a decomposition of the probabilities into principal, secondary, etc. effects.

Let us write $\log\left(P_{i_1 i_2}\right)$ as:

$$\log\left(P_{i_1 i_2}\right) = \mu + \alpha_1(i_1) + \alpha_2(i_2) + \beta_{12}(i_1, i_2), \quad i_1 = \{0, 1\}, \quad i_2 = \{0, 1\}. \qquad (5.3)$$

Here μ represents the *principal effect*, $\alpha_1(i_1)$ the *marginal effect* of the first variable, $\alpha_2(i_2)$ the marginal effect of the second variable, and $\beta_{12}(i_1, i_2)$ the *cross effect*; collectively these are known as interaction terms.

The following constraints are usually introduced to ensure uniqueness of the decomposition (5.3):

$$0 = \sum_{i_1} \alpha_1(i_1),$$

$$0 = \sum_{i_2} \alpha_2(i_2),$$

$$0 = \sum_{i_1} \beta_{12}(i_1, i_2),$$

$$0 = \sum_{i_2} \beta_{12}(i_1, i_2).$$

The first constraint, for example, indicates that the average effect of the first variable is nil.

Accounting for the constraints and defining:

$$\alpha_1 = \alpha_1(1), \quad \alpha_2 = \alpha_2(1), \quad \beta_{12} = \beta_{12}(1, 1),$$

we obtain:

$$\begin{aligned} \log(P_{00}) &= \mu - \alpha_1 - \alpha_2 + \beta_{12}, \\ \log(P_{01}) &= \mu - \alpha_1 + \alpha_2 - \beta_{12}, \\ \log(P_{10}) &= \mu + \alpha_1 - \alpha_2 - \beta_{12}, \\ \log(P_{11}) &= \mu + \alpha_1 + \alpha_2 + \beta_{12}. \end{aligned} \qquad (5.4)$$

In vector notation these equalities are written:

$$\log(\mathbf{P}) = \mu \begin{bmatrix} 1 \\ 1 \\ 1 \\ 1 \end{bmatrix} + \alpha_1 \begin{bmatrix} -1 \\ -1 \\ 1 \\ 1 \end{bmatrix} + \alpha_2 \begin{bmatrix} -1 \\ 1 \\ -1 \\ 1 \end{bmatrix} + \beta_{12} \begin{bmatrix} 1 \\ -1 \\ -1 \\ 1 \end{bmatrix}.$$

Here we have an instance in which the various terms $\mu, \alpha_1, \alpha_2, \beta_{12}$ constitute the coordinates of log (**P**) with respect to a base other than the familiar standard one. This base can easily be made explicit. Let U_0 and U_1 be the vectors:

$$\mathbf{U}_0 = \begin{pmatrix} 1 \\ 1 \end{pmatrix}, \quad \mathbf{U}_1 = \begin{pmatrix} -1 \\ 1 \end{pmatrix}.$$

Using $\otimes$ to denote the Kronecker product of matrices, we have:

$$\mathbf{U}_0 \otimes \mathbf{U}_0 = \begin{bmatrix} 1 \\ 1 \\ 1 \\ 1 \end{bmatrix}, \qquad \mathbf{U}_0 \otimes \mathbf{U}_1 = \begin{bmatrix} -1 \\ 1 \\ -1 \\ 1 \end{bmatrix},$$

$$\mathbf{U}_1 \otimes \mathbf{U}_0 = \begin{bmatrix} -1 \\ -1 \\ 1 \\ 1 \end{bmatrix}, \qquad \mathbf{U}_1 \otimes \mathbf{U}_1 = \begin{bmatrix} 1 \\ -1 \\ -1 \\ 1 \end{bmatrix}.$$

These vectors are orthogonal.

The new coordinates can obviously be expressed as functions of the old ones. Solving system (5.4) yields:

$$\begin{aligned}
\mu &= \frac{1}{4}\left[\log(P_{00}) + \log(P_{01}) + \log(P_{10}) + \log(P_{11})\right], \\
&= \log(P_{..}), \\
\alpha_1 &= \frac{1}{2}\left[\log(P_{10}) + \log(P_{11})\right] - \mu, \\
&= \left[\log(P_{1.})\right] - \left[\log(P_{..})\right], \\
\alpha_2 &= \frac{1}{2}\left[\log(P_{01}) + \log(P_{11})\right] - \mu, \\
&= \left[\log(P_{.1})\right] - \left[\log(P_{..})\right], \\
\beta_{12} &= \log(P_{11}) - \log(P_{.1}) - \log(P_{1.}) + \left[\log(P_{..})\right],
\end{aligned} \tag{5.5}$$

where:

$$\begin{aligned}
P_{1.} &= \frac{1}{2}(P_{11} + P_{10}), \\
P_{.1} &= \frac{1}{2}(P_{11} + P_{01}), \\
P_{..} &= \frac{1}{4}(P_{00} + P_{01} + P_{10} + P_{11}).
\end{aligned}$$

Remark 6: It is implied in the preceding derivations that the logarithms of the probabilities are not equal to zero. This assumption will be made henceforth.

5.2.2 Measures of Association

The coefficient of correlation provides a natural measure of the relationship between y_1 and y_2, having the desirable property of being invariant with respect to the coding of the variable (cf. exercise 6).

Using the $P_{1.}$ and $P_{.1}$ notation defined above, we have:

$$\begin{aligned}
\text{var}(y_1) &= P_{1.}(1 - P_{1.}), \\
\text{var}(y_2) &= P_{.1}(1 - P_{.1}), \\
\text{cov}(y_1, y_2) &= \text{E}[y_1 y_2 - \text{E}(y_1 y_2)], \\
&= P_{11} - P_{1.}P_{.1}, \\
&= P_{11} - (P_{11} + P_{10})(P_{11} + P_{01}), \\
&= P_{11}(1 - P_{11} - P_{10} - P_{01}) - P_{10}P_{01}, \\
&= P_{11}P_{00} - P_{10}P_{01}.
\end{aligned}$$

The correlation coefficient is:

$$\rho(y_1, y_2) = \frac{P_{11}P_{00} - P_{10}P_{01}}{\sqrt{P_{1.}(1 - P_{1.})P_{.1}(1 - P_{.1})}}.$$

The sign of the correlation coefficient depends on that of $P_{11}P_{00} - P_{10}P_{01}$, if it is equal to zero we have independence (which in this case is equivalent to the absence of correlation between y_1 and y_2).

Another natural measure of the correlation between y_1 and y_2 is given by the cross term β_{12} from the decomposition of log ($\mathbf{P}$). This coefficient is equal to:

$$\begin{aligned}
\beta_{12} = \log(P_{11}) &- \frac{1}{2}\left[\log(P_{01}) + \log(P_{11})\right] - \frac{1}{2}\left[\log(P_{10}) + \log(P_{11})\right] \\
&+ \frac{1}{4}\left[\log(P_{01}) + \log(P_{11}) + \log(P_{00}) + \log(P_{10})\right], \\
&= \frac{1}{4}\left[\log(P_{11}) + \log(P_{00}) - \log(P_{10}) - \log(P_{01})\right], \\
&= \frac{1}{4}\log\left(\frac{P_{11}P_{00}}{P_{10}P_{01}}\right).
\end{aligned}$$

Hence β_{12} has the same sign as $\rho(y_1, y_2)$.

Proposition 7: If $\beta_{12} > 0$ ($\beta_{12} < 0$), there exists a positive (negative) correlation between the variables. If $\beta_{12} = 0$, the variables are independent.

Consequently, the assumption of independence can be verified by testing whether the coefficient $\beta_{12} = 0$. One way we can do this is by applying a Wald test to the maximum-likelihood estimator for β_{12} from the saturated model. It can easily be verified that this is asymptotically equivalent to the usual χ^2 test for independence (cf. exercise 7).

The joint probabilities can be estimated under the assumption of independence. The maximum-likelihood estimators are:

$$\hat{p}_{i_1,i_2} = \frac{n_{i_1\cdot}}{n}\frac{n_{\cdot i_2}}{n}, \quad i_1 = \{0, 1\}, \quad i_2 = \{0, 1\},$$

where $n_{i_1\cdot} = \sum_{i_2} n_{i_1 i_2}$ and $n_{\cdot i_2} = \sum_{i_1} n_{i_1 i_2}$.

In practice, the test for independence may serve two purposes:

(i) to verify independence between two qualitative endogenous variables, in which case the structure of the model reduces from a joint distribution to the simpler case of two independent marginal distributions (cf. exercise 2).

(ii) to examine the relationship between a qualitative endogenous variable y_1 and a qualitative exogenous variable y_2. If the assumption of independence is borne out by the test, this explanatory variable has no place in the model.

5.2.3 *Observations on the Interpretation of the Interaction Term*

By way of analogy with the traditional analysis of variance (ANOVA) model, the terms $\mu, \alpha_1, \alpha_2, \beta_{12}$ are often called the principal effect (μ), the marginal effects (α_1, α_2), and the cross effect (β_{12}). It is important to bear in mind, however, that these terms do not have the same interpretation as they do in analysis of variance. In ANOVA, an endogenous variable is explained in terms of other qualitative variables. In our present analysis [the decomposition in equation (5.3)] we are examining the joint probabilities of the variables (y_1, y_2), which are expressed in terms of themselves. In other words, the relationship between the endogenous variables is under scrutiny. This implies that the model has no explanatory function and the "effects" are not subject to the usual interpretation.

There are, however, interesting interpretations to be made.

5.2.3.1 *Interpretation of the Sign of* α_1

From the set of equations in (5.5), the term α_1 is equal to:

$$\begin{aligned}\alpha_1 &= \frac{1}{2}\left[\log(P_{10})\right] + \log(P_{11}) \\ &\quad - \frac{1}{4}\left[\log(P_{10}) + \log(P_{11}) + \log(P_{01}) + \log(P_{00})\right], \\ &= \frac{1}{4}\log\left(\frac{P_{11}}{P_{00}}\frac{P_{10}}{P_{01}}\right).\end{aligned}$$

Notice the similarity between this expression and that for the second-order term:

$$\beta_{12} = \frac{1}{4} \log \left(\frac{P_{11}\, P_{00}}{P_{10}\, P_{01}} \right).$$

α_1 appears as a measure of association after the cells of the contingency table have been reordered. More precisely, let us define a dichotomous variable y_3 such that:

$$y_3 = \begin{cases} 1, & \text{if } y_1 = y_2 = 1 \text{ or } y_1 = y_2 = 0, \\ 0, & \text{otherwise.} \end{cases}$$

For example, $y_3 = (1 - y_1)(1 - y_2) + (y_1 y_2)$. Letting $P^*_{11}, P^*_{10}, P^*_{00}, P^*_{01}$ be the joint probabilities of (y_3, y_2), we have:

$$\alpha_1 = \frac{1}{4} \log \left(\frac{P^*_{11} P^*_{00}}{P^*_{10} P^*_{01}} \right) = \beta^*_{12},$$

where β^*_{12} is the cross term from the table constructed from the elements y_3 and y_2. We see that α_1, like β_{12}, is a measure of the relationship between variables.

To illustrate, let y_1 denote the purchase of a given good at time t and y_2 the purchase of the same good at time $t + 1$. $y_3 = 1$ signifies that the behaviour was the same over the two periods (i.e. the good was bought, or not bought, both times). $\alpha_1 = 0$ if the decision to purchase the good in period $t + 1$ is independent of a change in behaviour between the two periods.

Determining whether or not any of the values $\alpha_1, \alpha_2, \beta_{12}$ is nil constitutes an important step in the construction of the contingency tables – revealing which elements belong there.

5.2.3.2 *Relationship with Analysis of Variance*

Assume that we have information concerning the pass rates of a group of students writing an exam (y_1) and whether or not these students receive scholarships (y_2). Decomposition (5.3) yields the joint probabilities $P_{00}, P_{01}, P_{10}, P_{11}$.

In order to conduct a traditional analysis of variance study of the impact of receiving a scholarship on the probability of passing, we need to explain the pass rates of recipients and non-recipients. This model is constructed from the conditional probabilities:

$$\begin{aligned} P_{1|1} &= a + b_1 \quad \text{(success rate of recipients)}, \\ P_{1|0} &= a - b_1 \quad \text{(success rate of non-recipients)}, \end{aligned}$$

where a is the principal effect and b_1 is the first-order effect.

This yields:

$$\begin{aligned} b_1 &= \frac{P_{1|1} - P_{1|0}}{2}, \\ &= \frac{1}{2}\left[\frac{P_{11}}{P_{11} + P_{01}} - \frac{P_{10}}{P_{10} + P_{00}}\right], \\ &= \frac{1}{2}\left[\frac{P_{11}P_{00} - P_{01}P_{10}}{(P_{11} + P_{01})(P_{10} + P_{00})}\right]. \end{aligned}$$

Comparing this expression with that for β_{12}, we see that b_1 has the same sign as β_{12}. The cross term from the decomposition in equation (5.3) is thus a first-order effect in terms of analysis of variance.

5.3 The Case of Three Dichotomous Variables

The procedures from the previous section can easily be generalized to the case of three dichotomous variables. Furthermore, since this model is somewhat more complex, we can test assumptions other than simply the global independence of variables.

5.3.1 *The Saturated Model*

The distribution of (y_1, y_2, y_3) is summarized in the contingency table:

	y_3	0	1
$y_1 = 0$	$y_2 = 0$	P_{000}	P_{001}
	$y_2 = 1$	P_{010}	P_{011}
$y_1 = 1$	$y_2 = 0$	P_{100}	P_{101}
	$y_2 = 1$	P_{110}	P_{111}

There are eight joint probabilities such that:

$$\sum_{i_1=0}^{1}\sum_{i_2=0}^{1}\sum_{i_3=0}^{1} P_{i_1 i_2 i_3} = 1,$$

and the log-linear formulation of the saturated model is:

$$\begin{aligned} \log(\mathbf{P}) &\in \mathbb{R}^8, \\ \mathbf{e}'\mathbf{P} &= 1. \end{aligned}$$

Assume that we have n independent observations on the triple, and let $n_{i_1 i_2 i_3}$ be the number of observations for which $y_1 = i_1, y_2 = i_2, y_3 = i_3$. The maximum-likelihood estimators of the joint probabilities are:

$$\hat{P}_{i_1,i_2,i_3} = \frac{n_{i_1 i_2 i_3}}{n}, \quad i_1, i_2, i_3 = \{0, 1\}.$$

These can be decomposed in order to isolate to the various effects. There are now third-order cross effects:

$$\begin{aligned} P_{i_1 i_2 i_3} = \mu & \\ & + \alpha_1(i_1) + \alpha_2(i_2) + \alpha_3(i_3) \\ & + \beta_{12}(i_1, i_2) + \beta_{13}(i_1, i_3) + \beta_{23}(i_2, i_3) \\ & + \gamma_{123}(i_1, i_2, i_3). \end{aligned} \tag{5.6}$$

In order to ensure uniqueness, we impose:

$$\begin{aligned} \alpha_1(\cdot) &= \sum_{i_1} \alpha_1(i_1) = 0, \quad \alpha_2(\cdot) = \alpha_3(\cdot) = 0, \\ \beta_{12}(\cdot, i_2) &= \sum_{i_1} \beta_{12}(i_1, i_2) = 0, \quad \forall i_2, \quad \text{and, similarly} \\ \beta_{12}(i_1, \cdot) &= 0, \quad \forall i_1, \\ \beta_{13}(\cdot, i_3) &= \beta_{13}(i_1, \cdot) = \beta_{23}(\cdot, i_3) = \beta_{23}(i_2, \cdot) = 0, \\ \gamma_{123}(\cdot, i_2, i_3) &= \gamma_{123}(i_1, \cdot, i_3) = \gamma_{123}(i_1, i_2, \cdot) = 0. \end{aligned} \tag{5.7}$$

There are 27 effects in all (the principal effect, six first-order effects, twelve second-order effects, and eight third-order effects) as well as nineteen independent constraints (three on the first-order effects, nine on the second-order effects, and seven on the third-order effects). The formulation in equations (5.6) and (5.7) allows us to decompose any element of $\mathbb{R}^{27-19} = \mathbb{R}^8$.

To solve the equation system (5.7) we define:

$$\begin{aligned} &\alpha_1 = \alpha_1(1), \quad \alpha_2 = \alpha_2(1), \quad \alpha_3 = \alpha_3(1), \\ &\beta_{12} = \beta_{12}(1, 1), \quad \beta_{13} = \beta_{13}(1, 1), \quad \beta_{23} = \beta_{23}(1, 1), \\ &\gamma_{123} = \gamma_{123}(1, 1, 1), \end{aligned}$$

and let ϵ be a function defined by:

$$\epsilon(i) = \begin{cases} +1, & \text{if } i = 1, \\ -1, & \text{if } i = 0. \end{cases}$$

Using this notation, we have:

$$\begin{aligned} \alpha_j(i_j) &= \alpha_j \epsilon(i_j), \\ \beta_{j\ell}(i_j, i_\ell) &= \beta_{j\ell} \epsilon(i_j) \epsilon(i_\ell), \\ \gamma_{jk\ell}(i_j, i_k, i_\ell) &= \gamma_{jk\ell} \epsilon(i_j) \epsilon(i_k) \epsilon(i_\ell). \end{aligned} \tag{5.8}$$

This yields, for example:

$$\log(P_{111}) = \mu + \alpha_1 + \alpha_2 + \alpha_3 + \beta_{12} + \beta_{13} + \beta_{23} + \gamma_{123},$$
$$\log(P_{110}) = \mu + \alpha_1 + \alpha_2 - \alpha_3 + \beta_{12} - \beta_{13} - \beta_{23} - \gamma_{123},$$

etc.

The coordinates in the new base $(\mu, \alpha_1, \alpha_2, \alpha_3, \beta_{12}, \beta_{13}, \beta_{23}, \gamma_{123})$ can obviously be written in terms of $\log\left(P_{i_1 i_2 i_3}\right)$, yielding:

$$\begin{aligned}
\mu &= \log(P_{\cdots}),\\
\alpha_1 &= \log(P_{1\cdot\cdot}) - \log(P_{\cdots}),\\
\alpha_2 &= \log(P_{\cdot 1\cdot}) - \log(P_{\cdots}),\\
\alpha_3 &= \log(P_{\cdot\cdot 1}) - \log(P_{\cdots}),\\
\beta_{12} &= \log(P_{11\cdot}) - \log(P_{1\cdot\cdot}) - \log(P_{\cdot 1\cdot}) + \log(P_{\cdots}),\\
\beta_{13} &= \log(P_{1\cdot 1}) - \log(P_{1\cdot\cdot}) - \log(P_{\cdot\cdot 1}) + \log(P_{\cdots}),\\
\beta_{23} &= \log(P_{\cdot 11}) - \log(P_{\cdot 1\cdot}) - \log(P_{\cdot\cdot 1}) + \log(P_{\cdots}),\\
\gamma_{123} &= \log(P_{111}) - \log(P_{11\cdot}) - \log(P_{\cdot 11}) - \log(P_{1\cdot 1}) + \log(P_{1\cdot\cdot})\\
&\quad + \log(P_{\cdot 1\cdot}) + \log(P_{\cdot\cdot 1}) - \log(P_{\cdots}).
\end{aligned}$$

In these expressions the "·" in the subscripts indicates that we have taken the mean over the corresponding value, as on page 111. Thus, for example:

$$\log(P_{\cdot\cdot 1}) = \frac{1}{4}\sum_{i_1}\sum_{i_2}\log\left(P_{i_1 i_2 1}\right).$$

5.3.2 *Marginal and Conditional Distributions*

When we know the joint distribution of y_1, y_2, and y_3, we can derive the marginal and conditional distributions and also examine whether or not they are amenable to simple decompositions corresponding to initial effects.

5.3.2.1 *The Marginal Distribution of y_1*

This distribution is characterized by two probabilities:

$$\Pr(y_1 = 1) = P_{1\cdot\cdot} = \sum_{i_2}\sum_{i_3} P_{1 i_2 i_3},$$
$$\Pr(y_1 = 0) = P_{0\cdot\cdot} = \sum_{i_2}\sum_{i_3} P_{0 i_2 i_3}.$$

These can be decomposed in terms of the effects, yielding:

$$\log(P_{1\cdot\cdot}) = \tilde{\mu} + \tilde{\alpha}(1),$$
$$\log(P_{0\cdot\cdot}) = \tilde{\mu} + \tilde{\alpha}(0),$$

where $\tilde{\alpha}(1) + \tilde{\alpha}(0) = 0$.

These effects can, in turn, be expressed as functions of the effects occurring in the decomposition of the joint distribution:

$$\begin{aligned}
P_{1\cdot\cdot} &= e^{\tilde{\mu}+\tilde{\alpha}(1)}, \\
&= \sum_{i_2}\sum_{i_3} e^{\mu+\alpha_1(1)+\alpha_2(i_2)+\alpha_3(i_3)+\beta_{12}(1,i_2)+\beta_{13}(1,i_3)+\beta_{23}(i_2,i_3)+\gamma_{123}(1,i_2,i_3)}, \\
P_{0\cdot\cdot} &= e^{\tilde{\mu}+\tilde{\alpha}(0)}, \\
&= e^{\tilde{\mu}-\tilde{\alpha}(1)}, \\
&= \sum_{i_2}\sum_{i_3} e^{\mu+\alpha_1(0)+\alpha_2(i_2)+\alpha_3(i_3)+\beta_{12}(0,i_2)+\beta_{13}(0,i_3)+\beta_{23}(i_2,i_3)+\gamma_{123}(0,i_2,i_3)}.
\end{aligned}$$

Clearly, the expressions for $\tilde{\mu}$ and $\tilde{\alpha}$ (1) obtained from solving the preceding equations are not simple. They could also have been derived from the marginal distribution of (y_1, y_2).

5.3.2.2 The Conditional Distribution of y_1 Given (y_2, y_3)

We have:

$$\begin{aligned}
\Pr(y_1 = i_1 | y_2 = i_2, y_3 = i_3) &= \frac{P_{i_1 i_2 i_3}}{\sum_{i_1} P_{i_1 i_2 i_3}}, \\
&= \frac{e^{\alpha_1(i_1)+\beta_{12}(i_1,i_2)+\beta_{13}(i_1,i_3)+\gamma_{123}(i_1,i_2,i_3)}}{\sum_{i_1} e^{\alpha_1(i_1)+\beta_{12}(i_1,i_2)+\beta_{13}(i_1,i_3)+\gamma_{123}(i_1,i_2,i_3)}}.
\end{aligned}$$

Since:

$$\sum_{i_1} [\alpha_1(i_1) + \beta_{12}(i_1, i_2) + \beta_{13}(i_1, i_3) + \gamma_{123}(i_1, i_2, i_3)] = 0,$$

we conclude that:

$$\alpha_1(i_1) + \beta_{12}(i_1, i_2) + \beta_{13}(i_1, i_3) + \gamma_{123}(i_1, i_2, i_3)$$

is the first-order effect corresponding to this conditional distribution.

5.3.2.3 The Conditional Distribution of y_1 and y_2 Given y_3

We have:

$$\begin{aligned}
&\Pr(y_1 = i_1, y_2 = i_2 | y_3 = i_3) \\
&= \frac{P_{i_1 i_2 i_3}}{\sum_{i_1}\sum_{i_2} P_{i_1 i_2 i_3}}, \\
&= \frac{e^{\alpha_1(i_1)+\alpha_2(i_2)+\beta_{12}(i_1,i_2)+\beta_{13}(i_1,i_3)+\beta_{23}(i_2,i_3)+\gamma_{123}(i_1,i_2,i_3)}}{\sum_{i_1}\sum_{i_2} e^{\alpha_1(i_1)+\alpha_2(i_2)+\beta_{12}(i_1,i_2)+\beta_{13}(i_1,i_3)+\beta_{23}(i_2,i_3)+\gamma_{123}(i_1,i_2,i_3)}}.
\end{aligned}$$

Conditional on $y_3 = i_3$, we are interested in the distribution of a pair of dichotomous variables, with each probability decomposed into various-order effects:

principal, $\tilde{\mu}$, first-order, $\tilde{\alpha}_1(i_1)$ and $\tilde{\alpha}_2(i_2)$, and second-order, $\tilde{\beta}_{12}(i_1, i_2)$. We can easily verify that:

$$\begin{aligned}
\tilde{\alpha}_1(i_1) &= \alpha_1(i_1) + \beta_{13}(i_1, i_3),\\
\tilde{\alpha}_2(i_2) &= \alpha_2(i_2) + \beta_{23}(i_2, i_3),\\
\tilde{\beta}_{12}(i_1, i_2) &= \beta_{12}(i_1, i_2) + \gamma_{123}(i_1, i_2, i_3),
\end{aligned}$$

since $\tilde{\alpha}_1(\cdot) = \tilde{\alpha}_2(\cdot) = \beta_{12}(\cdot, i_2) = \beta_{12}(i_1, \cdot) = 0$.

5.3.3 *The Assumption of Independence*

5.3.3.1 *Independence Between y_1 and (y_2, y_3)*

If these variables are independent, the conditional distribution of y_1, given y_2 and y_3, does not depend on these latter variables. From the expression for this conditional distribution obtained in the previous section we derive:

$$\beta_{12}(i_1, i_2) = \beta_{13}(i_1, i_3) = \gamma_{123}(i_1, i_2, i_3) = 0, \quad \forall i_1, i_2, i_3$$

(cf. exercise 3). The same result holds, $\beta_{23}(i_2, i_3) = 0$, for the conditional distribution of y_2 given (y_1, y_3).

Conversely, if all the cross effects are nil, $P_{i_1 i_2 i_3}$ is proportional to $e^{\alpha_1(i_1)} e^{\alpha_2(i_2)} e^{\alpha_3(i_3)}$, which is the product of functions of i_1, i_2, and i_3, respectively. Hence the variables are independent.

Proposition 8: y_1, y_2, and y_3 are independent if all the cross effects β_{12}, β_{13}, β_{23}, and γ_{123} are nil.

5.3.3.2 *Independence of (y_1, y_2) Conditional on y_3*

Conditional on $y_3 = i_3$, y_1 and y_2 are independent if the cross effects in the joint distribution is nil. Thus:

$$\tilde{\beta}_{12}(i_1, i_2) = 0 \Leftrightarrow \begin{cases} 0 = \beta_{12}(i_1, i_2), \\ 0 = \gamma_{123}(i_1, i_2, i_3), \end{cases} \quad \forall i_1, i_2.$$

Notice that the fact that these variables are dichotomous implies that the foregoing conditions are true whether $i_3 = 1$ or $i_3 = 0$ [since $\gamma_{123}(i_1, i_2, 1) + \gamma_{123}(i_1, i_2, 0) = 0$]. The concept of conditional independence is not specific to a value of y_3.

Proposition 9: y_1 and y_2 are independent conditional on y_3 if and only if:

$$\begin{aligned} 0 &= \beta_{12}(i_1, i_2), \\ 0 &= \gamma_{123}(i_1, i_2, i_3), \end{aligned} \quad \forall i_1, i_2, i_3.$$

Variables such as (y_1, y_2), which are independent with respect to a third variable y_3, are not necessarily independent of each other. Given the assumption of conditional independence, the distribution of the pair (y_1, y_2) is:

$$P_{i_1 i_2 \cdot} = \sum_{i_3} e^{\mu+\alpha_1(i_1)+\alpha_2(i_2)+\alpha_3(i_3)+\beta_{13}(i_1,i_3)+\beta_{23}(i_2,i_3)},$$

which can not be decomposed into a function of i_1 multiplied by a function of i_2. We see from the form of $P_{i_1 i_2 \cdot}$ that y_1 and y_2 are related only over y_3. Let us now examine the marginal distribution of (y_2, y_3):

$$P_{\cdot i_2 i_3} = \sum_{i_1} e^{\mu+\alpha_1(i_1)+\alpha_2(i_2)+\alpha_3(i_3)+\beta_{13}(i_1,i_3)+\beta_{23}(i_2,i_3)}.$$

This probability can be written as:

$$P_{\cdot i_2 i_3} = e^{\tilde{\mu}+\tilde{\alpha}_2(i_2)+\tilde{\alpha}_3(i_3)+\tilde{\beta}_{23}(i_2,i_3)}.$$

Comparing the two expressions, we see that $\tilde{\beta}_{23}(i_2, i_3)$ is equal to $\beta_{23}(i_2, i_3)$. Assuming the conditional independence of (y_1, y_2) given y_3, we can study the relationship between y_2 and y_3 (y_1 and y_3) entirely on the base of the marginal distribution of (y_2, y_3) [(y_1, y_3)] (cf. exercise 9 for the analogous property for quantitative models).

5.3.3.3 *Independence Between* (y_1, y_2) *and* y_3

The pair (y_1, y_2) is independent of y_3 if the conditional distribution of (y_1, y_2), given that $y_3 = i_3$, does not depend on the value of i_3. Given the form of this conditional probability (cf. section 5.3.2), we have the proposition:

Proposition 10: The pair (y_1, y_2) is independent of y_3 if and only if:

$$\beta_{13}(i_1, i_3) = \beta_{23}(i_2, i_3) = \gamma_{123}(i_1, i_2, i_3) = 0, \quad \forall i_1, i_2, i_3.$$

In this case (y_1, y_2) and y_3 may be analysed separately.

5.3.3.4 *The Choice Between One and Two Independent of the Irrelevant Alternative Three*

Recall from chapter 4 that the choice between one and two is independent of three if:

$$\frac{P_{1|123}}{P_{2|123}} = \frac{P_{1|12}}{P_{2|12}}.$$

Assume that, instead of asking a survey subject to make a choice, we ask him to state for each option whether or not he likes it:

$$y_j = \begin{cases} 1, & \text{if he likes it,} \\ 0, & \text{otherwise.} \end{cases}$$

We can derive his preferences from the answers.

The individual strictly prefers one to two and three if $y_1 = 1$ and $y_2 = y_3 = 0$, he strictly prefers two to one and three if $y_1 = 0$, $y_2 = 1$, and $y_3 = 0$, and three to one and two if $y_1 = y_2 = 0$ and $y_3 = 1$. In all other cases he is undecided.

The probability that an individual will strictly prefer one to two and three, given that he is not undecided is:

$$P_{1|123} = \frac{P_{100}}{P_{100} + P_{010} + P_{001}}$$

and, by symmetry:

$$P_{2|123} = \frac{P_{010}}{P_{100} + P_{010} + P_{001}}.$$

Employing the same logic, we see that the probability that he will strictly prefer one to two given that he isn't indifferent between them is:

$$P_{1|12} = \frac{P_{100} + P_{101}}{P_{100} + P_{101} + P_{010} + P_{011}};$$

similarly:

$$P_{2|12} = \frac{P_{010} + P_{011}}{P_{100} + P_{101} + P_{010} + P_{011}}.$$

The condition $\frac{P_{1|123}}{P_{2|123}} = \frac{P_{1|12}}{P_{2|12}}$ becomes:

$$\frac{P_{100}}{P_{010}} = \frac{P_{100} + P_{101}}{P_{010} + P_{011}},$$

$$P_{100} P_{011} = P_{010} P_{101},$$

$$\log(P_{100}) + \log(P_{011}) = \log(P_{010}) + \log(P_{101}).$$

Decomposing the logarithms of the probabilities according to equation (5.8), we obtain:

$$\begin{aligned}(\mu + \alpha_1 - \alpha_2 - \alpha_3 - \beta_{12} - \beta_{13} + \beta_{23} + \gamma_{123}) \\ + (\mu - \alpha_1 + \alpha_2 + \alpha_3 - \beta_{12} - \beta_{13} + \beta_{23} - \gamma_{123}) \\ = (\mu - \alpha_1 + \alpha_2 - \alpha_3 - \beta_{12} + \beta_{13} - \beta_{23} + \gamma_{123}) \\ + (\mu + \alpha_1 - \alpha_2 + \alpha_3 - \beta_{12} + \beta_{13} - \beta_{23} - \gamma_{123}),\end{aligned}$$

$$\beta_{13} = \beta_{23}.$$

Proposition 11: The choice between alternatives one and two is independent of alternative three if alternative three has the same effect on the probability of choosing one as it does on the probability of choosing alternative two.

5.3.4 Estimation Under the Assumption of Independence

The various types of independence examined in section 5.3.3 can be tested with several techniques, including the likelihood-ratio test statistic. Application of these tests is facilitated by the fact that, under the assumption of independence, we can find an explicit formulation for the maximum-likelihood estimators.

5.3.4.1 Estimation Under the Assumption of the Independence of y_1, y_2 and y_3

The null hypothesis is:

$$H_0 : P_{i_1 i_2 i_3} = P_{i_1 ..} P_{. i_2 .} P_{.. i_3}, \quad \forall i_1, i_2, i_3,$$

under which the log-likelihood is written:

$$\begin{aligned}
\log(L_0) &= \sum_{i_1} \sum_{i_2} \sum_{i_3} n_{i_1 i_2 i_3} \log\left(P_{i_1 i_2 i_3}\right), \\
&= \sum_{i_1} \sum_{i_2} \sum_{i_3} n_{i_1 i_2 i_3} \left[\log\left(P_{i_1 ..}\right) + \log\left(P_{. i_2 .}\right) + \log\left(P_{.. i_3}\right)\right], \\
&= \sum_{i_1} n_{i_1 ..} \log\left(P_{i_1 ..}\right) + \sum_{i_2} n_{. i_2 .} \log\left(P_{. i_2 .}\right) + \sum_{i_3} n_{.. i_3} \log\left(P_{.. i_3}\right).
\end{aligned}$$

The maximization of $\log(L_0)$ under the constraints:

$$\sum_{i_1} \log\left(P_{i_1 ..}\right) = 1, \quad \sum_{i_2} \log\left(P_{. i_2 .}\right) = 1, \quad \sum_{i_3} \log\left(P_{.. i_3}\right) = 1,$$

yields:

$$\begin{aligned}
\hat{P}_{i_1 ..} &= \frac{n_{i_1 ..}}{n}, \quad \hat{P}_{. i_2 .} = \frac{n_{. i_2 .}}{n}, \quad \hat{P}_{.. i_3} = \frac{n_{.. i_3}}{n}, \\
\hat{P}_{i_1 i_2 i_3} &= \frac{n_{i_1 ..}}{n} \frac{n_{. i_2 .}}{n} \frac{n_{.. i_3}}{n}.
\end{aligned}$$

5.3.4.2 Estimation Under the Assumption of the Independence of (y_1, y_2) and y_3

Reasoning similar to that in the previous paragraphs gives us:

$$\hat{P}_{i_1 i_2 i_3} = \frac{n_{i_1 i_2 .}}{n} \frac{n_{.. i_3}}{n}.$$

5.3.4.3 Estimation Under the Assumption of Conditional Independence of (y_1, y_2) Given y_3

We denote $P_{i_1\cdot|i_3}$ the distribution of y_1 given $y_3 = i_3$ and $P_{\cdot i_2|i_3}$ the distribution of y_2 given $y_3 = i_3$. The null hypothesis is:

$$H_0 : P_{i_1 i_2 i_3} = P_{i_1\cdot|i_3} P_{\cdot i_2|i_3} P_{\cdot\cdot i_3}.$$

Hence:

$$\begin{aligned}
\log(L_0) &= \sum_{i_1}\sum_{i_2}\sum_{i_3} n_{i_1 i_2 i_3} \log\left(P_{i_1 i_2 i_3}\right), \\
&= \sum_{i_1}\sum_{i_2}\sum_{i_3} n_{i_1 i_2 i_3} \left[\log\left(P_{i_1\cdot|i_3}\right) + \log\left(P_{\cdot i_2|i_3}\right) + \log\left(P_{\cdot\cdot i_3}\right)\right], \\
&= \sum_{i_1}\sum_{i_3} n_{i_1\cdot i_3} \log\left(P_{i_1\cdot|i_3}\right) + \sum_{i_2}\sum_{i_3} n_{\cdot i_2 i_3} \log\left(P_{\cdot i_2|i_3}\right) \\
&\quad + \sum_{i_3} n_{\cdot\cdot i_3} \log\left(P_{\cdot\cdot i_3}\right).
\end{aligned}$$

This must be maximized under the constraints:

$$1 = \sum_{i_1} P_{i_1\cdot|i_3}, \quad \forall i_3,$$

$$1 = \sum_{i_2} P_{\cdot i_2|i_3}, \quad \forall i_3,$$

$$1 = \sum_{i_3} P_{\cdot\cdot i_3}.$$

And the solutions are:

$$\hat{P}_{i_1\cdot|i_3} = \frac{n_{i_1\cdot i_3}}{n_{\cdot\cdot i_3}}, \quad \hat{P}_{\cdot i_2|i_3} = \frac{n_{\cdot i_2 i_3}}{n_{\cdot\cdot i_3}}, \quad \hat{P}P_{\cdot\cdot i_3} = \frac{n_{\cdot\cdot i_3}}{n},$$

$$\hat{P}_{i_1 i_2 i_3} = \frac{n_{i_1\cdot i_3}}{n_{\cdot\cdot i_3}} \frac{n_{\cdot i_2 i_3}}{n_{\cdot\cdot i_3}} \frac{n_{\cdot\cdot i_3}}{n}.$$

5.3.4.4 Estimation Under the Assumption that the Choice Between y_1 and y_2 is Independent of y_3

We need to maximize the log-likelihood:

$$\sum_{i_1}\sum_{i_2}\sum_{i_3} n_{i_1 i_2 i_3} \log\left(P_{i_1 i_2 i_3}\right)$$

under the constraints:

$$1 = \sum_{i_1}\sum_{i_2}\sum_{i_3} P_{i_1 i_2 i_3},$$

$$0 = P_{100}P_{011} - P_{010}P_{101}.$$

Let λ and μ be the Lagrange multipliers associated with each of these constraints. The first-order conditions are:

$$0 = \frac{\partial \log (L)}{\partial P_{000}}, \qquad 0 = \frac{\partial \log (L)}{\partial P_{001}},$$
$$0 = \frac{\partial \log (L)}{\partial P_{010}}, \qquad 0 = \frac{\partial \log (L)}{\partial P_{011}},$$
$$0 = \frac{\partial \log (L)}{\partial P_{100}}, \qquad 0 = \frac{\partial \log (L)}{\partial P_{101}},$$
$$0 = \frac{\partial \log (L)}{\partial P_{110}}, \qquad 0 = \frac{\partial \log (L)}{\partial P_{111}},$$
$$0 = \frac{n_{000}}{P_{000}} - \lambda, \qquad 0 = \frac{n_{001}}{P_{001}} - \lambda,$$
$$0 = \frac{n_{110}}{P_{110}} - \lambda, \qquad 0 = \frac{n_{111}}{P_{111}} - \lambda,$$
$$0 = \frac{n_{010}}{P_{010}} - \lambda - \mu P_{101}, \qquad 0 = \frac{n_{011}}{P_{011}} - \lambda + \mu P_{100},$$
$$0 = \frac{n_{100}}{P_{100}} - \lambda + \mu P_{011}, \qquad 0 = \frac{n_{101}}{P_{101}} - \lambda - \mu P_{010}.$$

Multiplying each equation by the corresponding probability and summing yields:

$$\sum_{i_1} \sum_{i_2} \sum_{i_3} n_{i_1 i_2 i_3} - \lambda \sum_{i_1} \sum_{i_2} \sum_{i_3} P_{i_1 i_2 i_3} + 2\mu \left(P_{100} P_{011} - P_{101} P_{010} \right) = 0,$$

or:

$$n - \lambda = 0 \quad \Rightarrow \quad \lambda = n$$

We conclude that:

$$\hat{P}_{000} = \frac{n_{000}}{n},$$
$$\hat{P}_{001} = \frac{n_{001}}{n},$$
$$\hat{P}_{110} = \frac{n_{110}}{n},$$
$$\hat{P}_{111} = \frac{n_{111}}{n},$$

and:

$$0 = n_{010} - n P_{010} - \mu P_{101} P_{010},$$
$$0 = n_{011} - n P_{011} + \mu P_{100} P_{011},$$

$$0 = n_{100} - nP_{100} + \mu P_{100}P_{011},$$
$$0 = n_{101} - nP_{101} - \mu P_{101}P_{010}.$$

Combining the first and the last equations:

$$0 = n_{101} - nP_{101} - n_{010} - nP_{010},$$
$$P_{010} - P_{101} = \frac{n_{010}}{n} - \frac{n_{101}}{n},$$
$$P_{010} = \frac{n_{010}}{n} + a,$$
$$P_{101} = \frac{n_{101}}{n} + a,$$

where a is a constant whose value is to be determined. Similarly, combining the second and third equation, we obtain:

$$P_{011} = \frac{n_{011}}{n} + b,$$
$$P_{100} = \frac{n_{100}}{n} + b.$$

Now we sum the first two equations:

$$n_{010} + n_{011} - n\,(P_{010} + P_{011}) = 0 \Leftrightarrow a + b = 0.$$

The unknown parameter is defined by:

$$P_{100}P_{011} = P_{010}P_{101},$$
$$\left(\frac{n_{100}}{n} - a\right)\left(\frac{n_{011}}{n} - a\right) = \left(\frac{n_{010}}{n} + a\right)\left(\frac{n_{101}}{n} + a\right),$$
$$\frac{n_{100}n_{011}}{n^2} - \frac{n_{010}n_{101}}{n^2} = a\frac{n_{010} + n_{101} + n_{100} + n_{011}}{n},$$
$$a = \frac{n_{100}n_{011} - n_{010}n_{101}}{n\,(n_{010} + n_{101} + n_{100} + n_{011})}.$$

Hence:

$$\hat{P}_{010} = \frac{n_{010}}{n} + \frac{n_{100}n_{011} - n_{010}n_{101}}{n\,(n_{010} + n_{101} + n_{100} + n_{011})},$$
$$\hat{P}_{101} = \frac{n_{101}}{n} + \frac{n_{100}n_{011} - n_{010}n_{101}}{n\,(n_{010} + n_{101} + n_{100} + n_{011})},$$
$$\hat{P}_{011} = \frac{n_{011}}{n} - \frac{n_{100}n_{011} - n_{010}n_{101}}{n\,(n_{010} + n_{101} + n_{100} + n_{011})},$$
$$\hat{P}_{100} = \frac{n_{100}}{n} - \frac{n_{100}n_{011} - n_{010}n_{101}}{n\,(n_{010} + n_{101} + n_{100} + n_{011})}.$$

The probability of one being chosen when the available options are one and two is given by:

$$\hat{P}_{1|12} = \frac{\hat{P}_{100} + \hat{P}_{101}}{\hat{P}_{100} + \hat{P}_{101} + \hat{P}_{010} + \hat{P}_{011}},$$
$$= \frac{n_{100} + n_{101}}{n_{100} + n_{101} + n_{010} + n_{011}}.$$

Notice that the complicated term:

$$a = \frac{n_{100}n_{011} - n_{010}n_{101}}{n\,(n_{010} + n_{101} + n_{100} + n_{011})},$$

has disappeared.

5.4 Two Polychotomous Variables

This is the case of a (2×2) contingency table in which the two variables (y_1, y_2) can take I_1 and I_2 values respectively. These values are indexed $i_1 = 0, \ldots, I_1 - 1$ and $i_2 = 0, \ldots, I_2 - 1$.

The logarithms of the joint probabilities can be decomposed:

$$\log\left(P_{i_1 i_2}\right) = \mu + \alpha_1(i_1) + \alpha_2(i_2) + \beta_{12}(i_1, i_2), \tag{5.9}$$

where:

$$\alpha_1(\cdot) = \alpha_2(\cdot) = \beta_{12}(\cdot, i_2) = \beta_{12}(i_1, \cdot) = 0, \quad \forall i_1, i_2.$$

5.4.1 *Grouping*

In the polychotomous case we have a new possibility – grouping some of the values. Consider, for example, the case of y_1. We can form two groups, the first containing $\{0, 1\}$ and the other $\{2, \ldots, I_1 - 1\}$. The joint probabilities corresponding to this new classification are:

$$P_{\{0,1\},i_2} = P_{0,i_2} + P_{1,i_2},$$

or, using equation (5.9):

$$P_{\{0,1\},i_2} = \frac{e^{\alpha_2(i_2)}\left[e^{\alpha_1(0)+\beta_{12}(0,i_2)} + e^{\alpha_1(1)+\beta_{12}(1,i_2)}\right]}{\sum_{i_1}\sum_{i_2} e^{\alpha_1(i_1)+\alpha_2(i_2)+\beta_{12}(i_1,i_2)}}.$$

When these new probabilities are decomposed, the first-order term associated with the second variable is the same as before: $\tilde{\alpha}_2(i_2) = \alpha_2(i_2)$. The other effects $\tilde{\mu}, \tilde{\alpha}_1, \tilde{\beta}_{12}$ are rather complicated functions of the initial effects. This difficulty of expressing the new effects in terms of the old ones is a general feature, persisting even when the values are similar, i.e. when:

$$P_{0i_2} = P_{1i_2} \quad \Leftrightarrow \quad \begin{cases} \alpha_1(0) = \alpha_1(1) \\ \beta_{12}(0, i_2) = \beta_{12}(1, i_2) \end{cases}, \quad \forall i_2$$

In this case:

$$P_{\{0,1\},i_2} = \frac{2e^{\alpha_2(i_2)+\alpha_1(1)+\beta_{12}(1,i_2)}}{\sum_{i_1}\sum_{i_2} e^{\alpha_1(i_1)+\alpha_2(i_2)+\beta_{12}(i_1,i_2)}}.$$

Using the notation from equation (5.9) we can write:

$$\log\left(P_{\{0,1\},i_2}\right) = \mu + \alpha_1(1) + \alpha_2(i_2) + \beta_{12}(1, i_2) + \log(2),$$
$$\log\left(P_{i_1,i_2}\right) = \mu + \alpha_1(i_1) + \alpha_2(i_2) + \beta_{12}(i_1, i_2), \quad i_1 \geq 2.$$

And the new effects are given by:

$$\log\left(P_{\{0,1\},i_2}\right) = \tilde{\mu} + \tilde{\alpha}_1(1) + \alpha_2(i_2) + \tilde{\beta}_{12}(1, i_2),$$
$$\log\left(P_{i_1,i_2}\right) = \tilde{\mu} + \tilde{\alpha}_1(i_1) + \alpha_2(i_2) + \tilde{\beta}_{12}(i_1, i_2), \quad i_1 \geq 2.$$

The primary effect, $\tilde{\mu}$, found by taking the mean of the logarithms of the joint probabilities, is:

$$\begin{aligned}\tilde{\mu} &= \mu + \frac{\log(2)}{I_2(I_1-1)} + \frac{1}{I_1-1}\sum_{i_1=1}^{I_1-1}\alpha_1(i_1) + \frac{1}{I_2}\sum_{i_2=0}^{I_2-1}\alpha_2(i_2) \\ &\quad + \frac{1}{I_2(I_1-1)}\sum_{i_1=1}^{I_1-1}\sum_{i_2=0}^{I_2-1}\beta_{12}(i_1, i_2), \\ &= \mu + \frac{\log(2)}{I_2(I_1-1)} - \frac{\alpha_1(0)}{I_1-1}.\end{aligned}$$

The expressions for $\tilde{\alpha}_1$ and $\tilde{\beta}_{12}$ as functions of the initial effects are even more complicated. Clearly, an analysis of variance type decomposition is ill-suited to the study of grouped data.

When the values corresponding to the zero and one settings of the index are similar, however, the maximum-likelihood estimators are easily calculated. The null hypothesis:

$$H_0 : P_{0i_2} = P_{1i_2}, \quad \forall i_2,$$

can be tested using the likelihood-ratio test statistic.

Let $n_{i_1i_2}$ be the number of observations for which $y_1 = i_1$ and $y_2 = i_2$. Under the alternative hypothesis, the maximum-likelihood estimators are:

$$\hat{P}_{i_1i_2} = \frac{n_{i_1i_2}}{n},$$

and we maximize the log-likelihood equation:

$$\log(L) = \sum_{i_1=0}^{I_1-1} \sum_{i_2=0}^{I_2-1} n_{i_1 i_2} \log\left(\frac{n_{i_1 i_2}}{n}\right).$$

Under the null hypothesis, on the other hand, the maximum-likelihood estimators are:

$$\tilde{P}_{0,i_2} = \tilde{P}_{1,i_2} = \frac{n_{0i_2} + n_{1i_2}}{2n},$$

$$\tilde{P}_{i_1 i_2} = \frac{n_{i_1 i_2}}{n}, \quad \text{if} \quad i_1 \geq 2,$$

and the maximum of the log-likelihood solves:

$$\log(L_0) = \sum_{i_2=0}^{I_2-1} \left(n_{0i_2} + n_{1i_2}\right) \log\left(\frac{n_{0i_2} + n_{1i_2}}{2n}\right) + \sum_{i_1=0}^{I_1-1} \sum_{i_2=0}^{I_2-1} n_{i_1 i_2} \log\left(\frac{n_{i_1 i_2}}{n}\right).$$

Letting Λ represent the likelihood ratio we have:

$$- \log(\Lambda) = -2\left[\log(L_0) - \log(L)\right],$$

$$= -2 \sum_{i_2=0}^{I_2-1} \left[n_{0i_2} \log\left(\frac{n_{0i_2} + n_{1i_2}}{2n_{0i_2}}\right) + n_{1i_2} \log\left(\frac{n_{0i_2} + n_{1i_2}}{2n_{1i_2}}\right)\right].$$

This value is asymptotically distributed chi-square with $I_2 - 1$ degrees of freedom, since the null hypothesis is defined by $I_2 - 1$ independent constraints.

5.5 General Analysis of a Contingency Table

Our ability to decompose the logarithms of the joint probabilities into principal, first-order, second-order, etc., terms, combined with the fact that the some assumptions can be written simply as functions of these terms, allows us to generalize our analysis to an indeterminate number of qualitative variables. Consider q qualitative variables $y_1, \ldots, y_q$ assuming $I_1, \ldots, I_q$ values respectively. The joint distribution of these variables is characterized by the probabilities:

$$\Pr\left(y_1 = i_1, \ldots, y_q = i_q\right) = P_{i_1 \ldots i_q}, \quad i_1 = 0, \ldots, I_1 - 1, \quad \ldots, \quad i_q = 0, \ldots, I_q - 1.$$

These probabilities can be summarized in an $I_1 \times \ldots \times I_q$ contingency table.

5.5.1 An ANOVA-type Decomposition

In this decomposition the logarithms of the joint probabilities appear as the sums of the effects of different orders:

$$\begin{aligned}\log\left(P_{i_1\ldots i_q}\right) = \mu & \\ & + \alpha_1(i_1) + \ldots + \alpha_q\left(i_q\right) \\ & + \beta_{12}(i_1, i_2) + \ldots + \beta_{q-1,q}\left(i_{q-1}, i_q\right) \\ & + \ldots \\ & + \omega_{1,\ldots,q}\left(i_1, \ldots, i_q\right),\end{aligned} \tag{5.10}$$

with the usual condition that the means are zero when we sum over the index of any variable:

$$\begin{aligned} & 0 = \alpha_1(\cdot) = \alpha_2(\cdot) = \ldots = \alpha_q(\cdot), \\ & 0 = \beta_{12}(\cdot, i_2) = \beta_{12}(i_1, \cdot) = \ldots = \beta_{q-1,q}\left(\cdot, i_q\right), \\ & \qquad = \beta_{q-1,q}\left(i_{q-1}, \cdot\right), \\ & \quad \vdots \\ & 0 = \omega_{1,\ldots,q}\left(\cdot, i_2, \ldots, i_q\right) = \omega_{1,\ldots,q}\left(i_1, \cdot, i_3, \ldots, i_q\right), \\ & \qquad = \cdots = \omega_{1\ldots q}\left(i_1, i_2, \ldots, i_{q-1}, \cdot\right),\end{aligned} \tag{5.11}$$

This formulation generalizes those given in equations (5.4) and (5.6) for the case of two and three dichotomous variables respectively. We must now investigate whether every set, $\log\left(P_{i_1\ldots i_q}, i_1, \ldots, i_q\right)$, permits this type of decomposition.

Let us sort the vector $\log\left(P_{i_1\ldots i_q}\right)$ in the lexicographic order and denote it $\log(\mathbf{P})$:

$$\log(\mathbf{P}) = \begin{bmatrix} \log\left(P_{0,0,\ldots,0}\right) \\ \log\left(P_{0,\ldots,0,1}\right) \\ \vdots \\ \log\left(P_{0,\ldots,0,I_1-1}\right) \\ \log\left(P_{0,\ldots,0,1,0}\right) \\ \vdots \\ \log\left(P_{I_1-1,\ldots,I_q-1}\right) \end{bmatrix}.$$

The term $\log\left(P_{i_1\ldots i_q}\right)$ is the coordinate indexed:

$$i_1 I_2 I_3 \ldots I_q + i_2 I_3 I_4 \ldots I_q + \ldots + i_{q-1} I_q + i_q + 1.$$

Let the I_j-dimensional vectors $\mathbf{U}_0^j, \mathbf{U}_1^j, \ldots, \mathbf{U}_{I_j-1}^j$, $j = 1, \ldots, q$ be defined:

$$\mathbf{U}_0^j = \begin{bmatrix} 1 \\ 1 \\ \vdots \\ 1 \\ 1 \end{bmatrix}, \quad \mathbf{U}_1^j = \begin{bmatrix} -1 \\ 0 \\ \vdots \\ 0 \\ 1 \end{bmatrix}, \quad \mathbf{U}_2^j = \begin{bmatrix} 0 \\ -1 \\ \vdots \\ 0 \\ 1 \end{bmatrix}, \quad \ldots,$$

$$\mathbf{U}_{I_j-1}^j = \begin{bmatrix} 0 \\ 0 \\ \vdots \\ -1 \\ 1 \end{bmatrix}.$$

These vectors are independent and each is orthogonal to all the others.

We define:

$$\mathbf{U}_{i_1 i_2 \ldots i_q} = \mathbf{U}_{i_1}^1 \otimes \mathbf{U}_{i_2}^2 \otimes \ldots \otimes \mathbf{U}_{i_q}^q,$$

where the vectors $\left(\mathbf{U}_{i_1,\ldots,i_q}, i_1 = 0, \ldots, I_1 - 1, \quad \ldots, \quad i_q = 0, \ldots, I_q - 1\right)$ constitute a base of:

$$E = \mathbb{R}^{I_1 \times \ldots \times I_q},$$

and in which the vector log $(\mathbf{P})$ allows a unique decomposition. Notice that E is the sum of the orthogonal subspaces:

$$E_0 \text{ spanned by } \mathbf{U}_{0,0,\ldots,0} = \mathbf{U}_0^1 \otimes \mathbf{U}_0^2 \otimes \ldots \otimes \mathbf{U}_0^q,$$

$$E_1 \text{ spanned by } \mathbf{U}_{i_1,0,\ldots,0} = \mathbf{U}_{i_1}^1 \otimes \mathbf{U}_0^2 \otimes \ldots \otimes \mathbf{U}_0^q, \quad i_1 = 1, \ldots, I_1 - 1,$$

$$\vdots$$

$$E_q \text{ spanned by } \mathbf{U}_{0,\ldots,0,i_q} = \mathbf{U}_0^1 \otimes \mathbf{U}_0^2 \otimes \ldots \otimes \mathbf{U}_{i_q}^q, \quad i_q = 1, \ldots, I_q - 1,$$

$$E_{12} \text{ spanned by } \mathbf{U}_{i_1,i_2,\ldots,0} = \mathbf{U}_{i_1}^1 \otimes \mathbf{U}_{i_2}^2 \otimes \ldots \otimes \mathbf{U}_0^q, \quad i_1 = 1, \ldots, I_1 - 1, \; i_2 = 1, \ldots, I_2 - 1,$$

$$\vdots$$

$$E_{1,\ldots,q} \text{ spanned by } \mathbf{U}_{i_1,i_2,\ldots,i_q} = \mathbf{U}_{i_1}^1 \otimes \mathbf{U}_{i_2}^2 \otimes \ldots \otimes \mathbf{U}_{i_q}^q, \quad i_j = 1, \ldots, I_j - 1, \; j = 1, \ldots, q.$$

Thus, log (**P**) is the sum of orthogonal projections onto various subspaces. Denoting $\left[y_{i_1 \ldots i_q}\right]$ the vector with elements $y_{i_1 \ldots i_q}$, we can easily verify that the projection onto E_0 is:

$$\mathrm{proj}_{E_0}\left[\log\left(P_{i_1 \ldots i_q}\right)\right] = [\mu],$$

where μ is independent of $i_1 \ldots i_q$. The projection on E_1 is:

$$\mathrm{proj}_{E_1}\left[\log\left(P_{i_1 \ldots i_q}\right)\right] = [\alpha_1 (i_1)], \quad \alpha_1 (\cdot) = 0,$$

and so on up to $E_{1 \ldots q}$, where we have:

$$\mathrm{proj}_{E_{1,\ldots,q}}\left[\log\left(P_{i_1 \ldots i_q}\right)\right] = \left[\omega_{1,\ldots,q}\left(i_1, \ldots, i_q\right)\right],$$

with:

$$\omega_{1,\ldots,q}\left(\cdot, i_2, \ldots, i_q\right) = \ldots = \omega_{1,\ldots,q}\left(i_1, \ldots, i_{q-1}, \cdot\right) = 0.$$

Using this fact, we can easily derive the values of the various coordinates $\mu, \alpha_1 (i_1)$, etc. Thus:

$$\begin{aligned} \alpha_1 (i_1) &= \mathrm{proj}_{E_0 \otimes E_1}\left[\log\left(P_{i_1,\ldots,i_q}\right)\right] - \mathrm{proj}_{E_0}\left[\log\left(P_{i_1,\ldots,i_q}\right)\right], \\ &= \left[\log\left(P_{i_1 \ldots}\right) - \log\left(P_{\ldots}\right)\right]. \end{aligned}$$

The decomposition in equations (5.10) and (5.11) has a simpler form. When the variables are all dichotomous, the subspaces $E_0, E_1, \ldots, E_q, E_{12}, \ldots, E_{1 \ldots q}$ are one-dimensional and there exists only one independent effect corresponding to each of $\alpha_j, \beta_{j\ell}, \ldots, \omega_{1,\ldots,q}$.

Let:

$$\begin{aligned} \alpha_j &= \alpha_j (1), \\ \beta_{j\ell} &= \beta_{j\ell} (1, 1), \\ &\vdots \\ \omega_{1,\ldots,q} &= \omega_{1 \ldots q} (1, \ldots, 1), \end{aligned}$$

and let ϵ be a function such that:

$$\epsilon (i) = \begin{cases} 1, & \text{if } i = 1, \\ -1, & \text{if } i = 0. \end{cases}$$

In this special case, the decomposition (5.10) and (5.11) becomes:

$$
\begin{aligned}
\log\left(P_{i_1 \dots i_q}\right) = \mu & \\
& + \sum_{j=1}^{q} \alpha_j \epsilon\left(i_j\right) \\
& + \sum_{\ell=1}^{q} \sum_{j<\ell} \beta_{j\ell} \epsilon\left(i_j\right) \epsilon\left(i_\ell\right) \\
& + \dots \\
& + \omega_{1 \dots q} \epsilon\left(i_1\right) \dots \epsilon\left(i_q\right).
\end{aligned}
$$

We can determine the sign of a given effect by counting the number of variables determining it which assume the value zero. If this number is even, the sign is positive, otherwise it is negative.

5.5.2 *Conditional Distributions and the Assumption of Independence*

Conditional distributions derived from the joint probabilities $P_{i_1, \dots, i_q}$ allow for ANOVA type decompositions – they are simply written as sums of the various-order terms.

Consider a partition of $y_1, \dots, y_1$ into two subsets $a_1 = (y_1, \dots, y_k)$ and $a_2 = \left(y_{k+1}, \dots, y_q\right)$. Writing the joint probabilities according the form given in equation (5.10), we see that:

$$
\begin{aligned}
& \Pr\left(y_1 = i_1, \dots, y_k = i_k \mid y_{k+1} = i_{k+1}, \dots, y_q = i_q\right) \\
& = \frac{P_{i_1 \dots i_q}}{\sum_{i_1} \dots \sum_{i_k} P_{i_1 \dots i_q}}, \\
& = \frac{e^{\sum_j \alpha_j (i_j) + \sum_{\ell=1}^{q} \sum_{j<\ell} \beta_{j\ell}(i_j, i_\ell) + \dots + \omega_{1 \dots q}(i_1, \dots, i_q)}}{\sum_{i_1} \dots \sum_{i_k} e^{\sum_j \alpha_j (i_j) + \sum_{\ell=1}^{q} \sum_{j<\ell} \beta_{j\ell}(i_j, i_\ell) + \dots + \omega_{1 \dots q}(i_1, \dots, i_q)}}.
\end{aligned}
$$

We define:

$$
\eta_1 = \left\{i_1, \dots, i_k\right\}, \quad \eta_2 = \left\{i_{k+1}, \dots, i_q\right\},
$$

and let θ_{η_1} $\left(\theta_{\eta_2}\right)$ represent the sum of effects indexed by the values appearing in η_1 (η_2), and $\theta_{\eta_1 \eta_2}$ the sum of effects depending both on components of η_1 and

η_2. We have:

$$\begin{aligned}\Pr\left(y_1 = i_1, \dots, y_k = i_k \mid y_{k+1} = i_{k+1}, \dots, y_q = i_q\right) \\ = \frac{e^{\theta_{\eta_1}+\theta_{\eta_2}+\theta_{\eta_1\eta_2}}}{\sum_{\eta_1} e^{\theta_{\eta_1}+\theta_{\eta_2}+\theta_{\eta_1\eta_2}}}, \\ = \frac{e^{\theta_{\eta_1}+\theta_{\eta_1\eta_2}}}{\sum_{\eta_1} e^{\theta_{\eta_1}+\theta_{\eta_1\eta_2}}}.\end{aligned}$$

The decomposition of the conditional probability into the principal, first-order, etc. terms can now be found. If $\eta_2 = \left\{i_{k+1}, \dots, i_q\right\}$ is fixed, the principal term is:

$$\tilde{\mu} = -\log\left[\sum_{\eta_1} e^{\theta_{\eta_1}+\theta_{\eta_1\eta_2}}\right],$$

and the first-order term, $\tilde{\alpha}_j\left(i_j\right), j = 1, \dots, k$, is the sum of effects which only depend on η_1 over the intermediate term i_j:

$$\tilde{\alpha}_j\left(i_j\right) = \alpha_j\left(i_j\right) + \sum_{\ell\in\eta_2} \beta_{j\ell}\left(i_j, i_\ell\right) + \sum_{\ell,m\in\alpha_2}\sum_{\ell<m} \gamma_{j\ell m}\left(i_j, i_\ell, i_m\right) + \dots$$

The second-order term, $\tilde{\beta}_{j\ell}\left(i_j, i_\ell\right), \ell = 1, \dots, k, j = 1, \dots, \ell$, is obtained by summing the effects depending on η_1 over i_j, i_ℓ, and so on. Obviously, they generally depend on the values assumed by the variables in η_2.

Proposition 12: $a_1 = \{y_1, \dots, y_k\}$ and $a_2 = \left\{y_{k+1}, \dots, y_q\right\}$ are independent if and only if $\theta_{\eta_1\eta_2} = 0, \forall\eta_1, \eta_2$.

Proof: The necessary and sufficient condition is that the conditional probability of $\left\{y_1, \dots, y_k\right\}$, given $\left\{y_{k+1}, \dots, y_q\right\} = \eta_2$, does not depend on η_2. This obtains when $\theta_{\eta_1,\eta_2} = 0, \forall\eta_1\eta_2$. □

This proposition extends to cases of more that two groups. Consider, for example, the partition of $\left\{y_1, \dots, y_q\right\}$ into three subsets:

$$\begin{aligned} a_1 &= \left\{y_1, \dots, i_{k_1}\right\}, \\ a_2 &= \left\{y_{k_1+1}, \dots, y_{k_1+k_2}\right\}, \\ a_3 &= \left\{y_{k_1+k_2+1}, \dots, y_k\right\}, \end{aligned}$$

and let:

$$\begin{aligned} \eta_1 &= \left\{i_1, \dots, i_{k_1}\right\}, \\ \eta_2 &= \left\{i_{k_1+1}, \dots, i_{k_1+k_2}\right\}, \\ \eta_3 &= \left\{i_{k_1+k_2+1}, \dots, i_q\right\}, \end{aligned}$$

represent the corresponding indices. $\theta_{\eta_1}, \theta_{\eta_2}, \theta_{\eta_3}$ denote the sums of the effects with one index, $\theta_{\eta_1\eta_2}, \theta_{\eta_1\eta_3}, \theta_{\eta_2\eta_3}$ the sums over two effects, and $\theta_{\eta_1\eta_2\eta_3}$ incorporates all three.

According to propostion 12, a_1 is independent of $a_2 \cup a_3$ if and only if:

$$\theta_{\eta_1\eta_2} = \theta_{\eta_1\eta_3} = \theta_{\eta_1\eta_2\eta_3} = 0, \quad \forall \eta_1, \eta_2, \eta_3. \tag{5.12}$$

Under this assumption of independence between a_1 and $a_2 \cup a_3$, the marginal distribution of $a_2 \cup a_3$ is given by:

$$\begin{aligned}
\Pr(a_2 = \eta_2, a_3 = \eta_3) &= \sum_{\eta_1} \Pr(a_1 = \eta_1, a_2 = \eta_2, a_3 = \eta_3), \\
&= \sum_{\eta_1} e^{\theta_{\eta_1} + \theta_{\eta_2} + \theta_{\eta_3} + \theta_{\eta_2\eta_3}}, \\
&= e^{\theta_{\eta_2} + \theta_{\eta_3} + \theta_{\eta_2\eta_3} + \tilde{\mu}},
\end{aligned}$$

where $\tilde{\mu}$ is the principal term of this marginal distribution.

Proposition 13: a_1, a_2, and a_3 are globally independent if:

$$\theta_{\eta_1\eta_2} = \theta_{\eta_1\eta_3} = \theta_{\eta_2\eta_3} = \theta_{\eta_1\eta_2\eta_3} = 0, \quad \forall \eta_1, \eta_2, \eta_3.$$

Proof: If a_1, a_2, and a_3 are globally independent, then a_1 is independent of $a_2 \cup a_3$, and a_2 is independent of $a_1 \cup a_3$, satisfying the conditions in equation (5.12). Conversely, if these conditions are fulfilled, the joint distribution:

$$\begin{aligned}
\Pr(a_1 = \eta_1, a_2 = \eta_2, a_3 = \eta_3) &= e^{\mu + \theta_{\eta_1} + \theta_{\eta_2} + \theta_{\eta_3}}, \\
&= e^{\mu + \theta_{\eta_1}} e^{\theta_{\eta_2}} e^{\theta_{\eta_3}},
\end{aligned}$$

is the product of functions depending only on η_1 (η_2, η_3), so a_1, a_2, and a_3 are independent. □

Instead of examining the conditional distribution of a_1 given $a_2 \cup a_3$, we can focus on the distribution of $a_1 \cup a_2$ given a_3. We have:

$$\Pr(a_1 = \eta_1, a_2 = \eta_2 | a_3 = \eta_3) = e^{\tilde{\mu} + (\theta_{\eta_1} + \theta_{\eta_1\eta_3}) + (\theta_{\eta_2} + \theta_{\eta_2\eta_3}) + (\theta_{\eta_1\eta_2} + \theta_{\eta_1\eta_2\eta_3})},$$

where $\tilde{\mu}$ is the principal term of this distribution ($\tilde{\mu}$ depends on η_3).

Proposition 14: a_1 and a_2 are independent conditional on $a_3 = \eta_3$, if and only if:

$$\theta_{\eta_1\eta_2} = \theta_{\eta_1\eta_2\eta_3} = 0, \quad \forall \eta_1, \eta_2, \eta_3.$$

When a_1 and a_2 are conditionally independent with respect to a_3, the joint distribution of (a_1, a_3) is:

$$\Pr(a_1 = \eta_1, a_3 = \eta_3) = \sum_{\eta_2} e^{\mu+\theta_{\eta_1}+\theta_{\eta_2}+\theta_{\eta_3}+\theta_{\eta_1\eta_3}+\theta_{\eta_2\eta_3}},$$

$$= e^{\mu+\theta_{\eta_1}+\theta_{\eta_3}+\theta_{\eta_1\eta_3}} \sum_{\eta_2} e^{\theta_{\eta_2}+\theta_{\eta_2\eta_3}}.$$

We see that θ_{η_1} and $\theta_{\eta_1\eta_3}$ are the first-order and cross effects associated with the marginal distribution of a_1 respectively. When the assumption of conditional independence is satisfied we can analyse the relationship between a_1 and a_3 by studying the marginal distribution of $a_1 \cup a_3$.

5.6 The Log-Linear Model

5.6.1 Definition and Examples

In the most general version of the log-linear model (cf. Haberman [Hab74]) it is assumed that each observation consists of J independent vectors, $n_{kj}, k = 0, \ldots, K_j, j = 1, \ldots, J$, each of which is distributed multinomially $\mathcal{M}(n_j; P_{0j}, \ldots, P_{K_j,j})$.

The probabilities, P_{kj}, are obviously constrained by:

$$\sum_{k=0}^{K_j} P_{kj} = 1, \quad j = 1, \ldots, J.$$

These conditions can be written:

$$\boldsymbol{\nu}^{(j)} \cdot \mathbf{P} = 1, \quad j = 1, \ldots, J,$$

where $\mathbf{P}$ is the vector of all the probabilities:

$$\mathbf{P} = \left(P_{01}, P_{11}, \ldots, P_{k_1 1}, P_{02}, P_{12}, \ldots, P_{K_J J}\right),$$

and where $\boldsymbol{\nu}^{(j)}$ is a set of j vectors which contain ones and zeros with the j-th vector indexed $k = 0, \ldots, K_j$. $\boldsymbol{\nu}^{(j)}$ spans a subspace $\mathcal{N}$. Finally, log $(\mathbf{P})$ indicates the vector with members log (P_{kj}).

Definition 2: A model fitting the preceding description is log-linear if the vector log $(\mathbf{P})$ is constrained to belong to some space $\mathcal{M}$ containing $\mathcal{N}$.

This model, which is a generalization of the definition given in equation (5.1), allows for the simultaneous analysis of several contingency tables.

Assume, for example, that we have independent observations on two dichotomous variables y_{1t} and y_{2t} for T dates, $t = 1, \ldots, T$. If n_t is the number of observations for date t, the data can be summarized in T (2×2) frequency tables:

$y_{1t} \backslash y_{2t}$	0	1	
0	n_{00t}	n_{01t}	
1	n_{10t}	n_{11t}	
			n_t

The corresponding contingency table with the theoretical probabilities is:

$y_{1t} \backslash y_{2t}$	0	1
0	P_{00t}	P_{01t}
1	P_{10t}	P_{11t}

In this example we have $j = t$, $J = T$ and the indices k assume the values $(0, 0)$, $(0, 1)$, $(1, 0)$, and $(1, 1)$.

In section 5.2.2 we discussed how to formulate the hypothesis of independence for this type of (2×2) table, and we examined how this assumption could be tested. Given the fact that we now dispose of data for a number of dates, it is preferable to apply a global test to all the data. Under the assumption of independence, the probabilities are constrained by:

$$P_{00t} P_{11t} = P_{01t} P_{10t},$$

$$\log(P_{00t}) + \log(P_{11t}) = \log(P_{01t}) + \log(P_{10t}), \quad \forall t.$$

These conditions are of the form:

$$\log(\mathbf{P}) \in \mathcal{M}.$$

We can further verify that $\mathcal{M}$ contains the vector $\boldsymbol{\nu}^{(t)}$. In fact, $\boldsymbol{\nu}^{(t)}$ is such that:

$$\nu_{ii',\tau}^{(t)} = \begin{cases} 1, & \text{if } \tau = t, \forall i, i' = \{0, 1\}, \\ 0, & \text{otherwise.} \end{cases}$$

This yields:

$$\nu_{00\tau}^{(t)} + \nu_{11\tau}^{(t)} = \nu_{01\tau}^{(t)} + \nu_{10\tau}^{(t)}, \quad \forall \tau.$$

5.6.1.1 The Log-Linear and Logistic Models

Another model which gives rise to the log-linear form is the univariate polychotomous logit model (cf. sections 3.3 and 4.3.2). In this model we have a variable which can take $K + 1$ values and for which we have observations for

$j = 1, \ldots, J$ states of the world. The probability that the variable will assume the value k under conditions j is given by:

$$P_{kj} = \frac{\exp\left(\mathbf{x}_{kj}\mathbf{b}_j\right)}{\sum_{\ell=0}^{K} \exp\left(\mathbf{x}_{\ell j}\mathbf{b}_j\right)}, \quad k = 0, \ldots, K, \quad j = 1, \ldots, J.$$

These conditions can also be written:

$$\log\left(P_{kj}\right) = \mathbf{x}_{kj}\mathbf{b}_j + \alpha_j, \quad k = 0, \ldots, K, \quad j = 1, \ldots, J,$$

where the α_j-s are uniquely determined by the conditions:

$$\sum_{k=0}^{K} P_{kj} = 1.$$

Written like this, the univariate polychotomous logit model resembles a log-linear model. In fact, if we admit the possibility of imposing linearity conditions on the parameters $\mathbf{b}_j$ of the logit model, the only difference between the log-linear and the univariate polychotomous logit model is the fact that the number of values K_j assumed by the dependent variable may vary with the conditions j in the former case, but is fixed in the latter. This difference may be deemed irrelevant in most cases.

This virtual equivalence between the log-linear and the univariate polychotomous logit model clearly does not extend to other models such as: the probit model, the sequential logit model, the bivariate conditional logit model, etc.

5.6.2 *Some Theoretical Propositions*

From the formulation of the log-linear model given in definition 2 it is possible to establish some statistical results – calculation of exhaustive statistics and derivation of some properties of the maximum-likelihood estimator, for example. These properties are general and do not require specification of the base for $\mathcal{M}$. We do, however, specify this space to facilitate interpretation of the results for our examination of the logit model, and to simplify the ANOVA-type analysis.

Consider the likelihood associated with the log-linear model. It is given by:

$$L = \prod_{j=1}^{J} \left\{ \frac{n_j!}{\prod_{k=0}^{K_j} \left(n_{kj}\right)!} \right\} \exp\left[\sum_{j=1}^{J} \sum_{k=0}^{K_j} n_{kj} \log\left(P_{kj}\right) \right],$$

$$= \prod_{j=1}^{J} \frac{n_j!}{\prod_{k=o}^{K_j} \left(n_{kj}\right)!} \exp\langle \mathbf{n}, \log(\mathbf{P})\rangle,$$

where $\langle \cdot, \cdot \rangle$ designates the scalar product, and $\mathbf{n}$ the vector with elements n_{kj}.

Let $\mathcal{U}$ be the subspace orthogonal to $\mathcal{N}$ in $\mathcal{M}$, and $P_{\mathcal{M}}$, $P_{\mathcal{N}}$, and $P_{\mathcal{U}}$ be orthogonal projections onto $\mathcal{M}$, $\mathcal{N}$ and $\mathcal{U}$. Since log (**P**) is in $\mathcal{M}$, we have:

$$\begin{aligned}\langle \mathbf{n}, \log(\mathbf{P})\rangle &= \langle P_{\mathcal{M}}\mathbf{n}, \log(\mathbf{P})\rangle,\\ &= \langle P_{\mathcal{N}}\mathbf{n} + P_{\mathcal{U}}\mathbf{n}, P_{\mathcal{N}}\log(\mathbf{P}) + P_{\mathcal{N}}\log(\mathbf{P}) + P_{\mathcal{U}}\log(\mathbf{P})\rangle,\\ &= \langle P_{\mathcal{N}}\mathbf{n}, P_{\mathcal{N}}\log(\mathbf{P})\rangle + \langle P_{\mathcal{U}}\mathbf{n}, P_{\mathcal{U}}\log(\mathbf{P})\rangle,\\ &= \langle \mathbf{n}, P_{\mathcal{N}}\log(\mathbf{P})\rangle + \langle P_{\mathcal{U}}\mathbf{n}, P_{\mathcal{U}}\log(\mathbf{P})\rangle.\end{aligned}$$

The penultimate equality derives from the orthogonality of the subspaces $\mathcal{N}$ and $\mathcal{U}$. The vector $P_{\mathcal{N}}$ log (**P**) can be written:

$$P_{\mathcal{N}}\log(\mathbf{P}) = \sum_{j=1}^{J} \beta_j \boldsymbol{\nu}^{(j)}.$$

Now we impose the constraints $\langle \boldsymbol{\nu}^{(j)}, \mathbf{P}\rangle = 1, \forall j$, yielding:

$$\begin{aligned}\log(\mathbf{P}) &= P_{\mathcal{N}}\left[\log(\mathbf{P})\right] + P_{\mathcal{U}}\left[\log(\mathbf{P})\right],\\ &= \sum_{j=1}^{J} \beta_j \boldsymbol{\nu}^{(j)} + P_{\mathcal{U}}\log(\mathbf{P}).\end{aligned}$$

From this expression we see that the coordinates of **P** are of the form:

$$P_{kj} = \exp\left(\beta_j\right)\exp\left[P_{\mathcal{U}}\log\left(P_{kj}\right)\right].$$

Rewriting the constraints:

$$\begin{aligned}1 &= \langle \nu^{(j)}, \mathbf{P}\rangle,\\ 1 &= \sum_{k=0}^{K_j} P_{kj},\\ 1 &= \exp\left(\beta_j\right)\sum_{k=0}^{K_j}\exp\left[P_{\mathcal{U}}\log\left(P_{kj}\right)\right].\end{aligned}$$

Letting $\exp\left[P_{\mathcal{U}}\log(\mathbf{P})\right]$ denote the vector with $\exp\left[P_{\mathcal{U}}\log\left(P_{kj}\right)\right]$ as its elements, we find:

$$\exp\left(\beta_j\right) = \frac{1}{\langle \boldsymbol{\nu}^{(j)}, \exp\left[P_{\mathcal{U}}\log(\mathbf{P})\right]\rangle},$$

and thus:

$$\beta_j = -\log\langle \boldsymbol{\nu}^{(j)}, \exp\left[P_{\mathcal{U}}\log(\mathbf{P})\right]\rangle,$$

$$P_{\mathcal{N}} \log(\mathbf{P}) = \sum_{j=1}^{J} \beta_j \boldsymbol{\nu}^{(j)},$$

$$= -\sum_{j=1}^{J} \boldsymbol{\nu}^{(j)} \log\langle \boldsymbol{\nu}^{(j)}, \exp\left[P_{\mathcal{U}} \log(\mathbf{P})\right]\rangle.$$

This leads us to a new expression for the likelihood:

$$L = \prod_{j=1}^{J} \left[\frac{n_j!}{\prod_{k=0}^{K_j} n_{kj}!}\right] \exp\left\{ \langle P_{\mathcal{U}}\mathbf{n}, P_{\mathcal{U}} \log(\mathbf{P})\rangle \right.$$
$$\left. - \sum_{j=1}^{J} \langle \mathbf{n}, \nu^{(j)}\rangle \log\langle \nu^{(j)}, \exp\left[P_{\mathcal{U}} \log(\mathbf{P})\right]\rangle \right\},$$
$$= \prod_{j=1}^{J} \left[\frac{n_j!}{\prod_{k=0}^{K_j} n_{kj}!}\right] \exp\left\{ \langle P_{\mathcal{U}}\mathbf{n}, P_{\mathcal{U}} \log(\mathbf{P})\rangle \right.$$
$$\left. - \sum_{j=1}^{J} n_j \log\langle \nu^{(j)}, \exp\left[P_{\mathcal{U}} \log(\mathbf{P})\right]\rangle \right\}.$$

Examination of this formulation reveals that the "true" parameter, when the constraints are accounted for, is $P_{\mathcal{U}} \log(\mathbf{P})$. Furthermore, we see that the likelihood can be written as a function of *only* the observations:

$$\prod_{j=1}^{J} \frac{n_j!}{\prod_{k=0}^{K_j} n_{kj}!},$$

as a function of *only* the parameters:

$$\exp\left\{ -\sum_{j=1}^{J} n_j \log\langle \boldsymbol{\nu}^{(j)}, \exp\left[P_{\mathcal{U}} \log(\mathbf{P})\right]\rangle \right\},$$

and as a function of both the observations and the parameters:

$$\exp\langle P_{\mathcal{U}}\mathbf{n}, P_{\mathcal{U}} \log(\mathbf{P})\rangle.$$

Examining the cross term, we observe (cf. Monfort [1980]:

Proposition 15: The log-linear model is exponential, and the statistic $P_{\mathcal{U}}$ is *sufficient minimal* for the parameter $P_{\mathcal{U}} \log(\mathbf{P})$.

It is not always possible to find a maximum-likelihood estimator for the parameters of an exponential model. However, if the estimator exists, it is always unique and is obtained by solving the likelihood equations. Letting $\theta = P_{\mathcal{U}} \log(\mathbf{P})$, we can maximize the likelihood over $\theta \in \mathcal{U}$ or, equivalently, maximize:

$$\ell(\theta) = \langle \mathbf{n}, \theta \rangle - \sum_{j=1}^{J} n_j \log \langle \boldsymbol{\nu}^{(j)}, \exp(\theta) \rangle.$$

We easily find the differential of this expression:

$$\begin{aligned} d\ell(\theta) &= \sum_{j=1}^{J} \sum_{k=0}^{K_j} n_{kj} d\theta_{kj} - \sum_{j=1}^{J} n_j \frac{\sum_{k=0}^{K_j} \exp(\theta_{kj}) \, d\theta_{kj}}{\sum_{k=0}^{K_j} \exp(\theta_{kj})}, \\ &= \sum_{j=1}^{J} \sum_{k=0}^{K_j} \left(n_{kj} - n_j P_{kj}\right) d\theta_{kj}, \\ &= \langle d\theta, \mathbf{n} - m(\mathbf{P}) \rangle, \end{aligned}$$

where $m(\mathbf{P})$ is a vector of the means of the elements of $\mathbf{n}$ and where $d\theta \in \mathcal{U}$.

Proposition 16: When it exists, $\tilde{\mathbf{P}}$ – the maximum-likelihood estimator of $\mathbf{P}$ – is the unique solution to this equation system:

$$\begin{aligned} n - m\left(\tilde{\mathbf{P}}\right) &\in \mathcal{U}^{\perp}, \\ \tilde{\mathbf{P}} &\in \mathcal{N}, \\ \log\left(\tilde{\mathbf{P}}\right) &\in \mathcal{N}. \end{aligned}$$

Notice that in the special case of a single contingency table the expression $\mathbf{n} - m\left(\tilde{\mathbf{P}}\right) \in \mathcal{U}^{\perp}$ reduces to $\hat{\mathbf{P}} - \tilde{\mathbf{P}} \in \mathcal{U}^{\perp}$, where $\hat{\mathbf{P}}$ is the vector of empirical frequencies calculated from the observations. Consider, for example, a vector $\mathbf{x}$ in $\mathcal{M}$, $\hat{\mathbf{P}} - \tilde{\mathbf{P}}$ belongs to $\mathcal{U}^{\perp}$, but also to $\mathcal{N}^{\perp}$, so $\langle \mathbf{x}, \hat{\mathbf{P}} - \tilde{\mathbf{P}} \rangle = 0$ and the maximum-likelihood estimator of the function $\langle \mathbf{x}, \mathbf{P} \rangle$ is simply $\langle \mathbf{x}, \hat{\mathbf{P}} \rangle$. This explains why, in the cases examined in sections 5.2, 5.3, and 5.4, it was generally quite easy to find the maximum-likelihood estimators of the statistics (cf. exercise 7).

5.7 Applications

5.7.1 Business Cycle Studies

Among the most common applications of logit and log-linear models is the analysis of questionnaires with qualitative data. Surveys designed in this manner have the advantage of simplicity and tend to yield useful data very quickly. This is why qualitative questionnaires are frequently used for surveys in business cycle studies. These studies attempt to predict the evolution of certain economic indicators over the subsequent three or four months (or analyse this behaviour for the preceding period). When these surveys are conducted with heads of business as the sample group, the questions may be, for example:

(i) How have your prices P_t moved over the last three or four months?
(ii) What type of price changes, P_t^*, do you anticipate in the next three or four months?

The respondents are asked to choose among:

↗ "increase"
→ "no change"
↘ "decrease"

Similar questions are asked concerning their realized and anticipated level of production, how many orders they have or expect to receive, their expenses, their balance sheet, etc.

5.7.2 *Expected and Realized Values*

When information is simultaneously available on expected and realized changes of some economic variables (prices, for example) we can compare the two data sets and attempt to understand how executives form expectations. In a series of articles Koenig, Nerlove, Ottenwaelter, and Oudiz ([KNO81] and [Ner83]) proposed several log-linear models to describe the formation of expectations.

They estimated:

(i) Models of the conditional distribution of P_t^* given P_{t-q}^*, P_t – these are analogous to adaptive expectations models.
(ii) Models of the conditional distribution of P_t^* given P_{t-q}^*, P_t, analogous to extrapolative-type models.
(iii) They also introduced a generalized error correction mechanism, derived from the distribution of ΔP_t^* given $\mathrm{E}(P_t)$.

The variable ΔP_t^* – changes in expectations – is trichotomous and takes values according to:

P_t^* \ P_{t+1}^*	↗	→	↘
↗	=	+	+
→	−	=	+
↘	−	−	=

The variable $\epsilon\ (P_t)$ "error in expectation" or "surprise" is defined by:

$P_t^* \backslash P_t$	$\nearrow$	$\rightarrow$	$\searrow$
$\nearrow$	$=$	$+$	$+$
$\rightarrow$	$-$	$=$	$+$
$\searrow$	$-$	$-$	$=$

Studying these models may also allow us to determine the lag, q, which provides the strongest correlation between expectations and realizations. Knowledge of this value can allow us to make better use of the expressed expectations to obtain advance indicators of the true values for the following three or four months.

5.7.3 Price Adjustment Studies

Another application of data from business cycle studies was developed by Kawasaki-McMillan-Zimmerman ([KMZ83]). They wanted to test the hypothesis that companies react differently to demand changes depending on whether these changes are perceived as permanent or temporary. If the change is perceived as permanent, companies will tend to adjust both the price and the level of output. If the change is construed as temporary, however, only the level of production is altered.

Data for these studies comprised the following four qualitative, trichotomous variables:

(i) P_t: change in the price level between the previous and the current month.
(ii) Q_t: change in the quantity of output between the previous and the current month.
(iii) D_t: changes in the order book, this variable is used to establish short-term variations in demand.
(iv) G_t^*: anticipated change in the level of output for the next six months, this variable occurs as a proxy for long term changes in demand.

These variables are trichotomous and may assume the values $(\nearrow, \rightarrow, \searrow)$. The data is used to create two samples, one corresponding to observations for which G_{t-1}^* is "$\rightarrow$", i.e. no change in production, and a second sample in which the values of G_{t-1}^* and D_{t-1} are the same and indicate a real change, be it $\nearrow$ (increase) or $\searrow$ (decrease). For each of these sub-samples the authors estimate a conditional log-linear model on the ordered pair (P_t, Q_t) given D_{t-1}.

Estimating these models and applying tests of independence allow us to derive the following results from the data:

(i) A short-term shift in demand results in a price and / or production level change.
(ii) Variations in the price and quantity produced are greater for permanent than for temporary changes in demand.
(iii) Unlike permanent changes, temporary demand changes do not have a significant effect on price levels.

Exercises

5.1 Consider the dichotomous variable y assuming the values zero and one. Any order-maintaining coding of y can be written:

$$z = \begin{cases} \alpha, & \text{if } y = 0, \\ \beta, & \text{if } y = 1, \end{cases}$$

where $\beta > \alpha$. Show that z can be expressed as $z = ay + b$ with $a > 0$ and that the correlation between the two dichotomous variables y_1 and y_2 does not depend upon the coding (as long as it maintains the order).

5.2 Consider n independent observations on two dichotomous variables y_1 and y_2. Use the chi-square method to test for the independence between y_1 and y_2 (notice that the χ^2 formulation allows for significant simplification). Compare this with the test for $\beta_{12} = 0$.

5.3 Consider three dichotomous variables y_1, y_2 and y_3, such that y_1 and y_2 are independent of each other, and are independent conditional on y_3. Does global independence between the three variables y_1, y_2, y_3 obtain?

5.4 When two dichotomous variables are independent for any values of the explanatory variables, is seems reasonable to introduce a logistic model:

$$\Pr(y_1 = 0, y_2 = 0) = \frac{1}{1 + e^{\mathbf{x}_1 \mathbf{b}_1}} \frac{1}{1 + e^{\mathbf{x}_2 \mathbf{b}_2}},$$

$$\Pr(y_1 = 0, y_2 = 1) = \frac{1}{1 + e^{\mathbf{x}_1 \mathbf{b}_1}} \frac{e^{\mathbf{x}_2 \mathbf{b}_2}}{1 + e^{\mathbf{x}_2 \mathbf{b}_2}},$$

$$\Pr(y_1 = 1, y_2 = 0) = \frac{e^{\mathbf{x}_1 \mathbf{b}_1}}{1 + e^{\mathbf{x}_1 \mathbf{b}_1}} \frac{1}{1 + e^{\mathbf{x}_2 \mathbf{b}_2}},$$

$$\Pr(y_1 = 1, y_2 = 1) = \frac{e^{\mathbf{x}_1 \mathbf{b}_1}}{1 + e^{\mathbf{x}_1 \mathbf{b}_1}} \frac{e^{x_2 b_2}}{1 + e^{\mathbf{x}_2 \mathbf{b}_2}}.$$

Show that if we have n observations on the endogenous variables corresponding to several values of the exogenous variables, then full information maximum-likelihood estimation is equivalent to maximum likelihood applied to the marginal distributions.

5.5 Verify that if $\beta(i_1, i_2)$ does not depend on i_2, then we must have $\beta(i_1, i_2) = 0$.

5.6 Derive from equation (15) that every (2×2) array:

$$\begin{bmatrix} \log(P_{00}) & \log(P_{01}) \\ \log(P_{10}) & \log(P_{11}) \end{bmatrix}$$

is a combination of the tables:

$$\begin{bmatrix} 1 & 1 \\ 1 & 1 \end{bmatrix}, \begin{bmatrix} -1 & -1 \\ 1 & 1 \end{bmatrix}, \begin{bmatrix} -1 & 1 \\ -1 & 1 \end{bmatrix} \begin{bmatrix} -1 & -1 \\ -1 & 1 \end{bmatrix}.$$

Interpret the tables in this decomposition.

5.7 Consider the case of two polychotomous variables (cf. section 5.4.1). Find a test for the equality of the conditional distributions corresponding to two values of the first variable:

$$H_0 : \Pr(y_2 = i_2 | y_1 = 0) = \Pr(y_2 = i_2 | y_1 = 1), \quad \forall i_2.$$

5.8 Consider the conditional bivariate dichotomous logit model in section 4.3.2. Is this a log-linear model? Answer the same question for a sequential logit model.

5.9 Consider a (2×2) contingency table, and let the assumption of independence hold. Determine the subspace $\mathcal{M}$ associated with this log-linear model. Furthermore, using the procedures presented on page 140 show that the linear functions of the joint probabilities are none other that the marginal probabilities.

5.10 Sometimes the log-linear model is defined with the assumption that the mean, $m(\mathbf{P})$, of the n observations satisfies:

$$\log [m(\mathbf{P})] \in \mathcal{M}.$$

Show that if $\mathcal{N} \subset \mathcal{M}$ this condition is equivalent to $\log(\mathbf{P}) \in \mathcal{M}$.

5.11 Assume that the triple (y_1, y_2, y_3) is normally distributed. Furthermore, let y_1 and y_2 be independent conditional on y_3. What constraints does this condition impose on the parameters of the normal distribution? Find the conditional distribution of y_1 given y_3 and the conditional distribution of y_1 given y_2, y_3. Compare your results with those obtained in section 5.3.3.

6 Qualitative Panel Data

Time series data, or mixed time series and cross section data, are often analysed with the theory of processes. This procedure may, for example, be applied to linear models with serial correlation or with lagged endogenous variables – in the latter case the values assumed by the endogenous variables are described by a Markov process. Similar models can be built when the endogenous variable is qualitative; these derive from the theory of Markov chains (however, cf. section 2.8.3 for a different approach.)

It is beyond the scope of this chapter to develop a full treatment of this theory. Rather, we shall restrict our analysis to showing how it can be used to build qualitative models of time series and to studying estimation problems associated with this type of model.

6.1 Definition of a Markov Chain

Consider a qualitative variable **y** assuming J values, $j = 0, \ldots, J-1$, for which we have observations over a period of time, $t = 0, \ldots, T$. These observations $(y_0, y_1, \ldots, y_t, \ldots, y_T)$ have a joint distribution which can be characterized in several ways.

One approach is to postulate a priori the marginal distribution of y_0, the conditional distribution of y_1 given y_0, the conditional distribution of y_2 given (y_1, y_0), etc. We have:

$$\begin{aligned}
&\Pr(y_0 = j_0, \ldots, y_T = j_T) \\
&= \Pr(y_0 = j_0)\Pr(y_1 = j_1 \mid y_0 = j_0)\Pr(y_2 = j_2 \mid y_1 = j_1, y_0 = j_0) \\
&\quad \ldots \Pr(y_T = j_T \mid y_{T-1} = j_{T-1}, \ldots, y_0 = j_0).
\end{aligned}$$

Definition 3: $y_0, \ldots, y_T$ constitutes a first-order Markov chain if:

$$\begin{aligned}
&\Pr(y_t = j_t \mid y_{t-1} = j_{t-1}, \ldots, y_0 = j_0) \\
&\quad = \Pr(y_t = j_t \mid y_{t-1} = j_{t-1}), \quad \forall t, j_t, j_{t-1}, \ldots, j_0.
\end{aligned}$$

In other words, $y_0, \ldots, y_T$ is a Markov chain if y_t does not depend on previous values of $\mathbf{y}$ except through the intermediary effect of y_{t-1}. When this condition is satisfied the joint distribution is written:

$$\Pr(y_0 = j_0, \ldots, y_T = j_T) = \Pr(y_0 = j_0) \prod_{t=1}^{T} (y_t = j_t \,|\, y_{t-1} = j_{t-1}).$$

From here on we shall use the notation:

$P_{0 \ldots T}(j_0 \ldots j_T) = \mathrm{P}(y_0 = j_0, \ldots, y_T = j_T)$	the joint probability,
$P_t(j_t) = \mathrm{P}(y_t = j_t)$	the marginal probability of the j-th observation,
$P_{ij}(t) = \mathrm{P}(y_t = j \,|\, y_{t-1} = i)$	the probability that the value of y changes from i to j between $t-1$ and t.

Using this notation, we see that:

$$P_{0 \ldots T}(j_0, \ldots, j_T) = P_0(j_0) \prod_{t=1}^{T} P_{j_{t-1} j_t}(t),$$

$$P_t(j_t) = \sum_{j_0} \ldots \sum_{j_{t-1}} \left[P_0(j_0)\, P_{j_0 j_1}(1)\, P_{j_1 j_2}(2) \ldots P_{j_{t-1} j_t}(t) \right]. \quad (6.1)$$

Equation (6.1) can also be written in matrix form. Let P_t be a vector with J elements, $P_t(j)$, $j = 0, \ldots, J-1$, and let $\mathrm{P}(t)$ be a square $(J \times J)$ matrix with elements $P_{ij}(t)$, $i = 0, \ldots, J-1$, $j = 0, \ldots, J-1$. All the elements of $\mathrm{P}(t)$ are positive and the sum across any row equals one, since:

$$\sum_{j=0}^{J-1} P_{ij}(t) = \sum_{j=0}^{J-1} \mathrm{P}(y_t = j \,|\, y_{t-1} = i) = 1.$$

$\mathrm{P}(t)$ is called a transition matrix (from $t-1$ to t).

In matrix form the second equality of (6.1) becomes:

$$P_t = \mathrm{P}(t)' \, \mathrm{P}(t-1)' \ldots \mathrm{P}(1)' \, \mathbf{P}_0. \quad (6.2)$$

Definition 4: A Markov chain is called homogeneous if its transition matrix does not depend on time: $\mathrm{P}(t) = P$, $\forall t$.

In this case equation (6.2) becomes:

$$P_t = P_t' \mathbf{P}_0. \quad (6.3)$$

Remark 7: The first-order Markov process introduced in definition 3 is analogous to a quantitative linear model in which the endogenous variable is lagged by one period. To obtain the equivalent for higher-order lags, i.e. up to a duration of p, we write:

$$\begin{aligned} &\mathrm{P}\,(y_t = j_t \,|\, y_{t-1} = j_{t-1}, \ldots, y_0 = j_0) \\ &\quad = \mathrm{P}\left(y_t = j_t \,|\, y_{t-1} = j_{t-1}, \ldots, y_{t-p} = j_{t-p}\right). \end{aligned}$$

This is called a Markov chain of order p.

The issues we shall examine for $p = 1$ are easily generalized to the case of any positive integer p.

6.2 Independent Observations on a Markov Chain (Micro Data)

6.2.1 Maximum-Likelihood Estimation

Assume we have n independent observations on the process $(y_{i0}, \ldots, y_{iT})$, $i = 1, \ldots, n$. If we interpret the index i as corresponding to an individual, our data is a sample of individuals observed repeatedly over time. This is called *panel* data.

Denote $n_{0\ldots T}\,(j_0, \ldots, j_T)$ the number of observations for which $y_{i0} = j_0, \ldots, y_{iT} = j_T$, $n_t\,(j_t)$ the number for which $y_t = j_t$, and $n_{t-1,t}\,(j_{t-1}, j_t)$ the number for which $y_{t-1} = j_{t-1}$ and $y_t = j_t$. The distribution of the observations $(y_{i0}, \ldots, y_{iT})$, $i = 1, \ldots, n$ is given by:

$$\begin{aligned} L &= \prod_{j_0 \ldots j_T} \left[P_{0\ldots T}\,(j_0, \ldots, j_T)\right]^{n_{0\ldots T}(j_0 \ldots j_T)}, \\ &= \prod_{j_0 \ldots j_T} \left[P_0\,(j_0)\, P_{j_0 j_1}\,(1) \ldots P_{j_{T-1} j_T}\,(T)\right]^{n_{0\ldots T}(j_0 \ldots j_T)}, \\ &= \prod_{j_0} \left[P_0\,(j_0)\right]^{n_0(j_0)} \prod_{t=1}^{T} \prod_{j_{t-1}, j_t} \left[P_{j_{t-1}, j_t}\,(t)\right]^{n_{t-1,t}(j_{t-1}, j_t)}. \end{aligned}$$

This decomposition reveals that the set of values:

$$n_0\,(j_0),\; n_{t-1,t}\,(j_{t-1}, j_t), \quad \forall t, \forall j_{t-1}, j_t, j_0,$$

constitutes an exhaustive statistic for the problem.

The maximum-likelihood estimators of the probabilities $P_0\,(j_0)$ and $P_{j_{t-1}, j_t}\,(t)$ are obtained by maximizing:

$$\begin{aligned} \log\,(L) &= \sum_{j_0} n_0\,(j_0) \log\left[P_0\,(j_0)\right] \\ &\quad + \sum_{t=1}^{T} \sum_{j_{t-1}} \sum_{j_t} n_{t-1,t}\,(j_{t-1}, j_t) \log\left[P_{j_{t-1}, j_t}\,(t)\right] \end{aligned}$$

under the constraints:

$$1 = \sum_{j_0} P_0(j_0)$$

$$1 = \sum_{j_t} P_{j_{t-1},j_t}(t), \quad \forall t, \forall j_{t-1}.$$

This solves for:

$$\hat{P}_0(j_0) = \frac{n_0(j_0)}{n}, \tag{6.4}$$

$$\hat{P}_{j_{t-1},j_t}(t) = \frac{n_{t-1,t}(j_{t-1}, j_t)}{n_{t-1}(j_{t-1})}.$$

The maximum-likelihood estimators of the transition probabilities at time t are none other than the corresponding empirical frequencies.

6.2.2 *Properties of the Estimators*

To study the properties of aforementioned estimators we must first determine the values of $n_{0\ldots T}(j_0, \ldots, j_T)$, $n_{t-1,t}(j_{t-1}, j_t)$, and $n_t(j_t)$.

The variables $n_{0\ldots T}(j_0 \ldots j_T)$, $t = 0, \ldots, T$, $j_t = 0, \ldots, J-1$, have a multinomial distribution with parameters n, $P_{0\ldots T}(j_0, \ldots, j_T)\, n_{0\ldots T}(j_0 \ldots j_T)$, $t = 0, \ldots, T$, $j_t = 0, \ldots, J-1$.

Similarly, the distribution of $n_{t-1,t}(j_{t-1}, j_t)$, $j_{t-1} = 0, \ldots, J-1$, $j_t = 0, \ldots, J-1$ and the distribution of $n_t(j_t)$, $j_t = 0 \ldots J-1$ are both multinomial with parameters, n, $P_{t-1,t}(j_{t-1}, j_t)$, $j_{t-1} = 0, \ldots, J-1$, $j_t = 0, \ldots, J-1$ and n, $P_t(j_t)$, $j_t = 0, \ldots, J-1$ [where $P_{t-1,t}\left(j_{t-1}, j_t\right) = \Pr\left(y_{t-1} = j_{t-1}, y_t = j_t\right)$], respectively.

We can easily derive the conditional distribution of:

$$n_{t-1,t}(j_{t-1}, j_t), \quad j_{t-1} = 0, \ldots, J-1, \quad j_t = 0, \ldots, J-1,$$

given the values of:

$$n_{t-1}(j_{t-1}), \quad j_{t-1} = 0, \ldots, J-1,$$

yielding:

$$\Pr\left[n_{t-1,t}(j_{t-1}, j_t)\right] = \frac{\frac{n!}{\prod_{j_{t-1}}\prod_{j_t}[n_{t-1,t}(j_{t-1},j_t)]!}\prod_{j_{t-1}}\prod_{j_t}\left[P_{t-1,t}(j_{t-1}, j_t)\right]^{n_{t-1,t}(j_{t-1},j_t)}}{\frac{n!}{\prod_{j_{t-1}}[n_{t-1}(j_{t-1})]!}\prod_{j_{t-1}}[P_{t-1}(j_{t-1})]^{n_{t-1}(j_{t-1})}}, \tag{6.5}$$

where

$$n_{t-1}(j_{t-1}) = \sum_{j_t} n_{t-1,t}(j_{t-1}, j_t). \tag{6.6}$$

This conditional probability can be rewritten:

$$\prod_{j_{t-1}} \left\{ \frac{[n_{t-1}(j_{t-1})]!}{\prod_{j_t} [n_{t-1,t}(j_{t-1}, j_t)]!} \prod_{j_t} \left[\frac{P_{t-1,t}(j_{t-1}, j_t)}{P_{t-1}(j_{t-1})} \right]^{n_{t-1,t}(j_{t-1}, j_t)} \right\}$$

$$= \prod_{j_{t-1}} \left\{ \frac{[n_{t-1}(j_{t-1})]!}{\prod_{j_t} [n_{t-1,t}(j_{t-1}, j_t)]!} \prod_{j_t} [P_{j_{t-1}, j_t}(t)]^{n_{t-1,t}(j_{t-1}, j_t)} \right\}.$$

Proposition 17: Conditional on $n_{t-1}(j_{t-1})$, $j_{t-1} = 0, \ldots, J-1$ the variables:

$$n_{t-1,t}, (j_{t-1}, j_t), \quad j_t = 0, \ldots, J-1, \quad j_{t-1} = 0, \ldots, J-1$$

are independent and follow a multinomial distribution with parameters:

$$n_{t-1}(j_{t-1}), \quad P_{j_{t-1}, j_t}(t), \quad j_t = 0, \ldots, J-1, \quad j_{t-1} = 0, \ldots, J-1.$$

We immediately see that:

$$\begin{aligned}
\mathrm{E}\left[\hat{P}_{j_{t-1} j_t}(t)\right] &= \mathrm{E}\left[\frac{n_{t-1,t}(j_{t-1}, j_t)}{n_{t-1}(j_{t-1})}\right], \\
&= \mathrm{E}\left\{ \frac{1}{n_{t-1}(j_{t-1})} \mathrm{E}\left[n_{t-1,t}(j_{t-1}, j_t) \middle| n_{t-1}(j_{t-1}) \right] \right\}, \\
&= \mathrm{E}\left[P_{j_{t-1} j_t}(t)\right], \\
&= P_{j_{t-1} j_t}(t).
\end{aligned}$$

So the estimators of the transition probabilities are unbiased.

$$\begin{aligned}
\mathrm{var}\left[\hat{P}_{j_{t-1} j_t}(t)\right] &= \mathrm{E}\left\{ \mathrm{var}\left[\hat{P}_{j_{t-1} j_t}(t) \middle| n_{t-1}(j_{t-1}) \right] \right\} \\
&\qquad + \mathrm{var}\left\{ \mathrm{E}\left[\hat{P}_{j_{t-1} j_t}(t) \middle| n_{t-1}(j_{t-1}) \right] \right\}, \\
&= \mathrm{E}\left\{ \mathrm{var}\left[\hat{P}_{j_{t-1} j_t}(t) \middle| n_{t-1}(j_{t-1}) \right] \right\}, \\
&= \mathrm{E}\left[n_{t-1}(j_{t-1})\right] P_{j_{t-1} j_t}(t) \left[1 - P_{j_{t-1} j_t}(t)\right], \\
&= n P_{t-1}(j_{t-1}) P_{j_{t-1} j_t}(t) \left[1 - P_{j_{t-1} j_t}(t)\right].
\end{aligned}$$

Similarly:

$$\begin{aligned}
&\mathrm{cov}\left[\hat{P}_{j_{t-1} j_t}(t), \hat{P}_{j_{t-1} i_t}(t)\right] \\
&\quad = -\mathrm{E}\left\{ [n_{t-1}(j_{t-1})] P_{j_{t-1} j_t}(t) P_{j_{t-1} i_t}(t) \right\}, \\
&\quad = -n P_{t-1}(j_{t-1}) P_{j_{t-1} j_t}(t) P_{j_{t-1} i_t}(t), \quad \text{if } i_t \neq j_t, \\
&\quad = 0, \quad \text{if } i_{t-1} \neq j_{t-1}.
\end{aligned}$$

It remains to examine the relationship between the estimators of the transition probabilities for two different dates. To facilitate this analysis we assume n large. Asymptotically, the maximum-likelihood estimators:

$$\hat{P}_{j_{t-1}j_t}(t), \quad t = 1, \ldots, T, \quad j_{t-1} = 0, \ldots, J-1,$$
$$j_t = 0, \ldots, J-1,$$

have a multivariate normal distribution. Furthermore, notice that the constrained maximization of the log-likelihood is equivalent to a series of individual constrained maximizations with respect to the parameters: $P_0(j_0)$, $j_0 = 0, \ldots, J-1$, $P_{j_{t-1}j_t}(t)$, $j_{t-1} = 0, \ldots, J-1$, $j_t = 0, \ldots J-1$, $t = 1, \ldots, T$.

Hence the estimators of this family of parameters are asymptotically independent (cf. exercise 4).

Finally, we have:

Proposition 18: The variables:

$$\hat{P}_{j_{t-1}j_t}(t) = \frac{n_{t-1,t}(j_{t-1}, j_t)}{n_{t-1}(j_{t-1})},$$

for a given j_{t-1} and t, have the same asymptotic properties as the usual estimators of the probabilities for a multinomial distribution with parameters:

$$E[n_{t-1}(j_{t-1})] = nP_{t-1}(j_{t-1}), \left\{P_{j_{t-1}j_t}(t), j_t = 0, \ldots, J-1\right\}.$$

These variables are asymptotically independent for different values of j_{t-1} and t.

6.2.3 *Homogeneous Markov Chains*

In homogeneous Markov chains the transition probabilities do not depend on the date: $P_{ij}(t) = P_{ij}, \forall t$. The log-likelihood is given by:

$$\begin{aligned}
\log(L) &= \sum_{j_0} n_0(j_0)\log[P_0(j_0)] \\
&\quad + \sum_t \sum_{j_{t-1}} \sum_{j_t} n_{t-1,t}(j_{t-1}, j_t)\log\left(\hat{P}_{j_{t-1}j_t}\right), \\
&= \sum_{j_0} n_0(j_0)\log[P_0(j_0)] \\
&\quad + \sum_i \sum_j \left[\sum_t n_{t-1,t}(i, j)\right]\log\left(P_{ij}\right).
\end{aligned}$$

We maximize this under constraint of:

$$1 = \sum_{j_0} P_0(j_0),$$

$$1 = \sum_{j} P_{ij} \quad \forall i = 0, \ldots, J-1.$$

and solve:

$$\hat{P}_0(j_0) = \frac{n_0(j_0)}{n},$$

$$\hat{P}_{ij} = \frac{\sum_{t=1}^{T} n_{t-1,t}(i, j)}{\sum_{j=0}^{J-1} \sum_{t=1}^{T} n_{t-1,t}(i, j)}, \tag{6.7}$$

$$= \frac{\sum_{t=1}^{T} n_{t-1,t}(i, j)}{\sum_{t=1}^{T} n_{t-1}(i)},$$

where $\hat{P}_{ij}$ is a weighted average of the estimators obtained from solving a non-homogeneous Markov chain:

$$\hat{P}_{ij} = \sum_{t=1}^{T} \hat{P}_{ij}(t) \frac{n_{t-1}(i)}{\sum_{t=1}^{T} n_{t-1}(i)}.$$

Following the same reasoning as in section 6.2.2 (see Anderson-Goodman [AG57]) we can show that:

Proposition 19: The variables $\hat{P}_{ij}$ corresponding to a given value of the index i have the same asymptotic distribution as the usual estimators of the probabilities of a multinomial distribution with parameters:

$$E\left[\sum_{t=1}^{T} n_{t-1}(i)\right] = n \sum_{t=1}^{T} P_{t-1}(i) \quad \text{and} \quad P_{ij},\, j = 1, \ldots, J.$$

The variables associated with different values of i are asymptotically independent.

6.2.4 *Testing for Homogeneity*

Using our n observations, we can obviously test the assumption of homogeneity of the Markov chain. Let Λ be likelihood-ratio test statistic calculated under the null and the alternative hypotheses. We know that asymptotically $-2\log(\Lambda)$ is distributed chi-square with $J(J-1)(T-1)$ degrees of freedom. This is the number of independent constraints we have to impose on the $P_{ij}(t)$-s to ensure homogeneity.

In the example:

$$-2\log(\Lambda) = -2\sum_t \sum_{j_{t-1}} \sum_{j_t} n_{t-1,t}(j_{t-1}, j_t) \times \left\{\log\left(\hat{P}_{j_{t-1}j_t}\right) - \log\left[\hat{P}_{j_{t-1}j_t}(t)\right]\right\},$$
$$= -2\sum_t \sum_{j_{t-1}} \sum_{j_t} n_{t-1,t}(j_{t-1}, j_t) \times \log\left[1 + \frac{\hat{P}_{j_{t-1}j_t} - \hat{P}_{j_{t-1}j_t}(t)}{\hat{P}_{j_{t-1}j_t}(t)}\right]$$

is, under the null hypothesis, equal to:

$$-2\sum_t \sum_{j_{t-1}} \sum_{j_t} n_{t-1}(j_{t-1})\, \hat{P}_{j_{t-1}j_t}(t) \times \left\{\frac{\hat{P}_{j_{t-1}j_t} - \hat{P}_{j_{t-1}j_t}(t)}{\hat{P}_{j_{t-1}j_t}(t)} - \frac{1}{2}\left[\frac{\hat{P}_{j_{t-1}j_t} - \hat{P}_{j_{t-1}j_t}(t)}{\hat{P}_{j_{t-1}j_t}(t)}\right]^2\right\},$$
$$= \sum_t \sum_{j_{t-1}} n_{t-1}(j_{t-1}) \sum_{j_t} \frac{\left[\hat{P}_{j_{t-1}j_t} - \hat{P}_{j_{t-1}j_t}(t)\right]^2}{\hat{P}_{j_{t-1}j_t}(t)}.$$

This is a sum of chi-square statistics.

6.3 Independent Observations on a Markov Chain (Macro Data)

In the preceding section we assumed that we had individual observations for each date. Frequently, however, we only have values for $n_t(j)$, $j = 0, \ldots, J-1, t = 0, \ldots, T$, from which we cannot extract the individual values $n_{t-1,t}(i, j)$. We must re-examine the issue of estimation with this type of data.

In the subsequent argument we shall distinguish between two cases:

(i) Observations for all dates apply to the same collection of individuals, i.e. the same sample is followed for the duration of the measurement ("complete panel data"),

(ii) A new sample is taken for each period ("incomplete panel data").

6.3.1 Macro Data and Complete Panel Data

When studying the distribution of the observations $n_0(j_0), \ldots, n_T(j_T)$ it is of some use to examine the conditional distributions of the values for a given date

$t, n_t(j_t), j_t = 0, \ldots, J-1$, given our knowledge of the previous values:

$$n_{t-1}(j_{t-1}), \ldots, n_0(j_0), j_{t-1} = 0, \ldots, J-1, j_0 = 0, \ldots, J-1.$$

Since $n_t(j_t) = \sum_{j_{t-1}=0}^{J-1} n_{t-1,t}(j_{t-1}, j_t)$, proposition 17 gives us:

$$\begin{aligned} &\mathrm{E}\left[n_j(j_t) \middle| n_{t-1}(j_{t-1}), \ldots, n_0(j_0)\right] \\ &\quad = \mathrm{E}[n_t(j_t) | n_{t-1}(j_{t-1})], \\ &\quad = \sum_{j_{t-1}=0}^{J-1} \mathrm{E}\left[n_{t-1,t}(j_{t-1}, j_t) \middle| n_{t-1}(j_{t-1})\right], \\ &\quad = \sum_{j_{t-1}=0}^{J-1} P_{j_{t-1}j_t}(t)\, n_{t-1}(j_{t-1}), \end{aligned}$$

where $j_{t-1} = 0, j_{t-1} = 0, \ldots, J-1, j_0 = 0, \ldots, J-1$.

The conditional second moment of $n_t(j_t)$ is obtained in a similar manner:

$$\begin{aligned} &\mathrm{var}\,[n_t(j_t) | n_{t-1}(j_{t-1}), \ldots, n_0(j_0), j_{t-1} \\ &\quad = 0, \ldots, J-1, j_0 = 0, \ldots, J-1] \\ &\quad = \mathrm{var}\left[\sum_{j_{t-1}=0}^{J-1} n_{t-1,t}(j_{t-1}, j_t) \middle| n_{t-1}(j_{t-1}), j_{t-1} = 0, \ldots, J-1\right], \\ &\quad = \sum_{j_{t-1}=0}^{J-1} \mathrm{var}\left[n_{t-1,t}(j_{t-1}, j_t) \middle| n_{t-1}(j_{t-1})\right], \end{aligned}$$

because of the conditional independence of the $n_{t-1}(j_{t-1}, j_t)$-s corresponding to different indices j_{t-1}.

The expression given above is equal to:

$$\sum_{j_{t-1}=0}^{J-1} P_{j_{t-1}j_t}(t)\left[1 - P_{j_{t-1}j_t}(t)\right] n_{t-1}(j_{t-1}).$$

Furthermore, we see that:

$$\begin{aligned} &\mathrm{cov}\,[n_t(i_t), n_t(j_t) | n_{t-1}(j_{t-1}), \ldots, n_0(j_0)] \\ &\quad = \sum_{j_{t-1}=0}^{J-1} \left[-P_{j_{t-1}i_t}(t)\, P_{j_{t-1}j_t}(t)\, n_{t-1}(j_{t-1})\right], \end{aligned}$$

where $j_i = 0, \ldots, J-1, i = 0, \ldots, t-1$.

6.3.1.1 Estimating the Transition Probabilities

We are particularly interested in estimating the transition probabilities:

$$P_{j_{t-1}j_t}(t), t = 1, \ldots, T; \quad j_t = 0, \ldots, J-1.$$

The distribution of the observations $n_t(j_t)$, $j_t = 0, \ldots, J-1, t = 1, \ldots, T$ is somewhat complex, making application of the maximum-likelihood method difficult. An alternate approach is to use the expressions for the conditional expectations and variances which we just derived. We can write:

$$n_t(j_t) = \sum_{j_{t-1}=0}^{J-1} P_{j_{t-1}j_t}(t)\, n_{t-1}(j_{t-1}) + \epsilon_t(j_t), \tag{6.8}$$

with:

$$\begin{aligned} &\mathrm{E}[\epsilon_t(j_t) | n_{t-1}(j_{t-1}), j_{t-1} = 0, \ldots, J-1] = 0, \\ &\quad j_t = 0, \ldots, J-1, \quad t = 1, \ldots, T. \end{aligned}$$

This model is linear in the parameters $P_{j_{t-1}j_t}(t)$, so it seems reasonable to apply a least-squares approach. However, as the number of independent observations, $T(J-1)$, is less than the number of parameters to be estimated, $T \cdot J(J-1)$, this won't work unless we impose further constraints on the transition probabilities. One possible approach is to postulate that the Markov chain is homogeneous, $P_{j_{t-1}j_t}(t) = P_{j_{t-1}j_t}$. In this case there are $J(J-1)$ independent parameters and estimation is possible if $T \geq J$. The model becomes:

$$n_t(j) = \sum_{i=0}^{J-1} P_{ij} n_{t-1}(i) + \epsilon_t(j), \quad t, j \text{ variable}. \tag{6.9}$$

Notice that the variables $n_t(j_t)$ and the parameters P_{ij} satisfy the relationships:

$$\begin{aligned} n &= \sum_j n_t(j), \\ 1 &= \sum_j P_{ij}, \quad \forall i, \end{aligned}$$

and we can now apply ordinary least squares to equation (6.9) with the observations $n_t(j)$ corresponding to $j = 1, \ldots, J-1$. The parameters P_{ij}, for a given j, occur only in equations in which the endogenous variable assumes the value $n_t(j) = 1, \ldots, T$, so we may limit our attention to these equations to obtain the o.l.s. estimators. This model can be written in matrix form:

$$\begin{bmatrix} n_1(j) \\ n_2(j) \\ \vdots \\ n_T(j) \end{bmatrix} = \begin{bmatrix} n_0(1) & n_0(2) & \cdots & n_0(J-1) \\ n_1(1) & n_1(2) & \cdots & n_1(J-1) \\ \vdots & \vdots & \ddots & \vdots \\ n_{T-1}(1) & n_{T-1}(2) & \cdots & n_{T-1}(J-1) \end{bmatrix}$$

$$\times \begin{bmatrix} P_{1j} \\ P_{2j} \\ \vdots \\ P_{J-1,j} \end{bmatrix} + \begin{bmatrix} \epsilon_1(j) \\ \epsilon_2(j) \\ \vdots \\ \epsilon_T(j) \end{bmatrix}, \tag{6.10}$$

or, simplifying notation:

$$n(j) = \tilde{n} P_j + \epsilon(j).$$

The o.l.s. estimator for P_j is then:

$$\hat{P}_j = \left(\tilde{n}'\tilde{n}\right)^{-1} \tilde{n}' n(j). \tag{6.11}$$

This estimator is consistent but not asymptotically efficient, since the information contained in the conditional variance-covariance matrix of the disturbance term has not been incorporated.

In order to rectify this and improve our estimate we can perform the following three operations.

(i) Estimate P_j with ordinary least squares, yielding $\hat{P}_{ij}$.
(ii) Replace P_{ij} with $\hat{P}_{ij}$ in expression (6.10) to calculate an estimator of the conditional covariance matrix of the error term. The conditional variance for $\epsilon_t(j)$ is thus estimated with:

$$\widehat{\text{var}}\left[\epsilon_t(j) | n_{t-1}(i), i = 0, \ldots, J-1\right] = \sum_{i=1}^{J-1} \hat{P}_{ij}\left(1 - \hat{P}_{ij}\right) n_{t-1}(i),$$

and the covariances are:

$$\widehat{\text{cov}}\left[\epsilon_t(j), \epsilon_t(k) | n_{t-1}(i), i = 0, \ldots, J-1\right]$$
$$= \sum_{i=1}^{J-1} \left[-\hat{P}_{ij}\hat{P}_{ik} n_{t-1}(i)\right].$$

(iii) Apply generalized least squares to the model (6.9) with observations $n_t(j), t = 1, \ldots, T, j = 1, \ldots J-1$, by replacing the covariance matrix with its estimator from step (ii).

6.3.2 Macro Data and Incomplete Panel Data

In this case we still have data for the various values of the qualitative dependent variables, but we no longer take the values from the same sample on each date. More precisely, we consider an infinity of independent realizations of a homogeneous Markov chain $y_{it}, t = 1, \ldots, T, i \in I$ (where I is an infinite set) for each date t. We draw a sample of size m_t independently and equi-probably and observe the distribution of the elements of the sample from the values they assume. Denote $m_t(j)$ the number of individuals in the sample for whom y_t takes the value j. Clearly:

$$\sum_{j=0}^{J-1} m_t(j) = m_t.$$

Because the samples are drawn independently, the random vectors:

$$[m_t(0), \ldots, m_t(J-1)], \quad t = 1, \ldots, T,$$

are independent. The distribution of each of these vectors is multinomial with parameters $m_t, [P_t(0), \ldots, P_t(J-1)]$.

Remark 8: The parameters are $P_t(0), \ldots, P_t(J-1)$ because the universe I has an infinite number of members. If this universe had only a finite number of elements, N, the $P_t(j)$-s would be replaced with $\frac{N_t(j)}{N}$, where $N_t(j)$ is the number of individuals in I for whom $y_t = j$ (cf. McRae [McR77]). Since the $N_t(j)$-s are stochastic, this would complicate the analysis. From a practical perspective, if the sample size is large, the universe is even larger and there is no appreciable difference between the two approaches.

The distribution of the observations is easily found to be:

$$\prod_{t=1}^{T} \left\{ \frac{m_t!}{\prod_{j=0}^{J-1} m_t(j)!} \prod_{j=0}^{J-1} [P_t(j)]^{m_t(j)} \right\}.$$

Unfortunately, this expression is still complicated in the parameters [which, you will recall, are the initial probabilities, $P_0(j)$, and the transition] probabilities. Thus, in the case of a homogeneous chain, the parameters enter into

$P_t(j)$ in the form:

$$P_t(j) = \sum_{i_1=0}^{J-1} P_{i_1 j} P_{t-1}(i_1),$$
$$= \sum_{i_1=0}^{J-1} \sum_{i_2=0}^{J-1} \dots \sum_{i_t=0}^{J-1} P_{i_1 j} P_{i_2 i_1} \dots P_{i_t i_{t-1}} P_0(i_t).$$

Application of the maximum-likelihood method is thus hopeless when the number T is too large.

Another approach is to write the relationship:

$$P_t(j) = \sum_{i=0}^{J-1} P_{ij} P_{t-1}(i),$$

and replace the theoretical probabilities $P_t(j)$ in this equation with the observed frequencies:

$$\hat{P}_t(j) = \frac{m_t(j)}{m_t}.$$

This yields a linear model of the type:

$$\hat{P}_t(j) = \sum_{i-1}^{J-1} P_{ij} \hat{P}_{t-1}(i) + \epsilon_t(j). \tag{6.12}$$

What can we say about the disturbance term $\epsilon_t(j)$? Its mean is zero because:

$$\mathrm{E}[\epsilon_t(j)] = P_t(j) - \sum_{i=1}^{J-1} P_{ij} P_{t-1}(i) = 0.$$

It is also correlated with the variables $\hat{P}_{t-1}(i)$. We see this from the expression for the error:

$$\epsilon_t(j) = \hat{P}_t(j) - \sum_{i=0}^{J-1} P_{ij} \hat{P}_{t-1}(i),$$

and from the fact that $\hat{P}_t(j)$ is independent of $\hat{P}_{t-1}(i)$. This model is thus characterized by errors in the variables. However, as $m_t \to \infty, \forall t$, $\hat{P}_t(j)$ tends towards $P_t(j)$, $\hat{P}_{t-1}(j)$ towards $P_{t-1}(j)$, and $\epsilon_t(j)$ towards zero. Even though this is a model of errors in the variables, the o.l.s. estimator of P_{ij} derived from equation (6.12) (written for the indices $j = 1, \dots, J-1, t = 1, \dots, T$) is consistent. To give a more rigorous demonstration of this result, consider the form of this estimator:

$$\begin{pmatrix} \hat{P}_{0j} \\ \vdots \\ P_{J-1,j} \end{pmatrix} = \left[\begin{pmatrix} \hat{P}_0(0) & \cdots & \hat{P}_0(J-1) \\ \vdots & \ddots & \vdots \\ \hat{P}_{T-1}(0) & \cdots & \hat{P}_{T-1}(J-1) \end{pmatrix}' \right.$$

$$\left. \times \begin{pmatrix} \hat{P}_0(0) & \cdots & \hat{P}_0(J-1) \\ \vdots & \ddots & \vdots \\ \hat{P}_{T-1}(0) & \cdots & \hat{P}_{T-1}(J-1) \end{pmatrix} \right]^{-1}$$

$$\times \begin{pmatrix} \hat{P}_0(0) & \cdots & \hat{P}_0(J-1) \\ \vdots & \ddots & \vdots \\ \hat{P}_{T-1}(0) & \cdots & \hat{P}_{T-1}(J-1) \end{pmatrix}' \begin{pmatrix} \hat{P}_1(j) \\ \vdots \\ \hat{P}_T(j) \end{pmatrix}.$$

Since $\hat{P}_t(j)$ converges to $P_t(j)$, we conclude that the o.l.s. estimator converges to:

$$\left[\begin{pmatrix} P_0(0) & \cdots & P_0(J-1) \\ \vdots & \ddots & \vdots \\ P_{T-1}(0) & \cdots & P_{T-1}(J-1) \end{pmatrix}' \right.$$

$$\left. \times \begin{pmatrix} P_0(0) & \cdots & P_0(J-1) \\ \vdots & \ddots & \vdots \\ P_{T-1}(0) & \cdots & P_{T-1}(J-1) \end{pmatrix} \right]^{-1}$$

$$\times \begin{pmatrix} P_0(0) & \cdots & P_0(J-1) \\ \vdots & \ddots & \vdots \\ P_{T-1}(0) & \cdots & P_{T-1}(J-1) \end{pmatrix}' \begin{pmatrix} P_1(j) \\ \vdots \\ P_T(j) \end{pmatrix}.$$

Notice also that we can write:

$$\begin{pmatrix} P_1(j) \\ \vdots \\ P_T(j) \end{pmatrix} = \begin{pmatrix} P_0(0) & \cdots & P_0(J-1) \\ \vdots & \ddots & \vdots \\ P_{T-1}(0) & \cdots & P_{T-1}(J-1) \end{pmatrix} \begin{pmatrix} P_{0j} \\ \vdots \\ P_{J-1,j} \end{pmatrix}.$$

From this expression we can conclude that the o.l.s. estimators converge to the true values of the transition probabilities.

These estimators can be improved if we account for the information contained in the covariance matrix of $\epsilon_t(j)$ (cf. exercise 4). Because the expression for this matrix includes the unknown transition probabilities we begin by estimating them. One possible approach is as follows:

(i) Apply o.l.s. to equation (6.12) to obtain consistent estimators of the transition probabilities P_{ij}.
(ii) Find the covariance matrix for:

$$\epsilon_t(j) = \hat{P}_t(j) - \sum_{i=0}^{J-1} P_{ij} \hat{P}_{t-1}(i).$$

This matrix, depending on the quantities P_{ij} and $P_t(j)$, is estimated by replacing P_{ij} with its estimator derived in the preceding step, and replacing $P_t(j)$ by $\hat{P}_t(j)$.
(iii) Apply weighted least squares to equation (6.12) using our results from the previous step as the covariance matrix.

This estimation procedure yields asymptotically efficient estimators. (Gourieroux-Monfort-Trognon [GMT85]).

6.4 Transition Probabilities Depending on the Explanatory Variables

As the purpose of this book is to study models with explanatory variables, we shall consider transition probabilities which are functions of exogenous variables for an individual i at time t.

To simplify notation, we write the transition probabilities in logistic form. Thus, $P_{ijj'}(t)$, represents the probability that an individual i passes from state j to state j' during the interval between $t-1$ and t. This is written:

$$P_{ijj'}(t) = \frac{e^{x_{itjj'} b_{jj'}}}{\sum_{j'=0}^{J-1} e^{x_{itjj'} b_{jj'}}}.$$

Each row of the transition matrix constitutes a probability distribution, and is modelled with the logistic formulation. In order to ensure that the model is identified, we set $b_{j0} = 0, \forall j = 0, \ldots, J-1$. The explanatory variables generally depend on the states between which the transition takes place, j and j'.

We see that, in the dichotomous case, $j = 2$, the model is perfectly defined by:

$$P_{i01}(t) = \frac{e^{x_{it01} b_{01}}}{1 + e^{x_{it01} b_{01}}},$$

$$P_{i11}(t) = \frac{e^{x_{it11} b_{11}}}{1 + e^{x_{it11} b_{11}}},$$

where $i = 1, \ldots, n$, $t = 1, \ldots T$.

From here on we shall assume that the behaviour of different individuals is independent and is a function of the values of the exogenous variables.

6.4.1 *The Case of Micro Data*

Letting $n_{i,0\ldots T}(j_0, \ldots, j_T)$ represent a variable assuming the value one (1) if $y_{i0} = j_0, \ldots, y_{iT} = j_T$, and the value zero (0) otherwise, the distribution function for the observations:

$$n_{i0\ldots T}(j_0 \ldots j_T), \quad i = 1, \ldots, n, \quad \{j_0, \ldots, j_T\} = 0, \ldots, J-1,$$

conditional on the original state, is given by:

$$\prod_{i=1}^{n} \prod_{j_1 \ldots j_T} \left[P_{ij_0j_1}(1)\, P_{ij_1j_2}(2), \ldots, P_{ij_{T-1}j_T}(T)\right]^{n_{i,0,\ldots,T}(j_0,\ldots,j_T)}.$$

The log-likelihood is:

$$\begin{aligned}\log(L) &= \sum_{i=1}^{n} \sum_{j_1 \ldots j_T} n_{i0,\ldots,T}(j_0 \ldots j_T) \left\{\log\left[P_{ij_0j_1}(1)\right]\right. \\ &\quad \left. + \log\left[P_{ij_1j_2}(2)\right] + \ldots + \log\left[P_{ij_{T-1}j_T}(T)\right]\right\}, \\ &= \sum_{j} \sum_{j'} \log\left(L_{jj'}\right),\end{aligned}$$

where:

$$\begin{aligned}\log\left(L_{jj'}\right) &= \sum_{i} n_{i-1}(jj') \log\left[P_{ijj'}(1)\right] \\ &\quad + \sum_{i} n_{i12}(jj') \log\left[P_{ijj'}(2)\right] \\ &\quad + \ldots + \sum_{i} n_{i,T-1,T}(jj') \log\left[P_{ijj'}(T)\right],\end{aligned}$$

with:

$$n_{i,t-1,t}(jj') = \begin{cases} 1, & \text{if} \quad y_{i,t-1} = j \quad \text{and} \quad y_{i,t} = j', \\ 0, & \text{otherwise.}\end{cases}$$

Assuming that the parameters $\mathbf{b}_{jj'}$ are linearly independent, we see that $\sum_{j'} \log\left(L_{jj'}\right)$ depends only on the parameters $\mathbf{b}_{jj'}$, $j' = 1, \ldots, J-1$, and we can maximize the elements of $\sum_{j'} \log\left(L_{jj'}\right)$ individually. Clearly, this maximization results in nonlinear equations which must be solved using numeric methods.

As is usual in models of qualitative dependent variables, the quest for asymptotically efficient estimators is facilitated when we have repeated observations. This occurs when the number of different values assumed by the explanatory variables $x_{itjj'}$ is small relative to the number of observations $n(T+1)J^2$, in particular when the vector multiplication $x_{itjj'}\mathbf{b}_{jj'}$ is of the form $x_{ijj'}\alpha_{jj'} +$

$z_{tjj'}\beta_{jj'}$ where the vector $\mathbf{x}$ assumes K values $\tilde{\mathbf{x}}_k$, $k = 1, \ldots, K$ and where K is small relative to n (incorporating cross effects increases the number of values assumed by the explanatory variables considerably.)

The set of observations can be partitioned into K subsets $\wp_k$, $k = 1, \ldots, K$, corresponding to the individuals for whom $\mathbf{x}_i = \tilde{\mathbf{x}}_k$. Denote n_k the number of individuals in $\wp_k$, $n_{k,t-1,t}(j, j')$ the number of individuals in this subpopulation for whom $y_{it-1} = j$ and $y_{it} = j'$, and $n_{k,t-1}(j)$ the number for whom $y_{it-1} = j$.

The log-likelihood is:

$$\log(L) = \sum_{k=1}^{K} \sum_{t=1}^{T} \sum_{j,j'} n_{k,t-1,t}(j, j') \log\left[P_{k_{jj'}}(t)\right].$$

This reveals that, as in section 6.2.1, the values:

$$\hat{P}_{kjj'}(t) = \frac{n_{k,t-1,t}(j, j')}{n_{k,t-1}(j)},$$

constitute a family of exhaustive statistics for the parameters α and β from the expression for the transition probabilities.

As a consequence, when the n_k-s are large for all $k = 1, \ldots K$, we can base the estimation directly on the asymptotic distribution of the $\hat{P}_{kjj'}(t)$-s. According to proposition 17, we know that for different k, j, or t the variables $\hat{P}_{kjj'}(t)$ are asymptotically independent, and that:

$$\sqrt{n_k \hat{P}_{k,t-1}(j)} \begin{bmatrix} \hat{P}_{kj0}(t) - P_{kj0}(t) \\ \vdots \\ \hat{P}_{kj,J-1}(t) - P_{kj,J-1}(t) \end{bmatrix}$$

$$\sim^{asy} N\left[\begin{pmatrix} 0 \\ \vdots \\ 0 \end{pmatrix}, \quad \Lambda_{kj}(t)\right],$$

where:

$$\Lambda_{kj}(t)$$

$$= \begin{bmatrix} P_{kj0}(t)\left[1 - P_{kj0}(t)\right] & \cdots & \\ \vdots & \cdots & \\ -P_{kjj'}(t)\, P_{kjj''}(t) & \ddots & \\ \vdots & & P_{kj,J-1}(t)\left[1 - P_{kj,J-1}(t)\right] \end{bmatrix}.$$

We can apply the maximum-likelihood method to this asymptotically normal model. The estimation procedure is minimum chi-square.

It is preferable in this case, however, to generalize the Berkson method and estimate the asymptotic distribution of:

$$\begin{bmatrix} \log\left[\frac{\hat{P}_{kj1}(t)}{\hat{P}_{kj0}(t)}\right] \\ \vdots \\ \log\left[\frac{\hat{P}_{kj,J-1}(t)}{\hat{P}_{kj0}(t)}\right] \end{bmatrix}.$$

Since:

$$\begin{bmatrix} \log\left[\frac{\hat{P}_{kj1}(t)}{\hat{P}_{kj0}(t)}\right] \\ \vdots \\ \log\left[\frac{\hat{P}_{kj,J-1}(t)}{\hat{P}_{kj0}(t)}\right] \end{bmatrix} = \begin{bmatrix} x_{kj1}\alpha_{j1} + z_{tj1}\beta_{j1} \\ \vdots \\ x_{kj,J-1}\alpha_{j,J-1} + z_{tj,J-1}\beta_{j,J-1} \end{bmatrix},$$

the vector:

$$\sqrt{n_k \hat{P}_{k,t-1}(j)} \begin{bmatrix} \log\left[\frac{\hat{P}_{kj1}(t)}{\hat{P}_{kj0}(t)}\right] - x_{kj1}\alpha_{j1} - z_{tj1}\beta_{j1} \\ \vdots \\ \log\left[\frac{\hat{P}_{kj,J-1}(t)}{\hat{P}_{kj0}(t)}\right] - x_{kj,J-1}\alpha_{j,J-1} - z_{tj,J-1}\beta_{j,J-1} \end{bmatrix}$$

is asymptotically normal $N\left[0; \Omega_{kj}(t)\right]$ where $\Omega_{kj}(t) = A_{kj}(t)' \Lambda_{kj} A_{kj}(t)$. The matrix $A_{kj}(t)$ contains the partial derivatives of the transformed variables with respect to the original ones:

$$A_{kj}(t) = \begin{bmatrix} -\frac{1}{P_{kj0}(t)} & -\frac{1}{P_{kj0}(t)} & \cdots & -\frac{1}{P_{kj0}(t)} \\ \frac{1}{P_{kj1}(t)} & 0 & \cdots & \vdots \\ 0 & \frac{1}{P_{kj2}(t)} & \cdots & \vdots \\ \vdots & \vdots & \ddots & \vdots \\ 0 & 0 & \cdots & \frac{1}{P_{kj,J-1}(t)} \end{bmatrix}.$$

This new, asymptotically equivalent normal model is linear in the parameters α and β, so they can be estimated asymptotically efficiently using generalized least squares with the estimates $\hat{P}_{kjj'}(t)$ replacing the unknown $P_{kjj'}(t)$-s in $\Omega_{kj}(t)$ [GMT85].

Let's illustrate with the dichotomous case. After transformation we have:

$$\log\left[\frac{P_{k01}(t)}{P_{k00}(t)}\right] = x_{k01}\alpha_{01} + z_{t01}\beta_{01} + \epsilon_{k01}(t),$$

and

$$\log\left[\frac{P_{k11}(t)}{P_{k10}(t)}\right] = x_{k11}\alpha_{11} + z_{t11}\beta_{11} + \epsilon_{k11}(t).$$

The error terms are asymptotically independent with variance:

$$\mathrm{var}\left[\epsilon_{k01}(t)\right] = \frac{1}{n_k P_{k,t-1}(0)\, P_{k01}(t)\left[1 - P_{k01}(t)\right]},$$

$$\mathrm{var}\left[\epsilon_{k11}(t)\right] = \frac{1}{n_k P_{k,t-1}(1)\, P_{k11}(t)\left[1 - P_{k11}(t)\right]}.$$

We see that, in order to estimate the parameters $(\alpha_{01}, \beta_{01})$ and $(\alpha_{11}, \beta_{11})$, we individually estimate two separate simple dichotomous logit models (cf. chapter 2).

6.4.2 *The Case of Macro Data*

We shall limit our analysis to the case of complete panel data and assume that we have repeated observations. A relationship analogous to equation (6.9) can be postulated:

$$n_{kt}\left(j'\right) = \sum_{j=0}^{J-1} P_{kjj'}(t)\, n_{k,t-1}(j) + \epsilon_{kt}\left(j'\right),$$

$$j' = 1, \ldots, J-1, \quad t = 1, \ldots, T. \qquad (6.13)$$

A consistent estimator for the parameters $\alpha_{jj'}, \beta_{jj'}, j = 0, \ldots, J-1$ can be found using nonlinear least squares. We minimize the expression:

$$\sum_{k=1}^{K}\sum_{t=1}^{T}\left[n_{kt}\left(j'\right) - \sum_{j=0}^{J-1} P_{kjj'}(t)\, n_{k,t-1}(j)\right]^2, \quad j = 1, \ldots, J-1$$

with respect to $\alpha_{jj'}$ and $\beta_{jj'}$.

A particularly interesting case arises when all of the Markov chains are homogeneous, i.e. when the transition probabilities do not depend on time t. Under these conditions we can find an efficient estimator for $\alpha_{jj'}$. First of all, ignoring the logistic form of the transition probabilities, we find efficient and consistent estimators for the probabilities (denoted $\hat{P}_{kjj'}$) using the method described at the end of section 6.3.1. Next we use these estimators to construct an approximately linear model and to estimate the α_{jj}-s using a Berkson-type approach. This involves applying generalized least squares to the model:

$$\log\left(\frac{\hat{P}_{kjj'}}{\hat{P}_{kj0}}\right) = x_{kjj'}\alpha_{jj'} + u_{kjj'}, \begin{cases} j' = 1, \ldots, J-1, \\ j = 0, \ldots, J-1, \\ k = 1, \ldots, K. \end{cases}$$

6.5 Applications

In its most complete form, with variables indexed on time, the model developed in the preceding section has not yet been employed. Applications to date have essentially involved individual qualitative explanatory variables. This allows the model to be reduced to a homogeneous Markov chain for each category of individual.

Among possible uses for this model, we shall look at a study of unemployment and a dynamic approach to disequilibrium issues.

6.5.1 Unemployment Survey

Some agencies responsible for allocating unemployment insurance premiums keep records with panel-type data on recipients. For each individual, data may include information on items such as current job status: unemployed (receiving premiums) or employed (not receiving premiums), and a profile of the individual's characteristics – age, level of education, participation in training courses, etc. In addition to allowing for analysis of the bearing of certain individual characteristics ($\mathbf{x}_i$) or macroeconomic indicators ($\mathbf{z}_t$) on unemployment rates, this data can be analysed using a Markov chain and yield some very interesting and intuitive statistics.

6.5.1.1 Duration of Unemployment

We may, for example, derive the distribution of the duration of unemployment from knowledge of the transition probabilities. Consider an individual who is working at the date indexed zero and unemployed at time one. Denoting the state of being unemployed zero (0) and of being employed one (1), the duration of unemployment τ equals one with probability:

$$\Pr(\tau = 1) = P_{01}(2).$$

The probability that $\tau = 2$ is given by:

$$\Pr(\tau = 2) = [1 - P_{01}(2)]\, P_{01}(3).$$

And, in general, we have:

$$\Pr(\tau = k) = \prod_{\ell=1}^{k} [1 - P_{01}(\ell)]\, P_{01}(k+1).$$

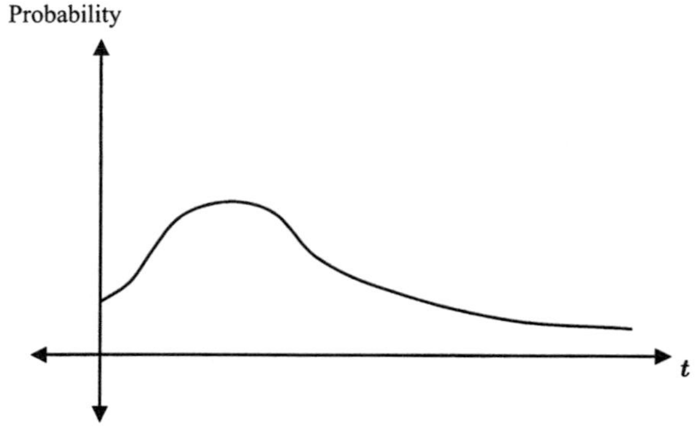

Fig. 6.1. Probability of finding work over time

In the special case of a homogeneous Markov chain this expression simplifies to:

$$\Pr(\tau = k) = (1 - P_{01})^{k-1} P_{01}.$$

So we see that the duration of unemployment follows a geometric distribution.

6.5.1.2 Survival Functions

Another interesting result occurs if we calculate so-called *survival functions* (the name derives from their association with studies of mortality). This type of function yields the probability of finding work following t periods of unemployment. The expression is:

$$\Pr\left(y_{i,t+1} = 1 \middle| y_{i,t} = 0, y_{i,t-1} = 0, \ldots, y_{i,0} = 0 \right).$$

In the case of a first-order Markov chain this reduces to $\Pr\left(y_{i,t+1} = 1 \middle| y_{i,t} = 0 \right)$. Clearly, this expression won't represent a higher-order Markov chain. Calculation of this function gives an idea of how the probability of finding work depends on the length of the preceding period of unemployment. *Ceteris paribus*, this function is graphed as depicted in fig. 6.1. This shape results from the fact that two effects are superimposed:

(i) a positive effect translating the efforts made by the unemployed person.
(ii) a negative impact on potential employers of the duration of unemployment.

These problems can also be studied using continuous time, but the difficulties are at least as great as in the present case. The reader is referred to chapter 12.

Table 6.1. *Marginal Probabilities of IR for different dates*

Date	Sample size	Keynesian unemployment %	Under consumption %	Classical unemployment %	Permanent inflation %
75 03	1,741	67.03	15.51	11.77	5.69
75 06	1,818	69.7	15.51	9.79	5
75 11	1,869	68.27	14.87	11.4	5.46
76 03	1,842	62.81	18.24	11.67	7.28
76 06	1,787	51.82	22.5	13.43	12.25
76 11	1,829	55.28	20.78	13.72	10.22
77 03	1,923	57.88	18.82	14.3	9
77 06	1,917	58.53	18.62	14.45	8.4
77 11	2,119	60.97	18.12	13.07	7.84
78 03	2,013	62.49	18.33	12.57	6.61
78 06	2,031	59.87	18.07	14.33	7.73
78 10	1,785	60.62	17.54	14.73	7.11
79 01	2,036	60.95	16.85	15.28	6.92
79 03	1,988	60.82	15.79	16.35	7.04
79 06	1,965	56.69	15.98	18.73	8.6
79 10	1,996	54.61	16.33	20.14	8.92
80 01	1,919	56.7	16.21	18.86	8.23
80 03	2,031	54.01	16.45	20.38	9.16
80 06	1,957	56.11	16.09	18.65	9.15
80 10	2,015	63.23	16.63	14.14	6
81 01	1,804	69.01	14.63	12.42	3.94
81 03	1,726	71.55	12.57	12.34	3.54
81 06	1,671	73.55	11.19	11.85	3.41
81 10	1,774	70.97	12.63	12.91	3.49
82 01	1,832	70.69	11.68	13.37	4.26
82 03	1,743	69.31	13.42	12.79	4.48
82 06	1,648	63.96	15.53	14.93	5.58

6.5.2 *The Evolution of Disequilibria*

In business cycle surveys corporate executives may be asked about constraints they are experiencing in obtaining supplies, recruiting personnel, in sales, and with credit. *A posteriori*, we can group them according to their responses.

This approach was used by Bouissou, Lafont, and Vuong [BLV86] using French data. The survey questions were:

IQ – "If you were to receive more orders could you increase production with your current capacity?"

If the response is "yes" ($IQ = 1$), that suggests that the company is constrained on the goods market. If the response is "no" ($IQ = 0$), it is not.

IL – "Are you currently experiencing difficulties recruiting?"

If the answer is "yes" ($IL = 1$), the company is probably undergoing difficulties finding suitable employees, if "no" ($IL = 0$) the opposite is true.

With this data we can categorize each company into one of four groups:

$IR = 0$	"Keynesian unemployment,"	if $IQ = 1$ and $IL = 0$,
$IR = 1$	"under-consumption,"	if $IQ = 1$ and $IL = 1$,
$IR = 2$	"classical unemployment,"	if $IQ = 0$ and $IL = 0$,
$IR = 3$	"permanent inflation,"	if $IQ = 0$ and $IL = 1$.

Table 6.1 provides an estimate of the evolution of the marginal probabilities of IR for the periods covered by the survey.

Of greater interest is the estimated matrix of transition probabilities obtained under the assumption of homogeneity:

$$\frac{1}{100}\begin{bmatrix} 85.82 & 24.69 & 24.31 & 12.13 \\ 7.00 & 64.24 & 2.74 & 18.53 \\ 5.73 & 2.32 & 65.45 & 14.51 \\ 1.45 & 8.75 & 7.51 & 54.84 \end{bmatrix}$$

From this matrix we see that there is significant inter-period stability in the classification of the companies. The probabilities of staying in the same group from one period to the next are shown in the diagonal, and we see that these are always quite high. Movement from one regime to another tends to be movement toward "Keynesian unemployment."

Exercises

6.1 Consider the dichotomous model at the end of section 6.4.1. Write out the expression for:

$$\frac{1}{T}\sum_{t=1}^{T}\log\left[\frac{\hat{P}_{k01}(t)}{\hat{P}_{k00}(t)}\right] - \frac{1}{T}\frac{1}{K}\sum_{t=1}^{T}\sum_{k=1}^{K}\log\left[\frac{\hat{P}_{k01}(t)}{\hat{P}_{k00}(t)}\right].$$

What are the properties of the estimator for α_{01} obtained by regressing this value on an explanatory variable defined:

$$x_{k01} - \frac{1}{K}\sum_{k=1}^{K} x_{k01}\,?$$

6.2 Let:

$$\log\left[\frac{\hat{P}_{k01}(t)}{\hat{P}_{k00}(t)}\right] = x_{k01}\alpha_{01t} + z_{t01}\beta_{01k} + \epsilon_{k01}(t)$$

represent a dichotomous model in which the parameters α are functions of time and β functions of the individuals' characteristics. Count the number of parameters and check whether the asymptotic results always obtain. Is it true that the test of the null hypothesis:

$$H_0 : \beta_{01k} = \mathbf{0},$$

where α_{01t} is independent of t, is equivalent to the assumption that the Markov chain corresponding to the k-th sub-population is homogeneous? How can we verify whether the impact of a given explanatory variable decreases over time?

6.3 Assume that the model describing the dichotomous observations is as follows:

$$\log\left[\frac{\hat{P}_{k01}(t)}{\hat{P}_{k00}(t)}\right] = x_{k01}\alpha_{01t} + z_{t01}\beta_{01k} + \epsilon_{k01}(t),$$

but that when estimating β_{01} we omit the term $x_{k01}\alpha_{01}$. Evaluate the resulting bias in the estimator for β_{01} and examine its sign.

6.4 Consider a statistical model with a set of parameters θ. The likelihood equation is:

$$L(\theta) = \prod_{k=1}^{K} L(\theta_k),$$

where the θ_k-s are linearly independent subsets of the parameter vector. Find the form of the matrix of second derivatives of the log-likelihood:

$$\frac{\partial^2 \log[L(\theta)]}{\partial\theta\partial\theta'}.$$

Using this information, show that the Fisher information matrix is block diagonal and that the maximum-likelihood estimators of the θ_k-s are not serially correlated.

6.5 Assume that we have micro-data on a homogeneous Markov chain with transition probabilities P_{ij}. Let $n_{it}(j)$ be a variable assuming the value one (1) if individual i is in state j at time t, and zero (0) otherwise. Verify that we can write:

$$n_{it}(j) = \sum_{j'=0}^{J-1} n_{i,t-1}(j') P_{j'j} + u_{it}(j),$$

where $u_{it}(j)$ is a disturbance term with mean zero.

Calculate the ordinary least squares estimator for $P_{j'j}$ from this model and verify that it is identical to the maximum-likelihood estimator derived from the micro-data.

6.6 Consider a series of $p+1$ random variables $Y_k^0, X_k^1, \ldots, X_k^p$. These vectors are all of the same (fixed) size, and asymptotically ($k \to \infty$):

$$\sqrt{k}\begin{bmatrix} Y_k - Y_\infty \\ X_k^1 - X_\infty^1 \\ X_k^p - X_\infty^p \end{bmatrix} \sim^{asy} N[0, \Omega],$$

where $Y_\infty^0, X_\infty^1, \ldots, X_\infty^p$ are constant unknown vectors satisfying:

$$Y_\infty = X_\infty^1 b_1 + \ldots + X_\infty^p b_p = X_\infty b.$$

Find the best estimator for b from the observations $Y_k, X_k^1, \ldots, X_k^p$. Given a symmetric p-dimensional matrix Λ, consider the estimator:

$$\beta_k(\Lambda) = \left(X_k' \Lambda^{-1} X_k\right)^{-1} X_k' \Lambda^{-1} Y_k.$$

(a) Show that:

$$\sqrt{k}\,[\beta_k(\Lambda) - b] = \left(X_\infty' \Lambda^{-1} X_\infty\right)^{-1} X_\infty' \Lambda^{-1} \sqrt{k}\,(Y_k - X_k b) + o_p$$

where o_p is a negligible residual.

(b) Show that asymptotically:

$$\sqrt{k}\left[\hat{b}_k(\Lambda) - b\right] \sim^{asy} N\left[0, \left(X_\infty' \Lambda^{-1} X_\infty\right)^{-1} X_\infty' \Lambda^{-1} \Sigma \Lambda^{-1} \left(X_\infty' \Lambda^{-1} X_\infty\right)^{-1}\right]$$

where Σ is the asymptotic covariance matrix of:

$$\sqrt{k}\epsilon_k = \sqrt{k}\,(Y_k - X_k b).$$

(c) Verify that the asymptotic variance of $\beta_k(\Lambda)$ is the smallest possible in the class of symmetric matrices for $\Lambda = \Sigma$. What is the corresponding estimator?

(d) Explain how these results apply to the case of incomplete macro panel data described in section 6.3.2.

7 The Tobit Model

7.1 Censored Observations

7.1.1 The Problem

The simple Tobit model was originally introduced to study how households allocate their income to the consumption of durable goods. This type of consumption has the peculiar feature that, at any point in time, expenditure on a given good may be any positive amount, but for many households it will be exactly zero as well. If we plot this type of data with income, y, on the abscissa and expenditure, e, on the ordinate, we obtain one cluster of points representing positive expenditures and another cluster strung along the y axis.

Clearly, a simple linear regression model, such as $e = a + by + u$, is inadequate for at least two reasons:

(i) The scatter diagram will be poorly represented by a function $e = a + by$, since it consists of two distinct parts.
(ii) The usual assumptions about continuously distributed disturbance terms are not appropriate in this situation. For instance, the probability of observing $e = 0$ is not equal to zero.

7.1.2 Evolution of a Stock

The unique form of this cluster of data is due to the fact that we do not observe actual consumption of the durable good, but only instances in which the consumer replenishes his stock. More precisely, let s_{t-1} represent the supply of the good held by the household in period $t-1$ and s_t^* the desired supply (total consumption) for period t. If s_{t-1} is consumed at the rate dv_t, then the following modification of the stock is called for:

$$e_t^* = s_t^* - (s_{t-1} - dv_t)\,.$$

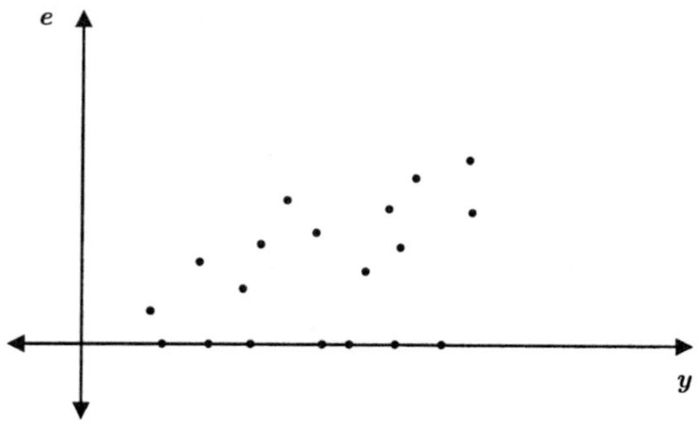

Fig. 7.1. Consumption of durable goods

Purchases for the period, e_t^*, are thus:

$$e_t = \begin{cases} e_t^*, & \text{if } e_t^* \geq 0, \\ 0, & \text{otherwise.} \end{cases}$$

Assuming that s_{t-1} and v_t are known, we may follow the usual procedure of modelling total consumption using a linear specification. We have:

$$e_t = \begin{cases} \mathbf{x_t b} - (s_{t-1} - dv_t) + u_t, & \text{if } \mathbf{x_t b} - (s_{t-1} - dv_t) + u_t \geq 0, \\ 0, & \text{otherwise,} \end{cases}$$

The values assumed by the variables $\mathbf{x_t}$, s_{t-1}, and dv_t will typically vary between households.

7.1.3 A Rationing Model

Rationing is a common phenomenon in economics. For example, we encounter rationing in the availability of certain consumption goods, in ceilings on assistance payments to households and businesses, in wage controls, etc.

Let y_i^* be the optimal choice of y for individual i in the absence of rationing, and assume that the choice of y is constrained to exceed some floor ℓ_i. Under rationing, the amount consumed will be:

$$y_i = \begin{cases} y_i^*, & \text{if } y_i^* \geq \ell_i, \\ \ell_i, & \text{otherwise.} \end{cases}$$

In the aforementioned examples the threshold, ℓ_i, is generally known and we can rewrite the model in terms of the difference $y_i - \ell_i$:

$$y_i - \ell_i = \begin{cases} y_i^* - \ell_i, & \text{if } y_i^* - \ell_i \geq 0, \\ 0, & \text{otherwise.} \end{cases}$$

This new formulation of the model is analogous to that obtained in section 7.1.2. The endogenous variable is always non-negative and assumes the value zero for many of the observations.

7.2 The Simple Tobit Model

7.2.1 Specification of the Model

For each observation i, $i = 1, \ldots, n$, the dependent variable is defined by:

$$y_i = \begin{cases} y_i^*, & \text{if } y_i^* \geq \ell_i, \\ \ell_i, & \text{otherwise}, \end{cases} \tag{7.1}$$

where $y_i^* = \mathbf{x}_i\mathbf{b} + u_i$. $\mathbf{b}$ is a vector of unknown parameters containing K elements, $\mathbf{x}_i$ is a vector comprising observations corresponding to the elements of $\mathbf{b}$, and the ℓ_i-s are the (known) thresholds.

To complete the model we have to specify the distribution of the error terms, u_i. We assume that these are independent and have conditional density functions f and distributions F which are the same for each u_i up to a scaling parameter s:

$$\frac{u_i}{s} \sim f.$$

The distribution of y_i is given by:

$$\begin{aligned} \Pr(y_i = \ell_i) &= \Pr\left(y_i^* < \ell_i\right), \\ &= \Pr\left(\frac{u_i}{s} < \frac{\ell_i}{s} - \frac{\mathbf{x}_i\mathbf{b}}{s}\right), \\ &= F\left(\frac{\ell_i}{s} - \frac{\mathbf{x}_i\mathbf{b}}{s}\right). \end{aligned}$$

Its density function on the interval (ℓ_i, ∞) is:

$$\frac{1}{s} f\left(\frac{y_i - \mathbf{x}_i\mathbf{b}}{s}\right).$$

If all the ℓ_i-s have a constant, known value, ℓ, and if the model $y_i^* = \mathbf{x}_i\mathbf{b} + u_i$ includes a constant term, we can simplify equation (7.1) by defining a new dependent variable $\tilde{y}_i = y_i - \ell$, yielding:

$$\tilde{y}_i = \begin{cases} \tilde{y}_i^*, & \text{if } \tilde{y}_i^* \geq 0, \\ 0, & \text{otherwise}, \end{cases} \tag{7.2}$$

with $\tilde{y}_i^* = \mathbf{x}_i\mathbf{b} - \ell + u_i = \mathbf{x}_i\boldsymbol{\beta} + u_i$.

Here we have reverted to a formulation in which the threshold values are identically equal to zero. To simplify the exposition in the remaining sections of this chapter we shall work with this special case.

7.2.2 *Combined Qualitative and Quantitative Models*

The model of equation (7.2) has two components: a qualitative aspect reflected in the division of the values of $\tilde{y}^*$ into strictly positive and zero-valued groups, and a quantitative part describing the range of positive values of $\tilde{y}_i$ for some settings of the index i.

Equation (7.2) can be viewed as a hybrid between standard quantitative regression models and dichotomous qualitative models such as:

$$z_{y_i^*} = \begin{cases} 1, & \text{if } y_i^* \geq 0, \\ 0, & \text{otherwise.} \end{cases}$$

Notice that there exists an inverse relationship between the amount of information we have about the value y^* and the degree to which the model is qualitative.

To analyse this model it seems reasonable to choose a distribution function with simple applications to both its quantitative and its qualitative aspects. The usual choice is the standard normal distribution (denoted Φ for the distribution function and φ for the density function), yielding the *Tobit Model.* Other distributions have been proposed, however – the logistic distribution (the qualitative aspect is then a logit model), the log-normal distribution (Amemiya-Boskin [AB74]), and the normal distribution subject to a Box-Cox transformation (Poirier [Poi77]), but these variations are rarely used.

7.2.3 *The Latent Variable*

The Tobit model is based on a variable (y^*) which is not always observed (the *latent* variable). Assumptions about its distribution cannot be tested with confidence from our observations on y. We find, however, that this variable is crucial for our analysis. Not only is it the introduction of the latent variable which allows us to formulate models of phenomena such as those described in sections 7.1.2 and 7.1.3, but it is required if we want to try and answer questions like "How does the fact that a household is not purchasing any of the good affect the rate at which it is running down its stock?" or "For how long will this household refrain from buying this good?" or "What impact will raising the ceiling have on social assistance disbursements?"

7.3 Least Squares Estimation

Even though the expression in equation (7.2) is not a linear regression model, we can estimate the parameter **b** by applying ordinary least squares to the entire sample or only to values for which $y_i > 0$ – the *complete observations.* Either procedure yields biased estimators, so we need to examine other techniques. This will be our focus in the following sections.

7.3.1 Application of O.L.S. to the Entire Sample

The ordinary least squares formulation is:

$$\beta = \left[\sum_{i=1}^{n} \mathbf{x}_i'\mathbf{x}_i\right]^{-1} \sum_{i=1}^{n} \mathbf{x}_i' y_i .$$

To find its expectation we require $\mathrm{E}[y_i]$. Using formulas from appendix 7.1, we obtain:

$$\mathrm{E}[y_i] = \mathrm{E}\left[(\mathbf{x}_i\mathbf{b} + u_i)\, z_{\mathbf{x}_i\mathbf{b}+u_i}\right],$$

or:

$$\mathrm{E}[y_i] = \mathbf{x}_i\mathbf{b}\Phi\left(\frac{\mathbf{x}_i\mathbf{b}}{s}\right) + s\varphi\left(\frac{\mathbf{x}_i\mathbf{b}}{s}\right).$$

Clearly $\mathrm{E}[\beta]$ is a nonlinear function of $\mathbf{b}$ and hence cannot be equal to $\mathbf{b}$; thus β is biased. This bias can be either positive or negative as demonstrated by the following example.

Given a model with a single explanatory variable ($K = 1$) we have:

$$\beta = \frac{\sum_{i=1}^{n} x_i y_i}{\sum_{i=1}^{n} x_i^2}.$$

If all the values of x_i, and the true value of b, are positive, we see that:

$$\mathrm{E}(\beta) = \frac{\sum_{i=1}^{n} x_i \mathrm{E}(\mathbf{y}_i)}{\sum_{i=1}^{n} x_i^2} \geq \frac{\sum_{i=1}^{n} x_i^2 b}{\sum_{i=1}^{n} x_i^2} = b.$$

Since $\mathrm{E}(y_i) \geq x_i b, \forall i$, b is overestimated. Conversely, if all values of x_i are negative b is underestimated.

7.3.2 Application of O.L.S. to the Complete Observations

The ordinary least squares formulation is:

$$\beta = \left(\sum_{i|y_i>0} \mathbf{x}_i'\mathbf{x}_i\right)^{-1} \left(\sum_{i|y_i>0} \mathbf{x}_i' y_i\right),$$

and its distribution is determined conditional on the fact that y_i is strictly positive for the retained observations:

$$\mathrm{E}(\beta) = \left(\sum_{i|y_i>0} \mathbf{x}_i'\mathbf{x}_i\right)^{-1} \sum_{i|y_i>0} \mathbf{x}_i'\mathrm{E}(y_i|\, y_i > 0).$$

Now it remains to calculate $\mathrm{E}(y_i \mid y_i > 0)$. The conditional distribution of y_i, given that $y_i > 0$ is continuous over the positive real numbers, yields the density function:

$$\frac{1}{s}\varphi\left(\frac{y_i - \mathbf{x}_i\mathbf{b}}{s}\right)\frac{1}{\Phi\left(\frac{\mathbf{x}_i\mathbf{b}}{s}\right)}.$$

The mean is derived in appendix 7.1:

$$\mathrm{E}(y_i \mid y_i > 0) = \mathbf{x}_i\mathbf{b} + s\frac{\varphi\left(\frac{\mathbf{x}_i\mathbf{b}}{s}\right)}{\Phi\left(\frac{\mathbf{x}_i\mathbf{b}}{s}\right)}.$$

Again we find that the ordinary least-squares estimator is biased, and that the bias may be negative or positive.

7.4 The Likelihood Function of the Simple Tobit Model

7.4.1 The Likelihood Function

Denote J_0 (J_1) the set of indices (i) for which $y_i = 0$ ($y_i > 0$). These sets contain n_0 and n_1 elements respectively.

Since the variables y_i are independent, the likelihood L is obtained by finding the product of the marginal distributions of the observations:

$$\begin{aligned} L &= \prod_{i \in J_0} \Phi\left(\frac{-\mathbf{x}_i\mathbf{b}}{s}\right) \prod_{i \in J_1} \frac{1}{s}\left[\varphi\left(\frac{y_i - \mathbf{x}_i\mathbf{b}}{s}\right)\right], \\ &= \prod_{i \in J_0} \Phi\left(\frac{-\mathbf{x}_i\mathbf{b}}{s}\right) \prod_{i \in J_1} \left\{\frac{1}{s\sqrt{2\pi}} \exp\left[-\frac{1}{2}\left(\frac{y_i - \mathbf{x}_i\mathbf{b}}{s}\right)^2\right]\right\}. \end{aligned}$$

The log-likelihood is easily derived:

$$\log(L) = \sum_{i \in J_0} \Phi\left(-\frac{\mathbf{x}_i\mathbf{b}}{s}\right) - \frac{n_1}{2}\log\left(2\pi s^2\right) - \frac{1}{2s^2}\sum_{i \in J_1}(y_i - \mathbf{x}_i\mathbf{b})^2.$$

7.4.2 Derivatives of the Log-likelihood

In order to simplify notation we adopt the following convention:

$$\begin{aligned} \Phi_i &= \Phi\left(\frac{-\mathbf{x}_i\mathbf{b}}{s}\right), \\ \varphi_i &= \frac{1}{s}\varphi\left(\frac{\mathbf{x}_i\mathbf{b}}{s}\right), \\ &= \frac{1}{s}\varphi\left(\frac{-\mathbf{x}_i\mathbf{b}}{s}\right). \end{aligned}$$

The first derivatives with respect to $\mathbf{b}$ and s^2 are:

$$\begin{aligned}\frac{\partial \log(L)}{\partial \mathbf{b}} &= -\sum_{J_0} \frac{\varphi_i}{\Phi_i}\mathbf{x}_i' + \frac{1}{s^2}\sum_{J_1}(y_i - \mathbf{x}_i\mathbf{b})\,\mathbf{x}_i', \\ \frac{\partial \log(L)}{\partial s^2} &= \frac{1}{2s^2}\sum_{J_0}\mathbf{x}_i\mathbf{b}\frac{\varphi_i}{\Phi_i} - \frac{n_1}{2s^2} + \frac{1}{2s^4}\sum_{J_1}(y_i - \mathbf{x}_i\mathbf{b})^2.\end{aligned} \tag{7.3}$$

The second-order partial derivatives are given by:

$$\frac{\partial^2 \log(L)}{\partial \mathbf{b}\partial \mathbf{b}'} = -\sum_{J_0}\frac{\varphi_i}{\Phi_i}\left(\varphi_i - \frac{\Phi_i}{s^2}\mathbf{x}_i\mathbf{b}\right)\mathbf{x}_i'\mathbf{x}_i - \frac{1}{s^2}\sum_{J_1}\mathbf{x}_i'\mathbf{x}_i,$$

$$\frac{\partial^2 \log(L)}{\partial s^2 \partial \mathbf{b}'} = -\frac{1}{2s^2}\sum_{J_0}\frac{\varphi_i}{\Phi_i^2}\left[\frac{\Phi_i}{s^2}(\mathbf{x}_i\mathbf{b})^2 - \Phi_i - \varphi_i\mathbf{x}_i\mathbf{b}\right]\mathbf{x}_i$$

$$-\frac{1}{s^4}\sum_{J_1}(y_i - \mathbf{x}_i\mathbf{b})\,\mathbf{x}_i,$$

$$\frac{\partial^2 \log(L)}{\partial \left(s^2\right)^2} = \frac{1}{4s^4}\sum_{J_0}\frac{\varphi_i}{\Phi_i^2}\left[\frac{\Phi_i}{s^2}(\mathbf{x}_i\mathbf{b})^3 - 3\Phi_i\mathbf{x}_i\mathbf{b} - \varphi_i(\mathbf{x}_i\mathbf{b})^2\right]$$

$$+\frac{n_1}{2s^4} - \frac{1}{s^6}\sum_{J_1}(y_i - \mathbf{x}_i\mathbf{b})^2.$$

7.4.3 *An Interesting Change of Parameters*

In the probit aspect of the Tobit model we can only identify $\frac{\mathbf{b}}{s}$, so this is what we solve for. Letting:

$$\mathbf{c} = \frac{\mathbf{b}}{s} \quad \text{and} \quad h = \frac{1}{s},$$

the log-likelihood is written:

$$\log(L) = \sum_{J_0}\log\left[\Phi(-\mathbf{x}_i\mathbf{c})\right] + n_1\log(h)$$

$$-\frac{n_1}{2}\log(2\pi) - \frac{1}{2}\sum_{J_1}(hy_i - \mathbf{x}_i\mathbf{c})^2.$$

Proposition 20: The log-likelihood is concave in $\mathbf{c}$ and h.

Proof: We know that the function $\log(L)$ is concave, because:

$$\frac{d^2\log[\Phi(x)]}{dx^2} = -\frac{\varphi(x)}{\Phi^2(x)}[x\Phi(x) + \varphi(x)],$$

is always negative. This result follows from the interpretation of $x\Phi(x)+\varphi(x)$ as the primitive of Φ, which is positive:

$$x\Phi(x)+\varphi(x)=\int_{-\infty}^{x}\Phi(t)\,dt.$$

So we see that the log-likelihood is the sum of concave functions, and is hence also concave. □

This translation of the parameters allows us to find much simpler expressions for the derivatives of the log-likelihood function.

For example, we have:

$$\frac{\partial \log(L)}{\partial \mathbf{c}}=-\sum_{J_0}\frac{\varphi(-\mathbf{x}_i\mathbf{c})}{\Phi(-\mathbf{x}_i\mathbf{c})}\mathbf{x}_i'+\sum_{J_1}(hy_i-\mathbf{x}_i\mathbf{c})\,\mathbf{x}_i',$$

$$\frac{\partial \log(L)}{\partial h}=\frac{n_1}{h}-\sum_{J_1}(hy_i-\mathbf{x}_i\mathbf{c})\,y_i,$$

and:

$$\frac{\partial^2 \log(L)}{\partial\mathbf{c}\partial\mathbf{c}'}=\sum_{J_0}\frac{\varphi(-\mathbf{x}_i\mathbf{c})}{\Phi(-\mathbf{x}_i\mathbf{c})}\left[\mathbf{x}_i\mathbf{c}-\frac{\varphi(-\mathbf{x}_i\mathbf{c})}{\Phi(-\mathbf{x}_i\mathbf{c})}\mathbf{x}_i'\mathbf{x}_i-\sum_{J_1}\mathbf{x}_i'\mathbf{x}_i,\right],$$

$$\frac{\partial^2 \log(L)}{\partial h\partial\mathbf{c}'}=\sum_{J_1}y_i\mathbf{x}_i,$$

$$\frac{\partial^2 \log(L)}{\partial h^2}=-\frac{n_1}{h^2}-\sum_{J_1}y_i^2.$$

7.5 The Maximum-Likelihood Method

7.5.1 *Properties of the Maximum-Likelihood Method*

This method yields values of the parameters which maximize the likelihood function or, equivalently, the log of the likelihood function. Denoting ζ and η the estimators for $\mathbf{c}$ and h respectively, proposition 20 reveals that the solution to the likelihood equations:

$$0=\frac{\partial \log(L)}{\partial \mathbf{c}},$$

$$0=\frac{\partial \log(L)}{\partial h},$$

is unique if it exists, and ζ and η are equal to the maximum-likelihood estimators of $\mathbf{c}$ and h.

Consequently, the maximum-likelihood estimators $\mathbf{b}$ and s^2 uniquely solve:

$$0 = \frac{\partial \log(L)}{\partial \mathbf{b}},$$
$$0 = \frac{\partial \log(L)}{\partial s^2},$$

and they satisfy:

$$\beta = \frac{\boldsymbol{\beta}}{\sigma} \quad \text{and} \quad \eta = \frac{1}{\sigma}.$$

As a result, we see that the estimation can proceed using the first-order conditions from differentiation with respect to $\mathbf{b}$ and s^2, or, more simply, with respect to $\mathbf{c}$ and h. Regardless which method is chosen, the first-order conditions cannot be solved analytically – we require numerical methods to find the estimators.

It can be shown that, under classical assumptions, an asymptotic solution to the likelihood equation always exists, and this estimator has the following characteristics:

$$\gamma \to \mathbf{g} \text{ as } n \to \infty, \text{ where:}$$

$$\mathbf{g} = \begin{pmatrix} \mathbf{b} \\ s^2 \end{pmatrix} \text{ or } \begin{pmatrix} \mathbf{c} \\ h \end{pmatrix}, \quad \text{and}$$
$$\gamma = \begin{pmatrix} \boldsymbol{\beta} \\ \sigma^2 \end{pmatrix} \text{ or } \begin{pmatrix} \zeta \\ \eta \end{pmatrix},$$

and

$$\gamma \rightsquigarrow N\left[\mathbf{g}; \mathrm{E}\left(-\frac{\partial^2 \log(L)}{\partial \mathbf{g}\partial \mathbf{g}'}\right)^{-1}\right]$$

It remains to specify the expression for the information matrices.

7.5.1.1 *Using the parameters* $\mathbf{b}$ *and* s^2

We have:

$$\mathrm{E}\left[\frac{-\partial^2 \log(L)}{\partial \mathbf{b}\partial \mathbf{b}'}\right] = \sum_{i=1}^{n}\left[\frac{\varphi_i}{\Phi_i}\left(\varphi_i - \frac{\Phi_i}{s^2}\mathbf{x}_i\mathbf{b}\right) + \frac{1+\Phi_i}{s^2}\right]\mathbf{x}_i'\mathbf{x}_i,$$

$$\mathrm{E}\left[\frac{-\partial^2 \log(L)}{\partial s^2\partial \mathbf{b}'}\right] = \sum_{i=1}^{n}\left\{\frac{1}{2s^2}\frac{\varphi_i}{\Phi_i}\left[\frac{\Phi_i}{s^2}(\mathbf{x}_i\mathbf{b})^2 - \Phi_i - \varphi_i\mathbf{x}_i\mathbf{b}\right] + \frac{\varphi_i}{s^3}\right\}\mathbf{x}_i,$$

$$\mathrm{E}\left[\frac{-\partial^2 \log(L)}{(\partial s^2)^2}\right]$$

$$= \sum_{i=1}^{n}\left\{-\frac{1}{4s^4}\frac{\varphi_i}{\Phi_i}\left[\frac{\Phi_i}{s^2}(\mathbf{x}_i\mathbf{b})^3 - 3\Phi_i\mathbf{x}_i\mathbf{b} - \varphi_i(\mathbf{x}_i\mathbf{b})^2\right]\right.$$

$$\left. - \frac{1-\Phi_i}{2s^4} + \frac{1}{s^6}\left[s^2(1-\Phi_i) - s\mathbf{x}_i\mathbf{b}\varphi_i\right]\right\}.$$

7.5.1.2 Using the parameters **c** *and h*

We have:

$$\mathrm{E}\left[\frac{-\partial^2 \log(L)}{\partial \mathbf{c}\partial \mathbf{c}'}\right] = \sum_{i=1}^{n}\left[-\varphi_i\left(\mathbf{x}_i\mathbf{c} - \frac{\varphi_i}{\Phi_i}\right) + 1 + \Phi_i\right]\mathbf{x}_i'\mathbf{x}_i,$$

$$\mathrm{E}\left[\frac{-\partial^2 \log(L)}{\partial h\partial \mathbf{c}'}\right] = \sum_{i=1}^{n} -\frac{1}{h}\left\{\mathbf{x}_i\mathbf{c}(1-\Phi i) + \varphi_i\right\}\mathbf{x}_i,$$

$$\mathrm{E}\left[\frac{-\partial^2 \log(L)}{\partial h^2}\right] = \sum_{i=1}^{n}\frac{1}{h^2}\left[2(1-\Phi_i) + (\mathbf{x}_i\mathbf{c})^2(1-\Phi_i) + \mathbf{x}_i\mathbf{c}\varphi\right],$$

where $\Phi_i = \Phi(-\mathbf{x}_i\mathbf{c})$ and $\varphi_i = \varphi(-\mathbf{x}_i\mathbf{c})$, as on page 177.

7.5.2 Algorithms

Solutions to the likelihood equations are obtained by iteration. In addition to the standard Newton-Raphson and Berndt-Hall-Hall-Hausman methods, we shall describe an algorithm which is more particularly suited to the Tobit model.

7.5.2.1 The Newton-Ralphson Algorithm

We begin with an arbitrary value for γ_0 and calculate the subsequent values using the following iteration formula:

$$\gamma_{n+1} \approx \gamma_n - \left\{\frac{\partial^2 \log[L(\mathbf{g})]}{\partial\gamma_n\partial\gamma_n'}\right\}^{-1}\frac{\partial \log[L(\mathbf{g})]}{\partial\gamma_n}. \tag{7.4}$$

This algorithm is increasing, as can be seen from proposition 20, so the series γ_n converges to the maximum-likelihood estimator γ.

7.5.2.2 The Berndt-Hall-Hall-Hausman Algorithm
The iterative formula is similar to equation (7.4):

$$\gamma_{n+1} \approx \gamma_n + \left\{ \sum_{i=1}^{n} \frac{\partial \log [L_i (\mathbf{g})]}{\partial \gamma_n} \frac{\partial \log [L_i (\mathbf{g})]}{\partial \gamma_n'} \right\}^{-1} \frac{\partial \log [L (\mathbf{g})]}{\partial \gamma_n},$$

where L_i is the density function for the i-th observation.

This method has the advantage that it only requires first-order partial derivatives. As in the previous case, this algorithm is increasing and hence consistent for the Tobit model.

7.5.2.3 The Fair Algorithm
We can also construct an iterative procedure directly from the likelihood equations:

$$0 = \frac{\partial \log (L)}{\partial \mathbf{c}},$$
$$0 = \frac{\partial \log (L)}{\partial h}.$$

Expressed as functions of $\mathbf{b}$ and s^2, these can be written:

$$\mathbf{b} = \left(\sum_{J_1} \mathbf{x}_i' \mathbf{x}_i \right)^{-1} \sum_{J_1} \mathbf{x}_i' y_i - s \left(\sum_{J_1} \mathbf{x}_i' \mathbf{x}_i \right)^{-1} \left[\sum_{J_0} \frac{\varphi \left(\frac{-\mathbf{x}_i \mathbf{b}}{s} \right)}{\Phi \left(\frac{-\mathbf{x}_i \mathbf{b}}{s} \right)} \mathbf{x}_i' \right],$$
$$s^2 = \frac{1}{n_1} \sum_{J_1} (y_i - \mathbf{x}_i \mathbf{b}) \, y_i,$$

or:

$$b = A_1 \left(\mathbf{b}, s^2 \right),$$
$$s^2 = A_2 (\mathbf{b}),$$

where A_1 and A_2 are known functions. The iterations are performed in the following manner. If β_n and σ_n^2 are the values obtained at the n-th iteration, the subsequent iteration yields:

$$\beta_{n+1} = A_1 \left(\beta_n, \sigma_n^2 \right), \quad \text{and}$$
$$\sigma_{n+1} = A_2 (\beta_{n+1}).$$

This algorithm will not necessarily converge, but when it does the result is the solution to the maximum-likelihood equations.

7.5.3 Finding the Initial Values

Application of the preceding algorithms necessitates selection of an initial value γ_0. The closer this is to the true value $\mathbf{g}$, the faster convergence will occur.

Generally, γ_0 is obtained using a method which is easier to apply, but less precise, than the maximum-likelihood procedure.

In the case of the Tobit model, one of the following methods may be used:

(i) Apply o.l.s. to the set of all observations. The initial bias in γ_0 will disappear when the iterative procedures are applied.
(ii) Apply o.l.s. to the censored observations.

Other methods can be used, but they will not significantly simplify the problem except in the case of repeated observations. For example:

(i) Consider the dichotomous probit model associated with the Tobit model and apply a Berkson-type procedure. Unfortunately, this will only yield an estimate of $\frac{\mathbf{b}}{s}$.
(ii) Apply a two-stage method for each of the quantitative and qualitative parts of the model (cf. section 7.6).
(iii) Apply a moments-based method (cf. section 7.7).

7.6 Two-Stage Estimation

7.6.1 The Method

The Two-stage method essentially consists of successively estimating first the qualitative, and then the quantitative aspects of the model.

7.6.1.1 First Step

The qualitative aspect of the model consists of the probit model with:

$$\Pr\left(z_{y_i} = 1\right) = \Pr\left(y_i > 0\right) = \Phi\left(\mathbf{x}_i \frac{\mathbf{b}}{s}\right) = \Phi\left(\mathbf{x}_i \mathbf{c}\right).$$

c can be estimated using one of the methods from chapter 2 (maximum likelihood, Berkson method, etc.) Let us denote the estimator derived at this stage $\boldsymbol{\zeta}$. It is important to recognize that this first step is simpler than direct maximum-likelihood estimation of the Tobit model in the case of repeated data.

7.6.1.2 Second Step

The quantitative part of the model corresponds to values of y_i for which $i \in J_1$. For these observations we can write:

$$y_i = \mathrm{E}\left(y_i \mid i \in J_1\right) + v_i,$$

where v_i has mean zero. From appendix 7.1:

$$\mathrm{E}\left(y_i \mid i \in J_1\right) = \mathrm{E}\left(y_i \mid y_i > 0\right) = \mathbf{x}_i \mathbf{b} + s \frac{\varphi\left(\frac{\mathbf{x}_i \mathbf{b}}{s}\right)}{\Phi\left(\frac{\mathbf{x}_i \mathbf{b}}{s}\right)}.$$

Replacing this conditional expectation by its expression, we obtain:

$$y_i = \mathbf{x}_i\mathbf{b} + s\frac{\varphi(\mathbf{x}_i\mathbf{c})}{\Phi(\mathbf{x}_i\mathbf{c})} + v_i,$$

or:

$$y_i = \mathbf{x}_i\mathbf{b} + s\frac{\varphi(\mathbf{x}_i\zeta)}{\Phi(\mathbf{x}_i\zeta)} + w_i,$$

where:

$$w_i = v_i + s\left[\frac{\varphi(\mathbf{x}_i\mathbf{c})}{\Phi(\mathbf{x}_i\mathbf{c})} - \frac{\varphi(\mathbf{x}_i\zeta)}{\Phi(\mathbf{x}_i\zeta)}\right].$$

In this formulation the quantitative part of the model appears as a linear function of **b** and s. Since ζ is a consistent estimator of **c**, the disturbance term w_i is asymptotically centered around zero, and the o.l.s. estimators for **b** and s obtained from regressing y on **x** and $\frac{\varphi(\mathbf{x}\zeta)}{\Phi(\mathbf{x}\zeta)}$ for the observations in J_1 converge to the true values asymptotically.

Notice, however, that for finite sample sizes the o.l.s. estimators are biased because the error term w_i is correlated with the explanatory variable $\frac{\varphi(\mathbf{x}_i\zeta)}{\Phi(\mathbf{x}_i\zeta)}$.

7.6.2 Using Weighted Least Squares for the Second Step

For the second step we can improve on the estimation by accounting for the form of the covariance matrix of the disturbance term w_i. We shall present a procedure for repeated observations, as this provides a relatively straightforward application and simple notation.

Let $\theta_j = \frac{n_j}{n}$, $j = 1, \ldots, J$, represent the proportion of independent experiments conducted under environmental conditions $\mathbf{x}_j$. The observations on the endogenous variables are:

$$y_{ij} = \begin{cases} \mathbf{x}_j\mathbf{b} + u_{ij}, & \text{if } \mathbf{x}_j\mathbf{b} + u_{ij} > 0, \\ 0, & \text{otherwise.} \end{cases}$$

For this step the linear model is written:

$$y_{ij} = \mathbf{x}_j\mathbf{b} + s\frac{\varphi(\mathbf{x}_j\zeta)}{\Phi(\mathbf{x}_j\zeta)} + w_{ij}, \quad j = 1, \ldots J, \quad i = 1, \ldots, n_j,$$

for $y_{ij} > 0$.

The explanatory aspect depends only on the index j, so we can group the observations corresponding to similar experiments. Let $\overline{y}_j^c$ represent the average value of the complete observations $(y_{ij} > 0)$ associated with the j-th experiment, and let $\overline{w}_j^c$ be the mean of the corresponding errors. The preceding model's estimate of the parameters is equivalent to:

$$\overline{y}_j^c = \mathbf{x}_j \mathbf{b} + s \frac{\varphi\left(\mathbf{x}_j \zeta\right)}{\Phi\left(\mathbf{x}_j \zeta\right)} + \overline{w}_j^c, \quad j = 1, \ldots, J.$$

Finding the variance-covariance matrix for $\overline{w}_j^c$, $j = 1, \ldots, J$, is somewhat more delicate, as it depends not only on $\overline{y}_j^c$ but also on ζ and on the correlation between ζ and $\overline{y}_j^c$. We simply sketch the procedure here, referring the reader to Heckman [Hec78] for the details.

When n tends to infinity, the asymptotic variance of the disturbance term is given by:

$$\begin{aligned}\mathrm{var}_{asy}\left(\sqrt{n}\overline{w}^c\right) &= D\left[\frac{\Phi^2 - \lambda\varphi}{\theta h^2 \Phi^3}\right] \\ &\quad + \frac{1}{h^2} D\left[\frac{\lambda\varphi}{\Phi^2}\right] X\left(X'\Omega^{-1}X\right)^{-1} X' D\left[\frac{\lambda\varphi}{\Phi^2}\right],\end{aligned}$$

where $D[\cdots]$ is a matrix with the elements in brackets on the diagonal and zeros elsewhere, and where:

$$X = \begin{bmatrix} \mathbf{x}_1 \\ \vdots \\ \mathbf{x}_J \end{bmatrix},$$

$$\Omega = D\left[F\Phi\left(\frac{1-\Phi}{\theta\varphi^2}\right)\right],$$

$$\varphi_j = \varphi\left(\mathbf{x}_j \mathbf{c}\right),$$

$$\Phi_j = \Phi\left(\mathbf{x}_j \mathbf{c}\right),$$

$$\lambda_j = \mathbf{x}_j \mathbf{c} \Phi\left(\mathbf{x}_j \mathbf{c}\right) + \varphi\left(\mathbf{x}_j \mathbf{c}\right).$$

This asymptotic covariance matrix is a function of the parameters $\mathbf{b}$ and s, which are themselves functions of $\mathbf{c}$ and h. To simplify notation we write $A = A(\mathbf{c}, h)$. Before applying generalized least squares to this approximately linear model we must replace the elements of A with their consistent estimators. The resulting matrix is denoted $\hat{A}$.

The two-stage estimator now has the form:

$$\begin{pmatrix} \beta \\ \sigma \end{pmatrix} = \left[(X\psi)' A (X, \psi)\right]^{-1} (X\psi)' \hat{A} \overline{y}_j^c.$$

where ψ is a column vector with elements $\frac{\varphi(\mathbf{x}_j\zeta)}{\Phi(\mathbf{x}_j\zeta)}$. The asymptotic covariance matrix for this estimator is defined by the usual expression:

$$\mathrm{var}_{asy}\left[\sqrt{n}\begin{pmatrix} \beta \\ \sigma \end{pmatrix}\right] = \left[(X\psi)' A^{-1} (X\psi)\right]^{-1}.$$

7.7 The Method of Asymptotic Least Squares

7.7.1 The Gourieroux-Monfort-Trognon [1985] Method

The method of moments provides another useful approach for the case of repeated observations. The "zero-" and first-order moments of y_{ij} are:

$$\begin{aligned} \Pr\left(y_{ij} > 0\right) &= \Phi\left(\frac{\mathbf{x}_j \mathbf{b}}{s}\right), \\ &= \Phi\left(\mathbf{x}_j \mathbf{c}\right), \\ \mathrm{E}\left(y_{ij}\right) &= \mathbf{x}_j \mathbf{b} \Phi\left(\frac{\mathbf{x}_j \mathbf{b}}{s}\right) + s\varphi\left(\frac{\mathbf{x}_j \mathbf{b}}{s}\right), \\ &= \frac{\mathbf{x}_j \mathbf{c}}{h} \Phi\left(\mathbf{x}_j \mathbf{c}\right) + \frac{1}{h}\varphi\left(\mathbf{x}_j \mathbf{c}\right). \end{aligned}$$

These moments can be approximated by the corresponding empirical frequencies:

$$\begin{aligned} \tau_j &= \frac{1}{n_j}\sum_{i=1}^{n_j} y_{ij}, \\ \overline{y}_j &= \frac{1}{n_j}\sum_{i=1}^{n_j} \overline{y}_{ij}. \end{aligned}$$

Thus, when n is sufficiently large, we have:

$$\begin{aligned} \tau_j &\approx \Phi\left(\mathbf{x}_j \mathbf{c}\right), \\ \overline{y}_j &\approx \mathbf{x}_j \frac{\mathbf{c}}{h} \Phi\left(\mathbf{x}_j \mathbf{c}\right) + \frac{1}{h}\varphi\left(\mathbf{x}_j \mathbf{c}\right), \end{aligned}$$

or:

$$\begin{aligned} \Phi^{-1}\left(\tau_j\right) &\approx \mathbf{x}_j \mathbf{c}, \\ h\overline{y}_j &\approx \tau_j \mathbf{x}_j \mathbf{c} + \varphi\left[\Phi^{-1}\left(\tau_j\right)\right]. \end{aligned}$$

Finally, we obtain a model which is linear in the parameters $\mathbf{c}$ and h:

$$\begin{aligned} \Phi^{-1}\left(\tau_j\right) &= \mathbf{x}_j \mathbf{c} + v_j^1, \\ \varphi\left[\Phi^{-1}\left(t_j\right)\right] &= -\tau_j \mathbf{x}_j \mathbf{c} + h\overline{y}_j + v_j^2. \end{aligned} \tag{7.5}$$

Once we have found the asymptotic covariance matrix of $\left(v_j^1, v_j^2\right)$, $j = 1, \ldots, J$, which is easily derived from the corresponding matrix for $\left(\tau_j, \overline{y}\right)$, $j = 1, \ldots, J$, weighted least squares can be applied to equation (7.5). This will yield consistent estimators of $\mathbf{c}$ and h, and, by extension, of $\mathbf{b}$ and s, since $\mathbf{c} = \frac{\mathbf{b}}{s}$ and $h = \frac{1}{s}$.

7.7.1.1 The Asymptotic Covariance Matrix of the Error Term

The disturbance terms $\left(v_j^1, v_j^2\right)$, $j = 1, \ldots, J$, are asymptotically correlated. We have:

$$\text{var}_{asy}\left[\sqrt{n}\begin{pmatrix} v_j^1 \\ v_j^2 \end{pmatrix}\right] = \frac{1}{\theta_j}\begin{pmatrix} \frac{\Phi_j(1-\Phi_j)}{\varphi_j^2} & -\frac{(1-\Phi_j)\lambda_j}{\varphi_j} \\ -\frac{(1-\Phi_j)\lambda_j}{\varphi_j} & \Phi_j + \mathbf{x}_j\mathbf{c}\lambda_j - \lambda_j^2 \end{pmatrix}. \quad (7.6)$$

7.7.2 *The Estimator*

Using Λ to denote the right hand side of equation (7.6), we replace the parameters with their consistent estimators and let $\hat{\Lambda}_j$ be the resulting matrix. The asymptotic least squares estimators for $\mathbf{c}$ and h are given by:

$$\begin{pmatrix} \varsigma \\ \eta \end{pmatrix} = \left(\sum_{j=1}^{J} Q_j' \hat{\Lambda}_j^{-1} Q_j\right)^{-1} \sum_{j=1}^{J} Q_j' \hat{\Lambda}_j^{-1} P_j, \quad (7.7)$$

where:

$$Q_j = \begin{pmatrix} \mathbf{x}_j & 0 \\ -\tau_j \mathbf{x}_j & \bar{y}_j \end{pmatrix},$$

and:

$$P_j = \begin{pmatrix} \Phi^{-1}(\tau_j) \\ \varphi\left[\Phi^{-1}(\tau_j)\right) \end{pmatrix}\Bigg].$$

The asymptotic covariance matrix for expression (7.7) is given by:

$$\text{var}_{asy}\left[\sqrt{n}\begin{pmatrix} \varsigma \\ \eta \end{pmatrix}\right] = \left[\sum_{j=1}^{J} \left(Q_j^{\infty}\right)' \Lambda_j^{-1} Q_j^{\infty}\right]^{-1},$$

where:

$$Q_j^{\infty} \equiv \lim_{n\to\infty} Q_j = \begin{pmatrix} \mathbf{x}_j & 0 \\ -\Phi_j \mathbf{x}_j & \mathrm{E}(y_{ij}) \end{pmatrix}.$$

Expanding this expression, we obtain:

$$\text{var}_{asy}\left[\sqrt{n}\begin{pmatrix} \varsigma \\ \eta \end{pmatrix}\right] = \begin{pmatrix} X'D\left\{\frac{\theta[\Phi(1-\Phi)+\lambda\varphi-\mathbf{x}\mathbf{c}\varphi]}{1-\Phi}\right\}X & X'D\left(-\frac{\theta\lambda}{h}\right)\mathbf{e} \\ \mathbf{e}'D\left(-\frac{\theta\lambda}{h}X\right) & e'D\left[\frac{\theta\Phi\lambda^2}{h^2(\Phi^2-\lambda\varphi)}\right]\mathbf{e} \end{pmatrix}\Bigg]^{-1},$$

where $\mathbf{e}$ is a vector consisting entirely of ones.

7.7.3 Comparison with Other Methods of Estimation

Proposition 21:

(i) The asymptotic least squares estimator is uniformly better than the two-stage estimator.

(ii) The asymptotic least squares estimator permits efficient estimation of a hyperplane of the parameters.

For a detailed proof, see [GMT85].

Obviously, these comparisons are based on the asymptotic properties of the methods, and we may wonder whether the results hold when the number of repetitions for each group is small. Simulations have shown that, in this case, the maximum-likelihood and asymptotic least-squares methods yield similar results. On the other hand, Heckman's method appears to be significantly less precise, particularly for estimation of the standard error, s.

7.8 The Generalized Tobit Model

7.8.1 Expenditure on Durable Goods

In the model of expenditures on durable goods described in section 7.1.2, the consumer simultaneously decided whether or not to purchase a certain good and how much to spend on it. Alternatively, we could assume that these decisions are taken sequentially.

First, the individual chooses whether or not to purchase the good. This decision can be described by a dichotomous qualitative choice model based on some criteria y_{2i}^*:

$$y_{2i}^* \geq 0, \quad \text{individual } i \text{ buys the good,}$$
$$y_{2i}^* < 0, \quad \text{he does not.}$$

Subsequently he determines how much he will spend, y_{1i}^*. The observed variable, y_i, is:

$$y_i = \begin{cases} y_{1i}, & \text{if } y_{2i} \geq 0, \\ 0, & \text{otherwise.} \end{cases} \tag{7.8}$$

This formulation generalizes the simple Tobit model (in which $y_{2i}^* = y_{1i}^*$). In particular, it allows us to analyse the degree of correlation between the two decisions.

7.8.2 Observations on Salaries

Let us examine a model of labour force participation and salary determination. An individual seeking work must determine which jobs to accept and which ones to reject. Let s_{1i}^* represent the salary offered, and s_{2i}^* the salary expected (the reservation wage). She will accept the job if $s_{1i}^* \geq s_{2i}^*$, in which case her salary will be $y_i = s_{1i}^*$. If she rejects the job offer, $s_{1i}^* < s_{2i}^*$, her salary will be $y_i = 0$.

$$y_i = \begin{cases} s_{1i}^*, & \text{if } s_{1i}^* \geq s_{2i}^*, \\ 0, & \text{otherwise.} \end{cases}$$

Given this formulation, we have a simple Tobit model with an unknown threshold s_{2i}^*. If we set $y_{1i}^* = s_{1i}^*$ and $y_{2i}^* = s_{1i}^* - s_{2i}^*$, we can rewrite this model in the form of equation (7.8).

Offered and expected wages are functions of the individual's characteristics. In the case of a married woman, for example, s_1^* may depend upon her level of education, age, etc., while s_2^* reflects the premium she places on staying home, the number of children at home, her husband's income, her age and level of education as well as other factors.

$$\begin{aligned} s_{1i}^* &= \mathbf{x}_{1i}\mathbf{b}_1 + u_{1i}, \\ s_{2i}^* &= \mathbf{x}_{2i}\mathbf{b}_2 + u_{2i}, \end{aligned}$$

where $\mathbf{x}_1$ and $\mathbf{x}_2$ may share some elements.

7.8.3 Non-Response

Frequently individuals will refuse or neglect to answer some questions on a questionnaire. Assume that we wish to find the mean m_1 of some characteristic y_1^*. Some people will not give this information, $y_{1i}^* = m_1 + u_{1i}$, and this propensity to conceal the facts is a function of certain traits $\mathbf{x}_2$. An answer will be provided if $y_{2i}^* = \mathbf{x}_{2i}\mathbf{b}_2 + u_{2i}$ is positive, otherwise not.

The survey results will hence be:

$$y_i = \begin{cases} y_{1i}^*, & \text{if } y_{2i}^* \geq 0, \\ \text{non-response}, & \text{otherwise.} \end{cases}$$

In this example we clearly see an endogenous variable which is both qualitative and quantitative. From here on we shall denote "non-response" as zero for compatibility with previous models.

Let us make the further assumption that the error terms, u_{1i} and u_{2i}, are independently and identically normally distributed:

$$(u_{1i}, u_{2i})' \sim N\left[\begin{pmatrix} 0 \\ 0 \end{pmatrix}, \begin{pmatrix} s_1^2 & rs_1s_2 \\ rs_1s_2 & s_2^2 \end{pmatrix}\right].$$

We can calculate the rate of non-response, τ, for individuals with characteristics

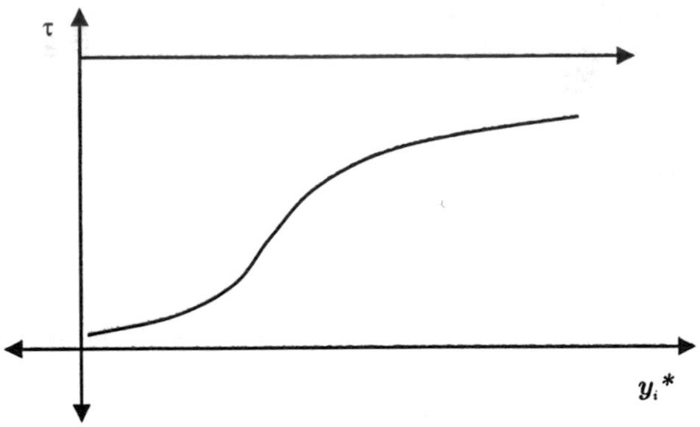

Fig. 7.2. Survey non-response when $\tau < 0$.

y_1^* and $\mathbf{x}_2$:

$$\tau = \Pr\left(y_{2i}^* < 0 \middle| y_{1i} = y_1^*\right),$$
$$= 1 - \Phi\left[\frac{r\frac{s_2}{s_1}\left(y_1^* - m_1\right) + \mathbf{x}_2\mathbf{b}_2}{s_2\sqrt{1-r^2}}\right].$$

For a set of individuals with the same characteristics $\mathbf{x}_2$, this rate is an increasing (decreasing) function of y_1^* when $r < 0$ $(r > 0)$. Rates of non-response for income-related questions which increase with income are captured well by this type of model.

Ordinary least squares estimation of m_1 on the complete observations, which implies using the approximation:

$$\mu_1 = \frac{\sum_{y_1 \neq 0} y_i}{n_1},$$

leads us to underestimate the true value of the mean when $r < 0$.

7.8.4 *Selectivity Bias*

In the preceding section we described a situation in which respondents do not answer one question while answering the others. In this case we know the vector of characteristics $\mathbf{x}_2$. Frequently we only have information on individuals who have filled out the questionnaire. Our observations are thus limited to those for whom $y_i = y_{1i}^*$.

Many examples of this phenomenon can be found: we have data on foreign workers only if they decided to emigrate, salaries only for individuals who are working, grades obtained by students who choose to take an exam, characteristics of job seekers registered with a government agency, responses to voluntary questionnaires only from people who agree to participate, etc.

Given that we have complete information on each observed individual, it is tempting to use o.l.s. to analyse the data. However, we have already seen that in some situations this procedure can lead to biased estimators. All of the examples we have listed conceal a selection process in the generation of the observed values – this is known as *self-selectivity*, while the resulting bias is known as the *selectivity bias*. Consider the model:

$$y_i = \begin{cases} y_{1i}^*, & \text{if } y_{2i}^* > 0, \\ 0, & \text{otherwise,} \end{cases}$$

where:

$$\begin{aligned} y_{1i}^* &= \mathbf{x}_{1i}\mathbf{b}_1 + u_{1i}, \\ y_{2i}^* &= \mathbf{x}_{2i}\mathbf{b}_2 + u_{2i}, \end{aligned}$$

and:

$$(u_{1i}, u_{2i})' \sim N\left[\begin{pmatrix} 0 \\ 0 \end{pmatrix}, \begin{pmatrix} s_1^2 & \rho s_1 s_2 \\ \rho s_1 s_2 & s_2^2 \end{pmatrix}\right].$$

The ordinary least squares estimator of $\mathbf{b}_1$ is unbiased if:

$$\mathrm{E}(y_i \mid y_i \neq 0) = \mathbf{x}_{1i}\mathbf{b}_1 \quad \Leftrightarrow \quad r s_1 \frac{\varphi\left(\frac{\mathbf{x}_{2i}\mathbf{b}_2}{s_2}\right)}{\Phi\left(\frac{\mathbf{x}_{2i}\mathbf{b}_2}{s_2}\right)} = 0 \quad \Leftrightarrow \quad r = 0.$$

As soon as the selection process incorporates any dependency on y_1^*, a bias is introduced which increases with $|r|$. This bias appears because some explanatory variables included in $\mathbf{x}_2$ have been omitted. In this sense, what we are dealing with can be considered a specification error.

While demonstrating the existence of this bias is quite straightforward from a mathematical perspective, its interpretation is less so. An example which helps to clarify this is given by a model of an individual's career profile, showing the evolution of salary, s, as a function of age, *age*.

Let this profile be for women and assume that it is represented by an approximately linear formulation:

$$s = a \cdot age + b + u.$$

If all women between the ages of sixteen and sixty years decided to work the observations would look as in figure 7.3.

In fact, women's labour force participation rates are highly dependent on age. In general, these rates are lower for women aged 16–20, 25–44, and 55–60. For

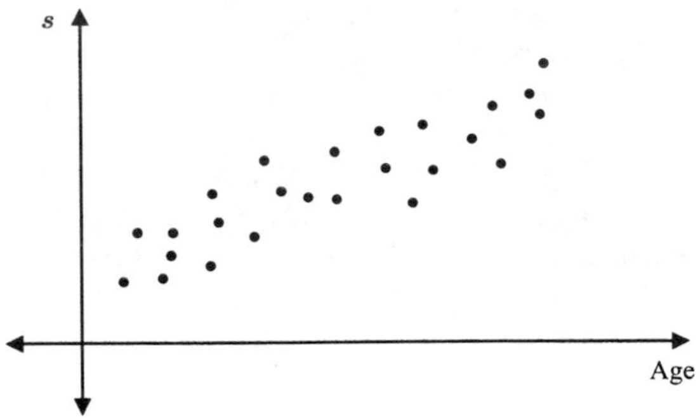

Fig. 7.3. Profile of evolution of women's incomes – all women working

the first group this is due to the fact that many women are still pursuing their studies. Hence observed salaries will, on average, be below what they would be if all women worked. Conversely, women between twenty-five and forty-four years of age who continue working are those whose salary is above average. The points which we observe will thus look approximately as in figure 7.4.

Visually, we can tell that least squares estimation will not provide a satisfactory fit to the data.

7.9 Estimation with the Generalized Tobit Model

7.9.1 The Likelihood Equation

We see that:

$$y_i = \begin{cases} y_{1i}^*, & \text{if } y_{2i}^* > 0, \\ 0, & \text{otherwise,} \end{cases}$$

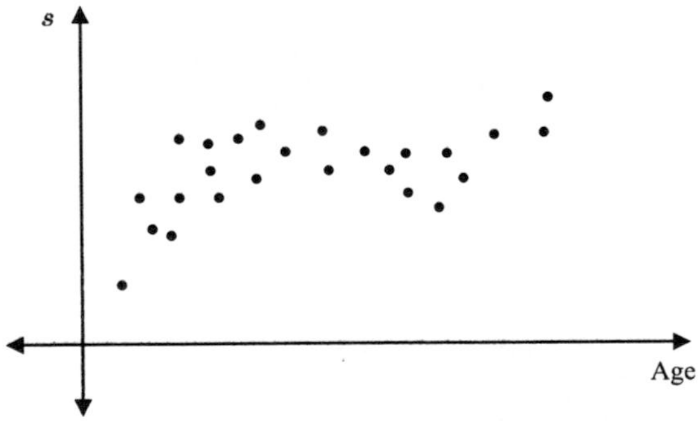

Fig. 7.4. Profile of the evolution of women's incomes – observed data

where:

$$y_{1i}^* = \mathbf{x}_{1i}\mathbf{b}_1 + u_{1i},$$
$$y_{2i}^* = \mathbf{x}_{2i}\mathbf{b}_2 + u_{2i},$$

and:

$$(u_{1i}, u_{2i})' \sim N\left[\begin{pmatrix} 0 \\ 0 \end{pmatrix}, \begin{pmatrix} s_1^2 & rs_1s_2 \\ rs_1s_2 & s_2^2 \end{pmatrix}\right].$$

Let J_0 denote the set of n_0 indices for which $y_i = 0$ and J_1 the complementary set with n_1 elements. The likelihood is given by:

$$L = \prod_{J_0} \Phi\left(\frac{-\mathbf{x}_{2i}\mathbf{b}_2}{s_2}\right) \prod_{J_1}\left[\frac{1}{s_1}\varphi\left(\frac{y_i - \mathbf{x}_{1i}\mathbf{b}_1}{s_1}\right)\right]$$
$$\times \prod_{J_1} \Phi\left\{\frac{1}{\sqrt{1-r^2}}\left[\frac{\mathbf{x}_{2i}\mathbf{b}_2}{s_2} + \frac{r}{s_1}(y_i - \mathbf{x}_{1i}\mathbf{b}_1)\right]\right\}.$$

$\mathbf{b}_2$ and s_2 only appear in this equation as $\frac{\mathbf{b}_2}{s_2}$, so there exists an identification problem – only r, s_1, $\mathbf{b}_1$, and $\frac{\mathbf{b}_2}{s_2}$ are determined.

As in the case of the simple Tobit model, it is useful to perform a translation of the parameters. We have:

$$h_1 = \frac{1}{s_1},$$
$$\mathbf{c}_1 = \frac{\mathbf{b}_1}{s_1},$$
$$\mathbf{c}_2 = \frac{\mathbf{b}_2}{s_2},$$

yielding:

$$\log(L) = \sum_{J_0} \log\left[\Phi\left(-\mathbf{x}_{2i}\mathbf{c}_2\right)\right] + n_1 \log(h_1)$$
$$+ \sum_{J_1} \log\left[\varphi\left(h_1 y_i - \mathbf{x}_{1i}\mathbf{c}_1\right)\right]$$
$$+ \sum_{J_1} \log \Phi\left\{\frac{1}{\sqrt{1-r^2}}\left[\mathbf{x}_{2i}\mathbf{c}_2 + r\left(h_1 y_i - \mathbf{x}_{1i}\mathbf{c}_1\right)\right]\right\}.$$

For a given value of r, this function is concave in h_1, $\mathbf{c}_1$, and $\mathbf{c}_2$.

7.9.2 The Maximum-Likelihood Method

The maximum-likelihood method is applied to this model in the usual manner and yields nonlinear equations which must be solved using numeric algorithms.

Notice, however, that is of some interest to modify the procedure in order to account for the partial concavity of the likelihood function with respect to h_1, $\mathbf{c}_1$, and $\mathbf{c}_2$ (when r is fixed). We can, for example, iterate over a series of values for r and maximize the likelihood function with respect to the other parameters at each step. We then retain the value of r corresponding to the greatest likelihood.

7.9.3 *Two-Stage Estimation*

It is always useful to have a simple estimation method, even if it is not efficient. In particular, we need to be able to evaluate the quality of the adjustment process, to see whether or not the model needs to be modified. Furthermore, simple models may provide starting values for the iterative algorithms of more complex ones. For example, the following procedure can be applied:

(i) Identify the model given above with the probit model, yielding:

$$\Pr\left(z_{y^*_{2i}} = 1\right) = \Pr\left(y^*_{2i} \geq 0\right),$$
$$= \Phi\left(\frac{\mathbf{x}_{2i}\mathbf{b}_2}{s_2}\right),$$

where:

$$z_{y^*_{2i}} = \begin{cases} 0, & \text{if } y^*_{2i} < 0, \\ 1, & \text{otherwise.} \end{cases}$$

This provides us with an estimator for $\mathbf{c}_2 = \frac{\mathbf{b}_2}{s_2}$, which we call $\boldsymbol{\zeta}_2$.

(ii) Having looked at the qualitative part of the model, we will now turn our attention to its quantitative aspect, corresponding to the indices $i \in J_1$:

$$\mathrm{E}\left(y_i \mid i \in J_1\right) = \mathbf{x}_{i1}\mathbf{b}_1 + rs_1 \frac{\varphi\left(\frac{\mathbf{x}_{2i}\mathbf{b}_2}{s_2}\right)}{\Phi\left(\frac{\mathbf{x}_{2i}\mathbf{b}_2}{s_2}\right)}.$$

Let:

$$\hat{\psi}_i = \frac{\varphi\left(\mathbf{x}_{2i}\boldsymbol{\zeta}_2\right)}{\Phi\left(\mathbf{x}_{2i}\boldsymbol{\zeta}_2\right)}.$$

We limit our sample to the elements in J_1 and regress y_i on $\mathbf{x}_{i1}$ and $\hat{\psi}_i$, obtaining estimators for $\mathbf{b}_1$ and rs_1 which are asymptotically unbiased but not efficient. In fact, the errors corresponding to this method are heteroscedastic, since:

$$\operatorname{var}\left(y_i \mid i \in J_1\right)$$
$$= s_1^2 + (s_1 r)^2 \left\{ -\mathbf{x}_{2i}\mathbf{c}_2 \frac{\varphi\left(\mathbf{x}_{2i}\mathbf{c}_2\right)}{\Phi\left(\mathbf{x}_{2i}\mathbf{c}_2\right)} - \left[\frac{\varphi\left(\mathbf{x}_{2i}\mathbf{c}_2\right)}{\Phi\left(\mathbf{x}_{2i}\mathbf{c}_2\right)}\right]^2 \right\}.$$

(iii) It remains to estimate s_1. For that we consider the residual, $\hat{v}_{1i}$, from the preceding regression:

$$\hat{v}_{1i} = y_i - \mathbf{x}_{1i}\boldsymbol{\beta}_1 - \rho\sigma_1\psi_i.$$

Since:

$$s_1^2 = \operatorname{var}(y_i \mid i \in J_1) + (s_1 r)^2 \left\{ \mathbf{x}_{2i}\mathbf{c}_2 \frac{\varphi(\mathbf{x}_{2i}\mathbf{c}_2)}{\Phi(\mathbf{x}_{2i}\mathbf{c}_2)} + \left[\frac{\varphi(\mathbf{x}_{2i}\mathbf{c}_2)}{\Phi(\mathbf{x}_{2i}\mathbf{c}_2)}\right]^2 \right\},$$

it follows that:

$$\sigma_1^2 = \frac{1}{n}\sum_{J_1} \hat{v}_{1i}^2 + \frac{(r\sigma_1)^2}{n_1}\sum_{J_1}\left(\mathbf{x}_{2i}\zeta_2\hat{\psi}_i + \hat{\psi}_i^2\right).$$

Under the usual assumptions this procedure yields consistent and asymptotically normal estimators. The variance-covariance matrix, which is not equal to the inverse of the Fisher information matrix, was estimated by Heckman.

7.10 Robustness of the Estimation Methods

One of the advantages of ordinary least squares as applied to the linear model is that it can be meaningfully used even in situations when the standard assumptions do not hold. This technique will yield good estimators even when, for example, the model is heteroscedastic, the disturbance terms are correlated, the endogenous variable is measured with error, an explanatory variable which is orthogonal to the included variables has been omitted, etc. Because of this feature we describe the o.l.s. model as robust.

Since the Tobit model derives directly from a linear model, it is reasonable to examine the estimation methods which we have introduced to see if they are characterized by the same robustness. As the estimators of this model cannot be expressed analytically, we shall look at this issue from the perspective of their asymptotic properties.

7.10.1 *Heteroscedasticity (Maddala-Nelson [MN75])*

Beginning with a simple example, we will show that the estimator $\boldsymbol{\beta}$ derived using equation (7.3) is not consistent when the disturbance term is heteroscedastic.

Assume that the observations are generated by the model:

$$y_i = \begin{cases} y_i^*, & \text{if } y_i^* > 0, \\ 0, & \text{otherwise,} \end{cases} \qquad i = 1, \ldots, 2n,$$

with $y_i^* = m_0 + u_i$. Among the $2n$ disturbances, the variance of the first n is s_0^2 while the variance of the remaining n is $4s_0^2$. Furthermore, we set the unknown true values of the parameters m_0 and s_0 equal to zero and one respectively. If we ignore the heteroscedasticity and estimate the parameters m and s using maximum-likelihood methods, we must maximize:

$$\begin{aligned}\frac{1}{n}\log(L_n) = \frac{1}{n}\sum_{i=1}^{n}\Big\{&\log\left[\Phi\left(\frac{-m}{s}\right)\right] z_{y_i^*} - \log\left(s\sqrt{2\pi}\right) z_{y_i^*} \\ &- \frac{1}{2s^2}(y_i - m)^2\left(1 - z_{y_i^*}\right)\Big\} \\ &+ \frac{1}{n}\sum_{i=n+1}^{2n}\Big\{\log\left[\Phi\left(\frac{-m}{s}\right)\right] z_{y_i^*} \\ &- \log\left(s\sqrt{2\pi}\right) z_{y_i^*} - \frac{1}{2s^2}(y_i - m)^2\left(1 - z_{y_i^*}\right)\Big\}.\end{aligned}$$

Asymptotically, the maximum-likelihood estimators converge towards the values of m and s which maximize:

$$\ell_\infty = \lim_{n\to\infty}\frac{1}{n}\log(L_n).$$

Applying the law of large numbers and defining a random ε which is distributed N (0, 1), we have:

$$\begin{aligned}\ell_\infty = \mathrm{E}\Big\{&\log\left[\Phi\left(\frac{-m}{s}\right)\right] z_\varepsilon - \log\left[s\sqrt{2\pi}\right] z_\varepsilon \\ &-\frac{1}{2s^2}(\varepsilon - m)^2(1 - z_\varepsilon)\Big\} \\ +\mathrm{E}\Big\{&\log\left[\Phi\left(\frac{-m}{s}\right) z_{2\varepsilon} - \log\left(s\sqrt{2\pi}\right) z_{2\varepsilon}\right. \\ &\left.-\frac{1}{2s^2}(2\varepsilon - m)^2 z_{2\varepsilon}\right]\Big\}, \\ = \log&\left[\Phi\left(\frac{-m}{s}\right)\right] - \log\left(s\sqrt{2\pi}\right) - \frac{m^2}{2s^2} + \frac{3m}{s^2\sqrt{2\pi}} - \frac{5}{2s^2}.\end{aligned}$$

where:

$$z_\varepsilon = \begin{cases} 0, & \text{if } \varepsilon \le 0, \\ 1, & \text{otherwise.}\end{cases}$$

Differentiating with respect to m and s and setting the derivative equal to zero, we obtain:

$$0 = \frac{\partial \ell_\infty}{\partial m} = -\frac{1}{s} \frac{\varphi\left(\frac{-m}{\varphi}\right)}{\Phi\left(\frac{-m}{s}\right)} - \frac{m}{s^2} + \frac{3}{s^2\sqrt{2\pi}},$$

$$0 = \frac{\partial \ell_\infty}{\partial s} = +\frac{m}{s^2} \frac{\varphi\left(\frac{-m}{s}\right)}{\Phi\left(\frac{-m}{s}\right)} - \frac{1}{s} + \frac{m^2}{s^3} - \frac{6m}{s^3\sqrt{2\pi}} + \frac{5}{s^3}.$$

If the estimator for m converges to $m_0 = 0$, then these two equations should have a common root:

$$0 = -\frac{1}{s} \frac{\varphi(0)}{\Phi(0)} + \frac{3}{s^2\sqrt{2\pi}},$$

$$0 = -\frac{1}{s} + \frac{5}{s^3},$$

implying:

$$0 = -2s + 3,$$

$$0 = -s^2 + 5,$$

which is, of course, impossible. Since we have arrived at a contradiction, we see that the maximum-likelihood estimator calculated under the assumption of homoscedasticity is not consistent.

To understand this, consider that, unlike in the linear case, we cannot estimate m independently of s^2. The error we made in our assumptions on the form of s^2 spills over into our estimation of m.

7.10.2 Errors in the Endogenous Variables

A similar experiment can be performed using a different modification of the Tobit model.

For example, let the quantitative part of the endogenous variable be measured with an error, v, such that:

$$\mathrm{E}(v) = 0,$$

$$\mathrm{var}(v) = s_v^2.$$

We have:

$$y_i = \begin{cases} y_i^* + v_i, & \text{if } y_i^* > 0, \\ 0, & \text{otherwise,} \end{cases}$$

where $y_i^* = \mathbf{x}_i\mathbf{b} + u_i$, $\mathrm{E}(u_i) = 0$, $\mathrm{var}(u_i) = s^2$ and where the variables u_i and

v_j are independent and normally distributed. When the measurement error, v, is normal, this model can be interpreted as a generalized Tobit model with the deterministic parts of y_{1i}^* and y_{2i}^* identical.

Application of the maximum-likelihood method in this situation will yield inconsistent estimators of m and s^2. Stapleton and Young [SY81] demonstrate and that, asymptotically, this technique leads to overestimation of the variance, and they use Monte Carlo trials to examine its impact on m.

7.11 Generalized Residuals and Tests

7.11.1 Interpretation of the Vector of Scores

Consider a linear Gaussian model with independent observations y_i^*, $i = 1, \ldots, n$, which are distributed $\mathrm{N}\left(\mathbf{x}_i\mathbf{b}, s^2\right)$. The log-likelihood associated with the i-th observation is:

$$\log\left[f\left(y_i^*; \mathbf{b}, s^2\right)\right] = -\frac{1}{2}\log\left(s^2\right) - \frac{1}{2}\log\left(2\pi\right) - \frac{1}{2s^2}\left(y_i^* - \mathbf{x}_i\mathbf{b}\right)^2.$$

The vector of scores is:

$$\begin{aligned}
\frac{\partial \log\left[f\left(y_i^*; \mathbf{b}, s^2\right)\right]}{\partial \mathbf{b}} &= \frac{1}{s^2}\mathbf{x}_i'\left(y_i^* - \mathbf{x}_i\mathbf{b}\right), \\
&= \frac{1}{s^2}\mathbf{x}_i' u_i, \\
\frac{\partial \log\left[f\left(y_i^*; \mathbf{b}, s^2\right)\right]}{\partial s^2} &= -\frac{1}{2s^2} + \frac{1}{2s^4}u_i^2, \\
&= \frac{1}{2s^2}\left(u_i^2 - s^2\right).
\end{aligned}$$

These are relatively simple functions of the errors, u_i, and we shall demonstrate that these expressions have analogues in the Tobit model. In order to keep the computations simple, we restrict our analysis to the case of the simple Tobit model.

Proposition 22: Consider the simple Tobit model defined by: $y_i = y_i^* z_{y_i^*}$, with the y_i^*-s independent and distributed $\mathrm{N}\left(\mathbf{x}_i\mathbf{b}, s^2\right)$. The vector of scores is given by:

$$\begin{aligned}
\frac{\partial \log\left(L\right)}{\partial \mathbf{b}} &= \frac{1}{s^2}\sum_{i=1}^{n}\mathbf{x}_i' E\left(u_i \mid y_i\right), \\
\frac{\partial \log\left(L\right)}{\partial s^2} &= \frac{1}{2s^2}\sum_{i=1}^{n}\left[E\left(u_i^2 \mid y_i\right) - s^2\right],
\end{aligned}$$

with $u_i = y_i^* - \mathbf{x}_i\mathbf{b}$.

All we need to do is replace the latent errors in the scores of the linear model with their estimates given the endogenous variables y_i.

Proof: Let us verify this for $\frac{\partial \log(L)}{\partial \mathbf{b}}$ by way of illustration. We know that:

$$\frac{\partial \log(L)}{\partial \mathbf{b}} = \frac{1}{s^2}\sum_{i=1}^{n} \mathbf{x}_i' \left\{ \left(1 - z_{y_i}\right)\left[-\frac{s\varphi\left(\frac{\mathbf{x}_i\mathbf{b}}{s}\right)}{\Phi\left(\frac{\mathbf{x}_i\mathbf{b}}{s}\right)}\right] + z_{y_i}\left(y_i - \mathbf{x}_i\mathbf{b}\right)\right\}.$$

where:

$$z_{y_i} = \begin{cases} 0, & \text{if } y_i \leq 0, \\ 1, & \text{otherwise.} \end{cases}$$

As to the estimated latent variable, if $y_i > 0$, we have:

$$\begin{aligned} \mathrm{E}(u_i | y_i) &= \mathrm{E}\left(y_i^* - \mathbf{x}_i\mathbf{b} \middle| y_i\right), \\ &= y_i^* - \mathbf{x}_i\mathbf{b}, \\ &= y_i - \mathbf{x}_i\mathbf{b}, \end{aligned}$$

and, if $y_i < 0$:

$$\begin{aligned} \mathrm{E}(u_i | y_i) &= \mathrm{E}\left(y_i^* - \mathbf{x}_i\mathbf{b} \middle| y_i^* < 0\right), \\ &= \mathrm{E}(u_i | u_i < -\mathbf{x}_i\mathbf{b}), \\ &= -\frac{s\varphi\left(\frac{\mathbf{x}_i\mathbf{b}}{s}\right)}{\Phi\left(\frac{\mathbf{x}_i\mathbf{b}}{s}\right)}. \end{aligned}$$

So the predicted form of the error is:

$$\mathrm{E}(u_i | y_i) = \left(1 - z_{y_i}\right)\left[-\frac{s\varphi\left(\frac{\mathbf{x}_i\mathbf{b}}{s}\right)}{\Phi\left(\frac{\mathbf{x}_i\mathbf{b}}{s}\right)}\right] + z_{y_i}\left(y_i - \mathbf{x}_i\mathbf{b}\right),$$

which is what we were looking for. Calculation of the score with respect to s^2 proceeds analogously. □

Notice that the predicted error is a function of y_i and $\mathbf{x}_i$ as well as of the parameters $\mathbf{b}$ and s^2:

$$\mathrm{E}(u_i | y_i) = \tilde{u}\left(y_i, \mathbf{x}_i; \mathbf{b}, s^2\right).$$

In the usual case of the linear model, we have:

$$\begin{aligned} \mathrm{E}\left(u_i \mid y_i\right) &= \mathrm{E}\left(u_i \mid y_i^*\right), \\ &= y_i - \mathbf{x}_i \mathbf{b}, \end{aligned}$$

and the error can be approximated by substituting $\boldsymbol{\beta}$ for $\mathbf{b}$. Generalization of this procedure to the Tobit model leads to the following definition.

Definition 5:

(i) We call first-order *generalized residuals* the approximations to the predicted latent variables given by:

$$\begin{aligned} \tilde{u}_i &= \tilde{u}_i\left(y_i, \mathbf{x}_i, \boldsymbol{\beta}, \sigma^2\right), \\ &= \mathrm{E}\left(u_i \mid y_i\right)\big|_{\mathbf{b}=\boldsymbol{\beta}, s^2=\sigma^2} . \end{aligned}$$

(ii) We call second-order *generalized residuals* the quantities:

$$\tilde{u}_i^{(2)} = \mathrm{E}\left(u_i^2 \mid y_i\right)_{\mathbf{b}=\boldsymbol{\beta}, s^2=\sigma^2} .$$

The first-order generalized residuals have the same asymptotic properties as the predicted errors $\mathrm{E}\left(u_i \mid y_i\right)$. In other words, they are asymptotically centred, since: $\mathrm{E}\left[\mathrm{E}\left(u_i \mid y_i\right)\right] = \mathrm{E}\left(u_i\right) = 0$.

Furthermore, these residuals are generally heteroscedastic: $\mathrm{var}\left[\mathrm{E}\left(u_i \mid y_i\right)\right]$ is not constant. This variance is, incidentally, always less that $\mathrm{var}\left(u_i\right)$. The first-order generalized residuals can be plotted on a "residuals graph" (cf. Chesher-Irish [CI87]) as in figure 7.5. We see that this graph has two distinct parts, representing the qualitative and the quantitative aspects of the Tobit model respectively.

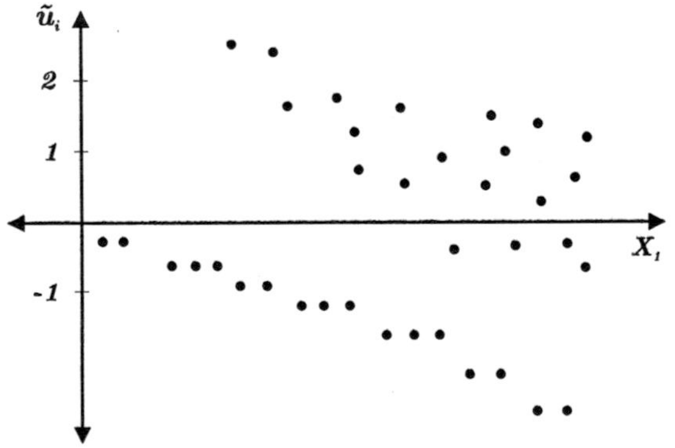

Fig. 7.5. Residuals Graph

7.11.2 Interpretation of the Likelihood Equations

The likelihood equations can easily be rewritten in terms of the generalized residuals, yielding:

$$0 = \sum_{i=1}^{n} \mathbf{x}_i' \tilde{u}_i,$$

$$\sigma^2 = \frac{1}{n} \sum_{i=1}^{n} \tilde{u}_i^{(2)},$$

where $\tilde{u}_i$ and $\tilde{u}_i^{(2)}$ are functions of $\boldsymbol{\beta}$, σ^2.

The first expression captures the orthogonality between the explanatory variables and the generalized residuals. It can be interpreted as a system of normal equations. The second shows that the estimator of the variance is the sum of squares of the predicted errors to within a factor of $\frac{1}{n}$:

$$\sigma^2 = \frac{1}{n} \left[\mathrm{E} \left(\sum_{i=1}^{n} u_i^2 | \, y_1, \ldots, y_n \right) \right]_{\mathbf{b}=\boldsymbol{\beta}, s^2=\sigma^2}.$$

In particular, the maximum-likelihood estimator of s^2 is always positive in the Tobit model.

7.11.3 Maximum-Score Test for Omitted Variables

Maximum-score tests of assumptions about the parameters of a Tobit model are based on the estimated score, and so are easily written in terms of the generalized residuals. Consider the test for omitted variables. The general hypothesis is:

$$y_i = y_i^* z_{y_i^*},$$

where $y_i^* \sim \mathrm{N}\left(\mathbf{x}_{i1}\mathbf{b}_1 + \mathbf{x}_{i2}\mathbf{b}_2, s^2\right)$, $i = 1, \ldots, n$, and the null hypothesis H_0 involves setting $\mathbf{b}_2 = 0$.

To derive the score test statistic we begin with:

$$\frac{\partial \log(L)}{\partial \mathbf{b}_2} \left[y; \boldsymbol{\beta}_1^c, \mathbf{0}, \left(\sigma^c\right)^2 \right] = \frac{1}{\sigma_0^2} \sum_{i=1}^{n} \mathbf{x}_{i2}' \tilde{u}_i^c,$$

where $\boldsymbol{\beta}_1^c$ and $(\sigma^c)^2$ are the constrained maximum-likelihood estimators and $\tilde{u}_i^c$ the generalized residuals corresponding to the constrained model.

The form of the statistic can be derived directly from this equation, yielding:

$$\xi_{ML} = \left(\sum_{i=1}^{n} \mathbf{x}_{i2} \tilde{u}_i^c \right) I^{22} \left(\sum_{i=1}^{n} \mathbf{x}_{i2}' \tilde{u}_i^c \right),$$

with:

$$I^{22} = \left\{ \sum_{i=1}^{n} \mathbf{x}'_{i2}\mathbf{x}_{i2} \left(\tilde{u}_i^c\right)^2 - \sum_{i=1}^{n} \mathbf{x}'_{i2}\mathbf{x}_{i1} \left(\tilde{u}_i^c\right)^2 \right.$$
$$\left. \times \left[\sum_{i=1}^{n} \mathbf{x}'_{i1}\mathbf{x}_{i1} \left(\tilde{u}_i^c\right)^2 \right]^{-1} \sum_{i=1}^{n} \mathbf{x}'_{i1}\mathbf{x}_{i2} \left(\tilde{u}_i^c\right) \right\}^{-1}.$$

To perform the test we:

$$\text{accept} \quad H_0 : (b_2 = 0) \text{ if } \xi_{ML} < \chi^2_{95\%} (\dim b_2),$$
$$\text{reject} \quad H_0 : (b_2 = 0) \text{ if } \xi_{ML} > \chi^2_{95\%} (\dim b_2).$$

Exercises

7.1 Examine the model with two thresholds defined by:

$$y_i = \begin{cases} 0, & \text{if } y_i^* < 0, \\ y_i^*, & \text{if } 0 \leq y_i^* < 10, \\ 10, & \text{if } 10 \leq y_i^*, \end{cases}$$

where $y_i^* = \mathbf{x}_i\mathbf{b} + u_i$.

7.2 Given a latent variable $y_i^* = \mathbf{x}_i\mathbf{b} + u_i$, consider the following three models:

(a) We observe all the values of y_i^*,

(b) We observe y_i^* if $y_i^* > 0$, otherwise we observe zero,

(c) We simply observe whether y_i^* is positive or negative.

Assume that the disturbance terms are independent and share the same distribution $\mathrm{N}\left(0, s^2\right)$. Write the likelihood functions for these three models and find their Fisher information matrices. Compare and contrast them.

7.3 Consider the model in equation (7.2). Suppose that the disturbance terms are independent and that the distribution of $\frac{u_i}{s}$ is logistic. Write the likelihood function for this model. Show that these equations have, at most, one solution, and that it is the global maximum of the likelihood.

7.4 The Truncated Model

Write the likelihood equation for a situation in which we only have observations on y for the complete observations. Is this likelihood concave in $\frac{1}{s}$ and $\frac{\mathbf{b}}{s}$?

7.5 It has been proposed that the consumption of rationed groceries be modelled with a truncated log-normal formulation? What justifications can you find for this specification?

7.6 For the simple Tobit model, explain how we can create adjusted values for y_i, denoted $\hat{y}_i$, and use the distance between $\hat{y}_i$ and y_i to evaluate the "quality" of the model.

7.7 Find a formula approximating the estimator for m in the simple Tobit model where $y_i^* = m + u_i$ and the error terms are independent and distributed $\mathrm{N}(0, 1)$.

7.8 Consider the model:

$$y_t^* = ax_t + b + \epsilon_t,$$

$$y_t = \begin{cases} y_t^*, & \text{if} \quad y_t^* > 0, \\ 0, & \text{otherwise.} \end{cases}$$

Assume that the pair (x_t, ϵ_t) are independent and distributed:

$$\mathrm{N}\left[\begin{pmatrix} m \\ 0 \end{pmatrix} \begin{pmatrix} s_x^2 & 0 \\ 0 & s^2 \end{pmatrix}\right].$$

Apply ordinary least squares to a regression of y on x and 1. The estimator for a is:

$$\tilde{a} = \frac{\widehat{\mathrm{cov}}\,(x, y)}{\widehat{\mathrm{var}}\,(x)},$$

verify that $\tilde{a}$ tends towards $a\mathrm{E}\,(y^* | \, y^* > 0)$. Use this information to derive a consistent estimator for a.

7.9 The Friction Model

Economic phenomena are often characterized by inertia. To illustrate, if the change in the return to a certain financial asset, Δr, is very small, changes in holdings of that asset for any given agent, ΔA_i, are quite likely to be nil. This may be due, for example, to transactions costs. The relationship between ΔA_i and Δr can thus be graphed as in figure 7.6:

The following model has been proposed to describe this situation:

$$y_{1i}^* = b_0' + x_i b + u_i,$$

$$y_{2i}^* = b_0'' + x_i b + u_i,$$

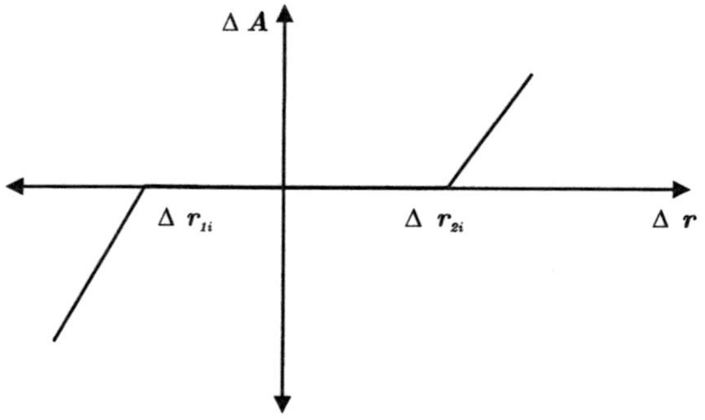

Fig. 7.6. Changes in holdings of financial assets

with $b''_0 < b'_0$. The observed endogenous variable is defined:

$$y_i = \begin{cases} y^*_{1i}, & \text{if } y^*_{1i} < 0, \\ 0, & \text{if } y^*_{1i} > 0 \quad \text{and} \quad y^*_{2i} < 0, \\ y^*_{2i}, & \text{if } y^*_{2i} > 0. \end{cases}$$

Discuss this model in the context of the financial assets problem, paying particular attention to the implied assumptions as they relate to the thresholds Δr_{1i} and Δr_{2i}. What significance can we attach to the fact that the equations for y^*_{1i} and y^*_{2i} contain the same error term u_i? why not use two different ones?

7.10 The Friction Model (continued)
Assume that the disturbances, u_i, are independent and share the same distribution $N\left(0, s^2\right)$. Write the distributions of the observations $y_i, i = 1, \ldots, n$, and derive the likelihood equations. Can you propose a two-stage method to estimate the parameters?

7.11 The Friction Model (end)
In order to allow the two thresholds to vary independently the model in exercise 7.9 has been modified to:

$$y_i = \begin{cases} y^*_{1i}, & \text{if } y^*_{1i} < v_i, \\ 0, & \text{if } y^*_{1i} > v_i \quad \text{and} \quad y^*_{2i} < w_i, \\ y^*_{2i}, & \text{if } y^*_{2i} > w_i, \end{cases}$$

where $v_i = x_{1i}b_1 + u_{1i}$ and $w_i = x_{2i}b_2 + u_{2i}$. What kind of joint distribution must we postulate for (u_{1i}, u_{2i}) if this model is to make sense? Suggest one. Does this model seem useful to you?

7.12 Assume that the qualitative part of the endogenous variable is determined by the following two criteria:

$$y^*_{2i} = x_{2i}b_2 + u_{2i},$$
$$y^*_{3i} = x_{3i}b_3 + u_{3i}.$$

The observed endogenous variable is:

$$y_i = \begin{cases} y^*_{1i}, & \text{if} y^*_{2i} > 0 \quad \text{and} \quad y^*_{3i} > 0, \\ 0, & \text{otherwise.} \end{cases}$$

Study this model.

7.13 Consider the Tobit model defined in section 8.2.1. Verify that the estimator for b_1 obtained by regressing $y_i, i = 1, \ldots n$ on x_{1i} is not consistent. Would it be if $\text{cov}\,(u_{1i}, u_{2i}) = 0$?

7.14 Consider again the Tobit model defined in section 8.2.1. Calculate $E\left(y^*_{2i} \mid y_i\right)$ and use this information to generate a prediction for the values assumed by the latent variable y^*_2.

7.15 How would we have to modify the likelihood if we observed y_i and y^*_{2i}?

Appendix 7.1 Moments of the Truncated Normal Distribution

We have:

$$y = \begin{cases} y^*, & \text{if } y^* > 0, \\ 0, & \text{otherwise,} \end{cases}$$

where $y^* \rightsquigarrow \mathrm{N}\left(m, \sigma^2\right)$.

This condition can be written:

$$y^* = m + \sigma\varepsilon,$$

with $\varepsilon \sim \mathrm{N}(0, 1)$.

(i)

$$\begin{aligned} \Pr(y > 0) &= \Pr\left(y^* > 0\right), \\ &= \Pr(m + \sigma\varepsilon > 0), \\ &= \Pr\left(\varepsilon > -\frac{m}{\sigma}\right), \\ &= 1 - \Phi\left(-\frac{m}{\sigma}\right), \\ &= \Phi\left(\frac{m}{\sigma}\right). \end{aligned}$$

$$\begin{aligned} \Pr(y < 0) &= \Phi\left(-\frac{m}{\sigma}\right), \\ &= 1 - \Phi\left(\frac{m}{\sigma}\right). \end{aligned}$$

(ii)

$$\begin{aligned} \mathrm{E}(y) &= \mathrm{E}\left(y^* z_{y>0}\right), \\ &= \mathrm{E}\left[(m + \sigma\varepsilon)\, z_{m+\sigma\varepsilon>0}\right], \\ &= m\Phi\left(\frac{m}{\sigma}\right) + \sigma\mathrm{E}\left(\varepsilon z_{\varepsilon>-\frac{m}{\sigma}}\right), \\ &= m\Phi\left(\frac{m}{\sigma}\right) + \sigma\int_{-\frac{m}{\sigma}}^{\infty} x\varphi(x)\, dx, \end{aligned}$$

$$= m\Phi\left(\frac{m}{\sigma}\right) + \sigma\varphi\left(-\frac{m}{\sigma}\right),$$
$$= m\Phi\left(\frac{m}{\sigma}\right) + \sigma\varphi\left(\frac{m}{\sigma}\right),$$

where:

$$z_\alpha = \begin{cases} 0, & \text{if } \alpha \leq 0, \\ 1, & \text{otherwise,} \end{cases}$$

and α represents some term or function.

(iii) $$\mathrm{E}\left[(y-m)\, z_{y>0}\right] = \mathrm{E}\left(y z_{y>0}\right) - m \Pr(y>0),$$
$$= \sigma\varphi\left(\frac{m}{\sigma}\right).$$

(iv) $$\mathrm{E}(y|\, y>0) = \frac{\mathrm{E}\left(y^* z_{y^*>0}\right)}{\Pr(y^*>0)},$$
$$= m + \sigma\frac{\varphi\left(\frac{m}{\sigma}\right)}{\Phi\left(\frac{m}{\sigma}\right)}.$$

(v) $$\mathrm{E}\left(y^2\right) = \mathrm{E}\left(y^* z_{y^*>0}\right),$$
$$= \mathrm{E}\left[(m+\sigma\varepsilon)^2 z_{m+\sigma\varepsilon>0}\right],$$
$$= m^2\Phi\left(\frac{m}{\sigma}\right) + 2m\sigma\varphi\left(\frac{m}{\sigma}\right) + \sigma^2\mathrm{E}\left(\varepsilon^2 z_{\varepsilon>-\frac{m}{\sigma}}\right).$$

Now:

$$\mathrm{E}\left(\varepsilon^2 z_{\varepsilon>-\frac{m}{\sigma}}\right) = \int_{-\frac{m}{\sigma}}^{\infty} x^2\varphi(x)\, dx,$$
$$= -\, x\varphi(x)|_{-\frac{m}{\sigma}}^{\infty} + \int_{-\frac{m}{\sigma}}^{\infty} \varphi(x)\, dx,$$
$$= -\frac{m}{\sigma}\varphi\left(\frac{m}{\sigma}\right) + \Phi\left(\frac{m}{\sigma}\right).$$

Thus:

$$\mathrm{E}\left(y^2\right) = m^2\Phi\left(\frac{m}{\sigma}\right) + m\sigma\varphi\left(\frac{m}{\sigma}\right) + \sigma^2\Phi\left(\frac{m}{\sigma}\right).$$

(vi) $$\mathrm{E}\left[(y-m)^2 z_{y>0}\right] = \mathrm{E}\left(y^2\right) - 2m\mathrm{E}(y) + m^2\Pr(y>0),$$
$$= \sigma^2\Phi\left(\frac{m}{\sigma}\right) - m\sigma\varphi\left(\frac{m}{\sigma}\right).$$

(vii) $$\begin{aligned}\operatorname{var}(y) &= \mathrm{E}\left(y^2\right) - [\mathrm{E}(y)]^2,\\ &= m^2\Phi\left(\frac{m}{\sigma}\right) + m\sigma\varphi\left(\frac{m}{\sigma}\right) + \sigma^2\Phi\left(\frac{m}{\sigma}\right) - m^2\Phi^2\left(\frac{m}{\sigma}\right)\\ &\quad - 2m\sigma\varphi\left(\frac{m}{\sigma}\right)\Phi\left(\frac{m}{\sigma}\right) - \sigma^2\varphi^2\left(\frac{m}{\sigma}\right).\end{aligned}$$

(viii) $$\begin{aligned}\operatorname{var}(y|\, y > 0) &= \mathrm{E}\left(y^2\middle|\, y > 0\right) - \left[\mathrm{E}\left(y^2\middle|\, y > 0\right)\right]^2\\ &= m^2 + m\sigma\frac{\varphi\left(\frac{m}{\sigma}\right)}{\Phi\left(\frac{m}{\sigma}\right)} + \sigma^2 - m^2\\ &\quad -2m\sigma\frac{\varphi\left(\frac{m}{\sigma}\right)}{\Phi\left(\frac{m}{\sigma}\right)} - \sigma^2\frac{\varphi^2\left(\frac{m}{\sigma}\right)}{\Phi^2\left(\frac{m}{\sigma}\right)},\\ &= \sigma^2 - m\sigma\frac{\varphi\left(\frac{m}{\sigma}\right)}{\Phi\left(\frac{m}{\sigma}\right)} - \sigma^2\frac{\varphi^2\left(\frac{m}{\sigma}\right)}{\Phi^2\left(\frac{m}{\sigma}\right)}.\end{aligned}$$

Appendix 7.2 Moments of the Truncated Normal Bivariate Distribution

Let:

$$\begin{pmatrix} y_1^* \\ y_2^* \end{pmatrix} \rightsquigarrow \mathrm{N}\left[\begin{pmatrix} m_1 \\ m_2 \end{pmatrix}\begin{pmatrix} \sigma_1^2 & \rho\sigma_1\sigma_2 \\ \rho\sigma_1\sigma_2 & \sigma_2^2 \end{pmatrix}\right].$$

We wish to calculate the conditional moments:

$$\mathrm{E}\left(y_1^* \middle| y_2^* > 0\right) \quad \text{and} \quad \mathrm{var}\left(y_1^* \middle| y_2^* > 0\right).$$

To do this it is of some interest to decompose y_1^* to isolate the conditional expectation of y_1^* given y_2^*.

$$\mathrm{E}\left(y_1^* \middle| y_2^*\right) = m_1 + \rho\frac{\sigma_1}{\sigma_2}\left(y_2^* - m_2\right).$$

We have:

$$\begin{aligned} y_1^* &= \mathrm{E}\left(y_1^* \middle| y_2^*\right) + v_1, \\ &= m_1 + \rho\frac{\sigma_1}{\sigma_2}\left(y_2^* - m_2\right) + v_1, \end{aligned}$$

where v_1 is some variable independent of y_2^*, with mean zero and variance: $\mathrm{var}\left(v_1\right) = \sigma_1^2\left(1-\rho^2\right)$.

$$\begin{aligned} \text{(i)} \qquad \mathrm{E}\left(y_1^* \middle| y_2^* > 0\right) &= \mathrm{E}\left[m_1 + \rho\frac{\sigma_1}{\sigma_2}\left(y_2^* - m_2\right) \middle| y_2^* > 0\right], \\ &\quad + \mathrm{E}\left(v_1 \middle| y_2^* > 0\right), \\ &= \mathrm{E}\left[m_1 + \rho\frac{\sigma_1}{\sigma_2}\left(y_2^* - m_2\right) \middle| y_2^* > 0\right], \\ &= m_1 + \rho\sigma_1\mathrm{E}\left(\frac{y_2^* - m_2}{\sigma_2} \middle| \frac{y_2^* - m_2}{\sigma_2} > -\frac{m_2}{\sigma_2}\right), \\ &= m_1 + \rho\sigma_1\frac{\varphi\left(\frac{m}{\sigma}\right)}{\Phi\left(\frac{m}{\sigma}\right)}, \end{aligned}$$

from appendix 7.1.

(ii)
$$\mathrm{E}\left[\left(y_1^*\right)^2\middle| y_2^* > 0\right]$$
$$= \mathrm{E}\left\{\left[m_1 + \rho\frac{\sigma_1}{\sigma_2}\left(y_2^* - m_2\right) + v_1\right]^2\middle| y_2^* > 0\right\},$$
$$= \mathrm{E}\left\{\left[m_1 + \rho\frac{\sigma_1}{\sigma_2}\left(y_2^* - m_2\right)\right]^2\middle| y_2^* > 0\right\}$$
$$+2\mathrm{E}\left\{\left[m_1 + \rho\frac{\sigma_1}{\sigma_2}\left(y_2^* - m_2\right)\right]v_1\middle| y_2^* > 0\right\}$$
$$+\mathrm{E}\left(v_1^2\middle| y_2^* > 0\right),$$
$$= \left\{\left[m_1 + \rho\frac{\sigma_1}{\sigma_2}\left(y_2^* - m_2\right) + v_1\right]^2\middle| y_2^* > 0\right\} + \mathrm{E}\left(v_1^2\right),$$
$$= m_1^2 + 2\rho m_1\sigma_1\mathrm{E}\left\{\frac{y_2^* - m_2}{\sigma_2}\middle| \frac{y_2^* - m_2}{\sigma_2} > \frac{m_2}{\sigma_2}\right\} + \mathrm{E}\left(v_1^2\right),$$
$$= m_1^2 + 2\rho m_1\sigma_1\frac{\varphi\left(\frac{m_2}{\sigma_2}\right)}{\Phi\left(\frac{m_2}{\sigma_2}\right)} + \rho_2\sigma_1^2\left[-\frac{m_2}{\sigma_2}\frac{\varphi\left(\frac{m_2}{\sigma_2}\right)}{\Phi\left(\frac{m_2}{\sigma_2}\right)} + 1\right]$$
$$+\sigma_1^2\left(1 - \rho^2\right),$$
$$= m_1^2 + 2\rho m_1\sigma_1\frac{\varphi\left(\frac{m_2}{\sigma_2}\right)}{\Phi\left(\frac{m_2}{\sigma_2}\right)} + \rho_2\sigma_1^2\left[-\frac{m_2}{\sigma_2}\frac{\varphi\left(\frac{m_2}{\sigma_2}\right)}{\Phi\left(\frac{m_2}{\sigma_2}\right)}\right] + \sigma_2^1.$$

(iii)
$$\mathrm{var}\left(y_1^*\middle| y_2^* > 0\right)$$
$$= \mathrm{E}\left[\left(y_1^*\right)^2\middle| y_2^* > 0\right] - \left[\mathrm{E}\left(y_1^*\middle| y_2^* > 0\right)\right]^2,$$
$$= \sigma_1^2 + \sigma_1^2\rho^2\left\{-\frac{m_2}{\sigma_2}\frac{\varphi\left(\frac{m_2}{\sigma_2}\right)}{\Phi\left(\frac{m_2}{\sigma_2}\right)} - \left[\frac{\varphi\left(\frac{m_2}{\sigma_2}\right)}{\Phi\left(\frac{m_2}{\sigma_2}\right)}\right]^2\right\},$$

from (i) and (ii).

8 Models of Market Disequilibrium

8.1 Observations on the Quantity Exchanged

8.1.1 The Model

In classical microeconomic analysis we assume that a good's market price and the quantity exchanged are determined as its price adjusts until supply and demand are equal. This equilibrium model is based on the supply, S, and demand, D, equations, which are functions of price, p :

$$D = g^1(p),$$
$$S = g^2(p),$$

and on an equilibrium condition:

$$D = S.$$

The equilibrium price, p^e, solves:

$$g^1(p) = g^2(p).$$

This solution is unique if both g^1 and g^2 are continuous, with the former strictly decreasing and the latter strictly increasing. The equilibrium amount exchanged is given by:

$$Q^e = g^1(p^e) = g^2(p^e).$$

Under these assumptions any observation (p^e, Q^e) is a point both on the demand, and on the supply, curves.

When prices are rigid and the market clearing price level cannot be attained, rationing appears. If the price is below equilibrium, demand will exceed supply and will not be fully satisfied. Conversely, if the price is too high, suppliers will have stocks which they cannot sell.

In disequilibrium the amount traded on the market will be less than or equal to $\min(D, S)$. In the analysis to follow we shall let $Q = \min(D, S)$, implying that agents have perfect knowledge of the market.

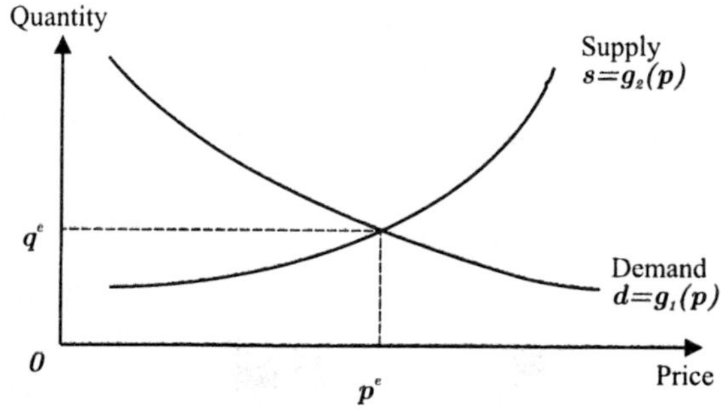

Fig. 8.1. Market clearing price and quantity

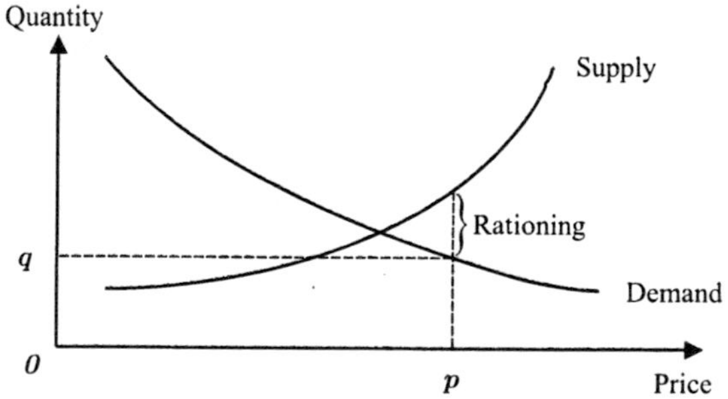

Fig. 8.2. Rationing

To complete the model we specify linear demand and supply functions, S_t and D_t, yielding the amount demanded and supplied (at time t) as functions of price, p_t, and of exogenous variables, $\mathbf{x}_t^1$ and $\mathbf{x}_t^2$, respectively:

$$\begin{aligned} D_t &= a_1 p_t + \mathbf{x}_t^1 \mathbf{b}_1 + u_{1t}, \\ S_t &= a_2 p_t + \mathbf{x}_t^2 \mathbf{b}_2 + u_{2t}, \end{aligned} \tag{8.1}$$

where $t = 1, \ldots, T$, $a_1 < 0$, $a_2 > 0$. u_{1t}, u_{2t} are disturbance terms which are uncorrelated over time and distributed:

$$N\left[\begin{pmatrix} 0 \\ 0 \end{pmatrix}, \begin{pmatrix} s_1^2 & r s_1 s_2 \\ r s_1 s_2 & s_2^2 \end{pmatrix}\right].$$

The observed variables are p_t, $\mathbf{x}_t^1$, $\mathbf{x}_t^2$, and the amount exchanged:

$$Q_t = \min(D_t, S_t). \tag{8.2}$$

Notice that demand and supply are not necessarily both observed. If $D_t \leq S_t$, we see demand, otherwise – supply. Finally, our model is:

$$Q_t = \min\left(a_1 p_t + \mathbf{x}_t^1 \mathbf{b}_1 + u_{1t}, a_2 p_t + \mathbf{x}_t^2 \mathbf{b}_2 + u_{2t}\right), \quad t = 1, \ldots, T,$$

which is obviously not linear in the parameters.

8.1.2 *Expectations on the Quantity Exchanged*

The introduction of disturbance terms reflects a degree of randomness in the behaviour of agents. On average, demand at any point in time, t is, $\mathrm{E}(D_t) = a_1 p_t + \mathbf{x}_t^1 \mathbf{b}_1$, while supply is $\mathrm{E}(S_t) = a_2 p_t + \mathbf{x}_t^2 \mathbf{b}_2$. The average amount traded is thus the minimum of two random variables with normal distributions:

$$\mathrm{E}(Q_t) = \mathrm{E}[\min(D_t, S_t)].$$

Since $\min(D_t, S_t) \le D_t$, we see immediately that $\mathrm{E}(Q_t) \le \mathrm{E}(D_t)$ and, by symmetry, $\mathrm{E}(Q_t) \le \mathrm{E}(S_t)$. This implies that:

$$\mathrm{E}(Q_t) \le \min[\mathrm{E}(D_t), \mathrm{E}(S_t)].$$

Letting $r = 0$, we find the expression for this expectation:

$$\mathrm{E}(Q_t) = d_t \Phi\left(\frac{s_t - d_t}{s}\right) + s_t \Phi\left(\frac{d_t - s_t}{s}\right) - s\varphi\left(\frac{s_t - d_t}{s}\right),$$

where $s_t = \mathrm{E}(S_t)$, $d_t = \mathrm{E}(D_t)$, and $s^2 = s_1^2 + s_2^2$.

This expectation can be rewritten in the following two formulations:

$$\mathrm{E}(Q_t) = s_t - s\left[\frac{s_t - d_t}{s}\Phi\left(\frac{s_t - d_t}{s}\right) + \varphi\left(\frac{s_t - d_t}{s}\right)\right], \tag{8.3}$$

$$\mathrm{E}(Q_t) = d_t - s\left[\frac{d_t - s_t}{s}\Phi\left(\frac{d_t - s_t}{s}\right) + \varphi\left(\frac{d_t - s_t}{s}\right)\right].$$

Since $y \in \mathbb{R}, \forall y$, we know that $y \cdot \Phi(y) + \varphi(y) \ge 0$, and consequently:

$$\mathrm{E}(Q_t) \le d_t = \mathrm{E}(D_t),$$
$$\mathrm{E}(Q_t) \le s_t = \mathrm{E}(S_t).$$

Furthermore,

$$\text{as } p_t \to +\infty, \quad d_t - s_t \to -\infty, \quad \mathrm{E}(Q_t) - d_t \to 0,$$
$$\text{as } p_t \to -\infty, \quad s_t - d_t \to -\infty, \quad \mathrm{E}(Q_t) - s_t \to 0.$$

The graph of the average quantity exchanged as a function of price is hence situated under the graph of $\min(d_t, s_t)$, and is bounded on top by this function as the price tends toward $\pm\infty$.

The distance between these two curves increases with s, i.e. with the variance of the disturbances in the supply and demand equations.

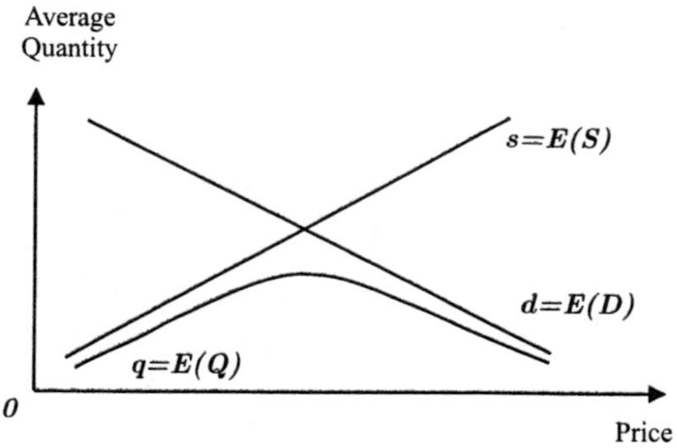

Fig. 8.3. Average quantity exchanged when S, D random

8.1.3 Likelihood Analysis

Denoting $g_t(d, s)$ the density function of the pair (D_t, S_t), we have:

$$\begin{aligned}\Pr(Q_t \in A) &= \Pr(Q_t \in A;\ D_t < S_t) + \Pr(Q_t \in A;\ D_t \geq S_t),\\ &= \Pr(D_t \in A;\ D_t < S_t) + \Pr(S_t \in A;\ D_t \geq S_t),\\ &= \int_A \left[\int_y^{\infty} g_t(y, z)\, dz\right] dy + \int_A \left[\int_y^{\infty} g_t(z, y)\, dz\right] dy,\\ &= \int_A \left[\int_y^{\infty} g_t(y, z)\, dz + \int_y^{\infty} g_t(z, y)\, dz\right] dy.\end{aligned}$$

The density function of Q_t is thus:

$$h_t(q) = \int_q^{\infty} g_t(q, z)\, dz + \int_q^{\infty} g_t(z, q)\, dz, \tag{8.4}$$

and hence, given the assumption of normality:

$$\begin{aligned}g_t(d, s) &= \frac{1}{2\pi\sqrt{\det \sum}}\\ &\quad \times \exp\left[-\frac{1}{2}\begin{pmatrix} d - a_1 p_t - \mathbf{x}_t^1 \mathbf{b}_1 \\ s - a_2 p_t - \mathbf{x}_t^2 \mathbf{b}_2\end{pmatrix}' \Sigma^{-1} \begin{pmatrix} d - a_1 p_t - \mathbf{x}_t^1 \mathbf{b}_1 \\ s - a_2 p_t - \mathbf{x}_t^2 \mathbf{b}_2\end{pmatrix}\right],\end{aligned}$$

where $\sum$ is the covariance matrix of the disturbance terms.

Using the independence of the Q_t-s, we derive the likelihood of the observations:

$$L = \prod_{t=1}^{T} h_t(q_t).$$

Applying maximum likelihood yields equations which are nonlinear in the parameters, necessitating the use of numerical algorithms. When the disturbances u_{1t} and u_{2t} are not correlated, the density function $h_t\ (q_t)$ is simply:

$$h_t\ (q_t) = \frac{1}{s_1}\varphi\left(\frac{a_1 p_t + \mathbf{x}_t^1 \mathbf{b}_1 - q_t}{s_1}\right)\Phi\left(\frac{a_2 p_t + \mathbf{x}_t^2 \mathbf{b}_2 - q_t}{s_2}\right) + \frac{1}{s_2}\varphi\left(\frac{a_2 p_t + \mathbf{x}_t^2 \mathbf{b}_2 - q_t}{s_2}\right)\Phi\left(\frac{a_1 p_t + \mathbf{x}_t^1 \mathbf{b}_1 - q_t}{s_1}\right).$$

Notice that maximum likelihood must be applied to this model with caution. The likelihood can always be driven to infinity by choosing parameters so that s_1 (or s_2) evaluates to zero. Consider the set of observations $\left(p_t, \mathbf{x}_t^1, q_t\right), t = 1, \ldots, T$, it is possible to find values for a_1 and $\mathbf{b}_1$ such that $a_1 p_t + \mathbf{x}_t^1 \mathbf{b}_1 - q_t \leq 0$ for all t, while $a_1 p_t + \mathbf{x}_t^1 \mathbf{b}_1 - q_t = 0$ for some $t = \tau$. Letting s_1 tend toward zero by assigning finite, positive values to a_2, $\mathbf{b}_2$, and s_2, the term:

$$\frac{1}{s_2}\varphi\left(\frac{a_2 p_t + \mathbf{x}_t^2 \mathbf{b}_2 - q_t}{s_2}\right)\Phi\left(\frac{a_1 p_t + \mathbf{x}_t^1 \mathbf{b}_1 - q_t}{s_1}\right),$$

is bounded for $\forall t$. On the other hand, if s_1 tends toward zero, the term:

$$\frac{1}{s_1}\varphi\left(\frac{a_1 p_t + \mathbf{x}_t^1 \mathbf{b}_1 - q_t}{s_1}\right)\Phi\left(\frac{a_2 p_t + \mathbf{x}_t^2 \mathbf{b}_2 - q_t}{s_2}\right)$$

tends toward zero for all $t \neq \tau$ and toward infinity for $t = \tau$.

As a result, the maximum likelihood evaluates to (plus) infinity. Two procedures can be used to prevent this occurrence, we can:

(i) estimate the parameters under the constraint that s_1 and s_2 are greater than some strictly positive value, or
(ii) restrict the domain and search for a local solution to the maximum likelihood equation.

It can be shown that there exists a local maximum which converges to the true value of the parameter.

8.1.4 Prediction[†]

Having estimated the disequilibrium model, we often wish to assign values to some of the latent variables in order to impute an economic interpretation to the results. At this point a decision must be made whether to incorporate the

[†] In this chapter the terms "predicting" is not used in the sense of forecasting. Rather, we predict, or "determine" whether a market is dominated by the demand or the supply side. This is referred to as the regime.

natural constraints on the variables. To simplify our calculations we assume that the disturbance terms are not serially correlated.

8.1.4.1 Determining the Regime

Since our observations only tell us how much of the good was exchanged, we have no way of knowing whether this corresponds to the demand, or to the supply, side of the market. To infer this information (i.e. the existence of excess demand or supply at time t) we need the value of an index:

$$z_t = \begin{cases} 1, & \text{if } D_t > S_t, \\ 0, & \text{otherwise.} \end{cases}$$

Unconstrained Prediction This prediction, $\hat{z}_t = k\,(Q_1, \ldots, Q_T)$, is the estimator closest to z_t:

$$\mathrm{E}\,(\hat{z}_t - z_t)^2 = \min_k \{\mathrm{E}\,[k\,(Q_1, \ldots, Q_T) - z_t]\}^2.$$

Clearly, this is equal to the conditional expectation of z_t, given $Q_1, \ldots, Q_T$:

$$\begin{aligned} \hat{z}_t &= \mathrm{E}\,(z_t |\, Q_1, \ldots, Q_T), \\ &= \mathrm{E}\,(z_t |\, Q) \text{ (because of independence over time)}, \\ &= \Pr\,(D_t > S_t |\, Q_t), \end{aligned}$$

yielding:

$$\Pr\,(D_t > S_t |\, Q_t = q_t) = \frac{\frac{1}{s_2}\varphi\left(\frac{a_2 p_t + \mathbf{x}_t^2 \mathbf{b}_2 - q_t}{s_2}\right)\Phi\left(\frac{a_1 p_t + \mathbf{x}_t^1 \mathbf{b}_1 - q_t}{s_1}\right)}{h_t\,(q_t)}.$$

To evaluate this probability we replace the parameters s_2, a_2, $\mathbf{b}_2$, etc. by their estimates.

Constrained Prediction Since the latent variable z_t can only assume the values zero or one, we may wish to impose this same property on the prediction $\tilde{z}_t$. To do this we solve:

$$\tilde{z}_t = \min_{k \in K_1} \{\mathrm{E}\,[k\,(Q_1, \ldots, Q_T) - z_t]\}^2,$$

where K_1 is the set of functions only assuming the values zero or one. Clearly the solution to this problem cannot be $\hat{z}_t$, since this variable may only take values in the open interval (0, 1). We can, however, use $\hat{z}_t$ to help us find an expression for $\tilde{z}_t$. Using the properties of conditional expectation, we have:

$$\mathrm{E}\,[k\,(Q_1, \ldots, Q_T) - z_t]^2 = \mathrm{E}\,[k\,(Q_1, \ldots, Q_t) - \hat{z}_t]^2 + \mathrm{E}\,(z_t - \hat{z}_t)^2.$$

Next we need the function closest to $\hat{z}_t$ whose range comprises only the values zero or one. The obvious choice is:

$$\tilde{z}_t = \begin{cases} 1, & \text{if } \hat{z}_t \geq \frac{1}{2}, \\ 0, & \text{otherwise.} \end{cases}$$

We conclude that the market is characterized by excess demand if this conditional probability is greater than one half (i.e. when the supply side dominates), and vice versa.

8.1.4.2 Determining the Quantity

Unconstrained Prediction of D_t and S_t $\hat{D}_t$ and $\hat{S}_t$ are equal to:

$$\hat{D}_t = \mathrm{E}\,(D_t \mid Q_t),$$
$$\hat{S}_t = \mathrm{E}\,(S_t \mid Q_t).$$

Since the calculation of these two quantities is obviously similar, we restrict our analysis to developing the first case as an example:

$$\begin{aligned} \mathrm{E}\,(D_t \mid Q_t = q) &= \Pr\,(D_t > S_t \mid Q_t = q)\,\mathrm{E}\,(S_t \mid Q_t = q,\, D_t > S_t) \\ &\quad + \Pr\,(D_t < S_t \mid Q_t = q)\,\mathrm{E}\,(D_t \mid Q_t = q,\, D_t < S_t), \\ &= \hat{z}_t \mathrm{E}\,(D_t \mid S_t = q,\, D_t > q) \\ &\quad + (1 - \hat{z}_t)\,\mathrm{E}\,(D_t \mid D_t = q,\, S_t > q), \\ &= \hat{z}_t \mathrm{E}\,(D_t \mid D_t > q) + (1 - \hat{z}_t)\,q. \end{aligned}$$

Now all that remains is to apply the equation for the mean of a truncated normal variable to obtain the desired prediction.

Constrained Prediction of D_t and S_t By construction, any observation Q_t will satisfy the equality $Q_t = \min\,(D_t, S_t)$. On the other hand, this will not be true for the fitted values $\hat{D}_t$ and $\hat{S}_t$. If we wish to impose this as a constraint and find new values, $\tilde{D}_t$ and $\tilde{S}_t$, we must solve the following problem:

$$\min_{k^1, k^2} \left\{ \mathrm{E}\left[k^1(Q_1, \ldots, Q_T) - D_t\right]^2 + \mathrm{E}\left[k^2(Q_1, \ldots, Q_T) - S_t\right]^2 \right\},$$

where the functions k^1 and k^2 are such that:

$$\min\left[k^1(Q_1, \ldots, Q_T),\, k^2(Q_1, \ldots, Q_T)\right] = Q_t.$$

Using reasoning analogous to that in the analysis of the regime, we see that the solution to this equation is equivalent to that of:

$$\min_{k^1, k^2} \left\{ \mathrm{E}\left[k^1(Q_1, \ldots, Q_T) - \hat{D}_t\right]^2 + \mathrm{E}\left[k^2(Q_1, \ldots, Q_T) - \hat{S}_t\right]^2 \right\}.$$

Several cases can be distinguished, depending on the relationship of the values of $\hat{D}_t$ and $\hat{S}_t$ to that of Q_t.

$$\begin{array}{llll}
\text{if} \quad \hat{D}_t > \hat{S}_t > Q_t, & \text{then} \quad \tilde{D}_t = \hat{D}_t & \text{and} & \tilde{S}_t = Q_t, \\
\text{if} \quad \hat{S}_t > \hat{D}_t > Q_t, & \text{then} \quad \tilde{D}_t = Q_t & \text{and} & \tilde{S}_t = S_t, \\
\text{if} \quad \max\left(\hat{S}_t, \hat{D}_t\right) < Q_t, & \text{then} \quad \tilde{D}_t = Q_t & \text{and} & \tilde{S}_t = Q_t.
\end{array}$$

Intuitively, we can see that the last case should be a rare occurrence if the model is correctly specified. In fact, observing this situation is a good indication that we need to rework our formulation.

Finally, notice that it is not impossible that predictions concerning the regime and the quantity, being derived independently, may be incompatible. For example, we may have:

$$\hat{z}_t > \frac{1}{2} \quad \text{and} \quad \hat{D}_t < \hat{S}_t.$$

8.1.4.3 Determining Equilibrium

We may also be interested in examining what the market would look like in equilibrium. This implies finding the market clearing price p_t^e and the corresponding quantity Q_t^e, values which can be derived directly from the equations for D_t and S_t, given a price p_t. In fact:

$$p_t^e = \frac{\mathbf{x}_t^2 \mathbf{b}_2 + u_{2t} - \mathbf{x}_t^1 \mathbf{b}_1 - u_{1t}}{a_1 - a_2},$$

$$p_t^e = \frac{S_t - D_t}{a_1 - a_2} + p_t.$$

Hence:

$$\hat{p}_t^e = \mathrm{E}\left(p_t^e \middle| Q_t\right) = p_t + \frac{\hat{S}_t - \hat{D}_t}{a_1 - a_2}.$$

8.2 Observations on the Regime and the Quantity Exchanged

8.2.1 The Model

In the disequilibrium model we examined in section 8.1, a good's price is considered fixed at any point in time and variable between periods. The trajectory of its evolution is a function of the nature of the observed disequilibria. As a first approximation, we may speculate that the price will increase in the case of excess demand and decrease under excess supply. Integrating this information into our model, we obtain:

$$\begin{aligned} D_t &= a_1 p_t + \mathbf{x}_t^1 \mathbf{b}_1 + u_{1t}, \\ S_t &= a_2 p_t + \mathbf{x}_t^2 \mathbf{b}_2 + u_{2t}, \\ Q_t &= \min(D_t, S_t), \\ \Delta p_t &\equiv p_{t+1} - p_t, \\ &= h(D_t - S_t), \end{aligned} \tag{8.5}$$

where h is an unknown monotonically increasing function.

Since we don't know h, the only information added by incorporating this function is the specification of the regime. If $\Delta p_t > 0$ we know that there is excess demand, while $\Delta p_t < 0$ implies excess supply.

We observe two endogenous variables, Q_t and z_t, or, equivalently, two truncated variables:

$$D_t^* = \begin{cases} D_t, & \text{if } D_t < S_t, \\ 0, & \text{otherwise,} \end{cases}$$
$$S_t^* = \begin{cases} S_t, & \text{if } S_t < D_t, \\ 0, & \text{otherwise.} \end{cases} \tag{8.6}$$

8.2.2 *Estimation Methods*

When a_1 or a_2 are non-zero, the quantity exchanged depends on the exogenous variables over the unknown function h. The likelihood also depends upon this function and is thus of no use.

The only case in which this model can be estimated is when current or past prices don't impact on the quantity demanded or supplied. Clearly, this is of little practical interest. In this situation the variables (D_t, S_t) are independent over time and characterized by a normal two-dimensional distribution which is a function of the parameters $\mathbf{b}_1, \mathbf{b}_2, \Sigma$. The associated marginal models are of the Tobit generalized form (cf. chapter 7), whose properties they share.

In particular, in this model applying ordinary least squares to a regression of D_t on $\mathbf{x}^1$ (for $D_t < S_t$) yields inconsistent estimators of the demand equation parameters. Consistent estimates of these parameters can be obtained, however, with the maximum-likelihood method (cf. exercise 3), or by expanding the two-stage method we examined in the context of the generalized Tobit model.

8.3 Predetermined Evolution of the Price

8.3.1 *The Model*

Our analysis in section 8.2 revealed that in order to simultaneously include prices in the supply and demand equations while accounting for the regime we need to specify the function h. In this section we shall define the price adjustment equation as:

$$\begin{aligned}\triangle p_t &\equiv p_{t+1} - p_t, \\ &= \lambda\,(D_t - S_t),\end{aligned} \tag{8.7}$$

where λ is a positive real number. Now the price at time t, equal to $p_t = p_{t-1} + \lambda\,(D_{t-1} - S_{t-1})$, is predetermined.

Equation (8.7) can now be used to eliminate price, p_t, from the supply and demand equations, yielding:

$$\begin{aligned}D_t - D_{t-1} &= a_1\,(p_t - p_{t-1}) + \mathbf{x}_t^1\mathbf{b}_1 - \mathbf{x}_{t-1}^1\mathbf{b}_1 + u_{1t} - u_{1,t-1}, \\ D_t - D_{t-1} &= a_1\lambda\,(D_{t-1} - S_{t-1}) + \mathbf{x}_t^1\mathbf{b}_1 - \mathbf{x}_{t-1}^1\mathbf{b}_1 + u_{1t} - u_{1,t-1}, \\ D_t &= (1 + a_1\lambda)\,D_{t-1} - a_1\lambda S_{t-1} \\ &\quad + \mathbf{x}_t^1\mathbf{b}_1 - \mathbf{x}_{t-1}^1\mathbf{b}_1 + u_{1t} - u_{1,t-1}.\end{aligned}$$

We see that the equation for D_t contains the endogenous lagged variables D_{t-1} and S_{t-1}. This introduces serial correlation between the quantities supplied and demanded at time t and their previous values.

8.3.2 *Estimation Methods*

We have seen that (D_t, S_t) are not uncorrelated over time. The same is true for the observable endogenous variables $(Q_t, \triangle p_t)$. To find the likelihood we first need the conditional density of (D_t, S_t) given $Q_{t-1}, \triangle p_{t-1}, Q_{t-2}, \triangle p_{t-2}, \ldots$ We can then derive the conditional distribution of Q_t and $\triangle p_t$ given their previous values.

Let $\psi\,(u_1, u_2)$ be a normal two-dimensional density function with mean $\begin{pmatrix}0\\0\end{pmatrix}$ and covariance matrix Σ. Given previous values of the observable endogenous variables, the conditional density of (D_t, S_t), denoted $g_t\,(d, s)$, is equal to:

$$g_t\,(d, s) = \psi\left(d - a_1 p_t - \mathbf{x}_t^1\mathbf{b}_1, s - a_2 p_t - \mathbf{x}_t^2\mathbf{b}_2\right).$$

Consequently, the conditional density function of $(Q_t, \triangle p_t)$ is:

$$h_t\,(q, \triangle p) = \frac{1}{\lambda}\left[z_{\triangle p}\left(q + \frac{\triangle p}{\lambda'}, q\right) + (1 - z_{\triangle p})\left(q, q - \frac{\triangle p}{\lambda}\right)\right],$$

where:

$$z_{\triangle p} = \begin{cases}1, & \text{if } \triangle p > 0, \\ 0, & \text{otherwise.}\end{cases}$$

The likelihood is:

$$L = \prod_{t=1}^{T} h_t\,(q_t, \triangle p_t),$$
$$= \prod_{t:\triangle p_t>0} \frac{1}{\lambda} g_t \left(q_t + \frac{\triangle p_t}{\lambda'}, q_t\right) \prod_{t:\triangle p_t\leq 0} \frac{1}{\lambda} g_t \left(q_t, q_t - \frac{\triangle p_t}{\lambda}\right).$$

This relatively simple likelihood is easy to maximize using an iterative algorithm. Incidentally, notice that initial values for the parameters can be found by applying instrumental least squares to the supply and demand equations after a preliminary transformation. We write:

$$Q_t = D_t - \frac{1}{\lambda} \triangle p_t z_{\triangle p_t},$$
$$= a_1 p_t + \mathbf{x}_t^1 \mathbf{b}_1 - \frac{1}{\lambda} \triangle p_t z_{\triangle p_t} + u_{1t}.$$

In these equations $\triangle p_t z_{\triangle p_t}$ (which incorporates p_{t+1}) is correlated with the disturbance term u_{1t}. The parameters, $a_1, \mathbf{b}_1, \frac{1}{\lambda}$ may, however, still be estimated consistently if we use instrumental least squares, with p_t, $\mathbf{x}_t^1$, and $\mathbf{x}_t^2$ as instruments. To ensure identification, the vector of explanatory variables for the supply equation, $\mathbf{x}^2$ must contain at least one variable not included in $\mathbf{x}^1$.

8.4 Endogenous Evolution of Prices

8.4.1 A Preliminary Model

Until now we have assumed that the price, p_t, is fixed at any point in time t. A disequilibrium state is also feasible if the price is allowed to adjust instantaneously, provided the change is not sufficient to produce equilibrium. In this case p_t is an endogenous variable correlated with the disturbance terms of the supply and demand functions.

The simplest model of this phenomenon is as follows:

$$\begin{aligned} D_t &= a_1 p_t + \mathbf{x}_t^1 \mathbf{b}_1 + u_{1t}, \\ S_t &= a_2 p_t + \mathbf{x}_t^2 \mathbf{b}_2 + u_{2t}, \\ Q_t &= \min(D_t, S_t), \\ \triangle p_t &= p_t - p_{t-1}, \\ &= \lambda (D_t - S_t), \end{aligned} \tag{8.8}$$

where λ is a positive parameter reflecting the rate at which the price adjusts. Notice also that the equation for $\triangle p_t$ has changed from the previous section. In this model quantities (D_t, S_t) depend on price, which itself depends upon quantities over the last equation in (8.8). Consequently, we simultaneously solve for three variables p_t, D_t, and S_t.

The price adjustment equation can be rewritten if we introduce the equilibrium price:

$$p_t^e = \frac{\mathbf{x}_t^2 \mathbf{b}_2 + u_{2t} - \mathbf{x}_t^1 \mathbf{b}_1 - u_{1t}}{a_1 - a_2}.$$

Furthermore:

$$\begin{aligned} D_t - S_t &= (a_1 - a_2)\, p_t + \mathbf{x}_t^1 \mathbf{b}_1 + u_{1t} - \mathbf{x}_t^2 \mathbf{b}_2 - u_{2t}, \\ &= (a_1 - a_2)\left(p_t - p_t^e\right). \end{aligned}$$

Substituting this for excess demand in the price adjustment equation yields:

$$\triangle p_t = p_t - p_{t-1} = \lambda\,(a_1 - a_2)\left(p_t - p_t^e\right).$$

Letting:

$$\mu = \frac{\lambda\,(a_2 - a_1)}{1 + \lambda\,(a_2 - a_1)},$$

we obtain:

$$p_t = (1 - \mu)\, p_{t-1} + \mu p_t^e. \tag{8.9}$$

Since $\lambda \geq 0$, $a_2 > 0$, and $a_1 < 0$, we see that μ is bounded by zero and one. Consequently, p_t lies between the previous period's actual price and the current period's equilibrium price.

8.4.2 *Estimation Methods*

8.4.2.1 *Instrumental Least-Squares Estimation*

The quantity exchanged, Q_t, can be written:

$$\begin{aligned} Q_t &= D_t\,(1 - z_t) + S_t z_t, \\ Q_t &= D_t + (S_t - D_t)\, z_t, \end{aligned}$$

where:

$$z_t = \begin{cases} 1, & \text{if } D_t > S_t, \\ 0, & \text{otherwise.} \end{cases}$$

as in section 8.1.4.

Using the price equation $D_t - S_t = \frac{1}{\lambda}\Delta p_t$, we obtain:

$$Q_t = a_1 p_t + \mathbf{x}_t^1 \mathbf{b}_1 - \frac{1}{\lambda}\Delta p_t z_{\Delta p_t} + u_{1t}. \tag{8.10}$$

Here we have a model which is linear in the parameters a_1, $\mathbf{b}_1$, and $\frac{1}{\lambda}$, and comprises two explanatory variables, p and $\Delta p_t z_{\Delta p_t}$ which are correlated with the error term u_1. Consistent estimators of these two parameters can be obtained with instrumental least squares, provided there are at least two explanatory variables in the supply function $(\mathbf{x}^2)$ not present in the demand function $(\mathbf{x}^1)$. The supply function parameters a_2 and $\mathbf{b}_2$ are obtained symmetrically:

$$\begin{aligned} Q_t &= S_t + (D_t - S_t)\left(1 - z_{\Delta p_t}\right), \\ &= a_2 p_t + \mathbf{x}_t^2 \mathbf{b}_2 + \frac{1}{\lambda}\Delta p_t \left(1 - z_{\Delta p_t}\right) + u_{2t}. \end{aligned}$$

Notice that applying instrumental least squares to this second equation will yield a different estimate of λ. We avoid this by estimating:

$$Q_t - \frac{1}{\hat{\lambda}}\Delta p_t \left(1 - z_{\Delta p_t}\right) = a_2 p_t + \mathbf{x}_t^2 \mathbf{b}_2 + v_{2t},$$

where $\hat{\lambda}$ is a consistent estimator of λ obtained in the first stage. For this procedure to work we require that the demand equation contains at least one exogenous variable not occurring in the supply equation.

8.4.2.2 *The Maximum-Likelihood Method*

Before deriving the density function of (Q_t, p_t) we need to find it for (D_t, S_t). Substituting our expression for D_t and S_t in terms of p_t into the supply and demand equations yields:

$$\begin{aligned} D_t &= a_1 p_{t-1} + a_1 \lambda (D_t - S_t) + \mathbf{x}_t^1 \mathbf{b}_1 + u_{1t}, \\ S_t &= a_2 p_{t-1} + a_2 \lambda (D_t - S_t) + \mathbf{x}_t^2 \mathbf{b}_2 + u_{2t}, \end{aligned}$$

or:

$$\begin{aligned} (1 - a_1\lambda) D_t + a_1 \lambda S_t &= a_1 p_{t-1} + \mathbf{x}_t^1 \mathbf{b}_1 + u_{1t}, \\ -a_2 \lambda D_t + (1 + a_2\lambda) S_t &= a_2 p_{t-1} + \mathbf{x}_t^2 \mathbf{b}_2 + u_{2t}. \end{aligned}$$

Now, (D_t, S_t) can be derived from the pair (u_{1t}, u_{2t}) as follows. The Jacobian of the transformation, $|J| = 1 + (a_2 - a_1)\lambda$ is always positive under the standard assumptions: $a_2 > 0$, $a_1 < 0$, and $\lambda \geq 0$. If $\psi(u_1, u_2)$ is the density function for the disturbance term, then the density of (D_t, S_t), conditional on previous values, is given by:

$$\begin{aligned} g_t(d, s) = [1 + (a_2 - a_1)\lambda]\, \psi\big[&(1 - a_1\lambda) d + a_1 \lambda s - a_1 p_{t-1} - \mathbf{x}_t^1 \mathbf{b}_1 \\ &- a_2 \lambda d + (1 + a_2\lambda) s - a_2 p_{t-1} - \mathbf{x}_t^2 \mathbf{b}_2\big]. \end{aligned}$$

As in section 8.3.2, the likelihood is given by:

$$L = \prod_{t:\Delta p_t > 0} \frac{1}{\lambda} g_t \left(q_t + \frac{1}{\lambda} \Delta p_t, q_t \right) \prod_{t:\Delta p_t \leq 0} \frac{1}{\lambda} g_t \left(q_t, q_t - \frac{1}{\lambda} \Delta p_t \right).$$

8.4.2.3 O.L.S. Estimation of the Price Adjustment Equation
The price adjustment equation is:

$$p_t = (1-\mu)\, p_{t-1} + \mu p_t^e,$$

$$p_t = (1-\mu)\, p_{t-1} + \mathbf{x}_t^2 \mathbf{b}_2 \frac{\mu}{a_1 - a_2} - \mathbf{x}_t^1 \mathbf{b}_1 \frac{\mu}{a_1 - a_2} + \frac{\mu}{a_1 - a_2} (u_{2t} - u_{1t})\,.$$

Since the variables p_{t-1}, $\mathbf{x}_t^2$, and $\mathbf{x}_t^1$ are not correlated with the disturbances u_{1t} and u_{2t}, we can apply ordinary least squares to this equation. This yields an estimate for μ which is important for the characterisation of equilibrium, as we shall see.

8.4.3 *The Assumption of Equilibrium*

Equilibrium in the market for a good is characterized by equality between the good's actual price p_t and its equilibrium price p_t^e. According to equation (8.9) this implies that $\mu = 1$, or equivalently – in terms of how fast price adjustment occurs – $\lambda = \infty$. As to the parameters, the existence of equilibrium is independent of time. Consequently, from equation system (8.8), if the market is in equilibrium during any period, it will be so all the time. This definition of an equilibrium model coincides with the statistical meaning of the term. From the likelihood equation in section 8.4.2, letting λ approach (plus) infinity yields:

$$L_{\lambda \to +\infty} = \prod_t (a_2 - a_1)\, \psi \left(q_t - a_1 p_t - \mathbf{x}_t^1 \mathbf{b}_1, q_t - a_2 p_t - \mathbf{x}_t^2 \mathbf{b}_2 \right),$$

which is none other than the likelihood corresponding to the equilibrium model.

In practice, it is often important to know whether or not the market in question is approximately in equilibrium. We can test this with the parameters, defining $H_0 : (\mu = 1) = (\lambda = +\infty)$. However, this hypothesis can not be tested using standard procedures, i.e. the likelihood-ratio test or the Student's t-test. The null hypothesis, $H_0 : \mu = 1$ applies to the boundary of the set of possible values assumed by $\mu\,[0, 1]$, and the appropriate test is one-sided. Consider the equation:

$$p_t - p_{t-1} = -\mu p_{t-1} + \mathbf{x}_t^2 \mathbf{b}_2 \frac{\mu}{a_1 - a_2} - \mathbf{x}_t^1 \mathbf{b}_1 \frac{\mu}{a_1 - a_2} + \frac{\mu}{a_1 - a_2} (u_{2t} - u_{1t}).$$

It is tempting to test the null hypothesis $H_0 : \mu = 1$ by comparing the calculated t-statistic for μ with 1.96 for a 95% probability. In fact, it must be compared to 1.64 for a one-sided test, leading us to reject the null hypothesis more frequently.

8.4.4 *A General Model*

A natural extension to the endogenous price equation involves incorporating exogenous variables and a disturbance term:

$$\begin{aligned} \Delta p_t &= p_t - p_{t-1}, \\ &= \lambda (D_t - S_t) + \mathbf{x}_t^3 \mathbf{b}_3 + u_{3t}. \end{aligned}$$

This formulation includes everything we have seen so far.

If $\lambda = 0$, if lagged values of supply and demand don't enter into $\mathbf{x}^3$, and if the disturbance term u_{3t} is independent of u_{1t} and u_{2t}, then price is completely exogenous. In this case the price adjustment equation contributes nothing, and we recover the model from section 8.1.

For the model in section 8.3, we let λ and the variance of u_{3t} be nil, and set $\mathbf{x}_t^3 \mathbf{b}_3 = \mu (D_{t-1} - S_{t-1})$.

Section 8.4 introduced a model corresponding to $\mathbf{b}_3 = 0$ and var $(u_{3t}) = 0$. The equilibrium model appears as a limiting case when we let λ tend to plus infinity.

The estimation methods described in these sections can easily be extended to account for the expanded price adjustment equation.

Exercises

8.1 Given the conditions under which the model in section 8.1 is identified. Verify that, even if it is identified, we still require a minimum number of observations on demand and supply to be able to estimate the parameters.

8.2 Would we modify our estimation methods in section 8.1 if the values of D_t and S_t were observed?

Consider the model in section 8.1 with $r = 0$ and $s_1^2 = s_2^2$. Find $\Pr(D_t > S_t)$. Show that $\Pr(D_t < S_t) > \frac{1}{2}$ if and only if $p_t^e > p_t$.

8.3 Let $a_1 = a_2 = 0$ in the model from section 8.2, and let $g_t(d, s)$ represent the density function of the pair D_t, S_t. Show that the likelihood of the model is:

$$L = \prod_{t:\Delta p_t > 0} \int_{q_t}^{\infty} g_t(z, q_t)\, dz \prod_{t:\Delta p_t \le 0} \int_{q_t}^{\infty} g_t(z, q_t)\, dz.$$

In this likelihood, isolate the information contributed by the q_t-s.

8.4 Show that equation (8.9) can be used to express the price p_t as a function of past and current equilibrium prices.

8.5 We can estimate the parameters of equation (8.10) by performing a regression of p_t on all of the exogenous variables in $\mathbf{x}_t^1$ and $\mathbf{x}_t^2$. Denoting $\hat{p}_t$ the resulting fitted value of p_t, we regress Q_t on $\hat{p}_t$, $\mathbf{x}_t^1$, and $\Delta \hat{p}_t z_{\Delta \hat{p}_t}$, where $\Delta \hat{p}_t = \hat{p}_t - \hat{p}_{t-1}$ and where $z_{\Delta \hat{p}_t}$ is defined:

$$z_{\hat{\delta}_t} = \begin{cases} 0, & \text{if } \hat{p}_t < 0, \\ 1, & \text{otherwise.} \end{cases}$$

Will this procedure yield consistent estimators?

8.6 Verify that when the equilibrium price p_t^e is independent of t, the price-adjustment equation $p_t = \mu p_{t-1} + (1 - \mu)\, p_t^e$, $0 \le \mu < 1$ ensures the convergence of p_t to the equilibrium price.

8.7 Consider the model in equations (8.5) and (8.6), letting the disturbance terms u_{1t} and u_{2t} be independent and distributed $\mathrm{N}\left(0, s_1^2\right)$ and $\mathrm{N}\left(0, s_2^2\right)$ respectively. Find $\mathrm{E}\left(D_t^* \middle| p_t\right)$ and $\mathrm{E}\left(S_t^* \middle| p_t\right)$. Conditional on the values of p_t, derive a two-stage method to estimate the parameters.

8.8 Assume that the demand and supply functions are normal linear equations:

$$D_t = a_1 p_t + \mathbf{x}_t^1 \mathbf{b}_1 + u_{1t},$$
$$S_t = a_2 p_t + \mathbf{x}_t^2 \mathbf{b}_2 + u_{2t},$$

where $t = 1, \ldots, T$ and:

$$(u_{1t}, u_{2t})' \sim_{asy} \mathrm{N}\left[\begin{pmatrix} 0 \\ 0 \end{pmatrix}, \begin{pmatrix} s_1^2 & 0 \\ 0 & s_2^2 \end{pmatrix}\right].$$

(a) Calculate $\mathrm{E}\left(Q_t \mid p_t, \mathbf{x}_t^1, \mathbf{x}_t^2\right)$ for the disequilibrium model $Q_t = \min(D_t, S_t)$ and for the equilibrium model $Q_t = D_t = S_t$.

(b) Use these results to derive a test for market equilibrium versus disequilibrium without building any super-models (cf. Davidson, R. and MacKinnon, J. [DM81])

9 Truncated Latent Variables Defined by a System of Simultaneous Equations

9.1 The General Model

In previous chapters we were primarily interested in the study of a single endogenous variable defined as a function of one or more latent variables. Often, however, we wish to study values assumed simultaneously by several endogenous variables, some of which may be limited while others are not. For that reason we now introduce simultaneous equation models.

The general structure of the type of model we shall be studying in this chapter is as follows:

(i) L latent variables, $y^* = \left(y_1^*, \ldots, y_\ell^*, \ldots, y_L^*\right)'$, are defined by a simultaneous equation system:

$$Ay^* = X\mathbf{b} + \mathbf{u}, \quad u \sim_{asy} \mathrm{N}(0, \Sigma). \tag{9.1}$$

(ii) One purpose these variables serve is to partition the observations, $i = 1, \ldots, n$, into K categories or regimes $J_1, \ldots, J_K$:

$$i \in J_k \Leftrightarrow \mathbf{y}^* \in \mathcal{C}_k, \tag{9.2}$$

where the $\mathcal{C}$-s are known sets constituting a partition of $\mathbb{R}^L$.

(iii) Finally, the observable variables, $y = \left(y_1, \ldots, y_p\right)'$, are obtained for each regime as known, affine functions of the latent variables:

$$y_i = D_k y_i^* + d_k, \quad i \in J_k. \tag{9.3}$$

Notice that, depending on the choice of $\mathcal{C}$ and of D_k, some latent variables may not contribute to the definition of the partitions or, for that matter, they may not be (even partially) observable. Nevertheless, the model in equations (9.1), (9.2), and (9.3) covers a great number of cases.

For example, if $L = p = 1$ and $K = 2$, we recover the dichotomous model:

$$y = \begin{cases} 1, & \text{if } y^* > 0, \\ 0, & \text{otherwise,} \end{cases}$$

and the simple Tobit model:

$$y = \begin{cases} y^*, & \text{if } y^* > 0, \\ 0, & \text{otherwise.} \end{cases}$$

When $p = 1$ and $L = K = 2$, we have the generalized Tobit model:

$$y = \begin{cases} y_1^*, & \text{if } y_2^* > 0, \\ 0, & \text{otherwise,} \end{cases}$$

and the disequilibrium model, defined:

$$y = \begin{cases} y_1^*, & \text{if} \quad y_2^* > y_1^*, \\ y_2^*, & \text{if} \quad y_1^* > y_2^*. \end{cases}$$

Some qualitative dichotomous models simultaneously describe the behaviour of several agents, for example:

$$y = \begin{cases} 1, & \text{if } y_1^* > 0 \text{ and } y_2^* > 0, \\ 0, & \text{otherwise.} \end{cases}$$

In all of these examples a single dependent variable is observed. If we now turn are attention to situations in which two dependent variables, y_1 and y_2, are simultaneously observed, we find that there are many more possible scenarios.

Thus, if $L = 2$, the formulation resembles the disequilibrium model with observations on the regime:

$$\left.\begin{matrix} y_1 = y_1^* \\ y_2 = 0 \end{matrix}\right\} \quad \text{if} \quad y_2^* > y_1^*, \qquad \text{and} \qquad \left.\begin{matrix} y_1 = 0 \\ y_2 = y_2^* \end{matrix}\right\} \quad \text{if} \quad y_1^* > y_2^*.$$

We also have various qualitative models, such as:

$$y_1 = \begin{cases} 1, & \text{if} \quad y_1^* > 0, \\ 0, & \text{if} \quad y_1^* < 0, \end{cases} \qquad \text{and} \qquad y_2 = \begin{cases} 1, & \text{if} \quad y_2^* > 0, \\ 0, & \text{if} \quad y_2^* < 0 \end{cases}$$

Some new models arise, in which we may, for example, simultaneously observe a qualitative and a quantitative model:

$$\left.\begin{matrix} y_1 = y_1^* \\ y_2 = 1 \end{matrix}\right\} \quad \text{if} \quad y_2^* > 0, \qquad \text{and} \qquad \left.\begin{matrix} y_1 = y_1^* \\ y_2 = 0 \end{matrix}\right\} \quad \text{if} \quad y_2^* < 0,$$

or a quantitative variable and a truncated variable:

$$\left.\begin{matrix} y_1 = y_1^*, \\ y_2 = y_2^*, \end{matrix}\right\} \quad \text{if} \quad y_2^* > 0, \qquad \text{and} \qquad \left.\begin{matrix} y_1 = y_1^* \\ y_2 = 0 \end{matrix}\right\} \quad \text{if} \quad y_2^* < 0.$$

9.2 Estimation Methods

If we wish to conduct a general inquiry into estimation procedures for the parameters A, $\mathbf{b}$ and Σ in equations (9.1), (9.2), and (9.3), we will find this specification rather difficult to manipulate. In this section we shall present estimation methods for models which are sufficiently simple to be usable in practice. Examples and applications are given in section 9.3.

There are several approaches to the issue of estimation, and we must choose one suitable to the particular form of our model. While this presentation focuses on simple models, these techniques can be expanded to apply to more complex ones. Notice, however, that any functional form incorporating normal distributions in more than three dimensions cannot be considered malleable at this point in time.

9.2.1 The Maximum-Likelihood Method

As usual, this method is of great use when applied to models with truncated dependent variables, yielding non linear likelihood equations which must be solved using numerical algorithms.

Before determining the likelihood, we must first find the distribution of the latent variables. Once these have been calculated, we can derive the distribution of the observable endogenous variables.

Thus, consider the model with latent variables defined:

$$\begin{aligned} y_{1i}^* &= a_1 y_{2i}^* + b_1 + \mathbf{b}_2 \mathbf{x}_i + u_{1i}, \\ y_{2i}^* &= a_2 y_{1i}^* + \mathbf{b}_3 \mathbf{z}_i + u_{2i}, \end{aligned} \tag{9.4}$$

where $\mathbf{x}$ and $\mathbf{z}$ are two exogenous variables and the disturbances are assumed independent: $u_{1i} \sim \mathrm{N}\left(0, s_1^2\right)$ and $u_{2i} \sim \mathrm{N}\left(0, s_2^2\right)$. The observed endogenous variables are:

$$\begin{aligned} y_{1i} &= y_{1i}^*, \\ y_{2i} &= \begin{cases} y_{2i}^*, & \text{if } y_{2i}^* > 0, \\ 0, & \text{otherwise.} \end{cases} \end{aligned} \tag{9.5}$$

To find the distribution of the latent variables, we rewrite equations (9.4) in their reduced form:

$$\begin{aligned} y_{1i}^* &= \frac{b_1}{1-a_1a_2} + \frac{\mathbf{b}_2}{1-a_1a_2}\mathbf{x}_i + \frac{a_1\mathbf{b}_3}{1-a_1a_2}\mathbf{z}_i + \frac{u_{1i}+a_1u_{2i}}{1-a_1a_2}, \\ y_{2i}^* &= \frac{a_2b_1}{1-a_1a_2} + \frac{a_2\mathbf{b}_2}{1-a_1a_2}\mathbf{x}_i + \frac{\mathbf{b}_3}{1-a_1a_2}\mathbf{z}_i + \frac{a_2u_{1i}+u_{2i}}{1-a_1a_2}. \end{aligned} \tag{9.6}$$

The distribution of the vector $\left(y_{1i}^*, y_{2i}^*\right)'$ is consequently seen to be normal bivariate. The means of the latent variables, m_{1i} and m_{2i}, are given by the deterministic parts of equation system (9.6), while their variances and covariances, denoted η_1^2, η_2^2 and $\eta_1\eta_2$, respectively, are:

$$\eta_1^2 = \frac{s_1^2 + a_1^2 s_2^2}{(1 - a_1 a_2)^2},$$

$$\eta_2^2 = \frac{a_2^2 s_1^2 + s_2^2}{(1 - a_1 a_2)^2},$$

$$r\eta_1\eta_2 = \frac{a_2 s_1^2 + a_1 s_2^2}{(1 - a_1 a_2)^2}.$$

From this we can directly derive the density function of the observable variables. The density of (y_{1i}, y_{2i}) is equal to that of the latent variables when $y_{2i} > 0$, and equal to:

$$\frac{1}{\eta_1}\varphi\left[\frac{y_{1i} - m_{1i}}{\eta_1}\right]\Phi\left[\frac{-m_{2i} + r\frac{\eta_2}{\eta_1}(y_{1i} - m_{1i})}{\eta_2\sqrt{1 - r^2}}\right],$$

when $y_{2i} = 0$.

The likelihood is a complicated function of the parameters of the structural equation (9.4), and it is preferable to perform a change of parameters before maximization. We can, for example, introduce new parameters such as:

$$a_1, a_2, \frac{b_1}{1 - a_1 a_2}, \frac{\mathbf{b}_2}{1 - a_1 a_2}, \frac{\mathbf{b}_3}{1 - a_1 a_2}, \eta_1, \eta_2, r.$$

While the likelihood in this model is bounded, that is not generally true. It may tend toward infinity, as we saw in section 8.1.3 during our examination of disequilibrium models. This occurs when the values assumed by the observable variables do not permit us to identify to which regime the data points correspond. This is the case, for example, in a model based on four latent variables y_1^*, y_2^*, y_3^*, and y_4^*, with observed variables:

$$y_1 = y_1^*,$$

$$y_2 = \begin{cases} y_2^*, & \text{if} \quad y_4^* > 0, \\ y_3^*, & \text{if} \quad y_4^* \leq 0. \end{cases}$$

9.2.2 *Two-Stage Regression in Stacked Regression Models*

When equation (9.1) represents a system of stacked regressions (i.e. $A = I$), the two-stage regression procedure permits a straightforward generalization.

Consider the model:

$$y_{1i}^* = \mathbf{x}_{1i}\mathbf{b}_1 + u_{1i},$$
$$y_{2i}^* = \mathbf{x}_{2i}\mathbf{b}_2 + u_{2i},$$
$$y_{3i}^* = \mathbf{x}_{3i}\mathbf{b}_3 + u_{3i},$$

with observed endogenous variables:

$$y_{1i} = \begin{cases} y_{1i}^*, & \text{if } y_{3i}^* > 0, \\ y_{2i}^*, & \text{if } y_{3i}^* \leq 0, \end{cases}$$

$$y_{2i} = \begin{cases} 1, & \text{if } y_{3i}^* > 0, \\ 0, & \text{if } y_{3i}^* \leq 0. \end{cases}$$

Equivalently, we can define:

$$z_{1i} = \begin{cases} y_{1i}^*, & \text{if } y_{3i}^* > 0, \\ 0, & \text{if } y_{3i}^* \leq 0, \end{cases}$$

$$z_{2i} = \begin{cases} 0, & \text{if } y_{3i}^* > 0, \\ y_{2i}^*, & \text{if } y_{3i}^* \leq 0. \end{cases}$$

This model is comprised of two generalized Tobit models which share a variable defining the regime.

For the first step, we estimate the probit aspect, i.e. the part of the model associated with the observations on y_{2i}. The second step consists of analysing the data corresponding to $z_{1i} \neq 0$ and $z_{2i} \neq 0$ separately, using the methods presented in chapter 7.

9.2.3 *Preliminary Estimation of the Reduced Form*

When equation (9.1) represents a true system of simultaneous equations, i.e. when the system is not recursive, estimation typically begins by examining the parameters of the equations of the reduced form. To illustrate, examine the model in expression (9.4) and (9.5). The reduced form, equation (9.6), can be rewritten:

$$y_{1i}^* = c_{11} + \mathbf{c}_{12}\mathbf{x}_i + \mathbf{c}_{13}\mathbf{z}_i + v_{1i},$$
$$y_{2i}^* = c_{21} + \mathbf{c}_{22}\mathbf{x}_i + \mathbf{c}_{23}\mathbf{z}_i + v_{2i},$$

with:

$$c_{11} = \frac{b_1}{1 - a_1 a_2}, \quad \mathbf{c}_{12} = \frac{\mathbf{b}_2}{1 - a_1 a_2}, \quad \mathbf{c}_{13} = \frac{a_1 \mathbf{b}_3}{1 - a_1 a_2},$$

$$c_{21} = \frac{a_2 b_1}{1 - a_1 a_2}, \quad \mathbf{c}_{22} = \frac{a_2 \mathbf{b}_2}{1 - a_1 a_2}, \quad \mathbf{c}_{23} = \frac{\mathbf{b}_3}{1 - a_1 a_2},$$

and:

$$\text{var}(v_{1i}) = \eta_1^2, \quad \text{var}(v_{2i}) = \eta_2^2, \quad \text{cov}(v_{1i}, v_{2i}) = r\eta_1\eta_2.$$

If we ignore the constraints on the parameters of the reduced-form equations, these can be estimated from the observations.

Thus, c_{11}, $\mathbf{c}_{12}$, $\mathbf{c}_{13}$, η_1 are found by regressing the variable y_1 $\left(= y_1^*\right)$ on the number one (1), on $\mathbf{x}$, and on $\mathbf{z}$ using ordinary least squares. The parameters of the second equation are found from the Tobit model:

$$y_{2i} = \begin{cases} y_{2i}^*, & \text{if } y_{2i}^* > 0, \\ 0, & \text{otherwise.} \end{cases}$$

Finally, the correlation, r, is obtained by examining the residuals of the estimate.

This procedure yields consistent estimates of the parameters, but it is clearly not efficient. It now remains to calculate the parameters of the structural equations – a_1, a_2, b_1, b_2, and b_3.

9.2.4 *Instrumental-Variables Estimation*

Let Γ represent the estimators of C. We can predict the values of the latent variables by:

$$\hat{y}_{1i}^* = \gamma_{11} + \boldsymbol{\gamma}_{12}\mathbf{x}_i + \boldsymbol{\gamma}_{13}\mathbf{z}_i,$$

and:

$$\hat{y}_{2i}^* = \boldsymbol{\gamma}_{21} + \boldsymbol{\gamma}_{22}\mathbf{x}_i + \boldsymbol{\gamma}_{23}\mathbf{z}_i.$$

Asymptotically, these variables are not correlated with the disturbances. Substituting the predicted values for y_{1i}^* and y_{2i}^* into the right-hand side of equation (9.4), we apply ordinary least squares to the first equation to estimate a_1, b_1, and $\mathbf{b}_2$, and Tobit to the second equation to obtain a_2 and b_3.

9.2.5 *Amemiya's Method*

This method consists of examining the relation h expressing the parameters C as functions of $(a_1, a_2, b_1, \mathbf{b}_2, \mathbf{b}_3)$:

$$C = h(a_1, a_2, b_1, \mathbf{b}_2, \mathbf{b}_3). \tag{9.7}$$

When the model is exactly identified, the application h is a bijection (i.e. has an inverse over its entire domain), and:

$$(\alpha_1, \alpha_2, \beta_1, \boldsymbol{\beta}_2, \boldsymbol{\beta}_3)' = h^{-1}(\Gamma),$$

provides a consistent estimator of the coefficients of the structural equations. In the general case, the model is overidentified, and equation (9.7) yields several estimates of the parameters $(a_1, a_2, b_1, \mathbf{b}_2, \mathbf{b}_3)$ in terms of C:

$$(a_1, a_2, b_1, \mathbf{b}_2, \mathbf{b}_3) = h^-(C),$$

where $h^- \in \mathcal{H}$ is a generalized inverse.

Every estimator defined by $h^-(C)$, $h^- \in \mathcal{H}$, is consistent, so we need to select the "best" one. Amemiya [Ame78] proposed the following course of action. For the model under consideration, equation (9.7) yields:

$$\begin{pmatrix} 1 & -a_1 \\ -a_2 & 1 \end{pmatrix} \begin{pmatrix} c_{11} & \mathbf{c}_{12} & \mathbf{c}_{13} \\ c_{21} & \mathbf{c}_{22} & \mathbf{c}_{23} \end{pmatrix} = \begin{pmatrix} b_1 & \mathbf{b}_2 & 0 \\ 0 & 0 & \mathbf{b}_3 \end{pmatrix}.$$

If we wish to inspect the parameters a_2 and $\mathbf{b}_3$ from the second equation of (9.4), we see that they are related to the parameters C by:

$$\begin{aligned} c_{21} &= a_2 c_{11}, \\ \mathbf{c}_{22} &= a_2 \mathbf{c}_{12}, \\ \mathbf{c}_{23} &= a_2 \mathbf{c}_{13} + \mathbf{b}_3. \end{aligned}$$

Replacing the C-s by their estimators, we obtain:

$$\begin{aligned} \gamma_{21} &= a_2 \gamma_{11} + \omega_{21}, \\ \boldsymbol{\gamma}_{22} &= a_2 \boldsymbol{\gamma}_{12} + \boldsymbol{\omega}_{22}, \\ \boldsymbol{\gamma}_{23} &= a_2 \boldsymbol{\gamma}_{13} + \mathbf{b}_3 + \boldsymbol{\omega}_{23}, \end{aligned}$$

where $\omega_{21} = \gamma_{21} - c_{21} + a_2 (c_{11} - \gamma_{11})$, and similarly for $\boldsymbol{\omega}_{22}$ and $\boldsymbol{\omega}_{23}$.

We can now estimate a_2 and $\mathbf{b}_3$ by regressing the vector $(\gamma_{21}, \boldsymbol{\gamma}_{22}, \boldsymbol{\gamma}_{23})'$ on the two vectors $(\gamma_{11}, \boldsymbol{\gamma}_{12}, \boldsymbol{\gamma}_{13})'$ and $(0, \mathbf{0}, \mathbf{1})'$ using o.l.s.

A variation on this method consists of applying weighted least squares in order to account for the information in the covariance matrix of the ω-s [GMT85]. This procedure, like that described in section 9.3.4, does not provide estimates of the variances and covariances of the disturbance terms.

9.3 Some Applications

9.3.1 Unionization and Salary Levels

The objective of this study is to describe the relationship between union membership and salaries. Each worker can decide whether or not to belong to a union, and will choose according to his or her preferences, the level of union dues, and the expected change in salary.

Let w_{si} and w_{ni} represent the salary an individual i receives depending on whether she does, or does not, belong to a union, respectively. She will decide to join a union if the increase in pay exceeds a threshold, ρ_i, which is a function of her characteristics:

$$\frac{w_{si} - w_{ni}}{w_{ni}} > \rho_i .$$

The relative increase can be approximated by $\log(w_{si}) - \log(w_{ni})$, and we shall use this expression to develop the model. The latent variables are given by:

$$\begin{aligned} \log(w_{si}) &= \mathbf{x}_{1i}\mathbf{b}_1 + u_{1i}, \\ \log(w_{ni}) &= \mathbf{x}_{2i}\mathbf{b}_2 + u_{2i}, \\ \rho_i &= \mathbf{x}_{3i}\mathbf{b}_3 + u_{3i}. \end{aligned}$$

The observed variables are, whether or not the individual is in a union (y_{1i}) and wages (y_{2i}):

$$\begin{aligned} y_{1i} &= 1, \\ y_{2i} &= \log(w_{si}), \end{aligned}$$

if $\log(w_{si}) - \log(w_{ni}) > \rho_i$, while:

$$\begin{aligned} y_{1i} &= 0, \\ y_{2i} &= \log(w_{ni}), \end{aligned}$$

if $\log(w_{si}) - \log(w_{ni}) < \rho_i$.

Here we have a qualitative observation on y_1 and truncated data on the two variables $\log(w_s)$ and $\log(w_n)$.

9.3.2 Agricultural Price Support

In order to guarantee a minimum income to farmers, the government may decide to intervene in the market. Consider an agricultural product with domestic demand and supply given by:

$$\begin{aligned} D_t &= a_1 p_t + \mathbf{x}_{1t}\mathbf{b}_1 + u_{1t}, \quad & a_1 < 0, \\ S_t &= a_2 p_t + \mathbf{x}_{2t}\mathbf{b}_2 + u_{2t}, \quad & a_2 > 0. \end{aligned}$$

If the government does not act, the market price and quantity will tend toward an equilibrium. In particular:

$$p_t = p_t^e = \frac{1}{a_2 - a_1}(\mathbf{x}_{1t}\mathbf{b}_t - \mathbf{x}_{2t}\mathbf{b}_2 + u_{1t} - u_{2t}).$$

Assume that a policy is adopted to ensure that the price does not fall below some floor p_t^s, which is set exogenously. If p_t^e is above the support threshold p_t^s there is no need for intervention. If, however, the market price is lower, the government steps in and begins buying the good, driving up the price until it reaches p_t^s. The domestic market can now be modelled as follows:

$$
\begin{aligned}
D_t &= a_1 p_t + \mathbf{x}_{1t}\mathbf{b}_t + u_{1t},\\
S_t &= a_2 p_t + \mathbf{x}_{2t}\mathbf{b}_2 + u_{2t},\\
p_t &= \max\left(p_t^e, p_t^s\right).
\end{aligned}
$$

This market incorporates two regimes:

(i) when $p_t^e \geq p_t^s$, $D_t = S_t$ and $p_t = p_t^e$.

(ii) when $p_t^e < p_t^s$, the quantity demanded by the government is $S_t - D_t > 0$, the amount exchanged is equal to the supply, and the observed price is $p_t = p_t^s$ (with p_t^s exogenous).

In the special case of supply S_t not depending on price p_t, we can explicitly solve the likelihood equations (cf. appendix 9.1).

9.3.3 Extensions of the Workforce Participation Model

Typically, models of work-force participation are based on the assumption that the individual can choose how many hours he desires to work, based on the prevailing hourly wage. This hypothesis is contradicted by evidence collected in household surveys, in which people often complain of being under-employed, either because they wish to work longer hours or because they are unemployed and would rather not be.

9.3.3.1 Labour Supply (The Double-Hurdle Model)

A model which incorporates the supply side was analysed by Blundell, Ham, and Meghir [BHM86]. The observations are generated by the system:

$$
h_i = \begin{cases} h_i^*, & \text{if } h_i^* > 0 \text{ and } D_i > 0,\\ 0, & \text{otherwise,} \end{cases}
$$

where h_i is the observed number of hours, h_i^* is the desired number of working hours, and D_i is a variable indicating whether or not the individual is employed.

This kind of model, based on two latent variables h_i^* and D_i, allows us to distinguish between three different groups of individuals: those whose work load corresponds to their desires $\left(h_i^* > 0, D_i > 0\right)$, those who are not working because they don't want to $\left(h_i^* < 0\right)$, and the unemployed who want to work $\left(h_i^* > 0, D_i \leq 0\right)$.

9.3.3.2 *Constraints on the Desired Hours*

In practice, the number of hours worked, h_i, may be less than desired, and people searching for work may accept jobs paying less than their expectations, suggesting that these conditions are deemed preferable to unemployment. This was modelled by Narendranathan and Nickell [NN86]. The reduced form of the econometric model corresponds to:

$$h_i = \begin{cases} h_i^*, & \text{if } D_i > 0 \text{ and } h_i^* > 0, \\ d_i, & \text{if } D_i < 0 \text{ and } C_i > 0, \\ 0, & \text{otherwise.} \end{cases}$$

Here D_i represents the supply constraint corresponding to the best possible job for the individual, while d_i is the salary which he will accept.

9.3.4 *Income and the Level of Education*

To analyse the effect of education on income it is necessary to account for individuals' choices. We postulate that this will be based, at least partially, on a maximization of expected future income.

In what follows we consider two types of education, denoted A and B, and assume that the program of studies A exceeds B in duration by an amount equal to S. The series $y^*(t)$, representing the stream of future income subsequent to completion of studies, is defined as a geometric growth curve. $\bar{y}$ is the salary earned upon entry onto the job market, and g^* is the rate of growth of income. These parameters depend upon individual i's characteristics. Letting graduation from studies B correspond to the beginning of working life, we have:

$$y_{ai}^*(t) = \begin{cases} 0, & \text{if } \; 0 < t < S, \\ \bar{y}_{ai}^* \exp\left[g_{ai}^*(t - S)\right], & \text{if } \; S < t, \end{cases}$$

$$y_{bi}^*(t) = \bar{y}_{bi}^* \exp\left[g_{bi}^*(t)\right] \quad \text{if } 0 < t.$$

Assume a discount factor, r_i, which is constant over time and individuals $\left(r_i > g_{ai}^*, g_{bi}^*\right)$, costless education, and an infinite time horizon. Total expected income over the course of the individual's working life is:

$$\begin{aligned} V_{ai} &= \int_S^\infty y_{ai}^*(t) \exp(-r_i t)\, dt, \\ &= \frac{\bar{y}_{ai}^*}{r_i - g_{ai}^*} \exp(-r_i S), \end{aligned}$$

in the case of study program A, and:

$$\begin{aligned} V_{bi} &= \int_0^\infty y_{bi}^*(t) \exp(-r_i t)\, dt, \\ &= \frac{\bar{y}_{bi}^*}{r_i - g_{bi}^*}, \end{aligned}$$

for program B.

Consequently, it follows that individual i chooses an education of type A if $V_{ai} > V_{bi}$ or, equivalently, if $I_i = \log\left(\frac{V_{ai}}{V_{bi}}\right)$ is positive. Linearizing the expression for a regime change, we find:

$$I_i = c_0 + c_1 \left[\log\left(\bar{y}_{ai}^*\right) - \log\left(\bar{y}_{bi}^*\right)\right] + c_2 g_{ai}^* + c_3 g_{bi}^* + c_4 r_i.$$

To complete the model, we set:

$$\begin{aligned} \log\left(\bar{y}_{ai}^*\right) &= \mathbf{x}_{i1}\mathbf{b}_1 + u_{i1}, \\ g_{ai}^* &= \mathbf{x}_{i2}\mathbf{b}_2 + u_{i2}, \\ \log\left(\bar{y}_{bi}^*\right) &= \mathbf{x}_{i3}\mathbf{b}_3 + u_{i3}, \\ g_{bi}^* &= \mathbf{x}_{i4}\mathbf{b}_4 + u_{i4}. \end{aligned}$$

It remains to specify how the observations are collected. Each individual is observed at two times in his working life, at the beginning and again twenty years later. This procedure provides data on the program of studies, the initial salary $\bar{y}_i$, and the rate of growth g_i. Mathematically, the endogenous observed variables are:

$$\left.\begin{aligned} \log\left(\bar{y}_{ai}\right) &= \log\left(\bar{y}_{ai}^*\right) \\ g_{ai} &= g_{ai}^* \\ \log\left(\bar{y}_{bi}\right) &= 0 \\ g_{bi} &= 0 \end{aligned}\right\} \quad \text{if } I_i > 0,$$

$$\left.\begin{aligned} \log\left(\bar{y}_{ai}\right) &= 0 \\ g_{ai} &= 0 \\ \log\left(\bar{y}_{bi}\right) &= \log\left(\bar{y}_{bi}^*\right) \\ g_{bi} &= g_{bi}^* \end{aligned}\right\} \quad \text{if } I_i < 0.$$

9.3.5 Rationing of Bank Loans

The model presented in this section was used to study the behaviour of the "Federal Home Loan Bank Board", an agency of the United States Government which advances money to financial institutions specializing in home ownership mortgages. We denote L the demand for homes, D the demand for advances, Q the actual amount disbursed, and R the rate of interest on this money. Let L, the demand for homes, be a function of advances given:

$$L = aQ + u,$$

where u incorporates the other exogenous explanatory variables as well as the disturbance term. Demand for advances, D, is a function of the interest rate:

$$D = bR + v.$$

We now wish to explain the behaviour of the government agency which sets Q and R. Defining the objective function as a quadratic loss function, we have:

$$V = \left(L - L^*\right)^2 + c\left(R - R^*\right)^2 + d\,(D - Q)^2.$$

The first term measures the difference between the demand for housing L and the demand desired by the funding agency, L^*. In the second term, R^* reflects various costs – this term ensures a degree of stability in the interest rate series R. Substituting the expressions for D and L into this equation, we obtain:

$$V = \left(aQ + u - L^*\right)^2 + c\left(R - R^*\right)^2 + d\,(bR + v - Q)^2.$$

This function is to be minimized, subject to the constraint:

$$Q \leq D \quad \Leftrightarrow \quad Q \leq bR + v.$$

We see that this model incorporates two regimes, depending on whether or not the constraint is binding.

9.3.5.1 The Constraint is not Binding

Q and R are obtained by setting the partial derivatives $\frac{\partial V}{\partial Q}$ and $\frac{\partial V}{\partial R}$ equal to zero:

$$0 = \frac{\partial V}{\partial Q} = 2a\left(aQ + u - L^*\right) - 2d\,(bR + v - Q),$$
$$0 = \frac{\partial V}{\partial R} = 2c\left(R - R^*\right) + 2bd\,(bR + v - Q).$$

Solving this system yields R and Q as linear functions of u, v, L^*, and R^*.

$$R = q_{11}u + q_{12}v + q_{13}L^* + q_{14}R^*,$$
$$Q = q_{21}u + q_{22}v + q_{23}L^* + q_{24}R^*,$$

where the coefficients $q_{11}, \ldots, q_{14}, q_{21}, \ldots, q_{21}$ are parameters of the initial values. In this case the regime is characterized by the inequality:

$$Q \leq bR + v, q_{21}u + q_{22}v + q_{23}L^* + q_{24}R^*,$$
$$\leq b\left(q_{11}u + q_{12}v + q_{13}L^* + q_{14}R^*\right) + v.$$

9.3.5.2 The Constraint is Binding

If the last inequality doesn't hold, Q is equal to $bR + v$ and the rate of interest is obtained by minimizing:

$$V = \left(abR + av + u - L^*\right)^2 + c\left(R - R^*\right)^2.$$

Solving $\frac{\partial V}{\partial R} = 0$ for R yields:

$$R = p_1 u + p_2 v + p_3 L^* + p_4 R^*,$$

and Q is derived by setting $bR + v = Q$.

We leave to the reader to verify that, when the observed variables are L, Q, and R, the model fits the pattern of equations (9.1), (9.2), and (9.3).

9.3.6 Estimating the Production Possibilities Frontier

9.3.6.1 The Usual Model

The production possibilities frontier is generally defined as the maximum level of output that can be generated from a given set of inputs. For simplicity, we shall use a Cobb-Douglas production function in our analysis:

$$y_{1i}^* = \log\left(Q_i^*\right) = \mathbf{x}_i \mathbf{b} + u_{1i},$$

where $i = 1, \ldots, n$, Q_i^* designates the maximum output, $\mathbf{x}_i$ contains the logs of the quantity of inputs, and u_{1i} is the disturbance term distributed $\mathrm{N}\left(0, s_1^2\right)$ by assumption.

Fitting empirical data directly to this type of model involves making the implicit assumption that firms achieve their optimum output. Phenomena such as friction and incomplete information may generate a degree of inefficiency, however. In this case, observations on a point in the production set will lie inside the production possibilities frontier:

$$y_i = \log\left(Q_i\right) < \log\left(Q_i^*\right) = \mathbf{x}_i \mathbf{b} + u_{1i}.$$

One way to account for this constraint involves introducing an additional error term which can only assume negative values.

$$\begin{aligned} y_i &= \log\left(Q_i\right), \\ &= \log\left(Q_i^*\right) + v_{2i}, \\ &= \mathbf{x}_i \mathbf{b} + u_i + v_{2i}, \end{aligned}$$

where $v_{2i} < 0$. This model differs from the classical regression model in that the error is composite and has an asymmetric distribution.

To complete this model, we must specify the distribution of the term, v_{2i}, representing the firm's inefficiency. In order to continue working with normal distributions we often specify that:

$$v_{2i} = -\,|u_{2i}|,$$

where u_{2i} is a normal variable distributed $\mathrm{N}\left(0, s_2^2\right)$, independent of u_{1i}.

The reduced form of the model is:

$$y_i = \mathbf{x}_i\mathbf{b} + u_{1i} - |u_{2i}|,$$

which is constructed from two normal variables (u_{1i}, u_{2i}) after truncation of the latter.

An absolute measure of inefficiency is found by taking the expectation of the added term, $\mathrm{E}\,|u_{2i}|$. Since this expectation is constant, we can readily see that the usual model is quite restrictive. In particular, it does not allow for inefficiency to depend on the level of production of the firm, nor upon the characteristics of the production process. Furthermore, it seems intuitively logical that the form of the inefficiency, i.e. our assumption about the distribution of v_{2i}, should depend on the nature of its primary causes. We now examine a macroeconomic model of inefficiency resulting from insufficient concentration in an industry.

9.3.6.2 A Macroeconomic Model of Inefficiency

Consider N firms, all with the same production function:

$$\begin{aligned} y_n &= \log(q_n), \\ &= a + \log(\mathbf{z}_n)\,\mathbf{b}, \\ &= a + \sum_{\ell=1}^{L} b_\ell \log(z_\ell), \end{aligned}$$

where ℓ indexes the elements of the input vector $\mathbf{z}$. Assume the firms to be technologically efficient from the microeconomic perspective, such that the quantities $(\mathbf{z}_n, q_n)$ for firm n, $n = 1, \ldots, N$, satisfy:

$$\log(q) = a_n + \log(\mathbf{z}_n)\,\mathbf{b}.$$

From a macroeconomic perspective, we see that to produce $Q = \sum_{n=1}^{N} q_n$, the firms collectively use $Z_\ell = \sum_{i=1}^{n} z_{\ell n}, \forall \ell$, inputs. In the case of increasing returns to scale, denoted $\sum_{\ell=1}^{L} b_\ell > 1$, we could increase total production by allocating all output to a single firm, thus increasing the level of concentration in the industry. Denoting this maximum output Q^*, we have $\log(Q^*) = a + \log(\mathbf{Z})\,\mathbf{b}$. The inefficiency associated with the lack of concentration is measured by the difference between Q and Q^*.

Explicit forms for the degree of inefficiency are obtained by specifying the distribution of production between the firms. To illustrate, assume that the input quantities $\mathbf{z}_n$ are independent with a log-normal distribution $\log(N\mathbf{z}_n) \sim \mathrm{N}(\mathbf{m}, \Sigma)$. The output quantities, q_n, are also independent and distributed log-normal:

$$\log(Nq_{\ell n}) + \left(\sum_{\ell=1}^{L} b_\ell - 1\right) \log(N) \sim \mathrm{N}\left(a + \mathbf{b}'\mathbf{m}, \mathbf{b}'\Sigma\mathbf{b}\right).$$

When the number of firms is sufficiently large, we can obtain reasonable approximations to Z, Q, and Q^*.

We begin by focusing on the quantities of inputs (ℓ, $\ell = 1, \ldots, L$) used. We have:

$$\begin{aligned} Z_\ell &= \sum_{n=1}^{N} z_{\ell n}, \\ &= \frac{1}{N} \sum_{n=1}^{N} \exp(v_{\ell n}), \end{aligned}$$

where the values $v_{\ell n}$, $n = 1, \ldots, N$, are independent and distributed $\mathrm{N}\left(m_\ell, s_\ell^2\right)$.

Application of the law of larger numbers yields:

$$\begin{aligned} Z_\ell &\approx \mathrm{E}\left[\exp(v_{\ell n})\right], \\ &\approx \exp\left(m_\ell + \frac{s_\ell^2}{2}\right). \end{aligned}$$

And the maximum output satisfies:

$$\begin{aligned} \log\left(Q^*\right) &= a + \sum_{\ell=1}^{L} b_\ell \log(Z_\ell), \\ &= a + \sum_{\ell=1}^{L} b_\ell \left(m_\ell + \frac{s_\ell^2}{2}\right). \end{aligned}$$

Similar reasoning allows us to find an approximate expression for real production Q. We have:

$$\begin{aligned} Q &= \sum_{n=1}^{N} q_n, \\ &= N^{1-\sum_{\ell=1}^{L} b_\ell} \frac{1}{N} \sum_{n=1}^{N} \exp(w_n), \end{aligned}$$

with the variables $w_n, n = 1, \ldots, N$ independent and identically distributed $\mathrm{N}\left(a + \mathbf{b}'m, \mathbf{b}'\Sigma\mathbf{b}\right)$. The law of large numbers allows us to write:

$$Q \approx N^{1-\sum_{\ell=1}^{L} b_\ell} \mathrm{E}\left(e^W\right),$$
$$\approx N^{1-\sum_{\ell=1}^{L} b_\ell} \exp\left(a + \mathbf{b}'\mathbf{m} + \frac{\mathbf{b}'\Sigma\mathbf{b}}{2}\right),$$

and we see the expression for $\log(Q^*)$ reappear in the equation for $\log(Q)$:

$$\log(Q) = \log\left(Q^*\right) + \left(1 - \sum_{\ell=1}^{L} b_\ell\right) N + \frac{\mathbf{b}'\Sigma\mathbf{b}}{2} - \sum_{\ell=1}^{L} \frac{b_\ell s_\ell^2}{2}.$$

To simplify, we impose that the matrix Σ is diagonal, yielding:

$$\log(Q) = \log\left(Q^*\right) + \left(1 - \sum_{\ell=1}^{L} b_\ell\right) N - \sum_{\ell=1}^{L} \frac{b_\ell\left(1 - b_\ell\right) s_\ell^2}{2},$$

$$\log\left(Q^*\right) = a + \sum_{\ell=1}^{L} b_\ell \log\left(Z_\ell\right).$$

We see that the additional term measuring inefficiency due to insufficient concentration is not constant over the agents, which may, for example, represent sectors. In particular, it depends upon the number of firms, N, in the sector, on the degree to which returns to scale $\left(\sum_{\ell=1}^{L} b_\ell - 1\right)$ are increasing, on the allocation of production between firms, $s_\ell^2, \ell = 1, \ldots, L$, and on the elasticities $b_\ell, \ell = 1, \ldots, L$.

9.4 The Maximum-Expectation (M.E.) Algorithm

We have already described several general algorithms used to numerically solve the likelihood equations. A further approach proposed by Dempster, Laird, and Rubin [DLR77] is of considerable interest for solving models of the form (9.1), (9.2), and (9.3).

9.4.1 Description of the Algorithm

This algorithm relies in a fundamental manner on the distribution assigned to the latent variables $\mathbf{y}^*$. In this section we shall denote this distribution $F^*(\mathbf{y}^*; \mathbf{t})$, and $F(\mathbf{y}; \mathbf{t})$ that of the observed variables. If the latent variables were observable, the parameters $\mathbf{t}$ could be estimated by an application of maximum likelihood to F^*:

$$\max_{\mathbf{t}} \left\{\log\left[F^*\left(\mathbf{y}^*; \mathbf{t}\right)\right]\right\}.$$

Since the latent variables are only partially known over the intermediary of the observed **y**-s, it seems reasonable to introduce the conditional expectation of $\log(F^*)$ given **y**. Specifically, we define the function:

$$Q(\boldsymbol{\theta}; t) = \mathrm{E}_t \left\{ \log \left[F^* \left(\mathbf{y}^*; \boldsymbol{\theta} \right) \middle| \mathbf{y} \right] \right\}.$$

where $\boldsymbol{\theta}$ is an estimator of the parameter vector **t**. The conditional expectation of $\log[F^*(\mathbf{y}^*; \boldsymbol{\theta})]$ is derived for the distribution corresponding to the value **t** of the parameter.

Each iteration of the algorithm comprises two steps: calculation of the expectation – step E, and maximization – step M. If $\boldsymbol{\theta}_p$ is the value obtained at the p-th iteration, the $(p+1)$-th iteration is as follows:

step E: calculate $Q(\boldsymbol{\theta}_p; t)$

step M: maximize with respect to $t : Q(\boldsymbol{\theta}_p; t)$.

Clearly, the function Q only needs to be derived once, and it is often relatively easy to find for models with truncated variables. This algorithm is of particular interest when maximizing Q is easier than directly maximizing of $\log[F^*(\mathbf{y}; \mathbf{t})]$.

9.4.2 An Example

To illustrate this procedure, consider the case of a simple Tobit model:

$$y_i^* = \mathbf{x}_i \mathbf{b} + u_i, \quad u_i \sim \mathrm{N}\left[0, s^2\right],$$

and:

$$y_i = \begin{cases} y_i^*, & \text{if } y_i^* > 0, \\ 0, & \text{otherwise.} \end{cases}$$

The distribution of the latent variable is:

$$\log\left[F\left(\mathbf{y}^*; \boldsymbol{\theta}\right)\right] = -\frac{n}{2}\log\left(\sigma^2\right) - \frac{n}{2}\log(2\pi) - \frac{1}{2\sigma^2}\sum_{i=1}^{n}\left(y_i^* - \mathbf{x}_i\boldsymbol{\beta}\right)^2,$$

and the function Q is derived as:

$$Q(\boldsymbol{\theta}, t) = -\frac{n}{2}\log\left(\sigma^2\right) - \frac{n}{2}\log(2\pi) - \frac{1}{2\sigma^2}\sum_{i=1}^{n}\mathrm{E}_t\left[\left(y_i^* - \mathbf{x}_i\boldsymbol{\beta}\right)^2 \middle| y_i\right].$$

Now, all we need to calculate is this last conditional expectation. If $y_i > 0$, we see that:

$$\mathrm{E}_t\left[\left(y_i^* - \mathbf{x}_i\boldsymbol{\beta}\right)^2 \middle| y_i\right] = (y_i - \mathbf{x}_i\boldsymbol{\beta})^2,$$

whereas if $y_i = 0$, we have:

$$\begin{aligned} &\mathrm{E}_t\left[\left(y_i^* - \mathbf{x}_i\boldsymbol{\beta}\right)\big|\, y_i\right] \\ &\quad = \mathrm{E}_t\left[\left(y_i^*\right)^2\Big|\, y_i^* < 0\right] - 2\mathbf{x}_i\boldsymbol{\beta}\mathrm{E}_t\left(y_i^*\big|\, y_i^* < 0\right) + (\mathbf{x}_i\boldsymbol{\beta})^2 . \end{aligned}$$

All that remains to do is replace the various conditional expectations by their expression (cf. chapter 7). To simplify notation, we write:

$$\begin{aligned} \lambda_i\left(\mathbf{b}, s^2\right) &= \mathrm{E}_t\left[\left(y_i^*\right)^2\Big|\, y_i^* < 0\right], \\ \mu_i\left(\mathbf{b}, s^2\right) &= \mathrm{E}_t\left(y_i^*\big|\, y_i^* < 0\right). \end{aligned}$$

Yielding:

$$\begin{aligned} Q\left[\boldsymbol{\theta}, t\right] = -\frac{n}{2}\log\left(\sigma^2\right) - \frac{n}{2}\log\left(2\pi\right) - \frac{1}{2\sigma^2}\sum_{J_1}^{n}\left(y_i^* - \mathbf{x}_i\boldsymbol{\beta}\right)^2 \\ - \frac{1}{2\sigma^2}\sum_{J_0}^{n}\left[\lambda_i - 2\mathbf{x}_i\boldsymbol{\beta}\mu_i + (\mathbf{x}_i\boldsymbol{\beta})^2\right]. \end{aligned}$$

It is obviously a simple matter to maximize this function over $\boldsymbol{\beta}$ and σ^2, as it is quadratic in $\boldsymbol{\beta}$ and solves explicitly for that variable. σ^2 is found with:

$$\sigma^2 = \frac{1}{n}\left\{\sum_{J_1}(y_i - \mathbf{x}_i\boldsymbol{\beta})^2 + \sum_{J_0}\left[\lambda_i - 2\mathbf{x}_i\boldsymbol{\beta}\mu_i + (\mathbf{x}_i\boldsymbol{\beta})^2\right]\right\}.$$

9.4.3 Convergence of the Algorithm

Proposition 23: The M.E. algorithm is increasing.

Proof: Denote $L(\mathbf{t}) = \log\left[F(\mathbf{y}, \mathbf{t})\right]$ and let $H(\boldsymbol{\theta}, t) = \mathrm{E_t}\{\log\left[F(\mathbf{y}^*|\, \mathbf{y}; \boldsymbol{\theta})|\, \mathbf{y}\right]\}$ be the conditional expectation of the log-likelihood of $\mathbf{y}^*$ given $\mathbf{y}$. Since:

$$\log\left[F^*\left(\mathbf{y}^*; \boldsymbol{\theta}\right)\right] = \log\left[F\left(\mathbf{y}^*\big|\, \mathbf{y}; \mathbf{t}\right)\right] + L(\boldsymbol{\theta}),$$

we take the conditional expectation of each element of the equation, yielding:

$$Q(\boldsymbol{\theta}, t) = H(\boldsymbol{\theta}, t) + L(\boldsymbol{\theta}).$$

We derive:

$$\begin{aligned} L\left(\boldsymbol{\theta}_{p+1}\right) - L\left(\boldsymbol{\theta}_p\right) = &\left[Q\left(\boldsymbol{\theta}_{p+1}, \boldsymbol{\theta}_p\right) - Q\left(\boldsymbol{\theta}_p, \boldsymbol{\theta}_p\right)\right] \\ &+ \left[H\left(\boldsymbol{\theta}_p, \boldsymbol{\theta}_p\right) - H\left(\boldsymbol{\theta}_{p+1}, \boldsymbol{\theta}_p\right)\right]. \end{aligned}$$

The first term is positive, since $\boldsymbol{\theta}_{p+1}$ is the maximum of $Q[\boldsymbol{\theta}, \mathbf{t}]$ with respect to $\boldsymbol{\theta}$, and the second term is also positive since $H(\boldsymbol{\theta}, t) \leq H(\mathbf{t}, \mathbf{t}), \forall \mathbf{t}, \boldsymbol{\theta}$ by Kullback's inequality.

Having shown that $L(\boldsymbol{\theta}_{p+1}) - L(\boldsymbol{\theta}_p)$ is positive, we conclude that the algorithm is increasing. □

Under some regularity conditions (Boyles [Boy73]) the following property can be shown to hold:

Proposition 24: The series $\boldsymbol{\theta}_p$ converges to the solution of the likelihood equations.

This convergence may be to maxima (local or global), or it may be to saddle points.

9.5 Lagrange Multiplier Tests

The results for generalized residuals and for the maximum-score tests which we developed in the chapter on the Tobit model can be applied to all the models considered in this chapter. This enables us to develop various tests for models of simultaneous equations, and specifically, tests of exogeneity.

9.5.1 The Expression for the Vector of Scores

The model presented in equations (9.1), (9.2), and (9.3) belongs to a larger class of models defined as follows:

(i) The latent model is a multi-dimensional Gaussian model:

$$y_i^* \sim_{asy} \mathrm{N}[m(x_i, t), \Omega_i(t)], \quad i = 1, \ldots, n,$$

where the variables y_i^* are independent.

(ii) The observable variables are derived from the latent variables over a known transformation g:

$$y_i = g(y_i^*).$$

In this type of model it is an easy matter to establish the relationship between the score associated with the latent model, i.e. the score of the log-likelihood equation $\log[F^*(\mathbf{y}^*; \mathbf{t})]$, and the score associated with the observable model – founded on $\log[F(\mathbf{y}; \mathbf{t})]$.

Proposition 25: The observable score is equal to the predicted latent score:

$$\frac{\partial \log [F(\mathbf{y}; \mathbf{t})]}{\partial \mathbf{t}} = E_{\mathbf{t}} \left\{ \frac{\partial \log [F^*(\mathbf{y}^*; \mathbf{t})]}{\partial \mathbf{t}} \middle| \mathbf{y} \right\}.$$

For a proof see Gourieroux, Monfort, Renault, and Trognon [GMRT86].

This property allows us to obtain a simple formulation for the score statistics. Assume we divide the parameters $\mathbf{t}$ into two groups, denoted $\mathbf{a}$ and $\mathbf{b}$, where the former enter into the mean while the latter define the variance.

The latent log-likelihood is:

$$\log \left[F^*\left(\mathbf{y}^*; \mathbf{t}\right)\right] = \sum_{i=1}^{n} \left(-\frac{G^*}{2} \log (2\pi) - \frac{1}{2} \log \{\det [\Omega_i (\mathbf{b})]\} \right.$$
$$\left. -\frac{1}{2} \sum_{i=1}^{n} \left[y_i^* - m(\mathbf{x}_i, \mathbf{a})\right]' \Omega_i^{-1} (\mathbf{b}) \left[y_i^* - m(\mathbf{x}_i, \mathbf{a})\right] \right).$$

We differentiate to obtain the latent score. Letting $u_i = y_i^* - m(\mathbf{x}_i, \mathbf{a})$ represent the latent error, we obtain:

$$\frac{\partial \log [F^*(\mathbf{y}^*, \mathbf{t})]}{\partial a_j} = \sum_{i=1}^{n} \frac{\partial m(\mathbf{x}_i, \mathbf{a})}{\partial a_j} \Omega_i^{-1} (\mathbf{b})\, u_i,$$

$$\frac{\partial \log [F^*(\mathbf{y}^*, \mathbf{t})]}{\partial b_j}$$
$$= -\frac{1}{2} \sum_{i=1}^{n} \mathrm{Tr} \left\{ \Omega_i^{-1} (\mathbf{b}) \left[I - u_i u_i' \Omega_i^{-1} (\mathbf{b})\right] \frac{\partial \Omega_i (\mathbf{b})}{\partial b_j} \right\}.$$

The observable scores are the predicted latent scores and are thus functions of the observations over the fitted errors (generalized first-order residuals) and over their squares (generalized second-order residuals).

$$\frac{\partial \log [F(\mathbf{y}; \mathbf{t})]}{\partial a_j} = \sum_{i=1}^{n} \frac{\partial m\left(\mathbf{x}_j, \mathbf{a}\right)'}{\partial a_j} \Omega_i^{-1} (\mathbf{b})\, \mathrm{E}\left(u_i \mid y_i\right),$$

$$\frac{\partial \log [F(\mathbf{y}; \mathbf{t})]}{\partial b_j}$$
$$= -\frac{1}{2} \sum_{i=1}^{n} \mathrm{Tr} \left\{ \Omega_i^{-1} (\mathbf{b}) \left[I - \mathrm{E}\left(u_i u_i' \mid y_i\right) \Omega_i^{-1} (\mathbf{b})\right] \frac{\partial \Omega_i (\mathbf{b})}{\partial b_i} \right\}.$$

9.5.2 Tests of Exogeneity

Consider a two-dimensional simultaneous equation model (cf. section 9.1). $\mathbf{y}_2^*$ may appear as an explanatory variable in the first equation (the equation for $\mathbf{y}_1^*$), and we may wonder whether or not this variable should be considered exogenous. Considering this question within a context of limited information, we have a model:

$$y_{1i}^* = a y_{2i}^* + \mathbf{x}_i \mathbf{b} + u_{1i},$$
$$y_{2i}^* = \mathbf{x}_i \mathbf{c}_1 + \mathbf{z}_i \mathbf{c}_2 + u_{2i},$$

where $\mathbf{z}_i$ represents explanatory variables occurring in the second equation and not in the first. The assumption that y_{2i}^* is exogenous constitutes the null hypothesis.

$$H_0 : \quad \begin{cases} 0 = \operatorname{cov}\left(\mathbf{y}_{2i}^*, u_{1i}\right), \\ 0 = \operatorname{cov}\left(u_{2i}, u_{1i}\right). \end{cases}$$

In order to facilitate evaluation of the vector of scores, it is of some interest to parametrized the variances with:

$$\Omega^{-1} = \begin{bmatrix} \omega^{11} & \omega^{12} \\ \omega^{21} & \omega^{22} \end{bmatrix}.$$

This allows us to reformulate H_0 as:

$$\omega^{12} = 0.$$

The latent score associated with ω^{12} is:

$$\frac{\partial \log\left[F^*\left(\mathbf{y}^*, \mathbf{t}\right)\right]}{\partial \omega^{12}}$$
$$= \frac{\partial}{\partial \omega^{12}} \sum_{i=1}^{n} \frac{1}{2} \log\left[\omega^{11}\omega^{22} - \left(\omega^{12}\right)^2\right] + \frac{\partial}{\partial \omega^{12}} \sum_{i=1}^{n} \left(-\omega^{12}\right)$$
$$\times \left(y_{1i}^* - a y_{2i}^* - \mathbf{x}_i \mathbf{b}\right)\left(y_{2i}^* - \mathbf{x}_i \mathbf{c}_1 - \mathbf{z}_i \mathbf{c}_2\right),$$
$$= \frac{-n\omega^{12}}{\omega^{11}\omega^{12} - \left(\omega^{12}\right)^2} - \sum_{i=1}^{n} u_{1i} u_{2i}.$$

The observable score, evaluated under the null hypothesis, is thus:

$$\left.\frac{\partial \log\left[F\left(\mathbf{y}; \mathbf{t}\right)\right]}{\partial \omega^{12}}\right|_{\omega^{12}=0} = -\sum_{i=1}^{n} \mathrm{E}_0\left(u_{1i} u_{2i} \mid y_i\right),$$

where E_0 signifies that the expectation is taken under the null hypothesis. Consequently, we see that the Lagrange multiplier test for the exogeneity of a variable is based upon the generalized cross residual.

The preceding expression for the score can be simplified significantly, though, if the latent variable y_2^* is observable. In that case we have:

$$\left.\frac{\partial \log [F(\mathbf{y}; \mathbf{t})]}{\partial \omega^{12}}\right|_{\omega^{12}=0} = -\sum_{i=1}^{n} \mathrm{E}(u_{1i} \mid y_i)\, u_{2i},$$

and only first-order residuals occur in the expression.

9.6 Models with Serial Correlation

Other general results can be obtained regarding correlation between the residuals.

9.6.1 *The Model*

Assume that the latent variables fit the model:

$$A y_t^* = \mathbf{x}_t \mathbf{b} + u_t, \quad t = 1, \ldots, T,$$

with error terms which are first-order auto-regressive:

$$u_t = R u_{t-1} + \epsilon_t.$$

R is a matrix of values which are strictly less than one and ϵ_t is Gaussian white noise with covariance matrix Ω.

The observable variables are derived from the latent variables by a mapping independent of the index t:

$$y_t = g\left(\mathbf{y}_t^*\right).$$

In the cases we have seen so far, the function g has been a linear piece-wise mapping.

9.6.2 *A Test for Serial Correlation*

Before using this model, we may wish to consider to what extent such a generalization is useful. To verify this, we need to test the hypothesis $H_0 : R = 0$, and, if possible, do so with the simplest estimators (i.e. the estimators corresponding to the null hypothesis being true). The Lagrange multiplier test allows us to answer this question, it is based on the statistic:

$$\xi = \left.\frac{\partial \log [F(\mathbf{y}; A, \mathbf{b}, \Omega, R)]}{\partial R}\right|_{A=\hat{A}_{ML}, \mathbf{b}=\beta_{ML}, \Omega=\hat{\Omega}_{ML}, R=0},$$

where $\hat{A}_{ML}$, β_{ML}, and $\hat{\Omega}_{ML}$ are the maximum-likelihood estimators of the parameters under the null hypothesis.

Calculation of the Lagrange multiplier statistic [GMT85] leads to the following test.

(i) Begin by estimating the fitted errors under the null hypothesis:

$$\tilde{u}_t\left(y_t;\, A, \mathbf{b}, \Omega\right) = \mathrm{E}_{A,\mathbf{b},\Omega,R=0}\left(u_t \mid y_t\right).$$

(ii) These predictions depend upon the unknown parameters, for which we substitute their maximum-likelihood estimators calculated under the null hypothesis, yielding:

$$\tilde{u}_t = u_t\left(y_t;\, \hat{A}_{ML}, \beta_{ML}, \hat{\Omega}_{ML}\right).$$

(iii) ξ is found by:

$$\xi = \left(\hat{\Omega}_{ML}^{-1} \otimes I\right) \sum_{t=2}^{T} \tilde{u}_t \otimes \tilde{u}_{t-1}.$$

This statistic is asymptotically normal and, in consequence, can be transformed to a test statistic with a χ^2 distribution, given by:

$$S_1 = \left(\sum_{t=2}^{T} \hat{\tilde{u}}_t \otimes \hat{\tilde{u}}_{t-1}\right)' \left[\sum_{t=2}^{T} \left(\hat{\tilde{u}}_t \hat{\tilde{u}}_t'\right) \otimes \left(\hat{\tilde{u}}_{t-1} \hat{\tilde{u}}_{t-1}'\right)\right]^{-1} \times \left(\sum_{t=2}^{T} \hat{\tilde{u}}_t \otimes \hat{\tilde{u}}_{t-1}\right).$$

S_1 is analogous to the Durbin-Watson statistic, the difference being that the latent residuals are replaced by their estimates given the observable variables.

Proposition 26: Let d be the dimension of the matrix R, and $\chi^2_{95\%}\left(d^2\right)$ the 95% confidence interval for the χ^2 distribution with d^2 degrees of freedom. The Lagrange multiplier test for the null hypothesis, $H_0 : R = 0$, consists of:

accept H_0, if $S_1 < \chi^2_{95\%}\left(d^2\right)$,
reject H_0, otherwise.

9.6.3 Estimation of A, **b**

If the test leads us to reject the null hypothesis $H_0 : R = 0$, we are left with the problem of how to estimate A and $\mathbf{b}$ in the presence of serial correlation. Under the alternative hypothesis the likelihood frequently has a complicated form involving as many integrals as there are observations. This makes it impossible to apply the maximum-likelihood method, even using numerical algorithms.

However, we may still achieve good estimates of A and b by making use the following proposition.

Proposition 27: The maximum-likelihood estimators $\hat{A}_{ML}$ and β_{ML} calculated under the null hypothesis retain the property of consistency even in the presence of autocorrelation.

For a proof see [GMT85].

This generalizes our results for the probit model (cf. chapter 2). Notice, however, that $\hat{\Omega}_{ML}$ is no longer a consistent estimator of Ω, and that the usual formulas for the variances of $\hat{A}_{ML}$ and β_{ML} do not obtain in the presence of serial correlation.

Exercises

9.1 Consider three latent variables defined by:

$$y_{ki}^* = \mathbf{x}_{ki}\mathbf{b}_k + u_{ki}, \quad k = 1, 2, 3,$$

and the model of regime changes with the observed variables:

$$y_i = \begin{cases} y_{1i}^*, & \text{if } y_{3i}^* > 0, \\ y_{2i}^*, & \text{if } y_{3i}^* < 0, \end{cases}$$

and:

$$z_i = \begin{cases} 1, & \text{if } y_{3i}^* > 0, \\ 0, & \text{otherwise.} \end{cases}$$

Write the likelihood for this model on the assumption that the disturbances are normally distributed. Under these conditions, can we estimate $\mathbf{b}_1$ from a regression of y_i on $\mathbf{x}_{1i}$ for all i such that $z_i = 1$?

9.2 In the following disequilibrium model supply, S_t, is assumed exogenous and known:

$$\begin{aligned} D_t &= a_1 p_t + \mathbf{x}_{1t}\mathbf{b}_1 + u_{1t}, \\ p_t - p_{t-1} &= \lambda (D_t - S_t) + u_{2t}, \\ Q_t &= \min (D_t, S_t). \end{aligned}$$

The endogenous, observed variables are Q_t and p_t. Show that this model fits into the framework of (9.1), (9.2) and (9.3) and suggest several ways to estimate the parameters.

9.3 Consider the model we examined in section 9.2.2, but now let the latent variables be defined recursively:

$$\begin{aligned} y_{1i}^* &= \mathbf{x}_{1i}\mathbf{b}_1 + u_{1i}, \\ y_{2i}^* &= a y_{1i}^* + \mathbf{x}_{2i}\mathbf{b}_2 + u_{2i}, \\ y_{3i}^* &= \mathbf{x}_{3i}\mathbf{b}_3 + u_{3i}. \end{aligned}$$

Show that the two-stage estimation method can easily be generalized to this case.

9.4 Discuss the problem of identification in the context of the model in (9.1), (9.2) and (9.3). Verify that for the parameters to be identified they must be in equation (9.1).

9.5 Find the likelihood defined by the following latent variables:

$$y_{ki}^* = m_k + u_{ki}, \quad i = 1, \ldots, n, \quad k = 1, 2, 3.$$

where the disturbances u_{ki} are independent and distributed $\mathrm{N}\left(0, \sigma_k^2\right)$ and where the observable variable is:

$$y_i = \begin{cases} y_{1i}^*, & \text{if } y_{3i}^* > 0, \\ y_{2i}^*, & \text{if } y_{3i}^* \leq 0. \end{cases}$$

Confirm that the maximum of this likelihood is infinite.

9.6 Write the likelihood for the model in section 9.3.2 when the error terms (u_{1t}, u_{2t}) are independent over time and follow the same bivariate normal distribution.

9.7 Under the assumptions of the model in the preceding question, verify that the distributions of p_t and $S_t - D_t$ are normal truncated. Derive an estimator other than maximum-likelihood for some of the model's parameters.

9.8 How would we write the model in section 9.3.2 if we only observe the quantity exchanged and the market price? Can all the parameters be estimated?

9.9 We wish to simultaneously study whether a family is a home-owner and how much money they spend on housing. Let $c_{1i} = \mathbf{x}_{1i}\mathbf{b}_1 + u_{1i}$ represent annual expenditure when they own their home, and $c_{2i} = \mathbf{x}_{2i}\mathbf{b}_2 + u_{2i}$ the cost of renting. Assume that the decision to purchase, $I_i = 1$, or to rent, $I_i = 0$, is given by:

$$I_i = \begin{cases} 1, & \text{if } \mathbf{x}_{3i}\mathbf{b}_3 + u_{3i} > 0, \\ 0, & \text{otherwise.} \end{cases}$$

If you have observations on whether or not the household is a home-owner and how much it spends on housing, find the likelihood for the model [assume that (u_{1i}, u_{2i}, u_{3i}) are independent and distributed $\mathrm{N}(0, \Sigma)$].

What information can be derived from testing the null hypothesis:

$$H_0 : \operatorname{cov}(u_1, u_2) = \operatorname{cov}(u_2, u_3) = 0?$$

Appendix 9.1 A Model with Price Floors – The Recursive Case

In models of agricultural production we generally postulate that supply is determined by price from the preceding period, p_{t-1}, not by the current price, p_t. This creates a lag between the point in time at which the farmer decides how much he will supply and the time at which it actually arrives on the market. Letting the disturbances of the supply and demand curves, u_{1t} and u_{2t} respectively, be independent over time, the lagged price p_{t-1} may be incorporated into the explanatory variables $\mathbf{x}_{2t}$ in the supply equation.

The model becomes:

$$\begin{aligned} D_t &= a_1 p_t + \mathbf{x}_{1t}\mathbf{b}_1 + u_{1t}, \quad a_1 < 0, \\ S_t &= \mathbf{x}_{2t}\mathbf{b}_2 + u_{2t}, \end{aligned}$$

where $t = 1, \dots T$. The observable variables are $D_t,\ S_t$, and the market price:

$$p_t = \max\left(p_t^e, p_t^s\right).$$

With u_{1t} and u_{2t} independently distributed $\mathrm{N}\left(0, s_1^2\right)$ and $\mathrm{N}\left(0, s_2^2\right)$ respectively, the likelihood is:

$$\begin{aligned} L = {} & T_1 \log(-a_1) - T\log(2\pi) - \frac{T}{2}\log\left(s_1^2\right) - \frac{T}{2}\log\left(s_2^2\right) \\ & - \frac{1}{2s_1^2}\sum_{t=1}^{T}(d_t - a_1 p_t - \mathbf{x}_{1t}\mathbf{b}_1)^2 - \frac{1}{2s_2^2}\sum_{t=1}^{T}(s_t - \mathbf{x}_{2t}\mathbf{b}_2)^2, \end{aligned}$$

where T_1 designates the number of periods in which the market is in equilibrium.

This log-likelihood can be decomposed into $L = L_1 + L_2$, with:

$$\begin{aligned} L_1 = {} & T_1 \log(-a_1) - \frac{T}{2}\log(2\pi) - \frac{T}{2}\log\left(s_1^2\right) \\ & - \frac{1}{2s_1^2}\sum_{i=1}^{T}(d_t - a_1 p_t - \mathbf{x}_{1t}\mathbf{b}_1)^2, \end{aligned}$$

and:

$$L_2 = -\frac{T}{2}\log(2\pi) - \frac{T}{2}\log\left(s_2^2\right) - \frac{1}{2s_2^2}\sum_{t=1}^{T}(s_t - \mathbf{x}_{2t}\mathbf{b}_2)^2 .$$

Since L_1 depends only on a_1, b_1, and s_1^2, and L_2 only on b_2 and s_2^2, we can easily find the maximum-likelihood estimators for these parameters by separately maximizing the two functions. This is straightforward for L_2. The maximum-likelihood estimator for b_2 (β_2) is obtained by applying o.l.s. to the supply equation, and the estimator σ_2^2 is then yielded by:

$$\sigma_2^2 = \frac{1}{T}\sum_{t=1}^{T}(s_t - \mathbf{x}_{2t}\beta_2)^2 .$$

To find the maximum-likelihood estimators of the other parameters $\left(a_1, b_1, s_1^2\right)$, we begin by solving for s_1^2, yielding:

$$\sigma_1^2(a_1, b_1) = \frac{1}{T}\sum_{t=1}^{T}(d_t - a_1 p_t - \mathbf{x}_{1t}\mathbf{b}_1)^2 .$$

Substituting $\sigma_1^2(a_1, b_1)$ for s_1^2 in L_1, we have:

$$L_1^c(a_1, \mathbf{b}_1) = T_1\log(-a_1) - \frac{T}{2}\log\sum_{t=1}^{T}(d_t - a_1 p_t - \mathbf{x}_{1t}\mathbf{b}_1)^2 + const.$$

To solve for b_1, we need to minimize:

$$\sum_{t=1}^{T}(d_t - a_1 pt_t - \mathbf{x}_{1t}\mathbf{b}_1)^2 ,$$

yielding:

$$\beta_1(a_1) = \left(X_1'X_1\right)^{-1}X_1'(d - a_1 p),$$

where X_1, d, and p are matrices whose rows consist of x_{1t}, d_t, p_t.

Substituting into $L_1^c(a_1, b_1)$, we obtain:

$$L_1^c(a_1) = T_1\log(-a_1) - \frac{T}{2}\log\left[\sum_{t=1}^{T}(\delta_t - a_1\Pi_t)^2\right] + const,$$

where δ_t and Π are defined:

$$\delta = \left[I - X_1\left(X_1'X_1\right)^{-1}X_1'\right]d,$$

$$\Pi = \left[I - X_1\left(X_1'X_1\right)^{-1}X_1'\right]p.$$

δ and Π are none other than the residuals from the regression of d and p on the columns of X_1.

Finally, it remains to maximize $\tilde{L}_1^c(a_1)$. The first order condition is:

$$T\frac{\sum_{t=1}^{T}\Pi_t(\delta_t - a_1\Pi_1)}{\sum_{t=1}^{T}(\delta_t - a_1 T_t)^2} + \frac{T_1}{a_1} = 0.$$

The maximum-likelihood estimator of a_1, α_1, is the solution to the second-order equation:

$$a_1^2(T_1 - T)\sum_{t=1}^{T}\Pi_t^2 + a_1(T - 2T_1)\sum_{t=1}^{T}\Pi_t\delta_t + T_1\sum_{t=1}^{T}\delta_t^2 = 0.$$

Ignoring the classical case of the equilibrium model ($T_1 = T$), we may assume that $T_1 - T < 0$. Consequently, the roots of the equation are real and of opposite signs. The negative solution is:

$$\alpha_1 = \frac{(2T_1 - T)\sum_{t=1}^{T}\Pi_t\delta_t + \sqrt{\Delta}}{2(T_1 - T)\sum_{t=1}^{T}\Pi_t^2}, \tag{A1.1}$$

with:

$$\Delta = (T - 2T_1)^2\left(\sum_{t=1}^{T}\Pi_t\delta_t\right)^2 - 4T_1(T_1 - T)\sum_{t=1}^{T}\Pi_t^2\sum_{t=1}^{T}\delta_t^2.$$

This solution corresponds to a maximum of $\tilde{L}_1^c$, since it is strictly concave in $a_1 < 0$.

In summary, the following steps yield the solution:

(i) apply ordinary least squares to the supply equation to obtain β_2 and σ_2^2.
(ii) regress d on X_1 and derive the vector of residuals δ.
(iii) regress p on X_1 and derive the vector of residuals Π.
(iv) calculate α_1 by means of the formula $(A1.1)$.
(v) finally, find β_1 and σ_1^2 by regressing the vector $d - \alpha_1 p$ on the columns in X_1.

10 Simultaneous Equation Systems with Truncated Latent Variables

10.1 The General Model

10.1.1 Description

The most general formulation of simultaneous equation systems with truncated latent variables is obtained when these variables are introduced into the equation system (9.1). The model is still defined on the basis of a set of latent values $\mathbf{y}^*$, and the observed variables are related to the latent variables over:

$$\mathbf{y} = D_k\mathbf{y}^* + \mathbf{d}_k, \quad \mathbf{y}^* \in \mathcal{C}, \quad k = 1, \ldots, K. \tag{10.1}$$

The definition of the latent variables is now written:

$$A\mathbf{y}^* + \Gamma\mathbf{y} = X\mathbf{b} + u. \tag{10.2}$$

Latent and observable variables are simultaneously defined, each in terms of the other. The model of equations (9.1), (9.2), and (9.3) is a special case of this one, resulting when we set $\Gamma = 0$.

10.1.2 The Problem of Consistency

Bearing the foregoing observations in mind, it is still of some interest to distinguish this model from that discussed in the previous chapter. In fact, this new formulation introduces an additional difficulty. The model in equations (9.2), (9.3), and (10.2) does not permit us to express the observable endogenous variables, $\mathbf{y}$, in terms of the exogenous variables and the disturbance terms. Consequently, the model does not define the values assumed by the endogenous variables, and hence is incomplete. In the standard terminology of simultaneous equation modelling, this system does not always yield a reduced form.

To obtain a reduced form we must express the latent variables in terms of the exogenous variables and the errors. This is accomplished by replacing $\mathbf{y}$ in equation (10.2) with an expression in $\mathbf{y}^*$, yielding:

$$Ay^* + \Gamma \sum_{k=1}^{K} \left(D_k \mathbf{y}^* + \mathbf{d}_k\right) z = X\mathbf{b} + u,$$

where:

$$z = \begin{cases} 1, & \text{if } \mathbf{y}^* \in C_k, \\ 0, & \text{if } \mathbf{y}^* \notin C_k. \end{cases}$$

We see that the reduced form exists (i.e. that the model is consistent), if and only if:

$$Ay^* + \Gamma \sum_{k=1}^{K} \left(D_k \mathbf{y}^* + \mathbf{d}_k\right) z$$

has an inverse.

Notice that this relation is piece-wise affine – hence the equivalence between consistency and invertibility. Before investigation the model's consistency further, we shall demonstrate the existence of relatively simple formulations which are not consistent.

Consider the bivariate qualitative model defined:

$$\begin{aligned} y_1^* &= a_1 y_2 + u_1, \\ y_2^* &= a_2 y_1 + u_2, \end{aligned} \tag{10.3}$$

$$y_1 = \begin{cases} y_1^*, & \text{if } y_1^* > 0, \\ 0, & \text{otherwise,} \end{cases} \qquad y_2 = \begin{cases} y_2^*, & \text{if } y_2^* > 0, \\ 0, & \text{otherwise.} \end{cases} \tag{10.4}$$

We see that:

(i) If $a_1 = a_2 = 2$, $u_1 > 0$, $u_2 > 0$ and $u_1 = u_2$, no solution exists for y_1 and y_2. Assume, for example, that $y_2 = 0$. The first equation in (10.3) reveals that $y_1^* > 0$ and, in consequence, $y_1^* = y_1$. Substituting back into the second equation of (10.3), we see that $y_2^* > 0$, hence $y_2 > 0$, which contradicts our assumption. By symmetry, $y_1 > 0$.
We now examine the case of both variables y_1 and y_2 assuming strictly positive values, y_1 and y_2 solve for:

$$\begin{aligned} y_1 &= 2y_2 + u_1, \\ y_2 &= 2y_1 + u_1, \end{aligned}$$

implying $y_1 = y_2 = -u_1 > 0$, contradicting the specification that $u_1 > 0$.

(ii) Another type of difficulty arises because this model may yield more than one solution. Letting $a_1 = a_2 = -2$ and $u_1 = u_2 = 1$, we see that:

$$\left(y_1^*, y_2^*\right) = \begin{cases} \left(\frac{1}{3}, \frac{1}{3}\right) \\ (1, -1) \\ (-1, 1) \end{cases}$$

are all solutions.

Turning now to a more thorough study of the model's consistency, we substitute the expression for the observable variables in terms of the latent variables into equation system (10.3), yielding:

$$y_1^* - a_1 y_2^* z_2 = u_1,$$
$$y_2^* - a_2 y_1^* z_1 = u_2,$$

where:

$$z_j = \begin{cases} 0, & \text{if } y_j^* \leq 0, \\ 1, & \text{if } y_j^* > 0, \end{cases} \qquad j = \{1, 2\}.$$

The piece-wise linear relation is:

$$\begin{pmatrix} 1 & -a_1 \\ -a_2 & 1 \end{pmatrix}, \quad \text{if } y_1^* > 0, \text{ and } y_2^* > 0 \Leftrightarrow \left(y_1^*, y_2^*\right) \in C_1,$$
$$\begin{pmatrix} 1 & -a_1 \\ 0 & 1 \end{pmatrix}, \quad \text{if } y_1^* < 0, \text{ and } y_2^* > 0 \Leftrightarrow \left(y_1^*, y_2^*\right) \in C_2,$$
$$\begin{pmatrix} 1 & 0 \\ 0 & 1 \end{pmatrix}, \quad \text{if } y_1^* < 0, \text{ and } y_2^* < 0 \Leftrightarrow \left(y_1^*, y_2^*\right) \in C_3,$$
$$\begin{pmatrix} 1 & 0 \\ -a_2 & 1 \end{pmatrix}, \quad \text{if } y_1^* > 0, \text{ and } y_2^* < 0 \Leftrightarrow \left(y_1^*, y_2^*\right) \in C_4,$$

and we must verify that each of these does indeed have an inverse.

The four cones C_1, C_2, C_3, C_4 are transformed by this relation to C_1', C_2', C_3', C_4'. These are, respectively, the positive cones generated by the vectors:

$$\begin{pmatrix} 1 \\ -a_2 \end{pmatrix}, \begin{pmatrix} -a_1 \\ 1 \end{pmatrix}; \quad \begin{pmatrix} -1 \\ 0 \end{pmatrix}, \begin{pmatrix} -a_1 \\ 1 \end{pmatrix};$$
$$\begin{pmatrix} -1 \\ 0 \end{pmatrix}, \begin{pmatrix} 0 \\ 1 \end{pmatrix}; \quad \begin{pmatrix} 1 \\ -a_2 \end{pmatrix}, \begin{pmatrix} 0 \\ -1 \end{pmatrix}.$$

Several possibilities arise:

(i) If $a_1 > 0$ and $a_2 < 0$, the cones look as represented in figure 10.1. Since the C_j'-s are disjoint and cover real R^2, the relation is one-to-one.

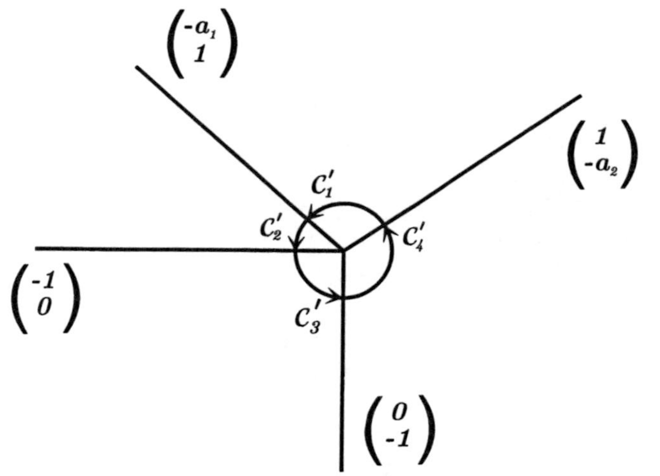

Fig. 10.1. $a_1 > 0, a_2 < 0$

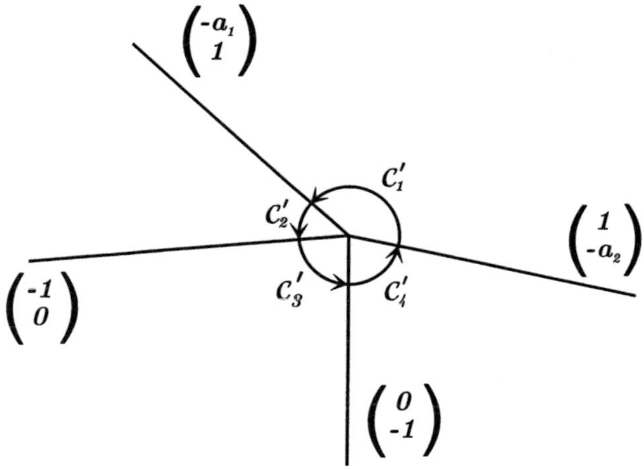

Fig. 10.2. $a_1 > 0, a_2 > 0, a_1a_2 < 1$

(ii) The case of $a_1 < 0$ and $a_2 > 0$ is symmetric and the relation is still a bijection.

(iii) If $a_1 > 0, a_2 > 0$ and $a_1a_2 < 1$,
the relation is again one-to-one (cf, figure 10.2).

(iv) The situation: $a_1 < 0, a_2 < 0$, and $a_1a_2 < 1$ is analogous.

(v) If $a_1 > 0, a_2 > 0$; and $a_1a_2 > 1$, the relation is neither one-to-one nor onto. The cones may have non-empty intersections, and hence multiple

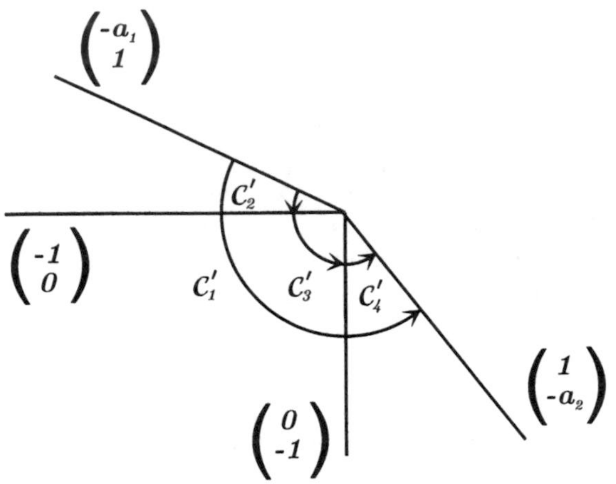

Fig. 10.3. $a_1 > 0, a_2 > 0, a_1a_2 > 1$

solutions $\left(y_1^*, y_2^*\right)$ for some values of (y_1, y_2) arise. Conversely, their union will not equal $\mathbb{R}^2$, implying that some values of (y_1, y_2) have no solution, as in figure 10.3

(vi) $a_1 < 0, a_2 < 0$, and $a_1a_2 > 1$ is analogous to item (v).

To summarize, the linear piece-wise application is not one-to-one unless $a_1a_2 < 1$, and constraints must be imposed on the coefficients to ensure the model's consistency.

10.1.3 Consistency Conditions

These conditions have been made explicit for two cases of practical importance.

Proposition 28: Assume that the regimes C_k are defined by the constraints $a_jy^* > 0$ or $a_jy^* < 0$, where $j = 1, \ldots, J$, and that the a_j-s are linearly independent. Consider a linearly piece-wise continuous function with matrix A_k for each C_k. The function has an inverse if, and only if, the determinants of the matrices A_k all have the same sign.

For a proof see Gourieroux-Laffont-Monfort [GMT80].

In the example, we see that the determinants of the matrices are $1-a_1a_2$, 1, 1, and 1 respectively, yielding the consistency condition $1 - a_1a_2 > 0$, which corresponds to what we found geometrically.

The other case for which we have determined the necessary and sufficient consistency conditions pertains to models in which the variables **y** from equation (10.2) are equal to the qualitative variables associated with the latent variables:

$$y_j = \begin{cases} 1, & \text{if } y_j^* > 0, \\ 0, & \text{otherwise.} \end{cases}$$

Proposition 29: The model in equation (10.2) is consistent if, and only if, it is possible to reorder the variables so that the matrix $A^{-1}\Gamma$ is triangular with zeros on the diagonal.

For a proof see Schmidt [Sch78].

This condition is equivalent to the assumption that equation system (10.2) is recursive. There exists one latent variable, y_{1j}^*, which can be expressed as a function of only the exogenous variables and a disturbance term; a second one, y_{2j}^*, which is a function of the exogenous variables, the disturbance term, and y_{1j}^*; and a third, y_{3j}^*, depending on y_{1j}^*, y_{j2}^*, etc.

An application of this proposition is given in section 10.2.2.

10.2 Some Examples

10.2.1 An Agricultural Model

This model was proposed by Quandt to describe the melon market in the United States. Market demand, D_t, is expressed as an inverse demand curve:

$$p_t = a_1 D_t + \mathbf{x}_{1t}\mathbf{b}_1 + u_{1t},$$

where p_t is the price of melons and $\mathbf{x}_{1t}$ a vector of explanatory variables. Supply, S_t, is a function of the quantity available, k_t, and of the quantity of melons which suppliers actually want to sell ℓ_t. k_t depends on:

(i) market price at the time of seeding (p_{t-1}), and
(ii) climate.

In other words, k_t is determined strictly by exogenous and lagged endogenous variables:

$$k_t = \mathbf{x}_{2t}\mathbf{b}_2 + u_{2t}.$$

while ℓ_t depends on the current price and other explanatory variables:

$$\ell_t = a_3 p_t + \mathbf{x}_{3t}\mathbf{b}_3 + u_{3t}.$$

Supply, S_t, is defined as the minimum of k_t and ℓ_t:

$$S_t = \min(k_t, \ell_t),$$

and, finally, the market is assumed in equilibrium, so that:

$$Q_t = D_t = S_t.$$

This model contains six latent variables $p_t, k_t, \ell_t, D_t, S_t$, and Q_t, the only observable endogenous variables are p_t and the quantity exchanged, Q_t.

In order for this model to make sense, the endogenous variables (observed or latent) must be well defined. Since Q_t, D_t, S_t are functions of k_t and ℓ_t, it is sufficient that we be able to express each of p_t, k_t, ℓ_t as unique functions of the exogenous variables and the disturbance terms. The resulting system is described by:

$$\begin{aligned} p_t &= a_1 \min(k_t, \ell_t) + \mathbf{x}_{1t}\mathbf{b}_1 + u_{1t}, \\ k_t &= \mathbf{x}_{2t}\mathbf{b}_2 + u_{2t}, \\ \ell_t &= a_3 p_t + \mathbf{x}_{3t}\mathbf{b}_3 + u_{3t}. \end{aligned}$$

This model comprises two regimes $\mathcal{C}_1$ and $\mathcal{C}_2$ such that:

$$\begin{aligned} \mathcal{C}_1 &= \{k_t > \ell_t\} \\ \mathcal{C}_2 &= \{k_t \leq \ell_t\}. \end{aligned}$$

Under regime $\mathcal{C}_1$ we have:

$$A_1 \begin{pmatrix} p_t \\ k_t \\ \ell_t \end{pmatrix} = \begin{pmatrix} x_{1t}b + u_{1t} \\ x_{2t}b_2 + u_{2t} \\ x_{3t}b_3 + u_{3t} \end{pmatrix}, \quad \text{where } A_1 = \begin{pmatrix} 1 & 0 & -a_1 \\ 0 & 1 & 0 \\ -a_3 & 0 & 1 \end{pmatrix},$$

and under $\mathcal{C}_2$:

$$A_2 \begin{pmatrix} p_t \\ k_t \\ \ell_t \end{pmatrix} = \begin{pmatrix} x_{1t}b + u_{1t} \\ x_{2t}b_2 + u_{2t} \\ x_{3t}b_3 + u_{3t} \end{pmatrix}, \quad \text{where } A_2 = \begin{pmatrix} 1 & -a_1 & 0 \\ 0 & 1 & 0 \\ -a_3 & 0 & 1 \end{pmatrix}.$$

The consistency conditions [cf. equation (10.1)] are satisfied if $\det(A_1)$ and $\det(A_2)$ are of the same sign, that is:

$$\det(A_1) \cdot \det(A_2) = 1 - a_1 a_3 > 0.$$

When this condition holds, we can unambiguously find the reduced form and derive the likelihood of the observations from the Jacobian.

10.2.2 A Model with Translations

Various economic phenomena can be explained by a model of the following type:

$$y_{1i}^* = \mathbf{x}_{1i}\mathbf{b}_1 + a_1 y_{2i}^* + c_1 y_{2i} + u_{1i},$$
$$y_{2i}^* = \mathbf{x}_{2i}\mathbf{b}_2 + a_2 y_{1i}^* + c_2 y_{2i} + u_{2i},$$

where:

$$y_{2i} = \begin{cases} 1, & \text{if } y_{2i}^* > 0, \\ 0, & \text{otherwise.} \end{cases}$$

Thus, for example, y_{1i}^* and y_{2i}^* could represent quantity exchanged and price in an equilibrium model. The two equations would then be the supply function and the inverse demand function respectively. When price y_{2i}^* exceeds a certain ceiling (zero here, but any constant value is possible) the government intervenes. This intervention may take the form of subsidies to economic agents to induce a shift in the supply and demand curves of c_1 and c_2.

This model satisfies the assumption of proposition 29. Expressing y_{1i}^* and y_{2i}^* as functions of y_{2i}, we have:

$$\begin{aligned} y_{1i}^* &= \frac{1}{1-a_1a_2}(c_1 + a_1c_2)\, y_{2i} \\ &\quad + \frac{1}{1-a_1a_2}(\mathbf{x}_{1i}\mathbf{b}_1 + a_1\mathbf{x}_{2i}\mathbf{b}_2) + \frac{u_{1i} + a_1u_{2i}}{1-a_1a_2}, \\ y_{2i}^* &= \frac{1}{1-a_1a_2}(a_2c_1 + c_2)\, y_{2i} \\ &\quad + \frac{1}{1-a_1a_2}(a_2\mathbf{x}_{1i}\mathbf{b}_1 + \mathbf{x}_{2i}\mathbf{b}_2) + \frac{a_2u_{1i} + u_{2i}}{1-a_1a_2}. \end{aligned}$$

Clearly, this system is recursive if, and only if, the coefficient of y_{2i} in the second equation is nil, i.e. if $a_2c_1 + c_2 = 0$. Here, in contrast to in our previous example, the condition appears in the form of an equality (as opposed to an inequality). We derive another expression of this condition by writing the matrix $A^{-1}\Gamma$ with the variables ordered (y_{1i}^*, y_{2i}^*):

$$A^{-1}\Gamma = \begin{bmatrix} 0 & \frac{1}{1-a_1a_2}(c_1 + a_1c_2) \\ 0 & \frac{1}{1-a_1a_2}(a_2c_1 + c_2) \end{bmatrix},$$

or in the order (y_{2i}^*, y_{1i}^*):

$$A^{-1}\Gamma = \begin{bmatrix} \frac{1}{1-a_1a_2}(a_2c_1 + c_2) & \frac{1}{1-a_1a_2}(c_1 + a_1c_2) \\ 0 & 0 \end{bmatrix}.$$

The condition $a_2c_1 + c_2 = 0$ ensures that at least one of the matrices (in this case, both) is triangular with zeros on the diagonal.

10.3 A Disequilibrium Model of Two Markets

10.3.1 The Model

This section focuses on a generalization to the two-market case of the disequilibrium model. This will allow us to describe the impact on one market of quantity constraints on the other.

Consider the standard model of a market for one good, a labour market, and two agents. The consumer acts as a buyer on the goods market and as a supplier on the labour market, while the firm supplies the good and demands labour. If demand for the good is insufficient the firm faces rationing in its supply of the good, being unable to produce and sell all it wants. Consequently, it hires less labour than desired, imposing rationing on the labour supply side in turn. Clearly, disequilibria in the two markets are not independent.

Disequilibrium market models are generally constructed on the basis of the notions of *effective* demand and supply. Several definitions exist for each of these concepts, and we shall use those which generate the simplest econometric model (cf. Gourieroux-Laffont-Monfort [GLM80] for a model based on another definition).

In our model the effective demand and supply schedules are those desired by the agents when they account for rationing on the other market. Let Q_1 (Q_2) represent the quantity exchanged on market one (two), assumed to be the minimum of the desired amounts:

$$Q_1 = \min(D_1, S_1),$$
$$Q_2 = \min(D_2, S_2).$$

The agent who demands on market one is squeezed by the quantity constraint Q_2 on market two. His demand, considering this constraint, is given by:

$$D_1 = a_1 Q_2 + \mathbf{x}_1\mathbf{b}_1 + u_1,$$

where the $\mathbf{x}_1$-s are exogenous variables. The other demand and supply schedules have analogous forms. Introducing the date of the observation, t, into our notation, we have:

$$\begin{aligned} D_{1t} &= a_1^1 Q_{2t} + \mathbf{x}_{1t}\mathbf{b}_1 + u_{1t}, \\ S_{1t} &= a_2^1 Q_{2t} + \mathbf{x}_{2t}\mathbf{b}_2 + u_{2t}, \\ D_{2t} &= a_1^2 Q_{1t} + \mathbf{x}_{3t}\mathbf{b}_3 + u_{3t}, \\ S_{2t} &= a_2^2 Q_{1t} + \mathbf{x}_{4t}\mathbf{b}_4 + u_{4t}, \end{aligned} \qquad (10.5)$$

where $t = 1, \ldots, T$.

$$Q_{1t} = \min(D_{1t}, S_{1t}),$$
$$Q_{2t} = \min(D_{2t}, S_{2t}). \tag{10.6}$$

The constrained market impacts on the other market over the coefficients $a_1^1, a_2^1, a_1^2, a_2^2$, called the *cross-over* coefficients. This model allows for four possible regimes at any given point in time, depending on whether or not each market is characterized by excess supply or by excess demand.

10.3.2 *Interpretation of the Consistency Conditions*

Equations (10.5) and (10.6) yield:

$$\begin{aligned} D_{1t} - a_1^1 \min(D_{2t}, S_{2t}) &= \mathbf{x}_{1t}\mathbf{b}_1 + u_{1t}, \\ S_{1t} - a_2^1 \min(D_{2t}, S_{2t}) &= \mathbf{x}_{2t}\mathbf{b}_2 + u_{2t}, \\ D_{2t} - a_1^2 \min(D_{1t}, S_{1t}) &= \mathbf{x}_{3t}\mathbf{b}_3 + u_{3t}, \\ S_{2t} - a_2^2 \min(D_{1t}, S_{1t}) &= \mathbf{x}_{4t}\mathbf{b}_4 + u_{4t}. \end{aligned}$$

The LHS appears as a mapping, g, piece-wise linear and continuous, onto $(D_{1t}, S_{1t}, D_{2t}, S_{2t})$. The matrices generated by g for each regime are as follows:

$$\text{for} \quad D_{1t} < S_{1t} \text{ and } D_{2t} < S_{2t} : A_1 = \begin{pmatrix} 1 & 0 & -a_1^1 & 0 \\ 0 & 1 & -a_2^1 & 0 \\ -a_1^2 & 0 & 1 & 0 \\ -a_2^2 & 0 & 0 & 1 \end{pmatrix},$$

$$\text{for} \quad D_{1t} < S_{1t} \text{ and } D_{2t} > S_{2t} : A_2 = \begin{pmatrix} 1 & 0 & 0 & -a_1^1 \\ 0 & 1 & 0 & -a_2^1 \\ -a_1^2 & 0 & 1 & 0 \\ -a_2^2 & 0 & 0 & 1 \end{pmatrix},$$

$$\text{for} \quad D_{1t} < S_{1t} \text{ and } D_{2t} < S_{2t} : A_3 = \begin{pmatrix} 1 & 0 & 0 & -a_1^1 \\ 0 & 1 & 0 & -a_2^1 \\ 0 & -a_1^2 & 1 & 0 \\ 0 & -a_2^2 & 0 & 1 \end{pmatrix},$$

$$\text{for} \quad D_{1t} < S_{1t} \text{ and } D_{2t} < S_{2t} : A_4 = \begin{pmatrix} 1 & 0 & -a_1^1 & 0 \\ 0 & 1 & -a_2^1 & 0 \\ 0 & -a_1^2 & 1 & 0 \\ 0 & -a_1^2 & 0 & 1 \end{pmatrix}.$$

Application of proposition 28 yields the following expression for the consistency condition:

$$1 - a_1^1 a_1^2, \quad 1 - a_1^1 a_2^2, \quad 1 - a_2^1 a_2^2, \quad 1 - a_2^1 a_2^2,$$

must all have the same sign. This condition is thus a function of the cross-over effects. Of these expressions, two involve only coefficients of the same agent:

$$1 - a_1^1 a_2^2 \quad \text{and} \quad 1 - a_2^1 a_1^2.$$

The usual assumptions about the concavity of utility functions imply that:

$$1 - a_1^1 a_2^2 > 0 \quad \text{and} \quad 1 - a_2^1 a_1^2 > 0.$$

Consequently, the two other expressions $1 - a_1^1 a_1^2$ and $1 - a_2^1 a_2^2$ must also be positive for the consistency criteria to obtain. It can be shown (cf. Gourieroux-Laffont-Monfort [GLM80]) that the constraints $1 - a_1^1 a_1^2 > 0$ and $1 - a_2^1 a_2^2 > 0$ are necessary and sufficient conditions for the stability of a quantity adjustment process.

Finally, notice that the consistency conditions which ensure the existence of a reduced form correspond, in terms of economic theory, to necessary and sufficient conditions for the existence of a unique equilibrium with a fixed price.

10.3.3 A Model with Endogenous Prices

We can expand the model in equations (10.5) and (10.6) by adding the following price adjustment equations for each market:

$$\begin{aligned} p_{1t} - p_{1t-1} &= \lambda_1 \left(D_{1t} - S_{1t}\right), \quad \lambda_1 > 0, \\ p_{2t} - p_{2t-1} &= \lambda_2 \left(D_{2t} - S_{2t}\right), \quad \lambda_2 > 0. \end{aligned} \tag{10.7}$$

As in the single equation case, this modification allows for the use of simpler estimation methods while facilitating a generalization of the model to include equilibrium as the limit case ($\lambda_1 = \lambda_2 = +\infty$).

The parameters of these equations can easily be estimated using instrumental least squares. We simply write:

$$\begin{aligned} Q_{1t} &= D_{1t} + (S_{1t} - D_{1t})\, z_{S_{1t} \le D_{1t}}, \\ Q_{1t} &= S_{1t} + (D_{1t} - S_{1t}) \left(1 - z_{S_{1t} \le D_{1t}}\right), \\ Q_{2t} &= D_{2t} + (S_{2t} - D_{2t})\, z_{S_{2t} \le D_{2t}}, \\ Q_{2t} &= S_{2t} + (D_{2t} - S_{2t}) \left(1 - z_{S_{2t} \le D_{2t}}\right), \end{aligned}$$

where:

$$z_{S_{2t} \le D_{2t}} = \begin{cases} 0, & \text{if } S_{2t} \le D_{2t}, \\ 1, & \text{otherwise.} \end{cases}$$

Equivalently:

$$Q_{1t} = a_1^1 Q_{2t} + \mathbf{x}_{1t}\mathbf{b}_1 + \frac{1}{\lambda_1}\left(p_{1,t-1} - p_{1t}\right) z_{p_{1t} > p_{1,t-1}} + u_{1t},$$

$$Q_{1t} = a_2^1 Q_{2t} + \mathbf{x}_{2t}\mathbf{b}_2 + \frac{1}{\lambda_1}\left(p_{1t} - p_{1,t-1}\right)\left(1 - z_{p_{1t} > p_{1,t-1}}\right) + u_{2t},$$

$$Q_{2t} = a_1^2 Q_{1t} + \mathbf{x}_{3t}\mathbf{b}_3 + \frac{1}{\lambda_2}\left(p_{2,t-1} - p_{2t}\right) z_{p_{1t} > p_{1,t-1}} + u_{3t},$$

$$Q_{2t} = a_2^2 Q_{1t} + \mathbf{x}_{4t}\mathbf{b}_4 + \frac{1}{\lambda_2}\left(p_{1t} - p_{1t-1}\right)\left(1 - z_{p_{1t} > p_{1,t-1}}\right) + u_{4t},$$

where:

$$z_{p_{1t} > p_{1,t-1}} = \begin{cases} 0, & \text{if } p_{1t} > p_{1,t-1}, \\ 1, & \text{otherwise.} \end{cases}$$

The first of these equations relates the endogenous variable Q_{1t} to the exogenous variables Q_{2t}, $\left(p_{1t} - p_{1,t-1}\right) z_{p_{1t} > p_{1,t-1}}$, p_{1t}, p_{2t} and to the exogenous variables in $\mathbf{x}_{1t}$. (Notice that p_{1t} and p_{2t} may occur in $\mathbf{x}_{1t}$). The parameters can be estimated by two-stage least squares.

10.4 Aggregation of Disequilibrium Markets

The disequilibrium models we introduced in chapter 8 and section 10.3 derive directly from the *microeconomic* theory of fixed prices, but they are estimated using *macroeconomic* data. Implicit in this approach is the assumption that within each market the quantity traded is equal to the minimum of the amount supplied and demanded. For a given period t (almost) all agents must be in the same regime. Now, we can clearly see from the data in section 6.5.2, derived from business cycle surveys, that this is rarely the case. In this section we shall turn our attention to the definition of more malleable specifications which explicitly account for aggregation, and derive a model incorporating continuous transition from a regime in which all suppliers are constrained to one in which this is true for all buyers.

10.4.1 Aggregation with No Crossover Effect

Consider a good which is simultaneously exchanged on several markets, indexed $i, i = 1, \ldots, n$. Demand on market i is denoted D_{it}, and supply S_{it}. The quantity traded at a given time is $Q_{it} = \min\left(D_{it}, S_{it}\right)$. Assume that there is no cross-over effect between markets; a buyer whose demand is not met in one market cannot make his purchase on another market. Under this arrangement, excess supply on one market can simultaneously coexist with excess demand on another. This structure allows us to derive a model with a number of macroeconomic features.

Global demand is given by:

$$D_t = \sum_{i=1}^{n} D_{it},$$

and global supply is:

$$S_t = \sum_{i=1}^{n} S_{it}.$$

The aggregate quantity exchanged is:

$$Q_t = \sum_{i=1}^{n} Q_{it}.$$

which is different from:

$$\min(D_t, S_t) = \min\left(\sum_{i=1}^{n} D_{it}, \sum_{i=1}^{n} S_{it}\right)$$

when markets characterized by excess demand coexist with markets in excess supply.

Let the proportion of markets in excess supply be:

$$\Pi_t = \frac{1}{n}\sum_{i=1}^{n} z_{S_{it}>D_{it}}.$$

where:

$$z_{S_{it}>D_{it}} = \begin{cases} 0, & \text{if } S_{it} > D_{it}, \\ 1, & \text{otherwise.} \end{cases}$$

Unfortunately, this macroeconomic formulation is not very tractable. One way to simplify it is to let the number of markets n tend to infinity while each individual market becomes infinitely small. We write:

$$D_{it} = \frac{d_{it}}{n},$$
$$S_{it} = \frac{s_{it}}{n},$$

and postulate that the empirical distribution of the variables $(d_{it}, s_{it}), i = 1, \ldots, n$ tends toward a density function $f_t(d, s)$. This formulation has the effect of incorporating the macroeconomic variables (for example, the price, p_t) into the moments of the distribution, and the microeconomic differences between markets into the density function.

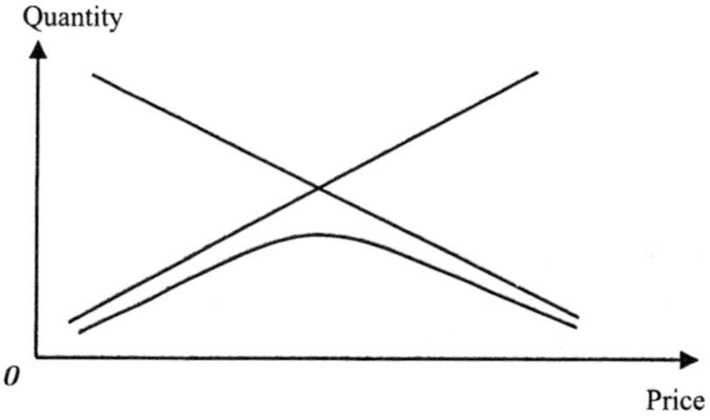

Fig. 10.4. Quantity exchanged and regime switching

As n tends to infinity the macroeconomic variables, whose observed values are the empirical means, tend toward the theoretical means associated with the limiting distribution f_t. Denoting the expectation of this distribution E_t, we obtain:

$$\begin{aligned} D_t &= \mathrm{E}_t\,(d), \\ S_t &= \mathrm{E}_t\,(s), \\ Q_t &= \mathrm{E}_t \min(d, s), \\ \Pi_t &= \mathrm{E}_t\,(z_{s>d}) = P_t\,(s > d). \end{aligned}$$

Example 9: Consider the case in which the limiting distribution is normal with mean:

$$\begin{aligned} D_t &= E_t\,(d), \\ S_t &= E_t\,(s), \end{aligned}$$

and with the second moments given by:

$$\begin{aligned} \sigma_1^2 &= \mathrm{var}_t\,(d), \\ \sigma_1^2 &= \mathrm{var}_t\,(s), \\ 0 &= \mathrm{cov}_t\,(d, s). \end{aligned}$$

Using our results from section 8.1.2, we see that the quantity exchanged is:

$$Q_t = S_t - \sigma \left[\frac{S_t - D_t}{\sigma} \Phi \left(\frac{S_t - D_t}{\sigma} \right) + \varphi \left(\frac{S_t - D_t}{\sigma} \right) \right],$$

with $\sigma^2 = \sigma_1^2 + \sigma_2^2$. When D_t and S_t are linear functions of the price p_t, the graph of the expectation is the same as it was in that section, but it now has a different interpretation:

The graph of the quantity exchanged is strictly below that of the function $\min(D_t, S_t)$, representing a continuous transition from a situation in which all buyers are constrained ($p_t \to -\infty$) to one in which all suppliers are ($p_t \to +\infty$).

Example 10: Clearly, we can postulate other functional forms for the limiting distribution, yielding different equations for the quantity exchanged. For example, using the C.E.S. function, we find:

$$Q_t = \left(D_t^r + S_t^r\right)^{\frac{1}{r}}, \quad r < 0.$$

In the limiting case: $r \to -\infty$, we revert to the model $Q_t = \min(D_t, S_t)$ – increasing values of r imply a greater degree of aggregation (cf. exercise 6).

10.4.2 Aggregation with Crossover Effects

The approach we have just examined can be generalized by introducing of the possibility of cross-over effects between markets. This implies that some buyers and some suppliers are active on more than one market simultaneously, and suggests that we must examine the allocation of rationing among agents. This case was studied by Gourieroux-Laroque [GL85].

Assume that economic agents (for example buyers) are active on all markets, and that their demand schedules are linear functions of the constraints. This entails constraints on the cross-over effects – constraints which are analogous to those we derived as consistency conditions. When these are satisfied we can demonstrate the existence and uniqueness of an equilibrium at a fixed price. In consequence, it is possible to obtain an explicit expression for the quantities Q_t and the proportions Π_t. These expressions depend on the distribution of excess demand $e = d - s$ between the markets. Let $\bar{e}_t = D_t - S_t$ be aggregate excess demand, σ^2 be the variance of e, F the distribution function of the associated normalized variable, defined by:

$$u = \frac{e - \bar{e}_t}{\sigma},$$

and g the function:

$$g(\Pi) = \mathrm{E}\left(u \cdot z_{u-F^{-1}(1-\Pi)}\right),$$

where:

$$z_{u-F^{-1}(1-\Pi)} = \begin{cases} 0, & \text{if } u - F^{-1}(1-\Pi) \le 0, \\ 1, & \text{otherwise.} \end{cases}$$

Solving the system for Q_t and Π_t yields:

$$\begin{aligned}
\frac{\bar{e}_t}{\sigma} &= -c\left[g\left(\Pi_t\right) - \Pi_t F^{-1}\left(1-\Pi_t\right)\right] \\
&\quad + c'\left[g\left(\Pi_t\right) + \left(1-\Pi_t\right) F^{-1}\left(1-\Pi_t\right)\right. \\
&\quad \left. - F^{-1}\left(1-\Pi_t\right)\right], \qquad (10.8) \\
Q_t &= D_t - (1-c)\,\sigma\left[g\left(\Pi_t\right) - \Pi_t F^{-1}\left(1-\Pi_t\right)\right], \\
&= S_t - \left(1-c'\right)\sigma\left[g\left(\Pi_t\right) + \left(1-\Pi_t\right) F^{-1}\left(1-\Pi_t\right)\right],
\end{aligned}$$

where c and c' are cross-over effect coefficients for buyers and sellers respectively. These coefficients are constrained by the closed interval $c, c' \in [0, 1]$.

In the simplest case, with D_t and S_t linear functions of price p_t (the former decreasing, the latter increasing), it can be shown that the graph of Q_t as a function of p_t is concave and asymptotically approaches the supply and demand curves (cf. exercise 7). It is thus analogous to the curve obtained in the aggregation model with no cross-over effects.

It is also of some interest to examine the evolution of this graph under differing specifications of the cross-over effects.

If $c = c' = 0$, there is no cross-over effect and we revert to the model of section 10.4.1. Increasing values of c and c' yield a graph approaching the function $\min\left(D_t, S_t\right)$. At the limit the graphs merge, indicating that agents move freely between markets.

10.4.3 Estimation

Given a formulation like the one in equations (10.8) , it is possible to simultaneously estimate the parameters of the supply and demand equations, as well as the coefficients of the cross-over effects. These coefficients can only be found to within a scale parameter, as they appear solely in the expressions $(1-c)\,\sigma$ and $\left(1-c'\right)\sigma$. Consequently, it is not possible to separate the cross-over effect from the variance $\left(\sigma^2\right)$ of the excess demand equation.

If the supply and demand functions are written:

$$\begin{aligned}
D_t &= a_1 p_t + \mathbf{x}_{1t}\mathbf{b}_1 + u_{1t}, \\
S_t &= a_2 p_t + \mathbf{x}_{2t}\mathbf{b}_2 + u_{2t},
\end{aligned}$$

we can substitute into equation (10.8), yielding:

$$\begin{aligned}
Q_t &= -(1-c)\,\sigma\left[g\left(\Pi_t\right) - \Pi_t F^{-1}\left(1-\Pi_t\right)\right] + a_1 p_t + \mathbf{x}_{1t}\mathbf{b}_1 + u_{1t}, \\
Q_t &= -\left(1-c'\right)\sigma\left[g\left(\Pi_t\right) + \left(1-\Pi_t\right) F^{-1}\left(1-\Pi_t\right)\right] \\
&\quad + a_2 p_t + \mathbf{x}_{2t}\mathbf{b}_2 + u_{2t}.
\end{aligned}$$

When Q_t (the quantity exchanged) and Π_t (the proportion of markets characterized by excess demand) are both observed, it is possible to estimate the parameters using two-stage least squares or maximum likelihood. If u_{1t} and u_{2t} are independent and follow a normal distribution with mean zero and variance σ_1^2 and σ_2^2, the likelihood is given by:

$$\ell(Q, \Pi) = \prod_{t=1}^{T} \ell_t(Q_t, \Pi_t),$$

where:

$$\begin{aligned} \ell(Q_t, \Pi_t) &= J_t \frac{1}{\sigma_1 \sigma_2} \varphi \left\{ \frac{Q_1 + (1-c)\sigma \left[g(\Pi_t) - \Pi_t F^{-1}(1-\Pi_t) - a_1 p_t - \mathbf{x}_{1t}\mathbf{b}_1 \right]}{\sigma_1} \right\} \\ &\times \varphi \left\{ \frac{Q_t + (1-c')\sigma \left[g(\Pi_t) + (1-\Pi_t) F^{-1}(1-\Pi_t) \right] - a_2 p_t - \mathbf{x}_{2t}\mathbf{b}_2}{\sigma_2} \right\} \end{aligned}$$

with the Jacobian:

$$J_t = \frac{\sigma}{f\left[F^{-1}(1-\Pi_t)\right]} \left[(1-c)\Pi_t + \left(1-c'\right)(1-\Pi_t) \right].$$

If only the quantity exchanged is observable we must integrate over Π_t to obtain the marginal distribution of Q_t. Usually, this must be done numerically.

Exercises

10.1 Find the likelihood of equation system (10.5) and (10.6). Do you think that this likelihood is usable if the prices in $\mathbf{x}_{1t}, \ldots, \mathbf{x}_{4t}$ are endogenous?

10.2 Under the assumptions in (10.5) and (10.6), find the probability of being in each regime. When do we have:

$$\Pr(D_{1t} < S_{1t}, D_{2t} < S_{2t}) = \Pr(D_{1t} < S_{1t}) \Pr(D_{2t} < S_{2t})?$$

10.3 Consider the system (10.5), (10.6), and (10.7) with the prices explicitly included in $\mathbf{x}_{1t}, \mathbf{x}_{2t}, \mathbf{x}_{3t}$, and $\mathbf{x}_{4t}$. Show that the model can be rewritten in terms only of the differences between actual and equilibrium quantities and actual and equilibrium prices.

10.4 From the preceding exercise, show that the price adjustment equation can be written exclusively as a function of current and lagged prices and of the equilibrium price. Verify that this equation is a piecewise linear recurrence function.

10.5 Consider the model in equations (10.5), (10.6) and (10.7), and assume that the values of the exogenous variables and the disturbances are known. Show that there exists a one-to-one relationship between $D_{1t}, S_{1t}, D_{2t}, S_{2t}$ and $Q_{1t}, Q_{2t}, p_{1t}, p_{2t}$ (don't forget that prices may occur in $\mathbf{x}_{1t}, \ldots, \mathbf{x}_{4t}$).

10.6 Assume that demand and supply follow a Weibull distribution with coefficients of proportionality d and s:

$$f(x) = \alpha x^{\alpha-1} \exp(-x^{\alpha}) z_{x>0}.$$

We have:

$$\frac{D_t}{d_t} \rightsquigarrow f,$$
$$\frac{S_t}{s_t} \rightsquigarrow f.$$

Assuming independence between D_t and S_t, calculate $\mathrm{E}(Q_t)$ as a function of d_t and s_t. Verify that the resulting equation is of the C.E.S. type. [cf. example 10].

10.7 (a) Show that (cf. section 10.4.2)

$$\frac{dg(\Pi)}{d\Pi} = F^{-1}(1-\Pi).$$

(b) Find the derivatives of:

$$-\alpha \left[g(\Pi) - \Pi F^{-1}(1-\Pi)\right]$$
$$+ a' \left[g(\Pi) + (1-\Pi) F^{-1}(1-\Pi)\right] - F^{-1}(1-\Pi),$$

and of:

$$g(\Pi) - \Pi F^{-1}(-\Pi).$$

What are the signs of these derivatives?

(c) Draw the graphs of Π as a function of p and of Q as a function of p for D and S linear functions of p.

10.8 Show that Π_t and Q_t tend toward limits as σ tends toward zero (or as α and α' tend toward one). What are these limits? Interpret your results.

11 The Econometrics of Discrete Positive Variables: the Poisson Model

11.1 Introduction

Data describing economic behaviour often consist of variables assuming a small number of positive values. For reasons analogous to those given in the introduction to chapter 2, the classical linear model is inadequate for the study of how these variables depend on other quantitative or qualitative variables: the scatter of observations is ill suited to a linear fit; the assumption of normality appears unjustified as the variable takes a small number of values (and does so with strictly positive probabilities); the predictive equations may, in fact, yield values which the variables cannot assume, etc.

The formulations proposed in the literature (El Sayyad [Say73], Lancaster [Lan76], Gilbert [Gil79], and Hausman-Hall-Griliches [GHH84]) postulate that the discrete variable follows a Poisson distribution whose parameters are determined by the exogenous variables. This distribution is clearly justified when the variable in question describes the number of occurrences of an event during a given time span and, of course, when all the usual assumptions underlying a Poisson process hold. The model is useful, for example, to describe how many flights will arrive at an airport on a given day as a function of the date; how many work-related accidents will occur in a firm as a function of the characteristics of that firm; the number of bankruptcies in a given industry, how many patent applications will be submitted in a given year (Hausman-Hall-Griliches [GHH84]), etc. This simple type of structure can also provide a good first approach to describing variables which do not fully meet the conditions of the Poisson model – particularly cases in which the assumption of independence between the present and the past does not hold. Thus, for example, it has been used to explain the number of times individuals change jobs over the course of a year (Gilbert [Gil79]).

11.2 The Simple Poisson Model

11.2.1 Description

Let y_i, $i = 1, \ldots, n$, represent n observations on the discrete variable assuming values in $\mathbb{N}$. In the simple model we assume that each of the variables y_i are independent and follow a Poisson distribution with parameters λ_i. These parameters depend on the values assumed by K exogenous variables: $\mathbf{x}_i = (x_{1i}, \ldots, x_{Ki})$ over:

$$\begin{aligned}\lambda_i &= \exp(\mathbf{x}_i \mathbf{b}),\\ &= \exp\left(\sum_{k=1}^{K} x_{ik} b_k\right),\end{aligned}$$

where the b_k-s are parameters.

The choice of this functional form to relate the parameters to the exogenous variables is justified in large part by the need to ensure that the values of λ_i are positive. We cannot, for example, use a linear formulation, $\lambda_i = \mathbf{x}_i \mathbf{b}$, as this requires imposing the constraint $\mathbf{x}_i \mathbf{b} \geq 0, \forall i$, on the parameters, which may very well lead to inconsistencies. Furthermore, when the $\mathbf{x}_k$-s are the logarithms of economic variables, $x_{ik} = \log(X_{ik})$, the parameter $\mathbf{b}_k$ is defined by:

$$b_k = \frac{\partial \log[\mathrm{E}(y_i)]}{\partial \log(X_{ik})},$$

and can be interpreted as an elasticity.

The mean and the variance of y_i are $\lambda_i = \exp(\mathbf{x}_i \mathbf{b})$, and the probability associated with an observation is:

$$\ell(y_i) = \frac{\exp(-\lambda_i)\, \lambda_i^{y_i}}{y_i\,!}.$$

The log-likelihood of the model is thus:

$$\begin{aligned}L(y; \mathbf{b}) &= \sum_{i=1}^{n} \log[\ell(y_i)],\\ &= -\sum_{i=1}^{n} \lambda_i + \sum_{i=1}^{n} y_i \log(\lambda_i) - \sum_{i=1}^{n} \log(y_i\,!),\\ &= -\sum_{i=1}^{n} \exp(\mathbf{x}_i \mathbf{b}) + \sum_{i=1}^{n} y_i \mathbf{x}_i \mathbf{b} - \sum_{i=1}^{n} \log(y_i\,!).\end{aligned}$$

Notice that this function is concave in $\mathbf{b}$.

11.2.2 The Maximum-Likelihood Method

The parameters of these equations can be estimated using the maximum-likelihood method:

$$\frac{\partial L}{\partial \mathbf{b}} = -\sum_{i=1}^{n} \mathbf{x}_i' \left[\exp(\mathbf{x}_i \mathbf{b}) - y_i\right] = 0.$$

This equation reflects the orthogonality between the explanatory variables, $\mathbf{x}_i$, and the residuals of the estimation, $\exp(\mathbf{x}_i \mathbf{b}) - y_i$.

Due to the strict concavity of the function L, the solution to this system of equations (β) assuming it exists (cf. exercise 7), is unique and defines a maximum. The Hessian is:

$$\frac{\partial^2 L}{\partial \mathbf{b} \partial \mathbf{b}'} = -\sum_{i=1}^{n} \mathbf{x}_i' \mathbf{x}_i \exp(\mathbf{x}_i \mathbf{b}).$$

From this expression we can derive the asymptotic variance-covariance matrix of the maximum-likelihood estimator:

$$\widehat{\text{var}}_{asy}(\beta) = \left[\sum_{i=1}^{n} \mathbf{x}_i' \mathbf{x}_i \exp(\mathbf{x}_i \beta)\right]^{-1}. \tag{11.1}$$

This model is easy to work with. In particular, the fact that it is strictly concave enables us to use standard maximization algorithms. Notice, incidentally, that when it contains a constant term, i.e. an exogenous variable equal to one, the likelihood equation becomes:

$$\sum_{i=1}^{n} \left[\exp(\mathbf{x}_i \beta) - y_i\right] = 0,$$

implying that the mean of the residuals of the estimation is zero. Comparison of numeric estimates of this mean with zero thus provides a useful measure of the precision of the algorithm.

11.3 The Poisson Model with Stochastic Coefficients

11.3.1 Description

The formulation we have just examined suffers from the limitation that, for a given $\mathbf{x}_i$, the variance of y_i cannot be determined independently of its mean. To avoid this difficulty we reformulate the model to include an additional random element:

$$\lambda_i = \exp(\mathbf{x}_i \mathbf{b} + \varepsilon_i).$$

This additional source of randomness, ε_i, captures various specification errors in the parameters λ_i – such as omitted explanatory variables which are independent of $\mathbf{x}_i$ – and we must be careful to distinguish this term from the initial error term. This latter reflects the fact that our observations on the data comprise an underlying stochastic element, while the former pertains to the randomness of the coefficients in our new model. To solve this model it is necessary to integrate over ε. The distribution of y_i, conditional on $\mathbf{x}_i$ and ε_i, is $\mathcal{P}(\lambda_i)$, from which we can derive the distribution of y_i conditional on $\mathbf{x}_i$:

$$\ell^*(y_i) = \int \frac{\exp\left[-\exp(\mathbf{x}_i\mathbf{b} + \varepsilon_i)\right]\left[\exp(\mathbf{x}_i\mathbf{b} + \varepsilon_i)\right]^{y_i} g(\varepsilon_i)\, d\varepsilon_i}{y_i!}, \tag{11.2}$$

where g is the density function of ε_i. If the ε_i-s are independent and identically distributed under g, we see that the log-likelihood is:

$$L^*(y; \mathbf{b}, g) = \sum_{i=1}^{n} \log\left[\ell^*(y_i)\right].$$

The expression for L^* clearly depends on the chosen distribution g of ε, and only when $\exp(\varepsilon)$ is assumed to follow a gamma distribution does it have a simple form.

11.3.2 Integration with Respect to the Gamma Distribution

Notice that if the model contains a constant term, we can always transform the error term such that the mean of $\exp(\varepsilon_i)$ is equal to one. Letting the distribution of $\exp(\varepsilon)$ be gamma with mean one and variance η^2, the density function is:

$$f(u) = \frac{u^{\frac{1}{\eta^2}-1} e^{-\frac{u}{\eta^2}}}{(\eta^2)^{\frac{1}{\eta^2}}\,\Gamma\left(\frac{1}{\eta^2}\right)}.$$

Integrating according to equation (11.2), we obtain a negative binomial distribution for ℓ^* :

$$\ell^*(y_i) = \frac{\Gamma\left(\frac{1}{\eta^2} + y_i\right)}{\Gamma\left(\frac{1}{\eta^2}\right)\Gamma(y_i + 1)} \frac{\left[\eta^2 \exp(\mathbf{x}_i\mathbf{b})\right]^{y_i}}{\left[1 + \eta^2 \exp(\mathbf{x}_i\mathbf{b})\right]^{y_i + \frac{1}{\eta^2}}}.$$

Now, the usual procedure is to maximize:

$$L^* = \sum_{i=1}^{n} \log\left[\ell^*(y_i)\right],$$

with respect to the parameters $\mathbf{b}$, η^2. Unfortunately, there are two problems associated with this procedure:

(i) Solving the likelihood equations and estimating their variances requires calculating the first and second derivatives of the gamma function numerically.
(ii) The estimates thus obtained are no longer well-behaved if the true distribution of $\exp(\varepsilon)$ is not gamma.

In consequence, we need to find estimation methods for the model with stochastic coefficients which are simpler to apply and yield consistent estimators for any distribution function g with mean one and variance η^2.

11.3.3 Calculating the Moments of y_i

As in the case of the classical linear model, it seems natural to search for methods which only involve the first two moments of the endogenous variables. These moments are easily found by decomposing the distribution conditional on ε_i. Assuming a specification error, ε_i, such that:

$$\begin{aligned} 1 &= \mathrm{E}\left[\exp(\varepsilon_i)\right], \\ \eta^2 &= \mathrm{var}\left[\exp(\varepsilon_i)\right], \end{aligned}$$

we see that:

$$\begin{aligned} \mathrm{E}(y_i) &= \mathrm{E}\left[\mathrm{E}(y_i \mid \varepsilon_i)\right], \\ &= \mathrm{E}\left[\exp(\mathbf{x}_i\mathbf{b} + \varepsilon_i)\right], \\ &= \exp(\mathbf{x}_i\mathbf{b})\,\mathrm{E}\left[\exp(\varepsilon_i)\right], \\ &= \exp(\mathbf{x}_i\mathbf{b}). \end{aligned}$$

Similarly:

$$\begin{aligned} \mathrm{var}(y_i) &= \mathrm{E}\left[\mathrm{var}(y_i \mid \varepsilon_i)\right] + \mathrm{var}\left[\mathrm{E}(y_i \mid \varepsilon_i)\right], \\ &= \mathrm{E}\left[\exp(\mathbf{x}_i\mathbf{b} + \varepsilon_i)\right] + \mathrm{var}\left[\exp(\mathbf{x}_i\mathbf{b} + \varepsilon_i)\right], \\ &= \exp(\mathbf{x}_i\mathbf{b})\,\mathrm{E}\left[\exp(\varepsilon_i)\right] + \exp(2\mathbf{x}_i\mathbf{b})\,\mathrm{var}\left[\exp(\varepsilon_i)\right], \\ &= \exp(\mathbf{x}_i\mathbf{b}) + \eta^2\exp(2\mathbf{x}_i\mathbf{b}). \end{aligned}$$

Use of the error term ε_i permits us to introduce the supplementary parameter η^2, and consequently the mean and the variance of y_i can vary independently, subject to $\text{var}(y_i) \geq \text{E}(y_i)$.

11.3.4 Some Estimation Methods

Various consistent estimation techniques which rely only on the first two moments are available. Here we shall present the main ones along with the respective asymptotic covariance matrices of the estimators. The proofs of convergence and asymptotic normality can be found in Gourieroux-Monfort-Trognon [1980].

11.3.4.1 The Ordinary Least Squares Method

The estimators $\boldsymbol{\beta}_{OLS}$ and $\hat{\eta}^2_{OLS}$ are obtained in two stages. $\boldsymbol{\beta}_{OLS}$ is defined as the solution to the minimization problem:

$$\min_{\mathbf{b}} \sum_{i=1}^{n} \left[y_i - \exp(\mathbf{x}_i \mathbf{b})\right]^2 .$$

We take advantage of the particular form of $\text{var}(y_i)$ to estimate η^2:

$$\text{var}(y_i) = \exp(\mathbf{x}_i \mathbf{b}) + \eta^2 \exp(2\mathbf{x}_i \mathbf{b}).$$

Denoting $\hat{u}_{1i} = y_i - \exp(\mathbf{x}_i \boldsymbol{\beta}_{OLS})$, we estimate η^2 by the coefficient of the regression of $\hat{u}^2_{1i} - \exp(\mathbf{x}_i \boldsymbol{\beta}_{OLS})$ on $(2\mathbf{x}_i \boldsymbol{\beta}_{OLS})$, that is:

$$\hat{\eta}^2_{OLS} = \frac{\sum_{i=1}^{n} \left[\hat{u}^2_{1i} - \exp(\mathbf{x}_i \boldsymbol{\beta}_{OLS})\right] \exp(2\mathbf{x}_i \boldsymbol{\beta}_{OLS})}{\sum_{i=1}^{n} \exp(4\mathbf{x}_i \boldsymbol{\beta}_{OLS})} .$$

These estimators are consistent. The asymptotic variance of $\boldsymbol{\beta}_{OLS}$ can be estimated by:

$$\begin{aligned} \widehat{\text{var}}_{asy}(\boldsymbol{\beta}_{OLS}) = & \left[\sum_{i=1}^{n} \mathbf{x}_i' \mathbf{x}_i \exp\left(2\mathbf{x}_i \boldsymbol{\beta}_{OLS}^{-1}\right)\right]^{-1} \\ & \times \left[\sum_{i=1}^{n} \mathbf{x}_i' \mathbf{x}_i \exp(2\mathbf{x}_i \boldsymbol{\beta}_{OLS})\right] \\ & \times \left[\exp(\mathbf{x}_1 \boldsymbol{\beta}_{OLS}) + \eta^2_{OLS} \exp(2\mathbf{x}_i \boldsymbol{\beta}_{OLS})\right] \\ & \times \left[\sum_{i=1}^{n} \mathbf{x}_i' \mathbf{x}_i \exp\left(2\mathbf{x}_i \hat{\boldsymbol{\beta}}_{OLS}\right)\right]^{-1} . \end{aligned} \qquad (11.3)$$

11.3.4.2 The Weighted Nonlinear Least Squares Method

The procedure in the previous section can be improved if we take into consideration the variances of the observations in our estimation of **b**, yielding a two-stage procedure. The estimator, $\boldsymbol{\beta}_w$, is the solution to the problem:

$$\min_{\mathbf{b}} \sum_{i=1}^{n} \frac{\left[y_i - \exp\left(\mathbf{x}_i \mathbf{b}\right)\right]^2}{\exp\left(\mathbf{x}_i \boldsymbol{\beta}_{OLS}\right) + \hat{\eta}_{OLS}^2 \exp\left(2\mathbf{x}_i \boldsymbol{\beta}_{OLS}\right)},$$

while the estimator for η^2 is:

$$\hat{\eta}_w^2 = \frac{\sum_{i=1}^{n} \left[\hat{u}_{2i}^2 - \exp\left(\mathbf{x}_i \boldsymbol{\beta}_w\right)\right] \exp\left(2\mathbf{x}_i \boldsymbol{\beta}_w\right)}{\sum_{i=1}^{n} \exp\left(4\mathbf{x}_i \boldsymbol{\beta}_w\right)},$$

where $\hat{u}_{2i} = y_i - \exp\left(\mathbf{x}_i \boldsymbol{\beta}_w\right)$.

These estimators are also consistent. An estimator for the asymptotic variance covariance matrix of $\boldsymbol{\beta}_w$ is given by:

$$\widehat{\text{var}}_{asy}\left(\boldsymbol{\beta}_w\right) = \left[\sum_{i=1}^{n} \frac{\mathbf{x}_i' \mathbf{x}_i \exp\left(2\mathbf{x}_i \boldsymbol{\beta}_w\right)}{\exp\left(\mathbf{x}_i \boldsymbol{\beta}_w\right) + \hat{\eta}_w^2 \exp\left(2\mathbf{x}_i \boldsymbol{\beta}_w\right)}\right]^{-1}. \tag{11.4}$$

The estimator $\boldsymbol{\beta}_w$ is asymptotically more precise than $\boldsymbol{\beta}_{OLS}$ (cf. exercise 2).

11.3.4.3 The Pseudo Maximum-Likelihood Method

This method consists of applying the maximum-likelihood method while treating y_i as if normally distributed, with mean:

$$\mathrm{E}\left(y_i\right) = \exp\left(\mathbf{x}_i \mathbf{b}\right),$$

and variance:

$$\text{var}\left(y_i\right) = \exp\left(\mathbf{x}_i \mathbf{b}\right) + \eta^2 \exp\left(2\mathbf{x}_i \mathbf{b}\right).$$

To obtain the estimators we maximize:

$$\max_{\mathbf{b}, \eta^2} \sum_{i=1}^{n} \psi\left(y_i, \mathbf{x}_i; \mathbf{b}, \eta^2\right),$$

with:

$$\psi\left(y_i, \mathbf{x}_i; \mathbf{b}, \eta^2\right) = -\frac{1}{2}\log\left(2\pi\right) - \frac{1}{2}\log\left[\exp\left(\mathbf{x}_i \mathbf{b}\right) + \eta^2 \exp\left(2\mathbf{x}_i \mathbf{b}\right)\right] - \frac{1}{2}\frac{\left[y_i - \exp\left(\mathbf{x}_i \mathbf{b}\right)\right]^2}{\exp\left(\mathbf{x}_i \mathbf{b}\right) + \eta^2 \exp\left(2\mathbf{x}_i \mathbf{b}\right)}.$$

The estimators, β_{PML} and $\hat{\eta}^2_{PML}$, are consistent, with asymptotic covariance matrix:

$$\widehat{\text{var}}_{asy}\left(\beta_{PML}\hat{\eta}^2_{PML}\right) = \sum_{i=1}^{n}\left[\frac{\partial^2\psi\left(y_i, \mathbf{x}_i; \mathbf{b}, \eta^2\right)}{\partial\left(\beta_{PML}, \hat{\eta}^2_{PML}\right)\partial\left(\beta_{PML}, \hat{\eta}^2_{PML}\right)}\right]^{-1}$$
$$\times\left[\sum_{i=1}^{n}\frac{\partial\psi\left(y_i, \mathbf{x}_i; \mathbf{b}, \eta^2\right)}{\partial\left(\beta_{PML}, \hat{\eta}^2_{PML}\right)}\frac{\partial\psi\left(y_i\mathbf{x}_i; \mathbf{b}, \eta^2\right)}{\partial\left(\beta_{PML}, \hat{\eta}^2_{PML}\right)}\right]$$
$$\times\left[\sum_{i=1}^{n}\frac{\partial^2\psi\left(y_i, \mathbf{x}_i; \mathbf{b}, \eta^2\right)}{\partial\left(\beta_{PML}, \hat{\eta}^2_{PML}\right)\partial\left(\beta_{PML}, \hat{\eta}^2_{PML}\right)}\right].$$

11.3.4.4 Pseudo-Maximum Likelihood Using the Poisson Distribution

Instead of postulating that the distribution of y_i is normal, we may calculate the maximum likelihood on the assumption that the y_i-s independently follow a Poisson distribution, $\mathcal{P}\left[\exp\left(\mathbf{x}_i\mathbf{b}\right)\right]$. The resulting estimator for $\mathbf{b}$ is clearly identical to the one yielded by the basic Poisson model. It is consistent even though we have ignored the specification error ε. However, the asymptotic variance of this estimator is no longer given by the equation (11.1). We must, in particular, take into consideration the fact the variance of y_i is no longer equal to its mean.

We have:

$$\widehat{\text{var}}_{asy}(\beta) = \left[\sum_{i=1}^{n}\mathbf{x}_i'\mathbf{x}_i \exp\left(\mathbf{x}_i\beta\right)\right]^{-1}\left\{\sum_{i=1}^{n}\mathbf{x}_i'\mathbf{x}_i\hat{\mathrm{E}}\left[\exp\left(\mathbf{x}_i\mathbf{b}\right) - y_i\right]^2\right\}$$
$$\times\left[\sum_{i=1}^{n}\mathbf{x}_i'\mathbf{x}_i \exp\left(\mathbf{x}_i\beta\right)\right]^{-1}.$$
$$= \left[\sum_{i=1}^{n}\mathbf{x}_i'\mathbf{x}_i \exp\left(\mathbf{x}_i\beta\right)\right]^{-1} + \eta^2\left[\sum_{i=1}^{n}\mathbf{x}_i'\mathbf{x}_i \exp\left(\mathbf{x}_i\beta\right),\right]^{-1}$$
$$\times\left[\sum_{i=1}^{n}\mathbf{x}_i'\mathbf{x}_i \exp\left(2\mathbf{x}_i\beta\right)\right]\left[\sum_{i=1}^{n}\mathbf{x}_i'\mathbf{x}_i \exp\left(\mathbf{x}_i\beta\right)\right]^{-1}.$$

This estimator obviously loses precision in the presence of specification error.

11.4 The Bivariate Poisson Model

11.4.1 The Probabilistic Model

In this section we shall present a generalization of the Poisson model with two discrete positive endogenous variables, y_1 and y_2. We begin with the standard assumptions of the Poisson distribution expanded to accommodate the bivariate case. These assumptions are as follows:

(i) $y_1(t)$ and $y_2(t)$ measure the frequency with which events of type one and type two occur respectively during the interval between 0 and t.
(ii) Occurances of any event between t and $t + dt$ are independent of any occurrences before t.
(iii) Between t and $t + dt$ one of the following may occur:
   (a) One event of type one and no event of type two, with probability $\lambda dt + 0(dt)$ [$0(dt)$ designates an infinitesimally small interval compared to dt],
   (b) One event of type two and no event of type one, with probability $\mu dt + 0(dt)$,
   (c) One event of type one and one event of type two, with probability $\nu dt + 0(dt)$,
   (d) No event, with probability $1 - \lambda dt - \mu dt - \nu dt + 0(dt)$.

Given these assumptions, we can easily find the distribution of the process $[y_1(t), y_2(t)]$. Observe that:

$$P_{n,m}(t) = \Pr[y_1(t) = n, y_2(t) = m], \quad n, m \in \boldsymbol{N},$$

and:

$$G(t, u, v) = \mathrm{E}\left[u^{y_1(t)} v^{y_2(t)}\right], \\ = \sum_n \sum_m P_{n,m}(t)\, u^n v^m,$$

is the moment generating function for $[y_1(t), y_2(t)]$. We have:

$$\begin{aligned} P_{n,m}(t + dt) = {} & P_{n,m}(t)\,[1 - \lambda\, dt - \mu\, dt - \nu\, dt + 0(dt)] \\ & + P_{n-1,m}(t)\,[\lambda\, dt + 0(dt)] \\ & + P_{n,m-1}(t)\,[\mu\, dt + 0(dt)] \\ & + P_{n-1,m-1}(t)\,[\nu\, dt + 0(dt)]. \end{aligned}$$

Taking the limit as $dt \to 0$, we obtain:

$$\frac{dP_{n,m}(t)}{dt} = (-\lambda - \mu - \nu) P_{n,m}(t) + \lambda P_{n-1,m}(t) + \mu P_{n,m-1}(t) + \nu P_{n-1,m-1}(t).$$

And, carrying this over to the moment generating function yields:

$$\frac{\partial G(t,u,v)}{\partial t} = (-\lambda - \mu - \nu + \lambda u + \mu v + \nu uv) G(t,u,v),$$
$$G(t,u,v) = \exp(-\lambda - \mu - \nu + \lambda u + \mu v + \nu uv) t.$$

Now we can derive the expression for the probabilities $P_{n,m}(t)$. Unfortunately, the resulting equations are not very tractable (cf. exercise 3). Consequently, it appears preferable to characterize the variables $y_1(t)$, $y_2(t)$ by their first two moments.

The moment generating function reveals that:

$$y_1(t) \sim \mathcal{P}[(\lambda + v)t],$$
$$y_2(t) \sim \mathcal{P}[(\mu + v)t],$$

and thus:

$$\mathrm{E}[y_1(t)] = \mathrm{var}[y_1(t)] = (\lambda + \nu)t,$$
$$\mathrm{E}[y_2(t)] = \mathrm{var}[y_2(t)] = (\mu + \nu)t.$$

The covariance between $y_1(t)$ and $y_2(t)$ follows from the second derivative of G:

$$\mathrm{E}[y_1(t)\, y_2(t)] = \left[\frac{\partial^2 G(t,u,v)}{\partial u \partial v}\right]_{u=1,v=1},$$
$$= \nu t + (\lambda + \nu)t(\mu + \nu)t,$$

and hence:

$$\mathrm{cov}[y_1(t), y_2(t)] = \nu t.$$

Notice that, when $\nu = 0$, the moment generating function of the pair $[y_1(t), y_2(t)]$ is equal to the product of the moment generating functions of $y_1(t)$ and $y_2(t)$:

$$G(t,u,v) = G(t,u,1)\, G(t,1,v),$$

and so the variables are independent. In this model the notions of uncorrelated and independent are synonymous.

11.4.2 The Econometric Model

Turning now to the econometric model, we begin by postulating that we have several independent observations $y_{1i}, y_{2i}, i = 1, \ldots, n$ on variables whose distributions correspond to those described in the previous section. These observations occur over a period of duration $t = 1$. This is, of course, a convention, any length of time could be used and incorporated into the parameters λ_i, μ_i, ν_i. To complete the model, it remains to specify the relationship between the parameters and the explanatory variables. By analogy to the stacked regression model we assume that the covariance between y_{1i} and y_{2i} is constant. Furthermore, we adopt an exponential form for the two other parameters, introducing into each a stochastic omitted-variable term:

$$\lambda_i = \exp(\mathbf{x}_i \mathbf{b} + \varepsilon_{1i}),$$
$$\mu_i = \exp(\mathbf{z}_i \mathbf{c} + \varepsilon_{2i}),$$
$$\nu_i = \nu,$$

where:

$$\begin{aligned} 1 &= \mathrm{E}\left[\exp(\varepsilon_{1i})\right] = \mathrm{E}\left[\exp(\varepsilon_{2i})\right], \\ \eta_1^2 &= \mathrm{var}\left[\exp(\varepsilon_{1i})\right], \\ \eta_2^2 &= \mathrm{var}\left[\exp(\varepsilon_{2i})\right], \\ \eta_{12} &= \mathrm{cov}\left[\exp(\varepsilon_{1i}), \exp(\varepsilon_{2i})\right]. \end{aligned} \tag{11.5}$$

Given the complex form of the probabilities $P_{n,m}$ (cf. exercise 3), it is clearly not practicable to integrate over the random terms $(\varepsilon_{1i}, \varepsilon_{2i})$ in order to apply the maximum-likelihood method. On the other hand, estimation methods based on the first two moments can easily be generalized. The moments of the observed variables are:

$$\mathrm{E}(y_{1i}) = \exp(\mathbf{x}_i \mathbf{b}) + \nu,$$

$$\mathrm{E}(y_{2i}) = \exp(\mathbf{z}_i \mathbf{c}) + \nu,$$

$$\begin{aligned} \mathrm{var}\begin{pmatrix} y_{1i} \\ y_{2i} \end{pmatrix} &= \begin{pmatrix} \exp(\mathbf{x}_i \mathbf{b}) & \nu \\ \nu & \exp(\mathbf{z}_i \mathbf{c}) \end{pmatrix} \\ &+ \begin{pmatrix} \exp(\mathbf{x}_i \mathbf{b}) & 0 \\ 0 & \exp(\mathbf{z}_i \mathbf{c}) \end{pmatrix} \begin{pmatrix} \eta_1^2 & \eta_{12} \\ \eta_{12} & \eta_2^2 \end{pmatrix} \\ &\times \begin{pmatrix} \exp(\mathbf{x}_i \mathbf{b}) & 0 \\ 0 & \exp(\mathbf{z}_i \mathbf{c}) \end{pmatrix}. \end{aligned}$$

The nonlinear least squares method consists of estimating $\mathbf{b}, \mathbf{c}$ and v by minimizing:

$$\min_{\mathbf{b},\mathbf{c},v} \sum_{i=1}^{n} \left[(y_{1i} - \exp(\mathbf{x}_i \mathbf{b}) - v)^2 + (y_{2i} - \exp(\mathbf{z}_i \mathbf{c}) - v)^2 \right],$$

and then performing a regression on the residuals to estimate $\eta_1^2, \eta_2^2, \eta_{12}$.

This method could also have been formulated so as to include in the first minimization the variance-covariance matrix of the observations. The pseudo maximum-likelihood method also allows for a straightforward generalization, based on a two-dimensional normal distribution.

Remark 9: At the estimation stage, it is usually necessary to solve for ν under the constraint $\nu \geq 0$. Similarly, the test of independence is one-sided, comparing $H_0 : \nu = 0$ with $H_1 : \nu > 0$. This constraint on ν is perfectly reasonable, as v reflects the relationship over time between the variables, and must be positive since the counters must increase with time. This constraint does not imply any restriction on the sign of the unconditional correlation between the variables (cf. exercise 4).

Remark 10: Notice, finally, that it would be possible to retain specifications other than the one given in equation (11.5), but that they would, in general, be more difficult to evaluate numerically (cf. exercise 5).

Exercises

11.1 It is sometimes stated that the simple Poisson model is ill-suited to typical econometric data since the empirical variance is usually greater than the empirical mean. What do you think of this observation?

11.2 Consider the simple Poisson model with a single explanatory variable. Using a procedure analogous to that in section 2.4.4, show that:

(a) the likelihood equation always has a solution if $\min(x_i) < 0 < \max(x_i)$, or,

(b) if this condition does not hold, a solution exists if and only if one of the observations on y is non-zero.

11.3 Let z be defined as:

$$z = \begin{cases} 1, & \text{if } y = 0, \\ 0, & \text{otherwise.} \end{cases}$$

where y is described by a simple Poisson model. Show that z follows a Gompertz distribution.

11.4 Find the first-order conditions satisfied by the estimator β_{OLS}.

11.5 Let the estimators in equations (11.3) and (11.4) be such that:

$$n \left[\widehat{\text{var}}_{asy}(\beta_{OLS}) - \text{var}_{asy}(\beta_{OLS}) \right] \to 0, \quad \text{if } n \to \infty$$

and:

$$n\left[\widehat{\text{var}}_{asy}(\beta_w) - \text{var}_{asy}(\beta_w)\right] \to 0, \quad \text{if } n \to \infty.$$

(a) Using the Gauss-Markov theorem show that, if X and Ω are (n, k)-dimensional and (n, n)-dimensional matrices respectively, we have:

$$\left(X'\Omega^{-1}X\right)^{-1} \ll \left(X'X\right)^{-1} X'\Omega X \left(X'X\right)^{-1}.$$

(b) Derive that:

$$\lim_{n\to\infty}\left[n\text{var}_{asy}(\beta_w)\right] \ll \lim_{n\to\infty}\left[n\text{var}_{asy}(\beta_{OLS})\right]$$

11.6 Consider the model introduced in section 11.4.1, show that:

$$P_{n,m}(t) = e^{(-\lambda-\mu-\nu)t} A_{n,m}(t),$$

with:

$$A_{n,m}(t) = \frac{t^{n+m}}{(n+m)!}\lambda^n\mu^m\frac{(n+m)!}{n!m!} + \frac{t^{n+m-1}}{(n+m-1)!}\lambda^{n-1}$$
$$\mu^{m-1}\nu\frac{(n+m+1)!}{(n-1)!(m-1)!} + \dots$$
$$+\frac{t^{n+m-p}}{(n+m-p)!}\lambda^{n-p}\mu^{m-p}\nu^p\frac{(n+m+p)!}{(n-p)!(m-p)!p!},$$

where $p = \min(n, m)$.

11.7 Given variables defined such that:

$$\text{cov}(y_{1i}, y_{2i} \mid \mathbf{x}_i) = v > 0,$$

show that it is simultaneously possible to have:

$$\text{cov}(y_{1i}, y_{2i}) < 0.$$

11.8 Discuss the following specifications:

(a)
$$\lambda_i = \exp(\mathbf{x}_i\mathbf{b} + \epsilon_{1i}),$$
$$\mu_i = \exp(\mathbf{z}_i\mathbf{c} + \epsilon_{2i}),$$
$$\nu_i = \exp(u_i d + \epsilon_{3i}).$$

(b)
$$\lambda_i + \nu_i = \exp(\mathbf{x}_i\mathbf{b} + \epsilon_{1i}),$$
$$\mu_i + \nu_i = \exp(\mathbf{z}_i\mathbf{c} + \epsilon_{2i}),$$
$$\nu_i = \nu.$$

(c)
$$\lambda_i + \nu_i = \exp(\mathbf{x}_i\mathbf{b} + \epsilon_{1i}),$$
$$\mu_i + \nu_i = \exp(\mathbf{z}_i\mathbf{c} + \epsilon_{2i}),$$
$$\nu_i = d\sqrt{\lambda_i + \nu_i}\sqrt{\mu_i + \nu_i}.$$

11.9 Discrete Panel Data

Let $y_{it}, t = 1, \ldots, T, i = 1, \ldots, n_t$ represent a set of independent variables following a Poisson distribution with parameters:

$$\lambda_{it} = \exp(\mathbf{x}_{it}\mathbf{b})$$

respectively.

(a) Find the distribution of:

$$y_{\cdot t} = \sum_{i=1}^{n_t} y_{it}.$$

(b) Derive the conditional distribution of $y_{it}, i = 1, \ldots, n_t$ given $y_{\cdot t}$. Show that the resulting conditional model is logit polychotomous. Relate this result to the usual procedure for estimating linear models with composite errors.

12 Duration Models

In the last chapter we presented various models suitable for describing duration-related data. These are used to analyse phenomena such as: how long a person remains unemployed, the length and size of bank overdrafts, the delay between successive purchases of a certain good, the life expectancy of certain types of vehicles depending on their characteristics, or the manner in which an employee rises through the ranks of a corporate hierarchy. The principal mathematical characteristics of these data is that they assume a series of positive values. Specification of the distribution of these processes is based upon the theory of renewal processes, the simplest example of which is the Poisson process. While it is beyond the scope of this chapter to develop this theory exhaustively, we shall present some of its aspects. This will allow us to establish the connection between duration models and some models developed in previous chapters: reservation wages (chapter 7), labour-market disequilibria (chapter 8), panel-data models (chapter 6), and Poisson models (chapter 11).

12.1 The Basic Models

12.1.1 Describing the Distribution of a Positive Real Variable

Let ζ be a duration variable distributed continuously over $\mathbb{R}^+$. In practice, this variable represents the time elapsed in a particular state (i.e. unemployment, position in a hierarchy, etc.), or separating two events (change of job, births, purchases, etc.)

We adopt the following notation:

(i) $f(t)$ is the density function for this variable (assumed strictly positive).
(ii) $F(t) = \int_0^t f(u)\,du$ is the corresponding distribution function.
(iii) $S(t) = 1 - F(t) = \int_t^{\infty} f(u)$ is the survival function.

The distribution of ζ is clearly characterized by any one of these three functions. There exist, however, further functions which may be used, and which possess interesting interpretations.

12.1.1.1 The Hazard Function

Definition 6: The hazard function, denoted λ, is defined as:

$$\lambda(t) = \frac{f(t)}{1 - F(t)} = \frac{f(t)}{S(t)},$$

and is interpreted as follows:

$$\begin{aligned}\lambda(t) &= \frac{f(t)}{S(t)},\\ &= \lim_{dt \to 0} \frac{1}{dt} \frac{\Pr(t < \zeta \leq t + dt)}{\Pr(t < \zeta)},\\ &= \lim_{dt \to 0} \frac{1}{dt} \Pr(t < \zeta \leq t + dt \,|\, \zeta > t).\end{aligned}$$

where $\lambda(t)$ is the *instantaneous rate of exit* from the state.

Proposition 30: The hazard function characterizes the distribution of ζ. We have:

$$S(t) = \exp\left[-\int_0^t \lambda(u)\, du\right], \quad t \in \mathbb{R}^+.$$

Proof: Clearly, if we find the equation for the survival function, we can derive a one-to-one mapping between S and λ, and hence show that the hazard function characterizes the distribution. Since:

$$f(t) = -\frac{dS(t)}{dt},$$

we have:

$$\begin{aligned}\lambda(t) &= -\frac{1}{S(t)} \frac{dS(t)}{dt},\\ &= -\frac{d}{dt} \log S(t).\end{aligned}$$

Integrating, and using the fact that $S(0) = 1$, we see that:

$$-\int_0^t \lambda(u)\, du = \log[S(t)],$$

and hence:

$$S(t) = \exp\left[-\int_0^t \lambda(u)\, du\right].$$

□

Examination of the expression for the survival function reveals that it contains a primitive of this function:

$$\Lambda(t) = \int_0^t \lambda(u)\, du.$$

This is called the *cumulative survival function.*

12.1.1.2 The Conditional Survival Function

The value of the hazard function is none other than the value, in t, of the conditional density of ζ given that $\zeta \geq t$. We shall examine this conditional distribution more thoroughly.

Definition 7: The *conditional survival function* is defined as:

$$S(t \mid t_0) = \Pr(\zeta > t + t_0 \mid \zeta > t_0).$$

This, in turn, can be expressed as a function of the survival function and the hazard function:

$$\begin{aligned} S(t \mid t_0) &= \frac{\Pr(\zeta > t + t_0)}{\Pr(\zeta > t_0)}, \\ &= \frac{S(t + t_0)}{S(t_0)}, \\ &= -\int_0^{t+t_0} \lambda(u)\, du + \int_0^{t_0} \lambda(u) du. \end{aligned}$$

Thus:

$$\begin{aligned} S(t \mid t_0) &= \exp\left[-\int_{t_0}^{t+t_0} \lambda(y)\, du\right], \\ &= \exp\{-[\Lambda(t + t_0) - \Lambda(t_0)]\}. \end{aligned} \quad (12.1)$$

12.1.1.3 The Remaining Mean Duration

We can also work with conditional expectations instead of probabilities. After a duration t has been spent in a state, the remaining time is $\zeta - t$, and the remaining mean duration is $\mathrm{E}(\zeta - t \mid \zeta > t)$.

Definition 8: The remaining mean duration is defined as:

$$r(t) = \mathrm{E}(\zeta - t \mid \zeta > t).$$

The expression for r from the survival function is:

$$
\begin{aligned}
r(t) &= \frac{1}{S(t)} \int_t^{\infty} (u - t)\, f(u)\, du, \\
&= -\frac{1}{S(t)} \int_t^{\infty} (u - t)\, dS(u), \\
&= \frac{1}{S(t)} \left\{ -(u - t)\, S(u)|_t^{\infty} + \int_t^{\infty} S(u)\, du \right\}, \\
&= \frac{1}{S(t)} \int_t^{\infty} S(u) du.
\end{aligned}
\tag{12.2}
$$

Proposition 31: The function r characterizes the distribution of the duration.

Proof: It suffices to express the survival function in terms of the function r. From equation (12.2) we see that:

$$
-\frac{1}{r(t)} = \frac{d}{dt} \log \left[\int_t^{\infty} S(u)\, du \right].
$$

After integrating:

$$
\int_0^t \frac{du}{r(u)} = -\log [S(u)\, du] + \log \int_t^{\infty} [S(u)\, du].
$$

Applying equation (12.2) , we find:

$$
r(0) = \int_0^{\infty} S(u)\, du,
$$

and hence:

$$
\int_0^t \frac{du}{r(u)} = -\log \left[\int_0^{\infty} S(u)\, du \right] + \log [r(0)],
$$

implying:

$$
\int_t^{\infty} S(u)\, du = r(0) \exp \left[-\int_0^t \frac{du}{r(u)} \right].
$$

Finally, differentiation yields:

$$
S(t) = \frac{r(0)}{r(t)} \exp \left[\int_0^t \frac{du}{r(u)} \right].
$$

□

12.1.2 Dependence over Time

12.1.2.1 Forms of the Hazard Function

The nature of the dependence of the hazard function upon time is often very important for the interpretation of the model.

Thus, if ζ designates the life expectancy of a machine, depreciation can be modelled using an increasing hazard function, reflecting the fact that the probability of breakdown increases with the machine's age.

If, on the other hand, ζ designates the duration of unemployment, a function which is decreasing for large values of t may be more appropriate. This is because workers who have been unemployment a long time frequently have greater difficulty finding a new job.

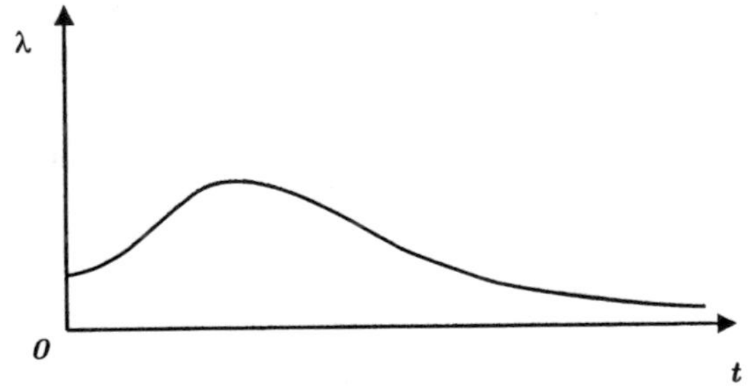

Fig. 12.1. Hazard function for unemployment duration

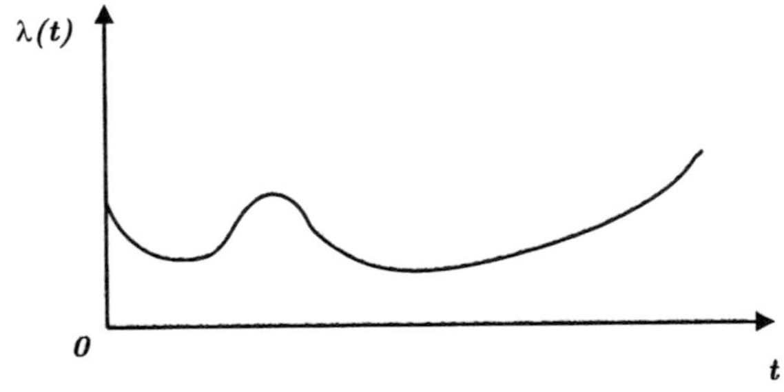

Fig. 12.2. Hazard function for mortality rates among French males

Generally, however, hazard functions are not monotonic. We have already seen in chapter 6 that hazard functions corresponding to unemployment duration are frequently first increasing and then decreasing. If we are interested in studying mortality rates of French males, we may wish to specify a hazard function (or mortality rate) as depicted in figure 12.2.

In addition to the expected increase as t becomes sufficiently large, there are two peaks: one corresponds to infant mortality ($t \approx 0$ years), while the second corresponds to motorcycle accident casualties ($t \approx 19$–20 years) .

12.1.2.2 The Case of Independence over Time

A limiting case is clearly one in which the hazard function is constant.

Definition 9: Independence over time holds if and only if $\lambda(t) = \lambda$, independent of t.

Since the hazard function is only one possible characterization of the distribution of the duration, the property of independence over time can also be expressed using the other functions F, S, r, etc.

Proposition 32: Independence over time can only hold if the distribution of the duration is exponential .

Proof: According to proposition 30, the condition $\lambda(t) = \lambda$ is equivalent to:

$$\begin{aligned} S(t) &= \exp\left[-\int_0^t \lambda(u)\, du\right], \\ &= \exp(-\lambda t), \end{aligned}$$

and this is, in fact, none other than an exponential survival function. □

This proposition explains the central role played by the exponential distribution in models of duration.

Proposition 33: Independence over time exists when the remaining mean duration is constant: $r(t) = r$.

Proof: According to equation (12.2), we have:

$$\begin{aligned} r(t) &= \frac{1}{S(t)} \int_t^\infty S(u)\, du, \\ &= \frac{1}{\exp(-\lambda t)} \int_t^\infty \exp(-\lambda u)\, du, \\ &= \frac{1}{\lambda}. \end{aligned}$$

□

Here we see that the remaining mean duration can be expressed as the reciprocal of the rate of change between states.

Finally, the conditional survival function is given by:

$$S(t \mid t_0) = \Pr(\zeta > t + t_0 \mid \zeta > t_0),$$

$$= \frac{S(t+t_0)}{S(t_0)},$$
$$= \frac{\exp[-\lambda(t+t_0)]}{\exp(-\lambda t_0)} + \exp(-\lambda t),$$
$$= S(t).$$

This is independent of the starting date t_0 – it is sometimes said that the exponential distribution is without memory.

12.1.2.3 Intertemporal Independence and Aggregation

The assumption of independence over time is not, in fact, very robust – it is susceptible, for example, to the simple aggregation of data. Take the case of a heterogeneous population of unemployed persons. These are classified by some index $v \in \mathbb{R}^+$ and distributed according to some rule $\Pi(v)$. The duration of unemployment for each individual is assumed to follow an exponential distribution: $S_v(t) = \exp[-\lambda(v)t]$, i.e. at the microeconomic level there exists intertemporal independence.

Let us look more closely at the situation of a typical individual in this population. The distribution of the duration of unemployment yields the following survival function:

$$\tilde{S}(t) = \int_0^\infty S_v(t)\,\pi(v)\,dv,$$
$$= \int_0^\infty \exp[-\lambda(v)t]\,\Pi(v)\,dv.$$

Applying definition (6) we derive the hazard function:

$$\tilde{\lambda}(t) = -\frac{1}{\tilde{S}(t)}\frac{d\tilde{S}(t)}{dt},$$
$$= \frac{\int_0^\infty \lambda(v)\exp[-\lambda(v)t]\,\Pi(v)\,dv}{\int_0^\infty \exp[-\lambda(v)t]\,\Pi(v)\,dv}.$$

Proposition 34: The hazard function obtained by aggregating a constant hazard function is monotonically decreasing.

Proof: Differentiating $\tilde{\lambda}$ with respect to t, we find:

$$\frac{d\tilde{\lambda}(t)}{dt} = \left(\int_0^\infty -\lambda(v)^2\exp[-\lambda(v)t]\,\Pi(v)\,dv\right.$$
$$\times \int_0^\infty \exp[-\lambda(v)t]\,\Pi(v)\,dv^2$$

$$+ \left\{ \int_0^\infty \lambda(v) - \exp[-\lambda(v)t]\,\Pi(v)\,dv \right\}\Bigg)$$

$$\times \frac{1}{\left\{\int_0^\infty \exp[-\lambda(v)t]\,\Pi(v)\,dv\right\}^2}.$$

Denoting:

$$\Pi_t(v) = \frac{\exp[-\lambda(v)t]\,\Pi(v)\,dv}{\int_0^\infty \exp[-\lambda(v)t]\,\Pi(v)\,dv},$$

we can write:

$$\frac{d\tilde{\lambda}(t)}{dt} = -\int_0^\infty \lambda(v)^2\,\Pi_t(v)\,dv + \left[\int_0^\infty \lambda(v)\,\Pi_t(v)\,dv\right]^2,$$

which expression, according to the Schwartz inequality, is negative. □

The interpretation of this result is straightforward. On average, those individuals who are the earliest to leave the state of unemployment are those with high values of $\lambda(v)$ (i.e. those who are movers), while those who remain have low values of $\lambda(v)$ (i.e. stayers). This explains why the rate of exit $\tilde{\lambda}(t)$ decreases over time. This phenomenon is known by the term *mover-stayer* or *heterogeneity bias*.

12.1.3 Some Parametric Models

A variety of probability distributions have been used to model duration, each characterized by its ability to approximate various formulations of the hazard function and by its ease of use. The most popular distributions currently used belong to the Weibull, log-normal, and gamma families of exponential functions. We shall describe the principal properties of these families of functions.

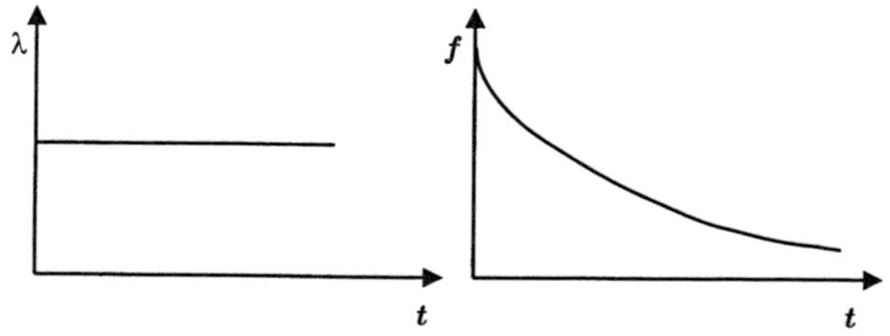

Fig. 12.3. Exponential distributions

12.1.3.1 Exponential Distributions

As we have seen, these models reflect independence over time. This family depends upon a positive parameter λ, and its various derivations are:

$$f(t) = \lambda \exp(-\lambda t),$$
$$F(t) = 1 - \exp(-\lambda t),$$
$$S(t) = \exp(-\lambda t),$$
$$\lambda(t) = \lambda,$$
$$r(t) = \frac{1}{\lambda}.$$

The first two moments of the duration are:

$$\mathrm{E}(\zeta) = \frac{1}{\lambda},$$
$$\mathrm{var}(\zeta) = \frac{1}{\lambda^2}.$$

Notice that the parameter is inversely related to time.

12.1.3.2 Mixed Exponential Distributions

We shall examine the simplest case of aggregation with respect to two sub-populations. The density function is:

$$f(t) = \pi_1 a_1 \exp(-a_1 t) + \pi_2 a_2 \exp(-a_2 t),$$

with $a_1 > 0$, $a_2 > 0$, $\pi_1 \geq 0$, $\pi_2 \geq 0$, and $\pi_1 + \pi_2 = 1$. The corresponding survival function is derived from a mix of exponentially distributed survival functions parametrized by a_1 and a_2:

$$S(t) = \pi_1 \exp(-a_1 t) + \pi_2 \exp(-a_2 t).$$

The mean of the duration is given by:

$$\mathrm{E}(\zeta) = \frac{\pi_1}{a_1} + \frac{\pi_2}{a_2},$$

and the variance:

$$\mathrm{var}(\zeta) = \frac{\pi_1(1+\pi_2)}{a_1^2} \frac{\pi_1(1+\pi_1)}{a_2^2} - \frac{2\pi_1\pi_2}{a_1 a_2}.$$

Using definition 6, we obtain the hazard function:

$$\begin{aligned}
\lambda(t) &= \frac{f(t)}{S(t)}, \\
&= \frac{\pi_1 a_1 \exp(-a_1 t) + \pi_2 a_2 \exp(-a_2 t)}{\pi_1 \exp(-a_t t)\, \pi_2 \exp(-a_2 t)}, \\
&= \frac{\pi_1 a_1 + \pi_2 a_2 \exp[-(a_2 - a_1)]\, t}{\pi_1 + \pi_2 \exp[-(a_2 - a_1)]\, t}.
\end{aligned}$$

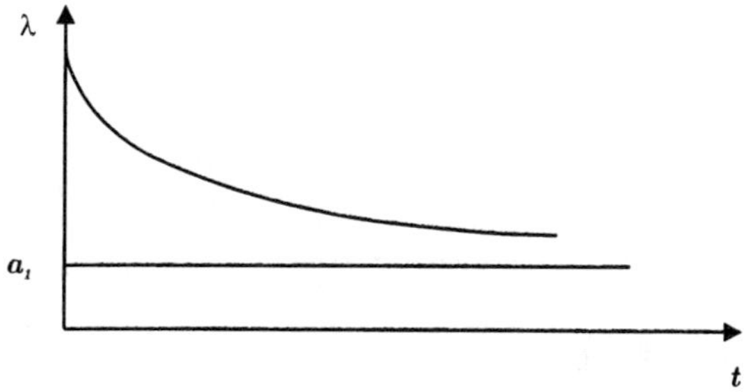

Fig. 12.4. Mixed exponential distribution for $a_2 > a_1$

Examining the case of $a_2 > a_1$ we immediately see that the hazard function is linear-fractional in $\exp[-(a_2 - a_1)]\,t$ and decreasing, which is compatible with the phenomenon of mover-stayer. The value of the function at zero is $\pi_1 a_1 + \pi_2 a_2$, and it tends to zero as t tends to plus infinity.

The case of $a_2 > a_1$ is depicted in figure 12.4.

The remaining duration is defined by:

$$
\begin{aligned}
r(t) &= \frac{1}{S(t)} \int_t^{\infty} S(u)\, du, \\
&= \frac{\frac{\pi_1}{a_1} \exp(-a_1 t) + \frac{\pi_2}{a_2} \exp(-a_2 t)}{\pi_1 \exp(-a_1 t) + \pi_2 \exp(-a_2 t)}.
\end{aligned}
$$

This function is increasing in t.

12.1.3.3 The Gamma Distribution

The family of gamma distributions is indexed by two positive parameters, denoted a and v. The density function is:

$$
f(t) = \frac{a^v t^{v-1} \exp(-a_2 t)}{\Gamma(v)}.
$$

The first two moments are:

$$
\begin{aligned}
\mathrm{E}(\zeta) &= \frac{v}{a}, \\
\mathrm{var}(\zeta) &= \frac{v}{a^2}.
\end{aligned}
$$

The hazard function must be expressed by means of integrals, yielding:

$$
\begin{aligned}
\lambda(t) &= \frac{f(t)}{S(t)}, \\
&= \frac{t^{v-1} \exp(-at)}{\int_t^{\infty} u^{v-1} \exp(-au)\, du},
\end{aligned}
$$

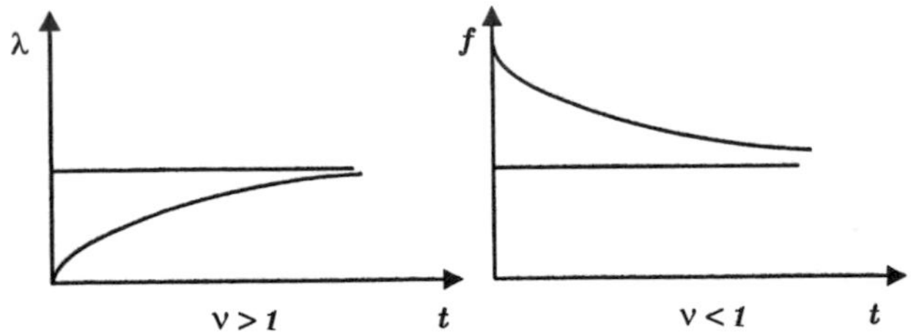

Fig. 12.5. Gamma distribution for $v > 1$ and $v < 1$

$$= \frac{1}{\int_t^\infty \left[\frac{u}{t}\right]^{v-1} \exp\left[-a\left(u-t\right)\right] du},$$

$$= \frac{1}{\int_t^\infty \left[\frac{u}{t}+1\right]^{v-1} \exp\left(-au\right) du}.$$

The evolution of this function depends on the values assumed by the parameter v relative to one:

$v > 1$ — the function λ is increasing from zero to a.
$v = 1$ — the model reduces to the exponential case and the hazard function is constant.
$v < 1$ — the function λ is decreasing from $+\infty$ to a.

12.1.3.4 The Weibull Distribution

Another two-parameter generalization of the exponential distribution is the family of Weibull distributions. Duration, ζ, is assumed distributed exponentially with parameter a, where $a > 0$. The survival function is thus:

$$S(t) = \exp\left(-at^b\right),$$

and the density:

$$f(t) = abt^{b-1} \exp\left(-at^b\right).$$

This yields a very simple hazard function:

$$\lambda(t) = abt^{b-1},$$

which can assume one of the shapes in figure 12.6 depending on b's value relative to one.

When this function is increasing, an important difference with the gamma distribution appears. The hazard function does not approach an asymptote and hence, for large t, the model cannot be approximated by one with independence over time.

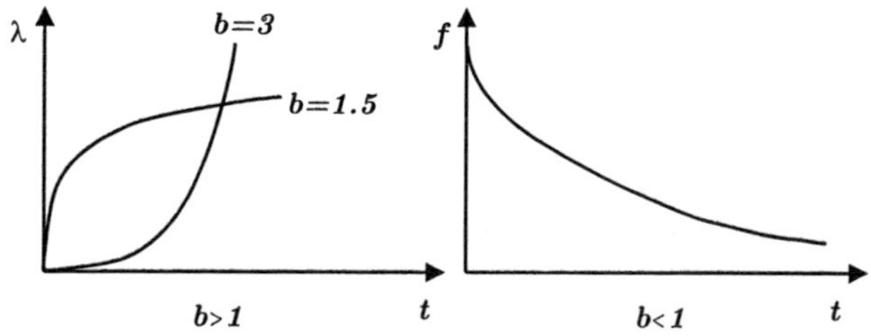

Fig. 12.6. Weibull distribution

12.1.3.5 Log-Normal Distributions

The models we presented in the previous section, some of which are quite easy to apply, do not allow for hazard functions which are increasing and then decreasing. Log-normal distributions yield this form.

The duration is specified such that log (ζ) follows a log-normal distribution N $(m; \sigma^2)$. The density derives immediately from the normal distribution by a change of variables:

$$\begin{aligned} f(t) &= \frac{1}{\sigma t \sqrt{2\pi}} \exp\left\{-\frac{1}{2\sigma^2}\left[\log(t) - m\right]^2\right\}, \\ &= \frac{1}{\sigma t}\varphi\left[\frac{\log(t) - m}{\sigma}\right]. \end{aligned}$$

The survival function is:

$$S(t) = 1 - \Phi\left[\frac{\log(t) - m}{\sigma}\right].$$

Using the Mill ratio, we obtain the hazard function:

$$\lambda(t) = \frac{1}{t}\frac{\varphi\left[\frac{\log(t) - m}{\sigma}\right]}{1 - \Phi\left[\frac{\log(t) - m}{\sigma}\right]}.$$

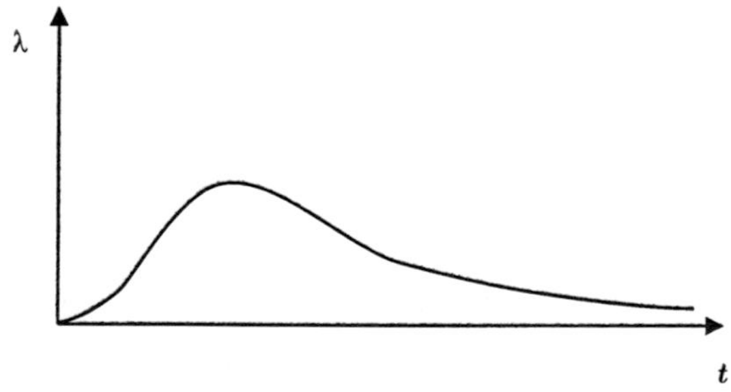

Fig. 12.7. Log-normal distribution

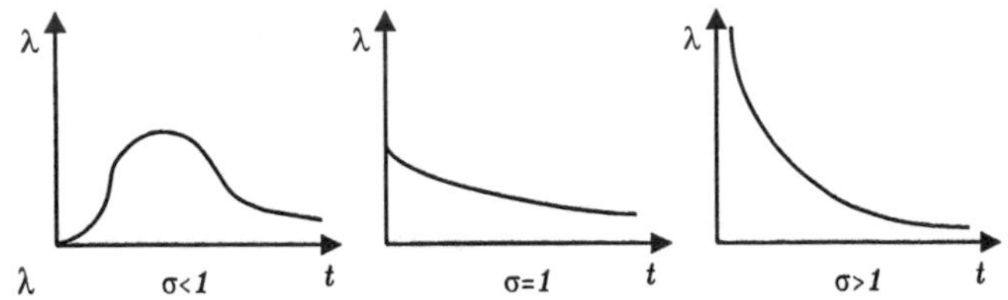

Fig. 12.8. Log-logistic distributions

This function is nil for $t = 0$, increases toward a maximum and then falls off toward zero.

12.1.3.6 Log-Logistic Distributions

By analogy to the logit model, we can rework the model in section 12.1.3.5, substituting the logistic distribution for the normal.

Denoting $F(t) = \frac{1}{1+\exp(-t)}$ the corresponding distribution, and recalling that $f(t) = F(t)[1 - F(t)]$, we have:

$$\begin{aligned}\lambda(t) &= \frac{1}{t}\frac{1}{\sigma}\frac{f\left[\frac{\log(t)-m}{\sigma}\right]}{1-F\left[\frac{\log(t)-m}{\sigma}\right]},\\ &= \frac{1}{t}\frac{1}{\sigma}F\left[\frac{\log(t)-m}{\sigma}\right].\end{aligned}$$

This expression can be simplified by introducing the parameter $a = \exp\left(-\frac{m}{\sigma}\right)$. We have:

$$\begin{aligned}\lambda(t) &= \frac{1}{t}\frac{1}{\sigma}F\left[\frac{\log(t)}{\sigma} + \log(a)\right],\\ &= \frac{1}{\sigma t}F\left[\log\left(at^{\frac{1}{\sigma}}\right)\right],\\ &= \frac{1}{\sigma t}\frac{at^{\frac{1}{\sigma}}}{1+at^{\frac{1}{\sigma}}},\\ &= \frac{a}{\sigma}\frac{t^{\frac{1}{\sigma}-1}}{1+at^{\frac{1}{\sigma}}}.\end{aligned}$$

We obtain various shapes depending on the magnitude of σ relative to one, as in figure 12.8.

12.1.4 General Methods for Constructing Other Families of Distributions

We shall now examine the possibility of transforming the distributions introduced in the preceding section to obtain further duration models. Some of these transformations have already been hinted at.

Let $f(t; v)$, $\lambda(t; v)$, and $S(t; v)$ represent a family of distributions, parametrized by v, which will serve as the basis for our manipulation.

12.1.4.1 Aggregation

Assuming that v is stochastic, with a distribution parametrized by α: $\pi(v; \alpha)$, we can directly generalize the aggregation of exponential distributions. The new density function is:

$$\tilde{f}(t; a) = \int_v f(t; \alpha)\, \pi(v; \alpha)\, dv,$$

the survival function is:

$$\tilde{S}(t; \alpha) = \int_v S(t; \alpha)\, dv,$$

and the hazard function is:

$$\begin{aligned}
\tilde{\lambda}(t; \alpha) &= \frac{\tilde{f}(t; \alpha)}{\tilde{S}(t; \alpha)}, \\
&= \frac{\int_v \tilde{f}(t; v)\, \pi(v; \alpha)\, dv}{\int_v S(t; v)\, \pi(v; \alpha)\, dv}, \\
&= \int_v \lambda(t; v) \frac{S(t; v)\, \pi(v; \alpha)}{\int_v S(t; v)\, \pi(v; \alpha)} dv.
\end{aligned}$$

Proposition 35: Denoting E_α^t the expectation calculated with respected to the density:

$$\frac{S(t; v)\, \pi(v; \alpha)}{\int_v S(t; v)\, \pi(v; \alpha)\, dv},$$

we have $\tilde{\lambda}(t; \alpha) = \mathrm{E}_\alpha^t \lambda(t; \alpha)$.

The aggregate hazard function appears as the mean of the individual hazard functions, being calculated over the remaining individuals at date t.

Example 11: In certain cases the integrals can be evaluated analytically, yielding an explicit function for the new density $\tilde{f}$. Thus, for example, the family based on the exponential distribution $f(t; v) = v \exp(-vt)$ and the distribution of the parameter v of the gamma distribution yields:

$$\pi(v; a; \nu) = \frac{a^\nu v^{\nu-1} \exp(-av)}{\Gamma(\gamma)} z_{v>0}, \quad \gamma > 0,\ a > 0.$$

where:

$$z_{v>0} = \begin{cases} 0, & \text{if } v \leq 0, \\ 1, & \text{otherwise.} \end{cases}$$

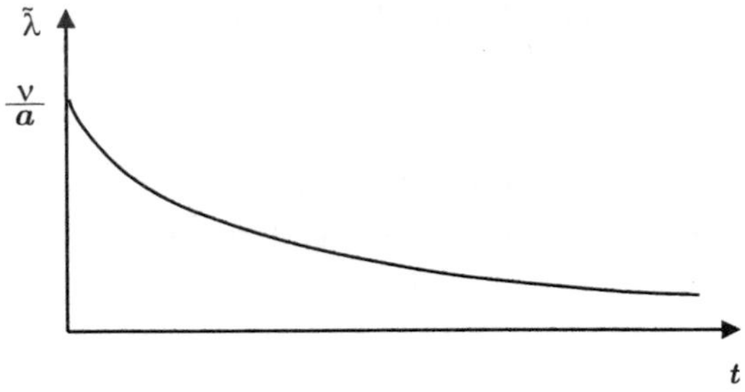

Fig. 12.9. Aggregate hazard for exponential distribution

Example 12: Aggregating, we obtain:

$$\begin{aligned}
\tilde{f}(t; a, v) &= \int_0^{\infty} \frac{v \exp(-vt)\, a^{\nu} v^{\nu-1} \exp(-av)}{\Gamma(\nu)} dv, \\
&= \frac{a^{\nu}}{\Gamma(\nu)} \int_0^{\infty} v^{(\nu+1)-1} \exp(-v)(a+t)\, dv, \\
&= \frac{\Gamma(\nu+1)}{\Gamma(\gamma)} \frac{a^{\nu}}{(a+t)^{\nu+1}}, \\
&= \frac{\nu a^{\nu}}{(a+t)^{\nu+1}}.
\end{aligned}$$

This is a Pareto-type distribution, whose survival and hazard functions are given by:

$$\begin{aligned}
\tilde{S}(t; a, \nu) &= \frac{a^{\nu}}{(t+a)^{\nu}}, \\
&= \frac{1}{\left(1+\frac{t}{a}\right)^{\nu}}, \\
\tilde{\lambda}(t; a, \nu) &= \frac{\nu}{a+t},
\end{aligned}$$

respectively.

12.1.4.2 Proportional Hazard Model (Lehman Family, or Cox Model)

The new family is derived from the old by the following transformations:

$$\begin{aligned}
\tilde{S}(t; a, v) &= S(t; v)^{a}, \\
\tilde{f}(t; a, v) &= aS(t; v)^{a-1} f(t; v), \\
\tilde{\lambda}(t; a, v) &= a\lambda(t; v), \quad a > 0.
\end{aligned}$$

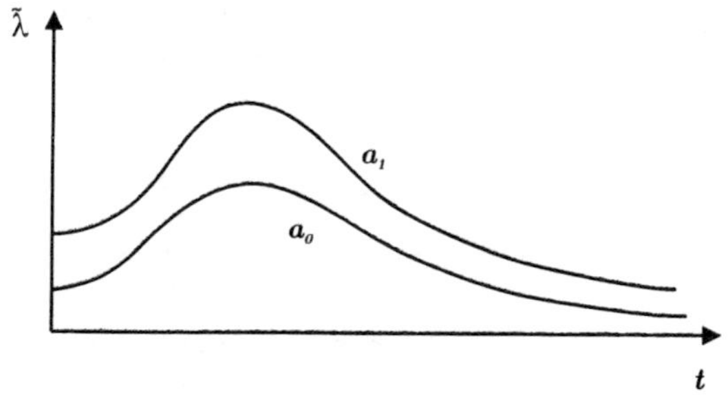

Fig. 12.10. Proportional hazard model

This last equation gives the family its name. When the auxiliary parameter a varies, the hazard functions can be derived from each other.

12.1.4.3 Increasing Transformations of the Duration Variable

Finally, many other distributions, fitting into one of the classical families, can be created from increasing transformations of the duration variable $h_a(\zeta)$. We write:

$$\tilde{S}(t; v, a) = S\left[h_a^{-1}(t); v\right],$$

$$\tilde{f}(t; v, a) = \frac{1}{\frac{dh_a}{dx}\left[h_a^{-1}(t)\right]} f\left[h_a^{-1}(t); v\right],$$

$$\tilde{\lambda}(t; v, a) = \frac{1}{\frac{dh_a}{dx}\left[h_a^{-1}(t)\right]} \lambda\left[h_a^{-1}(t); v\right].$$

Example 13: We can perform this type of transformation in order to obtain a more tractable formulation of the hazard function. Thus, starting from an exponential distribution $\lambda(t; v) = v$, we see that:

$$\tilde{\lambda}(t; v, a) = \frac{v}{\frac{dh_a}{dx}\left[h_a^{-1}(t)\right]}$$

varies along with the derivative $\frac{dh_a}{dx}$. Consequently, we obtain hazard functions with increasing and decreasing phases by choosing monotonic transformations which are sometimes concave and sometimes convex.

12.1.5 Comparing Distributions

If we wish to make explicit the interpretations of some parameters occurring in these families of distributions, it is useful to establishing a series of pre-orderings of the distributions of the positive variables. For example, assume that the variable ζ represents a person's life expectancy and that we wish to define binary relationships describing his "preference to reach old age."

12.1.5.1 First-Order Stochastic Dominance

The most representative relation in this class is defined here.

Definition 10: The distribution f^* first-order dominates the distribution f if and only if, for every positive increasing function V, we have:

$$\mathrm{E}^* [V(\zeta)] = \int_0^\infty V(t)\, f^*(t)\, dt \geq \mathrm{E}[V(\zeta)],$$
$$= \int_0^\infty V(t)\, f(t)\, dt.$$

The function V is to be interpreted as a utility function, and the fact that it is increasing indicates a desire to live as long as possible. The pre-ordering implies that f^* is preferred to f for all utility functions V. This pre-ordering yields a simple characterization of the survival function.

Proposition 36: f^* first-order dominates f if and only if $S^*(t) \geq S(t)$.

f^* is unambiguously preferred to f if and only if the probability of attaining old age, that it, attaining an age above t, is consistently higher with f^* than with f.

Proof: *Necessary condition*: Let us postulate a utility function:

$$V_t(u) = \begin{cases} 0, & \text{if } u < t, \\ 1, & \text{otherwise.} \end{cases}$$

If f^* dominates f, we have:

$$\mathrm{E}^* [V_t(\zeta)] = \overset{*}{\Pr}(\zeta \geq t) = S^*(t) \geq \mathrm{E}[V_t(\zeta)] = \Pr(\zeta \geq t) = S(t).$$

Sufficient condition: Conversely, it can easily be shown that any positive, increasing function V can be written as the increasing limit of linear combinations of $z_{u \geq t}$. Formulating the inequality in terms of these functions allows us to derive the inequality for any increasing function V. □

12.1.5.2 Dominance in Hazard Functions

An alternative definition of the preference for age can be derived directly from examination of the hazard functions. Recall that we have defined $\lambda(t)$ as the mortality rate at age t.

Definition 11: f^* dominates f for hazard functions if and only if:

$$\lambda(t) = \lambda^*(t), \quad \forall t.$$

f^* is preferred if it corresponds to a mortality rate which is consistently lower. In order to establish the connection with first-order dominance we require the following proposition.

Proposition 37:

(i) f^* dominates f for hazard functions if and only if:

$$S(t \mid t_0) \geq S(t \mid t_0), \quad \forall t \geq 0, \; t_0 \geq 0.$$

(ii) This condition is equivalent to:

$$\mathrm{E}^*[V(\zeta) \mid \zeta \geq t_0] \geq \mathrm{E}[V(\zeta) \mid \zeta \geq t_0],$$

with $\forall t_0$, V positive increasing.

Proof:

(i) The fact that parts one and two of proposition 37 are equivalent follows directly from proposition 36, so we will focus our efforts on proving part one.

(ii) Necessary conditions for part one:
Letting $\lambda(t) \geq \lambda^*(t)$, $\forall t$, we integrate to obtain:

$$\int_{t_0}^{t+t_0} \lambda(u)\, du \geq \int_{t_o}^{t+t_0} \lambda^*(u)\, du.$$

and expression (12.1) for the conditional survival function allows us to write:

$$S^*(t \mid t_0) \geq S(t \mid t_0), \quad \forall t \geq 0, \; t_0 \geq 0.$$

(iii) Sufficient conditions for part two:
As:

$$S^*(t \mid t_0) \geq S(t \mid t_0,), \quad \forall t \geq 0, \; t_0 \geq 0,$$

we also have:

$$\lim_{t \to 0} \frac{1}{t}\left[S^*(t \mid t_0) - 1\right] \geq \lim_{t \to 0} \frac{1}{t}\left[S(t \mid t_0 - 1)\right].$$

And our result follows from the equality:

$$\lim_{t\to 0} \frac{1}{t}\left[S(t|t_0) - 1\right] = \lim_{t\to 0} \frac{1}{t}\left\{\exp\left[-\int_{t_0}^{t_0+1} \lambda(u)\,du - 1\right]\right\},$$
$$= -\lambda(t_0).$$

□

So we see that first-order stochastic dominance is a special case, in which preference for old age is considered only at birth. This relation is less restrictive.

Corollary 1: If f^* first-order dominates f for the hazard functions, then f^* dominates f.

12.1.5.3 Conditional Dominance

Finally, proposition 37 suggests the following generalization.

Proposition 38: f^* dominates f conditionally if and only if:

$$\mathrm{E}^*\left[V(\zeta)|\,\zeta \in A\right] \geq \mathrm{E}\left[V(\zeta)|\,\zeta \in A\right],$$

for all positive, increasing V and for all $A \in I\!R^+$.

It immediately follows that this new pre-ordering is more restrictive than the simple comparison of hazard functions.

Corollary 2: If f^* dominates f conditionally, then f^* dominates f for the hazard functions.

This pre-ordering is easily applicable, as it reduces to the comparison of numeric functions.

Proposition 39: f^* dominates f conditionally if and only if:

$$\frac{d \log f^*(t)}{dt} \geq \frac{d \log f(t)}{dt}, \quad \forall t \geq 0.$$

Proof:

(i) Notice, first of all, that proposition 38 can equivalently be written with the variable ζ or another variable $x = h(\zeta)$. Denoting G and G^* the distributions of x corresponding to F and F^* respectively, we see that G is none other that the uniform distribution over $[0, 1]$. The characterization becomes:

$$\mathrm{E}^* [V(x) | x \in A] \geq \mathrm{E}[V(x) | x \in A],$$

for any positive increasing function V defined over $[0, 1]$. For any subset of $[0, 1]$, A, the inverse distributions are given by: $G(x) = x$, $G^*(x) = F^*\left[F^{-1}(x)\right]$. The corresponding density functions are:

$$g(x) = 1,$$
$$g^*(x) = \frac{f^*\left[F^{-1}(x)\right]}{f\left[F^{-1}(x)\right]}.$$

(ii) Integrating over the forms we have obtained yields:

$$\mathrm{E}^* [V(x) | x \in A]$$
$$= \frac{\int_A V(x) g^*(x) dx}{\int_A g^*(x)} \geq \mathrm{E}[V(x) | x \in A] \frac{\int_A V(x) dx}{\int_A dx},$$
$$0 \leq \frac{\int_A V(x) g^*(x) dx}{\int_A g^*(x) dx} - \frac{\int_A V(x) dx}{\int_A dx} \frac{\int_A g^*(x) dx}{\int_A dx},$$
$$0 \leq \mathrm{cov}_A \left[V(x), g^*(x)\right],$$

where cov_A is the covariance calculated with respect to the uniform distribution of A.

(iii) If the function g^* is increasing, we can calculate the covariance between two increasing functions V and g^*, which will necessarily be positive (cf. exercise 4).

(iv) Conversely, if g^* is not always increasing we will be able to find an interval, A_0, over which it is decreasing (for convenience we assume that g^* is continuously differentiable.) Over this interval A_0 we have: $\mathrm{cov}_{A_0} [V(X), g^*(X)] < 0$, as in exercise 4. In this case the inequalities which are characteristic of the relationship of conditional dominance will not all hold.

(v) In summary, we have established that f^* dominates f conditional on whether g^* is increasing. This condition is equivalent to:

$$\log\left[g^*(x)\right] = \log\left\{f^*\left[F^{-1}(x)\right]\right\} - \log\left\{f\left[F^{-1}(x)\right]\right\}$$

increasing in x, or, since the slope of F^{-1} is positive, to:

$$\log\left[f^*(t)\right] - \log[f(t)]$$

increasing in t. Differentiating, we obtain:

$$\frac{d\ \log[f^*(t)]}{dt} \geq \frac{d\ \log[f(t)]}{dt}, \quad \forall t \geq 0. \qquad \square$$

Remark 11: The preceding proposition is formulated in terms of the derivative of the log-density function. This function:

$$\frac{d\ \log[f(t)]}{dt}$$

is clearly characteristic of the distribution of the duration ζ, since the constant of integration is unambiguously determined by the constraint $\int_0^\infty f(t)\,dt = 1$. This function has some appeal for our study of duration problems. Furthermore, notice that the distributions for which it is constant is the set of all exponential distributions.

12.1.5.4 Examples

Example 14: The family of Weibull distributions corresponds to the density $f(t) = abt^{b-1}\exp\left(-at^b\right)$. We have:

$$\begin{aligned}\frac{d\ \log[f(t)]}{dt} &= \frac{d}{dt}\left[\log(a) + \log(b) + (b-1)\log(t) - at^b\right],\\ &= \frac{b-1}{t} - abt^{b-1}.\end{aligned}$$

The fact that this derivative is decreasing in a provides us with a measure of the degree of conditional dominance.

If $a > a_0$:

$$\frac{d\ \log[f(t;a,b)]}{dt} \leq \frac{d\ \log[f(t;a_0,b)]}{dt},$$

and $f(t;a_0,b)$ dominates $f(t;a,b)$ conditionally.

Example 15: In the case of Pareto distributions, we have:

$$\begin{aligned}f(t;a,\nu) &= \frac{\nu a^\nu}{(a+t)^{\nu+1}},\\ \frac{d\ \log[f(t;a,\nu)]}{dt} &= \frac{d}{dt}\left[\log(\nu) + \nu\log(a) - (\nu+1)\log(t+a)\right],\\ &= -\frac{\nu+1}{t+a}.\end{aligned}$$

We see that this function is increasing in a and decreasing in ν. Therefore, if

$\nu_0 \leq \nu$ and $a_0 \geq a$, the distribution $f(t; a_0, \nu_0)$ conditionally dominates the distribution $f(t; a, \nu)$.

Example 16: Consider two distributions derived from the family of exponential distributions by aggregation. In order to ensure different degrees of heterogeneity we introduce two independent random variables ν and α, such that ν and $\nu + \alpha$ are positive and α has mean zero. Define:

$$S(t) = \mathrm{E}\left[\exp(-\nu t)\right],$$
$$S^*(t) = \mathrm{E}\{\exp[-(\nu + a)t]\}.$$

$S^*(t)$ is characterized by a greater degree of heterogeneity because, conditional on ν, the parameter $\nu+\alpha$ is distributed with a mean of ν rather than being strictly equal to ν..

Using the assumption of independence, we obtain:

$$\begin{aligned} S^*(t) &= \mathrm{E}\left[\exp(-\nu t)\right] \mathrm{E}\left[\exp(-\alpha t)\right], \\ &= S(t)\, \mathrm{E}\left[\exp(-\alpha t)\right], \end{aligned}$$

yielding:

$$\begin{aligned} \frac{d\,\lambda^*(t)}{dt} &= -\frac{d^2 \log[S^*(t)]}{dt^2} - \frac{d^2 \log\left\{\mathrm{E}\left[\exp(-\alpha t)\right]\right\}}{dt^2}, \\ &= \frac{d\,\lambda(t)}{dt} - \frac{d^2 \log\left\{\mathrm{E}\left[\exp(-\alpha t)\right]\right\}}{dt^2}. \end{aligned}$$

Using exactly the same approach as in proposition 34, we see that:

$$0 \geq -\frac{d^2 \log\left\{\mathrm{E}\left[\exp(-\alpha t)\right]\right\}}{dt^2},$$

and, consequently, that:

$$\frac{d\,\lambda^*(t)}{dt} \leq \frac{d\,\lambda(t)}{dt}.$$

Furthermore, we have:

$$\begin{aligned} \lambda^*(t) &= -\frac{d \log[S^*(t)]}{dt}, \\ &= \frac{\mathrm{E}\left[\nu \exp(-\alpha t)\right] + \mathrm{E}\left[\exp(-\nu t)\right] \mathrm{E}\left[\alpha \exp(-\alpha t)\right]}{\mathrm{E}\left[\exp(-\nu t)\right] \mathrm{E}\left[\exp(-\alpha t)\right]}. \end{aligned}$$

Letting $t = 0$ in this expression, and using the fact that $\mathrm{E}(\alpha) = 0$, we see that: $\lambda^*(0) = \mathrm{E}(\nu) = \lambda(0)$. This equality, combined with:

$$\frac{d\,\lambda^*(t)}{dt} \leq \frac{d\,\lambda(t)}{dt},$$

allows us to conclude (by integration) that the hazard function λ^* is always situated underneath the hazard function λ.

In conclusion, we see that for hazard functions, a greater degree of heterogeneity implies dominance.

12.2 Discrete vs. Continuous Time

The question may arise as to whether our choice of continuous time in the preceding section is truly appropriate. For example, we may wish to consider cases in which values assumed by the duration are restricted to multiples of some length μ. In this case, the distribution of the duration is discrete on $\boldsymbol{N}$. We shall develop such a model, which can be considered a special case of the panel data models in chapter 6 – corresponding to a transition between two states. The characteristics of the discrete model are analogous to those of the continuous-time model.

In the following section we examine what happens to the discrete model as the unit of time, μ, tends to zero, permitting us to interpret the continuous-time model as a limiting case of the discrete time case.

12.2.1 Discrete-Time Models

The duration variable, ζ, may assume several values $(k\mu,\ k \in \boldsymbol{N})$. At any point in time, k, the probability of leaving the state is given by $\Pr(k),\ k \in \boldsymbol{N}$. This probability is analogous to the hazard function, λ, introduced in the continuous time case.

Derivation of the distribution of the duration is straightforward. The elementary probabilities are:

$$\begin{aligned} q_k &= \Pr(\zeta = k\mu), \\ &= [1 - \Pr(0)][1 - \Pr(1)] \cdots [1 - \Pr(k-1)] \Pr(k), \end{aligned}$$

and the survival function is:

$$\begin{aligned} 1 - Q_k &= \Pr(k \geq k\mu), \\ &= [1 - \Pr(0)][1 - \Pr(1)] \ldots [1 - \Pr(k-1)]. \end{aligned}$$

These two functions, q and Q, are respectively analogous to the functions f and S from the continuous case.

We immediately observe that:

(i) $\Pr(k) = \frac{q_k}{1-Q_k}$, as in definition 6 ,

(ii) $1 - Q_k = \exp\left\{-\sum_{j=0}^{k-1} \log\left[\frac{1}{1-\Pr(j)}\right]\right\}$, as in proposition 30.

Example 17: If the rate of exit, $\Pr(k)$, is constant: $\Pr(k) = P,\ \forall k$, we have:

$$\begin{aligned} q_k &= (1-P)^k P, \\ 1 - Q_k &= (1-P)^k. \end{aligned}$$

The distribution of the duration is geometric and parametrized by P. This distribution corresponds to the exponential distribution we examined in the continuous time case.

Example 18: An example of a decreasing rate of exit is given by:

$$\Pr(k) = 1 - \exp(-ak - b), \quad a < 0,\ b > 0.$$

Given this choice for the function P, the survival function is:

$$\begin{aligned} 1 - Q_k &= [1 - \Pr(0)] \cdots [1 - \Pr(k-1)], \\ &= \prod_{j=0}^{k-1} \exp(-aj - b), \\ &= \exp\left(-a \sum_{j=0}^{k-1} j - kb\right), \\ &= \exp\left[-a \frac{k(k-1)}{2} - kb\right]. \end{aligned}$$

12.2.2 Comparison of Continuous- and Discrete-Time Models

The chosen unit of time is very important in discrete-time modelling, especially with respect to its impact on the probability of exit. We should, in consequence, use the notation $\Pr(\mu, k)$ instead of $\Pr(k)$.

It is reasonable to conclude that, as the unit of time μ tends to zero, the corresponding probability will also tend to zero. More precisely, we postulate that:

$$\lim_{\mu \to 0} \frac{1}{\mu} \Pr\left(\mu, \frac{t}{\mu}\right) = \lambda(t).$$

where $\lambda(t)$ is the virtually instantaneous rate of exit for the interval $[t, t+\mu]$.

Let us examine the limit of the survival function under these conditions. With μ very small and t fixed, we have:

$$\begin{aligned}
\Pr(\zeta \geq t) &= 1 - Q_{t|\mu}, \\
&\approx \exp\left\{-\sum_{j=0}^{\frac{t}{\mu}-1} \log\left[\frac{1}{1-\Pr(\mu, j)}\right]\right\}, \\
&\approx \exp\left[-\sum_{j=0}^{\frac{t}{\mu}-1} p(\mu, j)\right], \quad \text{since } \Pr(\mu, j) \approx 0, \\
&\approx \exp\left[-\sum_{j=0}^{\frac{t}{\mu}-1} \mu\lambda(\mu j)\right], \\
&\approx \exp\left[-\int_0^t \lambda(u)\, du\right],
\end{aligned}$$

approximating the integral with a Riemann sum. So the relation reduces to the one we found for continuous time.

Example 19: When $\Pr(\mu, k)$ is constant in k, the condition on the virtually instantaneous rate can be written:

$$\Pr(\mu, k) = \lambda\mu.$$

This expression directly leads us to the following formulation of the geometrically distributed survival function:

$$\begin{aligned}
\Pr(\zeta \geq t) &= 1 - Q_{t|\mu} = (1-\lambda\mu)^{t|\mu}, \\
&\approx \exp\left[\frac{t}{\mu}\log(1-\lambda\mu)\right], \\
&\approx \exp(-\lambda t),
\end{aligned}$$

which is none other that the survival function of the exponential distribution.

12.3 Explanatory Models

12.3.1 Various Types of Covariates

The forms for the hazard functions introduced in section 12.1 are essentially of a descriptive nature. If we wish to examine the exogenous variables and understand their influence, we must incorporate them into the distribution of the duration.

We may, at this point, distinguish between several types of explanatory variables, each raising specific issues regarding specification and estimation. We shall assume that the observed durations ζ_i, $i = 1, \ldots, n$, are for different individuals $i = 1, \ldots, n$.

(i) Variables Depending on the Individual – Some covariates will be independent of time and distributed exclusively according to the index corresponding to the individual, i. Denoting these variables $\mathbf{x}_i$, we see that their value remains fixed over the entire range of time examined. In the case of unemployment duration studies, these variables may include, for example: sex, initial level of education, previous salaries and accumulated experience, and any other factors which are strictly historical.

(ii) Time-Varying Covariates – Other variables are known functions of time. In practice, these types of variables are quite rare. The standard example is the individual's age, which is a simple transformation on the index t. The variable age may, incidentally, be decomposed into two elements: the person's age at the beginning of the study (which is a characteristic of the individual and independent of t), and the evolution of the individual's age over the course of the study. This second element is clearly not distinct from the index t, and in consequence this case reduces to that discussed in the preceding paragraph.

(iii) There also exists a group of variables which depend on time, but whose evolution is partially unknown. This group may include variables which are uniquely indexed by time, such as the unemployment rate. Another possibility is that these variables may be indexed by time and the individual, examples include: the number of children, the amount of government assistance received, the local unemployment rate, etc. These variables are usually observed intermittently, i.e. at discrete intervals. We denote them $\mathbf{z}_i = z_i(t)$.

12.3.2 The Distribution of the Explanatory Variables Conditional on the Observations

12.3.2.1 The Case of Explanatory Variables Depending on the Individual

We shall introduce these variables, $\mathbf{x}_i$, into the distribution and parametrize them with $\boldsymbol{\theta}$. The hazard and survival functions for individual i are given by:

$$\begin{aligned}
\lambda_i(t) &= \lambda(\mathbf{x}_i; t; \boldsymbol{\theta}), \\
S_i(t) &= S(\mathbf{x}_i; t; \boldsymbol{\theta}), \\
&= \exp\left[-\int_0^t \lambda(\mathbf{x}_i; u; \boldsymbol{\theta})\, du\right].
\end{aligned}$$

If the distribution of the duration is selected from among the Weibull, gamma, log-normal, etc. families of distributions, we have seen that the hazard function already incorporates parameters. Some of these may be important for our interpretation in terms of increasing or decreasing dependence on time. Frequently it is over these parameters that $\mathbf{x}_i$ and $\boldsymbol{\theta}$ enter into the distribution.

Consequently, the family of exponential distributions depends on a parameter λ such that $\frac{1}{\lambda}$ defines the average duration. As this parameter is positive, it is clearly impossible to make it a linear function of the explanatory variables. In order to conserve this property of positiveness, and to establish an analogy with the simple Poisson model (cf. chapter 11), we postulate:

$$\lambda_i = \exp(\mathbf{x}_i\boldsymbol{\beta}),$$
$$\frac{1}{\lambda_i} = \exp(-\mathbf{x}_i\boldsymbol{\beta}),$$

with $\boldsymbol{\theta} = \boldsymbol{\beta}$. This yields the survival function:

$$S_i(t) = \exp\left[-\exp(\mathbf{x}_i\boldsymbol{\beta})\,t\right].$$

Example 20: In the same vein, for Weibull distributions we can specify:

$$\lambda_i(t;\boldsymbol{\theta}) = bt^{b-1}\exp(\mathbf{x}_i\boldsymbol{\beta}),$$
$$S_i(t;\boldsymbol{\theta}) = \exp\left[-\exp(\mathbf{x}_i\boldsymbol{\beta})\,t^b\right], \quad \boldsymbol{\theta} = \left(b, \beta'\right)'.$$

In the two preceding examples, a modification of the exogenous variables is sufficient to generate a new hazard function. This can be generalized as follows.

Definition 12: A model is said to be a *proportional risk model* if and only if the hazard function can be decomposed into:

$$\lambda_i(t) = g(t, b)\,h(\mathbf{x}_i, \boldsymbol{\beta}), \quad \boldsymbol{\theta} = \left(b', \beta'\right)'.$$

It is clear, however, that this condition is quite restrictive.

Consequently, in the case of a log-normal model, it is not possible to make the maximum of the function λ depend on the values of the explanatory variables. This can, however, be done using the following formulation.

Definition 13: A model is said to be an *accelerated risk model* if and only if the hazard function can be written:

$$\lambda_i(t) = g\left[t\,h(\mathbf{x}_i\boldsymbol{\beta}), b\right] h(\mathbf{x}_i, \boldsymbol{\beta}).$$

Finally, we may wish to make the direction of the evolution of λ depend upon the values of $\mathbf{x}_i$. Taking the Weibull distribution as an example, $\lambda(t) = abt^{b-1}$, we need to introduce the variables into the parameter b.

12.3.2.2 *The Case of Time-Varying Covariates*

In this case we have hazard and survival functions as follows:

$$\lambda_i(t) = \lambda_i[\mathbf{x}_i; z_i(t), u; \boldsymbol{\theta}],$$
$$S_i(t) = \exp\left\{\int_0^t \lambda_i[\mathbf{x}_i; z_i(u), u; \boldsymbol{\theta}]\,du\right\},$$
$$= \lambda_i\left[\mathbf{x}_i; z_i(\underline{t}), t; \boldsymbol{\theta}\right],$$

where the notation $z_i(\underline{t})$ implies dependency on all values of $\mathbf{z}_i$ previous to t. Consequently, when the rate of exit depends on the flow variables $\mathbf{z}_i$, the survival function incorporates a cumulative function of $\mathbf{z}_i$ which can be integrated anew.

The foregoing expressions cannot be used, however, if the exogenous variables, $z_i(t)$, are only observed at discrete intervals.

We shall assume from here on that the values are known for regular intervals – for example, years. The intervals of the observation are denoted $t_0,\ t_0+1,\ t_0+2, \ldots, t_0+k, \ldots,$ where $-1 \le t_0 < 0$. This latter statement follows from the fact that the first observation, which is indexed with zero by convention, will not necessarily fall at the beginning of the year, and hence t_0 is the most recent observation preceding the period of study. Given this, we can approximate the evolution of the unknown $z_i(t)$ with $z_i(t_0),\ z_i(t_0+1), \ldots, z_i(t_0+k), \ldots$

Two simple solutions suggest themselves.

(i) The first one is to replace the function $z_i(t)$ with a step function. For example, we may define a date t such that $t - t_0 \equiv k$, mod 1. Now:

$$z_i^*(t) = z_i(t_0+k)$$

is the last observed value, and:

$$z_i^*(t) = \frac{1}{2}\left[z_i(t_0+k) + z_i(t_0+k+1)\right]$$

is the mean of the values bracketing the study period.

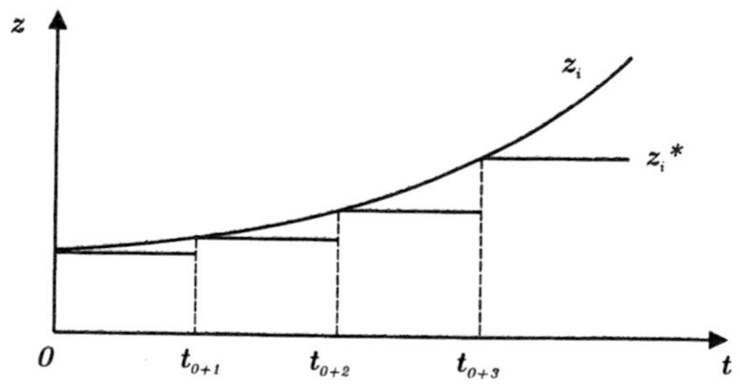

Fig. 12.11. Step function approximation to $z_i(t)$

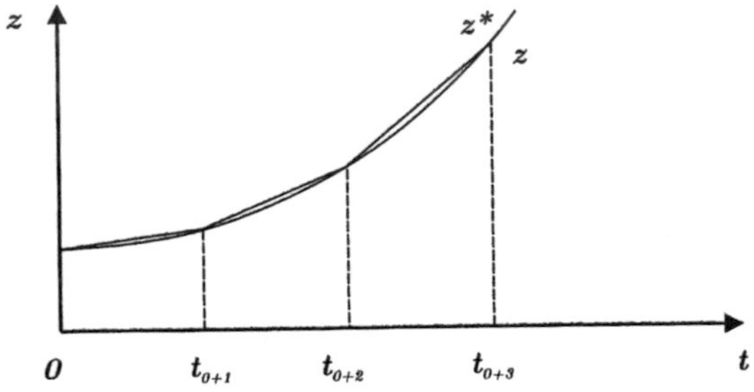

Fig. 12.12. Continuous function approximation to $z_i(t)$

Inspection of figure 12.11 reveals that this method will lead to underestimation of $\mathbf{z}_i$, and consequently the estimates of the parameters of the hazard function will be biased downward. The extent of this bias will depend upon the shape of $z_i\,(t)$ and on the distance between the observations.

(ii) We can also approximate the variable $\mathbf{z}_i$ with a continuous piece-wise linear function. This approach tends to be significantly more precise than the preceding, but it is computationally much more demanding.

If we replace $\mathbf{z}_i$ with an approximation $\mathbf{z}_i^*$, we must also modify the associated hazard and survival functions. To illustrate, consider the approximation:

$$z_i^*\,(t) = z_i\,(t_0 + k)\,, \quad \text{if } t - t_0 \equiv k, \text{mod } 1.$$

It follows that we can write:

$$\begin{aligned}\lambda_i^*\,(t) &= \lambda\left[\mathbf{x}_i;\, z_i^*\,(t)\,,t,\boldsymbol{\theta}\right],\\ &= \lambda\,[\mathbf{x}_i;\, z_i\,(t_0+k), t;\, \boldsymbol{\theta}]\,, \quad \text{if } t - t_0 \equiv k, \text{mod } 1.\end{aligned}$$

The approximated survival function is derived by integration:

$$\begin{aligned}S_i^*\,(t) &= \exp\left\{-\int_0^t \lambda_i^*\,(u)\,du\right\},\\ &= \exp\left\{-\int_0^{t_0+1} \lambda\,[\mathbf{x}_i;\, z_i\,(t_0)\,,u;\,\boldsymbol{\theta}]\,du\right.\\ &\quad -\sum_{j=1}^{k-1}\int_{t_0+j}^{t_0+j+1} \lambda\,[\mathbf{x}_i;\, z_i\,(t_0+j)\,,u;\,\boldsymbol{\theta}]\\ &\quad \left.-\int_{t_0+k}^{t} \lambda_i\,[\mathbf{x}_i;\, z_i\,(t_0+k)\,,u;\,\boldsymbol{\theta}]\right\}.\end{aligned}$$

The function $\tilde{S}$ is obtained by integration with z fixed:

$$\tilde{S}\,(\mathbf{x};\, z;\, t,\boldsymbol{\theta}) = \exp\left[-\int_0^t \lambda\,(\mathbf{x}, z;\, u;\,\boldsymbol{\theta})\right] du.$$

We have:

$$S_i^*(t) = \exp\Bigg\{ - \tilde{S}[\mathbf{x}_i; z_i(t_0), t_0 + 1; \boldsymbol{\theta}] \\ - \sum_{j=1}^{k-1} \big[\tilde{S}(\mathbf{x}_i; z_i(t_0 + j); t_0 + j + 1; \boldsymbol{\theta}) \\ -\tilde{S}(\mathbf{x}_i; z_i(t_0 + j); t_0 + j, \boldsymbol{\theta})\big] \\ - \big[\tilde{S}(\mathbf{x}_i; z_i(t_0 + k); t, \boldsymbol{\theta}) \\ -\tilde{S}(\mathbf{x}_i; z_i(t_0 + k); t_0 + k, \boldsymbol{\theta})\big] \Bigg\}.$$

The form obtained for the survival function is intermediate between that corresponding to the continuous- and the discrete-time models. The discrete aspect is manifest in the term:

$$\sum_{j=1}^{k-1} \big\{\tilde{S}[\mathbf{x}_i; z_i(t_0 + j); t_0 + j + 1; \boldsymbol{\theta}] \\ - \tilde{S}[\mathbf{x}_i; z_i(t_0 + j); t_0 + j, \boldsymbol{\theta}]\big\},$$

and the continuous part in the other two terms. In essence, the fact that our observations on some variables are of a discrete nature implies that we must work with a discrete model.

12.4 Estimation

12.4.1 Truncation on the RHS

Data used in econometric time-series studies are often in the form of panel data measured over a fixed period of time. Suppose, for example, that we have unemployment data for the period extending from January 1994 to December 1994, we can distinguish between four types of observations:

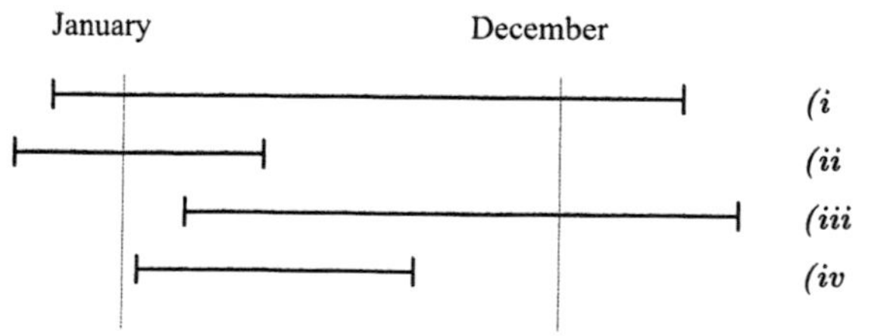

Fig. 12.13. Evolution of unemployment

(i) Individuals who are unemployed in January and remain unemployed in December.
(ii) Individuals who are unemployed in January and find a job during the year.
(iii) Individuals who are employed in January and lose their job during the year.
(iv) Individuals who lose a job and then find another during the year.

For simplicity we assume that no one goes through several stages of employment and unemployment in one year. Graphically, these cases are represented in figure 12.13.

Those individuals who were unemployed at the beginning of the study period can be questioned, and a certain amount of information concerning their employment history collected; for example: when did they lose their last job, what was their profession, etc. Given this supplementary information, two types of data can be distinguished. For groups two and four we know the duration of their unemployment by the end of the year. For groups one and three, on the other hand, we do not. This latter group is said to be truncated on the RHS, the former group is not truncated.

To account for this, we shall introduce a dummy variable, d_i, for each individual, i, to indicate whether or not this person's data is truncated.

$$d_i = \begin{cases} 1, & \text{if not truncated,} \\ 0, & \text{otherwise.} \end{cases}$$

We also denote the subsets of complete and truncated observations $\Im_1$ and $\Im_0$ respectively.

Furthermore, let T_i be the date on which unemployment begins, ζ_i the duration of unemployment, and y_i the overlap between the period of unemployment and the study period, given that this latter ends at T.

The ensuing model is based on the latent variables T_i and ζ_i. The observed variables, d_i and y_i, are related to the latent variables by:

$$T_i + \zeta_i < T \Rightarrow \qquad \begin{cases} d_i = 1, \\ y_i = \zeta_i, \end{cases}$$

$$T_i + \zeta_i > T \Rightarrow \qquad \begin{cases} d_i = 0, \\ y_i = T - T_i. \end{cases}$$

We see that the distribution of the pair (y_i, d_i), conditional on T_i, is given by:

$$\ell_i\,(y_i, d_i) = f_i\,(y_i)^{d_i}\; S_i\,(y_i)^{1-d_i}.$$

We can refer to the definition of the hazard function to rewrite this equation:

$$\ell_i\,(y_i, d_i) = \lambda_i\,(y_i)^{d_i}\; S_i\,(y_i).$$

Assuming independence between individual observations, we can write the log-likelihood function, conditional on the values of the explanatory variables, as:

$$\log\left[L\left(y;d\right)\right]=\sum_{i=1}^{n}\log\left[\ell_i\left(y_i,d_i\right)\right],$$
$$=\sum_{i=1}^{n}d_i\log\left[\lambda_i\left(y_i\right)\right]+\sum_{i=1}^{n}\log\left[S_i\left(y_i\right)\right],$$
$$=\sum_{i\in J_1}\log\left[\lambda_i\left(y_i\right)\right]+\sum_{i=1}^{n}\log\left[S_i\left(y_i\right)\right]. \tag{12.3}$$

This is quite similar to the Tobit model we saw in chapter 7, the principal difference being that the Tobit model is based on the normal distribution, while this one is not.

12.4.2 Maximum-Likelihood Estimation

In the interest of keeping our notation simple, the data we shall use to present the principal estimation techniques will only incorporate explanatory variables pertaining to the individual. We have:

$$\lambda_i\left(y_i\right)=\lambda\left(\mathbf{x}_i;y_i;\boldsymbol{\theta}\right),$$
$$S_i\left(y_i\right)=S\left(\mathbf{x}_i;y_i;\boldsymbol{\theta}\right),$$
$$=\exp\left[-\int_0^{y_i}\lambda\left(\mathbf{x}_i;u,\boldsymbol{\theta}\right)du\right],$$
$$\log\left[L\left(\theta\right)\right]=\sum_{i\in J_1}\log\left[\lambda\left(\mathbf{x}_i,y_i;\boldsymbol{\theta}\right)\right]+\sum_{i=1}^{n}\log\left[S\left(\mathbf{x}_i;y_i;\boldsymbol{\theta}\right)\right],$$
$$=\sum_{i\in J_1}\log\left[\lambda\left(\mathbf{x}_i,y_i;\boldsymbol{\theta}\right)\right]-\sum_{i=1}^{n}\int_0^{y_i}\lambda\left(\mathbf{x}_i;y;\boldsymbol{\theta}\right)du.$$

To apply the maximum-likelihood estimation procedure we write out the first-order conditions:

$$0=\frac{\partial\log\left[L\left(\boldsymbol{\theta}\right)\right]}{\partial\boldsymbol{\theta}},$$
$$=\sum_{i\in J_1}\frac{\partial\log\left[\lambda\left(\mathbf{x}_i,y_i;\boldsymbol{\theta}\right)\right]}{\partial\boldsymbol{\theta}}-\sum_{i=1}^{n}\int_0^{y_i}\frac{\partial}{\partial\boldsymbol{\theta}}\lambda\left(\mathbf{x}_i;u;\boldsymbol{\theta}\right)du,$$

assuming that the derivative under the integral exists.

Under the standard assumptions of regularity, the estimator $\hat{\boldsymbol{\theta}}$ yielded by this expression exists asymptotically, and it is consistent, asymptotically efficient, and asymptotically normal.

This general formulation does not, however, yield first-order conditions, or a Fisher information matrix, which are easy to simplify. For this reason we shall now turn our attention to analysing specific models, namely the Weibull model, the decomposable model, and the proportional hazard model.

12.4.2.1 The Weibull Model

The Weibull model, in which the explanatory variables are introduced over a coefficient of affinity, yields the following expression:

$$\lambda\,(t;\boldsymbol{\theta}) = bt^{b-1}\exp\,(\mathbf{x}\boldsymbol{\beta}).$$

This model contains two types of parameters: the $\boldsymbol{\beta}$ -parameters which measure the effect of the explanatory variables, and the b-parameter. The likelihood is given by:

$$\begin{aligned}
\log\,[L\,(\boldsymbol{\theta})] &= \sum_{i\in J_1}\log\left[by_i^{b-1}\exp\,(\mathbf{x}_i\boldsymbol{\beta})\right] \\
&\quad + \sum_{i=1}^{n}\log\left\{\exp\left[\exp\,(\mathbf{x}_i\boldsymbol{\beta})\,y_i^b\right]\right\}, \\
&= \sum_{i\in J_1}\log\,(b) + \sum_{i\in J_1}(b-1)\log\,(y_i) \\
&\quad + \sum_{i\in J_1}\mathbf{x}_i\boldsymbol{\beta} - \sum_{i=1}^{n}\exp\,(\mathbf{x}_i\boldsymbol{\beta})\,y_i^b, \\
&= n_1\log\,(b) + (b-1)\sum_{i\in J_1}\log\,(y_i) \\
&\quad + \sum_{i\in J_1}\mathbf{x}_i\boldsymbol{\beta} - \sum_{i=1}^{n}\exp\,(\mathbf{x}_i\boldsymbol{\beta})\,y_i^b.
\end{aligned}$$

n_1 denotes the number of observations in J_1, that is the number of complete observations.

Remark 12: In the case of the exponential model, i.e. when $b = 1$, the log-likelihood reduces to:

$$\log\,[L\,(\boldsymbol{\theta})] = \sum_{i\in J_1}\mathbf{x}_i\boldsymbol{\beta} - \sum_{i=1}^{n} y_i\exp\,(\mathbf{x}_i\boldsymbol{\beta}).$$

If there is no truncation, we have:

$$\log\left[L\left(\boldsymbol{\theta}\right)\right] = \sum_{i=1}^{n}\left[\mathbf{x}_i\boldsymbol{\beta} - y_i \exp\left(\mathbf{x}_i\boldsymbol{\beta}\right)\right].$$

The log-likelihood of the Weibull model depends upon the two types of parameters, $\boldsymbol{\beta}$ and b, which it incorporates, and it is of some interest to separate them when we write the first-order conditions. The vector of scores is:

$$\frac{\partial \log\left[L\left(\boldsymbol{\theta}\right)\right]}{\partial\boldsymbol{\beta}} = \sum_{i\in J_1}\mathbf{x}_i' - \sum_{i=1}^{n}\mathbf{x}_i' \exp\left(\mathbf{x}_i\boldsymbol{\beta}\right) y_i^b,$$

$$\frac{\partial \log\left[L\left(\boldsymbol{\theta}\right)\right]}{\partial b} = \frac{n_1}{b} + \sum_{i\in J_1}\log\left(y_i\right) - \sum_{i=1}^{n}\log\left(y_i\right)\exp\left(\mathbf{x}_i\boldsymbol{\beta}\right) y_i^b.$$

The likelihood equations:

$$0 = \frac{\partial \log\left[L\left(\hat{\boldsymbol{\theta}}\right)\right]}{\partial\boldsymbol{\beta}},$$

$$0 = \frac{\partial \log\left[L\left(\hat{\boldsymbol{\theta}}\right)\right]}{\partial b},$$

cannot be solved analytically. Even in this simple case the solution must be found numerically.

Remark 13: In the case of the exponential model, where $b = 1$, the estimator, $\hat{\boldsymbol{\beta}}_0$, for the parameter $\boldsymbol{\beta}$, is the solution to:

$$0 = \frac{\partial \log\left[L\left(\hat{\boldsymbol{\beta}}_0\right)\right]}{\partial\boldsymbol{\beta}} = \sum_{i\in J_1}\mathbf{x}_i' - \sum_{i=1}^{n}\mathbf{x}_i' \exp\left(\mathbf{x}_i\hat{\boldsymbol{\beta}}_0\right) y_i.$$

Remark 14: When there is no truncation, the first equation of the Weibull log-likelihood model becomes:

$$0 = \sum_{i=1}^{n}\mathbf{x}_i' \exp\left(\mathbf{x}_i\hat{\boldsymbol{\beta}}\right)\left[\exp\left(-\mathbf{x}_i\hat{\boldsymbol{\beta}}\right) - y_i^{\hat{b}}\right].$$

In this case, we have $\mathrm{E}\left(y_i^b\right) = \exp\left(-\mathbf{x}_i\boldsymbol{\beta}\right)$ and this equation becomes:

$$0 = \sum_{i=1}^{n}\mathbf{x}_i' \exp\left(\mathbf{x}_i\hat{\boldsymbol{\beta}}\right)\left[y_i^{\hat{b}} - \widehat{\mathrm{E}}\left(y_i^b\right)\right],$$

which can be interpreted as a condition of orthogonality between the explanatory variables, $\mathbf{x}$, and the estimated residuals corresponding to y^b for the scalar product associated with diag $\left[\exp\left(\mathbf{x}\hat{\beta}\right)\right]$.

Example 21: The simplest case, when the only explanatory variable is the constant, corresponds to the sampling model in a truncated Weibull distribution. In this case we have:

$$0 = \frac{\partial \log [L(\boldsymbol{\theta})]}{\partial \boldsymbol{\beta}} = n_1 - \exp\left[\hat{\beta}\right] \sum_{i=1}^{n} y_i^{\hat{b}},$$

$$0 = \frac{\partial \log [L(\boldsymbol{\theta})]}{\partial \mathbf{b}} = \frac{n_1}{\hat{b}} + \sum_{i \in J_1} \log(y_i) - \exp\left[\hat{\beta} \sum_{i=1}^{n} \log\left(y_i y_i^{\hat{b}}\right)\right].$$

Inspection of the first equation reveals that: $\exp(-\boldsymbol{\beta}) = \frac{1}{n_1} \sum_{i=1}^{n} y_i^{\hat{b}}$. Substituting into the second equation, we obtain an implicit function yielding $\hat{b}$:

$$0 = \frac{n_1}{\hat{b}} + \sum_{i \in J_1} \log(y_i) - \left[\frac{1}{n_1} \sum_{i=1}^{n} y_i^{\hat{b}}\right]^{-1} \sum_{i=1}^{n} \log\left(y_i y_i^{\hat{b}}\right).$$

The precision of the maximum-likelihood estimator may be estimated by:

$$-\frac{\partial^2 \log\left[L\left(\hat{\theta}\right)\right]}{\partial \theta \partial \theta'}.$$

The second derivatives of the log-likelihood are:

$$\frac{\partial^2 \log [L(\boldsymbol{\theta})]}{\partial \boldsymbol{\beta} \partial \boldsymbol{\beta}'} = -\sum_{i=1}^{n} \mathbf{x}_i' \mathbf{x}_i \exp(\mathbf{x}_i \boldsymbol{\beta})\, y_i^b,$$

$$\frac{\partial^2 \log [L(\boldsymbol{\theta})]}{\partial \boldsymbol{\beta} \partial b} = -\sum_{i=1}^{n} \mathbf{x}_i' \log\left(y_i y_i^b\right) \exp(\mathbf{x}_i \boldsymbol{\beta}),$$

$$\frac{\partial^2 \log [L(\boldsymbol{\theta})]}{\partial b^2} = -\frac{n_1}{b^2} - \sum_{i=1}^{n} \left[\log(y_i)\right]^2 \exp(\mathbf{x}_i \boldsymbol{\beta})\, y_i^b.$$

12.4.2.2 The Decomposable Model

Sometimes the estimation is simpler than in the foregoing example. This occurs when the hazard function contains a separation between the observations, y, and the parameters, $\boldsymbol{\beta}$:

$$\begin{aligned}\lambda_i(y_i; \boldsymbol{\beta}) &= \sum_{k=1}^{K} g_{ik}(\boldsymbol{\beta})\, h_{0ik}(y) + h_{1i}(y_i),\\ &= g_i'(\boldsymbol{\beta})\, h_{0i}(y_i) + h_{1i}(y_i).\end{aligned}$$

Denoting the primitives of h_{0i} and h_{1i} by H_{0i} and H_{1i} respectively, and noting that they are nil for $y_i = 0$, we find that the corresponding density functions and survival functions are:

$$\begin{aligned} f_i(y_i;\beta) &= \left[g_i'(\beta)\,h_{0i}(y_i) + h_{1i}(y_i)\right] \\ &\quad \times \exp\left\{-\left[g_i'(\beta)\,H_{0i}(y_i) + H_{1i}(y_i)\right]\right\}, \\ S_i(y_i;\beta) &= \exp\left\{-\left[g_i'(\beta)\,H_{0i}(y_i) + H_{1i}(y_i)\right]\right\}. \end{aligned}$$

We calculate the first and second derivatives of the marginal log-likelihoods:

$$\begin{aligned} \log\left[L_i(y_i,\beta)\right] &= \log\left[f_i(y_i,\beta)\right] z_{i\in J_1} + \log\left[S_i(y_i,\beta)\right]\left(1 - z_{i\in J_1}\right), \\ &= \frac{\frac{\partial g_i'(\beta)}{\partial \beta} h_{0i}(y_i)}{g_i'(\beta)\,h_{0i}(y_i) + h_{1i}(y_i)} z_{i\in J_1} - \frac{\partial g_i'(\beta)}{\partial \beta} H_{0i}(y_i), \\ &= \frac{\partial g_i'(\beta)}{\partial \beta}\left[\frac{h_{0i}(y_i)}{\lambda_i(y_i;\beta)} z_{i\in J_1} - H_{0i}(y_i)\right]. \end{aligned}$$

As the vector of scores is nil, the following lemma suggests itself:

Lemma 5: For a decomposable model:

$$0 = \mathrm{E}_i\left[\frac{h_{0i}(Y_i)}{\lambda_i(Y_i;\beta)} Z_i - H_{0i}(Y_i)\right].$$

The second derivative is:

$$\begin{aligned} \frac{\partial^2 \log\left[L_i(y_i;\beta)\right]}{\partial\beta\partial\beta'} &= \sum_{k=1}^{K} \frac{\partial g_{ik}(\beta)}{\partial\beta\partial\beta'}\left[\frac{h_{0i}(y_i)}{\lambda_i(y_i;\beta)} z_{i\in J_1} - H_{0i}(y_i)\right] \\ &\quad - \frac{\left[\frac{\partial g_i'(\beta)}{\partial\beta} h_{0i}(y_i)\right]^2}{\left[\lambda_i(y_i;\beta)\right]^2} z_{i\in J_1}. \end{aligned}$$

Taking expectations with respect to the distribution of Y_i conditional on the values assumed by the exogenous variables, and using lemma 5, we obtain the following result.

Proposition 40: For the decomposable model, the asymptotic precision of the maximum-likelihood estimator is approximately given by:

$$\operatorname{var}\left(\hat\beta\right) \approx \left\{\sum_{i=1}^{n} \frac{\left[\frac{\partial g_i'(\beta)}{\partial\beta} h_{0i}(y_i)\right]^2}{\lambda_i(y_i;\beta)^2} z_{i\in J_1}\right\}^{-1}.$$

Since the functions g and h_0 are given, we can vary the function h_1, and over it the hazard function. We see intuitively that, the larger this function, the greater the imprecision of the estimator.

On the other hand, as we have seen in preceding sections, the comparability of hazard functions is closely linked to the notion of heterogeneity. We shall examine what happens to our results when they are applied to a model derived from aggregating exponential models.

The survival function is:

$$S_i(y_i, \beta) = \int_v \exp\left\{-\left[v + \exp(\mathbf{x}_i\beta)\right] y_i \pi\right\} dv,$$

$$= \exp\left[-y_i \exp(\mathbf{x}_i\beta)\right] \int_v \exp(-vy_i\pi)\, dv.$$

Denoting $\Psi(y)$ the moment generating function associated with the distribution π, we find:

$$\log[S_i(y_i, \beta)] = \exp(\mathbf{x}_i\beta),$$
$$= -y_i \exp(\mathbf{x}_i\beta) + \log[\Psi(y_i)].$$

This is a decomposable model with:

$$g_i(\beta) = \exp(\mathbf{x}_i\beta),$$
$$H_{0i}(y_i) = y_i,$$
$$H_{1i}(y_i) = -\log[\Psi(y_i)].$$

Direct application of lemma 5 yields the following result.

Proposition 41: For a model derived from an exponential model by heterogeneity we have:

$$\mathrm{E}_i\left[\frac{z_{i\in J_1}}{\lambda_i(Y_i; \beta)}\right] = \mathrm{E}_i(Y_i).$$

In particular, applying this formula to the case of non-truncated variables, we see that the mean of the inverse of the hazard function is equal to the mean duration:

$$\mathrm{E}_i\left[\frac{1}{\lambda_i(\zeta_i; \beta)}\right] = \mathrm{E}_i(\zeta_i).$$

This formula constitutes a direct generalization of the relationship between the mean duration and the hazard rate established in the case of temporal independence (cf. proposition 33)

Proposition 40 takes the form:

$$\operatorname{var}\left(\hat{\boldsymbol{\beta}}\right) \approx \left(\sum_{i=1}^{n} \mathbf{x}_i' \mathbf{x}_i \exp\left(2\mathbf{x}_i \boldsymbol{\beta}\right) \mathrm{E}\left\{\frac{1}{\left[\lambda_i\left(y_i \boldsymbol{\beta}\right)\right]^2}\right\}\right)^{-1}.$$

Proposition 42: For a model derived from an exponential model we have:

$$\operatorname{var}\left(\hat{\boldsymbol{\beta}}\right) \approx \left(\sum_{i=1}^{n} \mathbf{x}_i' \mathbf{x}_i \exp\left(2\mathbf{x}_i \boldsymbol{\beta}\right) \mathrm{E}_i \left\{\frac{z_{i \in J_1}}{\exp\left(\mathbf{x}_i \boldsymbol{\beta}\right) - \frac{\partial \log[\Psi(Y_i)]}{\partial y_i}}\right\}\right)^{-1}.$$

The term:

$$-\frac{\partial \log\left[\Psi\left(Y_i\right)\right]}{\partial y_i}$$

brings out the effect of heterogeneity.

Finally, there is a corollary for $\Psi = 1$ which is a classical result of studies of duration models:

Corollary 3: In the case of the exponential model, we have:

$$\operatorname{var}\left(\hat{\boldsymbol{\beta}}\right) \approx \left[\sum_{i=1}^{n} \mathbf{x}_i' \mathbf{x}_i \pi_i\right]^{-1},$$

with $\pi_i = \mathrm{E}\left(z_{i \in J_1}\right)$.

This matrix is similar to the one we know from the linear model, except that each observation in the current one is weighted by its probability of being censored.

12.4.2.3 Proportional Hazard Models

After transformation of the endogenous variables, some duration models can be rewritten in a simpler form. A particular case of this is found in proportional hazard models, in which explanatory variables are introduced over exponential functions.

Let the hazard function be:

$$\lambda\left(\mathbf{x}_i; t; \boldsymbol{\beta}\right) = \exp\left(-\mathbf{x}_i \boldsymbol{\beta}\right) \lambda_0(t), \tag{12.4}$$

where λ_0 designates the base hazard. The corresponding survival function is:

$$S\left(\mathbf{x}_i; t; \boldsymbol{\beta}\right) = \exp\left[-\exp\left(-\mathbf{x}_i \boldsymbol{\beta}\right) \Lambda_0(t)\right],$$

where Λ_0 designates the cumulative base hazard.

We now introduce the following transformation of the duration variable ζ_i :

$$U = \log \Lambda_0 (\zeta_i) - \mathbf{x}_i \boldsymbol{\beta}.$$

We have:

$$\begin{aligned}
\Pr (U_i > u_i) &= \Pr \{\log [\Lambda_0 (\zeta_i)] - \mathbf{x}_i \boldsymbol{\beta} > u_i\}, \\
&= \Pr \left\{ \zeta > \Lambda_0^{-1} \left[\exp (\mathbf{x}_i \boldsymbol{\beta}) \exp (u_i) \right] \right\}, \\
&= \exp \left[- \exp (u_i) \right],
\end{aligned}$$

which derives from the expression for the survival function, S.

Thus, the initial model associated with the observations $(\zeta_i, \mathbf{x}_i)$ can be reformulated as:

$$\log [\Lambda_0 (\zeta_i)] = \mathbf{x}_i \boldsymbol{\beta} + u_i, \quad i = 1, \ldots, n, \tag{12.5}$$

where u_i follows the Gompertz distribution, with density $g(u) = \exp(u) \exp\left[-\exp(u)\right]$. This resembles a linear model, but it should be noted that the error term is not centered (the mean is approximately $\mathrm{E}[u] = -0.57$) – nor is it normally distributed.

This form lends itself to several applications. We may, for example, find certain simplifications in the likelihood equations or in the expression for the information matrix. In particular, the vector of scores is often amenable to introduction of generalized residuals, which form the basis for the test procedures. Furthermore, least squares type estimation procedures, while not efficient, may sometimes yield consistent estimators.

Example 22: Assume that we have uncensored data. We regress the transformed variable $\log [\Lambda_0 (\zeta_i)]$ on the explanatory variables $\mathbf{x}_i$ to obtain the parameter vector $\boldsymbol{\beta}$. The estimator is:

$$\tilde{\boldsymbol{\beta}} = \left(\sum_{i=1}^{n} \mathbf{x}_i' \mathbf{x}_i \right)^{-1} \sum_{i=1}^{n} \mathbf{x}_i' \log [\Lambda_0 (\zeta_i)].$$

Since u_i is not centered, this estimator is consistent for all elements except the constant. Also, we can introduce residuals $\tilde{u}_i = \log [\Lambda_0 (\zeta_i)] - \tilde{\boldsymbol{\beta}}$, which are approximations to the variables $u_i - \mathrm{E}(u_i)$, and which are centered.

In fact, the formulation introduced in equation (12.5) is not always the most appropriate. Notice, for example, that the transformed variable $\Lambda_0 (\zeta_1)$ is such that:

$$\Lambda_0 (\zeta_i) = \exp (\mathbf{x}_i \boldsymbol{\beta}) \exp (u_i),$$

where $\exp (u_i)$ follows an exponential distribution. Since the mean of this last distribution is equal to one, we have:

$$\Lambda_0(\zeta_i) = \exp(\mathbf{x}_i\boldsymbol{\beta}) + w_i, \tag{12.6}$$

with $\mathrm{E}(w_i) = 0$. This is an econometric model which is nonlinear in the parameter $\boldsymbol{\beta}$.

In the uncensored case, application of this second model leads us quite naturally to introduce the nonlinear least squares estimator $\tilde{\boldsymbol{\beta}}$, solution to the problem:

$$\min_{\boldsymbol{\beta}} \sum_{i=1}^{n} \left[\Lambda_0(\zeta_i) - \exp(\mathbf{x}_i\boldsymbol{\beta})\right]^2,$$

and to the residuals:

$$\tilde{w}_i = \Lambda_0(\zeta_i) - \exp\left(\mathbf{x}_i\tilde{\boldsymbol{\beta}}\right).$$

The simplest way to determine which of the two representations, equations (12.5) or (12.6), is better suited to the proportional hazard model is to write out the log-likelihood function associated with the model. It is given by:

$$\begin{aligned}\log\left[L^*(\boldsymbol{\beta})\right] &= \sum_{i=1}^{n} \log\left[\exp(-\mathbf{x}_i\boldsymbol{\beta})\,\lambda_0(\zeta_i)\right] \\ &\quad + \sum_{i=1}^{n} \log\left\{\exp\left[-\exp(-\mathbf{x}_i\boldsymbol{\beta})\,\Lambda_0(\zeta_i)\right]\right\}, \\ &= \sum_{i=1}^{n} \{-\mathbf{x}_i\boldsymbol{\beta} + \log[\lambda_0(\zeta_i)]\} - \sum_{i=1}^{n} \exp(-\mathbf{x}_i\boldsymbol{\beta})\,\Lambda_0(\zeta_i).\end{aligned}$$

The corresponding vector of scores is:

$$\begin{aligned}\frac{\partial \log[L^*(\boldsymbol{\beta})]}{\partial\boldsymbol{\beta}} &= \sum_{i=1}^{n} \mathbf{x}_i'\left[-1 + \exp(-\mathbf{x}_i\boldsymbol{\beta})\,\Lambda_0(\zeta_i)\right], \\ &= \sum_{i=1}^{n} \mathbf{x}_i' \exp(-\mathbf{x}_i\boldsymbol{\beta})\left[\Lambda_0(\zeta_i) - \exp(\mathbf{x}_i\boldsymbol{\beta})\right], \\ &= \sum_{i=1}^{n} \mathbf{x}_i' \exp(-\mathbf{x}_i\boldsymbol{\beta})\, w_i.\end{aligned}$$

Similarly, in the uncensored case, the likelihood equations, given by:

$$\frac{\partial \log\left[L^*\left(\hat{\boldsymbol{\beta}}\right)\right]}{\partial\boldsymbol{\beta}} = \sum_{i=1}^{n} \mathbf{x}_i' \exp(-\mathbf{x}_i\boldsymbol{\beta})\,\hat{w}_i = 0,$$

signify the conditions of orthogonality between the explanatory variables $\mathbf{x}_i$

and the residuals:

$$\hat{w}_i = \Lambda_0(\zeta_i) - \exp\left(\mathbf{x}_i\hat{\beta}\right)$$

associated with the formulation of equation (12.6) and estimated by maximum likelihood.

Remark 15: When the observations are censored, the score $\frac{\partial \log(L)}{\partial \beta}$ associated with the observable variables y_i, $i = 1, \ldots, n$ can be derived from the latent score, given by:

$$\frac{\partial \log[L(\beta)]}{\partial \beta} = \mathrm{E}\left[\frac{\partial \log[L^*(\beta)]}{\partial \beta}\middle| Y_1, \ldots, Y_n\right].$$

This evaluates to:

$$\frac{\partial \log[L(\beta)]}{\partial \beta} = \sum_{i=1}^{n} \mathbf{x}_i' \exp(-\mathbf{x}_i\beta)\, \mathrm{E}_\beta\left[\Lambda_0(\zeta_i) - \exp(\mathbf{x}_i\beta) | Y_i\right],$$

yielding the generalized residuals:

$$\tilde{w} = \left(\mathrm{E}_b\left[\Lambda_0(\zeta_i) - \exp(\mathbf{x}_i\beta) | Y_i\right]\right)_{\beta=\hat{\beta}}.$$

12.4.2.4 Test for the Exponential Distribution

The family of Weibull distributions includes the exponential distribution, where $b = 1$, as a special case. So we may wish to test the hypothesis $H_0 : b = 1$. This allows us to determine whether the hazard function is constant or monotonic.

This test may be performed with the usual methods: the Wald test, the maximum-score test, or the likelihood-ratio test. No real simplifications are possible for the calculation of these statistics. As an example we calculate the statistics for the simple case of observations which are i.i.d. and uncensored.

Example 23: From example 21, the vector of scores $\frac{\partial \log(L)}{\partial b}$, evaluated at $b = 1$, is given by:

$$\frac{\partial \log[L(\beta; 1)]}{\partial b} = n + \sum_{i=1}^{n} \log(y_i) - \exp(\beta) \sum_{i=1}^{n} y_i \log(y_i).$$

$\hat{\beta}_0$, the estimator of β calculated under the null hypothesis, is:

$$\exp\left(\hat{\beta}_0\right) = \frac{n}{\sum_{i=1}^{n} y_i}.$$

Substituting into the score expression, we have:

$$\frac{\partial \log [L(\beta;1)]}{\partial b} = n + \sum_{i=1}^{n} \log(y_i) - n\frac{\sum_{i=1}^{n} y_i \log(y_i)}{\sum_{i=1}^{n} y_i},$$
$$= \frac{y}{n}\left\{\bar{y} - \operatorname{cov}\left[y, \log(y)\right]\right\}.$$

Under the null hypothesis, the asymptotic variance of this score can be found using the Fisher information matrix:

$$\operatorname{var}_{asy}\left[\frac{1}{\sqrt{n}}\frac{\partial \log[L(\beta;1)]}{\partial b}\right] = I_{bb} - \frac{I_{b\beta}^2}{I_{\beta\beta}}.$$

We leave to the reader to verify that its value is consistently estimated by:

$$\hat{\eta}^2 = n + \sum_{i=1}^{n}\left(\exp\left(\hat{\beta}_0 y_i\right)\left\{\log\left[\exp\left(\hat{\beta}_0 y_i\right)\right]^2\right\}\right)$$
$$- \frac{\exp\left(2\hat{\beta}_0\right)}{n}\left\{\sum_{i=1}^{n} y_i \log\left[\exp\left(\hat{\beta}_0 y_i\right)\right]\right\}^2.$$

To apply the maximum-score test we accept the null hypothesis ($b = 1$) if:

$$\frac{1}{\sqrt{n}}\frac{\partial \log(L)}{\partial b}\left(\hat{\beta}_0; 1\right) < 2,$$

and reject it otherwise.

12.5 Models with Heterogeneity

In the models we have just examined, it has been assumed that the exogenous variables were measured without error, that no variables were omitted, etc. In other words, we ignored modelling errors. To account for this possibility, we need to introduce a parameter of heterogeneity.

12.5.1 Some Properties of Models with Heterogeneity

We begin by presenting a general formulation for these models, by specifying the direction of the heterogeneity bias, and by giving a precise description of the mover-stayer model.

12.5.1.1 The Relationship Between Aggregated and Disaggregated Models

Consider a population of individuals, for example the unemployed, with unobservable characteristics categorized into groups $v, v \in \mathcal{V}$. The population may be divided into several sub-populations, $\mathcal{P}_v$, where $\mathcal{P}_v$ is comprised of individuals with characteristics v. This grouping of individuals into the various sub-populations is summarized by the distribution of heterogeneity $\pi\,(dv)$.

At the disaggregated level, the distribution of the duration for individuals characterized by v is given by the following functions:

(i) $S\,(t;\,v)$ – the disaggregated survival function,
(ii) $\lambda\,(t;\,v)$ – the disaggregated hazard function,
(iii) $r\,(t;\,v)$ – the average remaining disaggregated duration.

It is important to recognize that the distribution of heterogeneity of the population changes over time. Some members of the population of the unemployed will, with time, find a job, for example. This change occurs each time that a spell of unemployment ends, i.e. each time that a duration is observed. As the rate at which individuals leave unemployment is not constant across the sub-populations, it is likely that the distribution of heterogeneity depends upon the date. Let us denote this dependence upon time, t, with $\pi_t\,(dv)$.

This distribution is easy to find. The proportion of individuals remaining unemployed at time t is $S\,(t;\,v)$. We find:

$$\pi_t\,(dv) = \frac{S\,(t;\,v)\,\pi\,(dv)}{\int_{\mathcal{V}} S\,(t;\,v)\,\pi\,(dv)}. \tag{12.7}$$

From here on we denote E_t, var_t, cov_t the expectation, variance, and covariance with respect to the distribution π_t.

So far, we have described the distribution of the duration in disaggregated terms, now we shall examine the aggregate distribution, that is for an individual drawn at random from the whole population $\mathcal{P} = \cup_{\mathcal{V}} \mathcal{P}_v$. The aggregate survival function is given by:

$$\tilde{S}\,(t) = \int_{\mathcal{V}} S\,(t;\,v)\,\pi\,(dv),$$

and the average hazard functions are yielded by:

$$\tilde{\lambda}\,(t) = \frac{-d \log\left[\tilde{S}\,(t)\right]}{dt},$$

$$\tilde{r}\,(t) = \frac{1}{\tilde{S}\,(t)} \int_t^{\infty} \tilde{S}\,(u)\,du.$$

The following result provides the relationship between the aggregate and disaggregated functions. The first part of this proposition has already been demonstrated in proposition 35, the second part is left as an exercise for the reader.

Proposition 43:

$$\tilde{\lambda}(t) = \mathrm{E}_t[\lambda(t; v)],$$
$$\tilde{r}(t) = \mathrm{E}_t[r(t; v)].$$

12.5.1.2 Heterogeneity Bias

These simple relationships provide the basis for our analysis of the functions at the aggregate and disaggregated levels. We shall make use of the following lemma:

Lemma 6: Let $g(t; v)$ be differentiable with respect to t, we have:

$$\frac{\partial}{\partial t}\mathrm{E}_t[g(t; v)] = \mathrm{E}_t\left[\frac{\partial g(t; v)}{\partial t}\right] - \mathrm{cov}_t[g(t; v), \lambda(t; v)].$$

Proof: We have:

$$\frac{\partial}{\partial t}\mathrm{E}_t[g(t; v)] = \int_{\mathcal{V}} g(g; v)\, \pi(t; v)\, dv,$$

where $\pi(t; v)$ is the density function for $\pi_t(dv)$. Applying the product rule to the terms under the integral, we obtain:

$$\begin{aligned}
&\frac{\partial}{\partial t}\mathrm{E}_t[g(t; v)] \\
&= \int_{\mathcal{V}} \frac{\partial}{\partial t} g(t; v)\, \pi(t; v)\, dv + \int_{\mathcal{V}} g(t; v) \frac{\partial}{\partial t}\pi(t; v)\, dv, \\
&= \mathrm{E}_t\left[\frac{\partial}{\partial t} g(t; v)\right] + \int_{\mathcal{V}} g(t; v) \frac{\partial}{\partial t}\left[\frac{S(t; v)\, \pi(v)}{\int_{\mathcal{V}} S(t; v)\, \pi(v)\, dv}\right] dv, \\
&= \mathrm{E}_t\left[\frac{\partial}{\partial t} g(t; v)\right] + \int_{\mathcal{V}} g(t; v) \left\{ - \frac{f(t; v)\, \pi(v)}{\int_{\mathcal{V}} S(t; v)\, \pi(v)\, dv} \right. \\
&\quad \left. + \frac{S(t; v)\, \pi(v) \int_{\mathcal{V}} f(t; v)\, \pi(v)\, dv}{\left[\int_{\mathcal{V}} S(t; v)\, \pi(v)\, dv\right]^2} \right\} dv, \\
&= \mathrm{E}_t\left[\frac{\partial}{\partial t} g(t; v)\right] + \int_{\mathcal{V}} g(t; v) \left[- \lambda(t; v)\, \pi(t; v) \right. \\
&\quad \left. + \pi(t; v) \int_{\mathcal{V}} \lambda(t; v)\, \pi(t; v)\, dv \right] dv,
\end{aligned}$$

$$= \mathrm{E}_t \left[\frac{\partial}{\partial t} g(t; v) \right] - \mathrm{E}_t \left[g(t; v) \lambda(t; v) \right]$$

$$+ \mathrm{E}_t \left[g(t; v) \right] \mathrm{E}_t \lambda(t; v),$$

$$= \mathrm{E}_t \left[\frac{\partial}{\partial t} g(t; v) \right] - \mathrm{cov}_t \left[g(t; v), \lambda(t; v) \right]. \qquad \square$$

This formula can be applied directly to the equations:

$$g(t; v) = \lambda(t; v),$$
$$r(t; v) = \lambda(t; v).$$

Corollary 4:

$$\frac{d\tilde{\lambda}(t)}{dt} = \frac{\partial}{\partial t} \mathrm{E}_t \lambda(t; v),$$
$$= \mathrm{E}_t \frac{\partial}{\partial t} \lambda(t; v) - \mathrm{var}_t \left[\lambda(t; v) \right].$$

If we wish to analyse the evolution of the mean of the individual hazard functions, it appears natural to begin with the aggregate hazard function. The preceding corollary shows, however, that this leads to an underestimation, since:

$$\mathrm{E}_t \frac{\partial}{\partial t} \lambda(t; v) \geq \frac{d\tilde{\lambda}(t)}{dt}.$$

This heterogeneity bias depends exclusively on the variability of the hazard function.

Remark 16: If we have intertemporal independence at the disaggregated level, i.e. $\lambda(t; v) = \lambda(v)$, then:

$$\frac{d\tilde{\lambda}(t)}{dt} = -\mathrm{var}\left[\lambda(v) \right] \leq 0,$$

reflecting the negative relationship presented in proposition 34.

Corollary 5: If the heterogeneity is constant, and if the mapping $v \to \lambda(t; v)$ is increasing for all t, then:

$$\mathrm{E}_t \frac{\partial}{\partial t} r(t; v) \leq \frac{d\tilde{r}(t)}{dt}.$$

For a proof see exercise 10.

This result is analogous to the one we found for the hazard function. The apparently reasonable approximation to the evolving mean of the remaining individual durations, $\frac{d\bar{r}(t)}{dt}$, actually constitutes an overestimate.

Remark 17: When intertemporal independence obtains at the level of the individual, we see that $\frac{d\bar{r}(t)}{dt} \geq 0$, and we conclude that the average remaining duration is increasing.

12.5.1.3 Evolution of the Distribution of Heterogeneity

Finally, we can compare the distribution of heterogeneity at two different dates.

Proposition 44: Let the coefficient of heterogeneity be constant and the mapping $v \rightarrow \lambda(t; v)$ increasing for all t. Then, if $t' > t$, the distribution π_t first-order dominates $\pi_{t'}$.

Proof:

(i) Let $g(v)$ be an increasing function in v. Applying lemma 6, with $g(t; v) = g(v)$, we have:

$$\frac{\partial}{\partial t} \mathrm{E}[g(v)] = \mathrm{E}_t \left[\frac{\partial g(v)}{\partial t} \right] - \mathrm{cov}_t [g(v), \lambda(t; v)],$$
$$= -\mathrm{cov}_t [g(v), \lambda(t; v)].$$

This value is less than zero, since it represents the negation of two functions which are increasing in the same variable, v (cf. exercise 4).

(ii) So we see that the application of $t \rightarrow \mathrm{E}_t[g(v)]$ is decreasing. Consequently, we have established that for any increasing function g and for any two dates t and t', we have:

$$\mathrm{E}_t[g(v)] \geq \mathrm{E}_{t'}[g(v)].$$

According to definition 10, this implies that π_t first-order dominates $\pi_{t'}$. □

From proposition 36, the condition of first-order stochastic dominance may be summarized using the allocation functions associated with the distributions of heterogeneity. These functions are:

$$Q_t(v) = \int_0^v \pi_t(dv),$$

where we assume that v is positive.

Let $Q_{t'}(v) \geq Q_t(v)$, $\forall t' \geq t$, $\forall v$. Since the hazard function increases with v, these inequalities clearly describe the mathematical formulation of the mover-stayer model. The proportion of stayers increases with time regardless of the specific definition of stayers, that is, the limit value v chosen to distinguish between stayers and movers.

We have seen that in some cases direct calculation of the distribution of the duration is possible. For example, if the disaggregated distribution is exponential $\lambda(t; v) = v$, and the distribution of heterogeneity is gamma, then:

$$\pi(v) = \frac{a^v v^{v-1}(-av)}{\Gamma(v)}.$$

We have already established, cf. example 11, that the aggregate duration follows a Pareto distribution:

$$\tilde{S}(t) = \frac{1}{\left(1+\frac{t}{a}\right)^v}.$$

The distribution of heterogeneity at time t has the density function:

$$\pi(t; v) = \exp(-vt)\frac{a^v v^{v-1}\exp(-av)}{\Gamma(v)},$$

$$\left[\int_0^\infty \exp(-vt)\frac{a^v v^{v-1}\exp(av)}{\Gamma(v)}dv\right]^{-1}$$

$$= \frac{(a+t)^{v-1}\exp(-v)(a+t)v^{v-1}}{\Gamma(v)}.$$

At time t, $\frac{v}{(a+t)}$ follows a gamma distribution parametrized by v. The cumulative functions shift toward a line parallel to the abscissa as t increases. Over this period the population becomes increasingly homogeneous, and at the limit, when $t = +\infty$, there is no differentiation at all – the distributions of heterogeneity converge to zero.

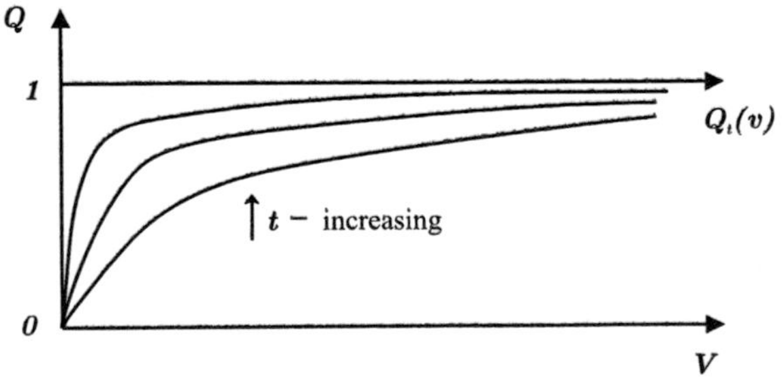

Fig. 12.14. Distribution of heterogeneity – gamma function

12.5.2 *Consequences of Ignoring Heterogeneity*

Failing to account for the phenomenon of heterogeneity may result in a significant bias in parameter estimates. We have examined these types of biases in the case of the evolution of the hazard and the average duration functions.

Certain types of parametric models allow us to perform very precise tests for bias. We shall examine the case with independent, uncensored observations on duration which we denote $Y_i,\ i = 1, \dots, n$. These data fit an underlying model of proportional hazard with heterogeneity. The individual hazard function is:

$$\lambda\,(\mathbf{x}; t; v; \boldsymbol{\beta}) = \exp\,(-\mathbf{x}\boldsymbol{\beta} + v)\,\lambda_0\,(t),$$

where the distribution of the factor of heterogeneity is given by π.

This model can be expressed in the following linear formulation:

$$\log\,[\Lambda_0\,(Y_i)] = \mathbf{x}_i\boldsymbol{\beta} + u_i + v_i, \quad i = 1, \dots, n, \tag{12.8}$$

where u_i and v_i are independent with distributions:

$$g\,(u) = \exp\,(u)\exp\left[-\exp\,(u)\right], \quad \text{and} \quad \pi,$$

respectively.

Assume that we proceed to use maximum likelihood to estimate the parameter $\boldsymbol{\beta}$, but forget about the presence of the heterogeneity factor. The estimator we obtain, $\hat{\boldsymbol{\beta}}_0$, is determined from a misspecified model:

$$\log\,[\Lambda_0\,(y_i)] = \mathbf{x}_i\boldsymbol{\beta} + u_i, \quad i = 1, \dots, n.$$

A demonstration of the following result is provided in appendix 12.1.

If the model contains a constant term:

$$\mathbf{x}_i\boldsymbol{\beta} = c + \mathbf{x}_i^*\mathbf{d},$$

and if c and $\mathbf{d}$ are estimated using maximum likelihood without considering the issue of heterogeneity:

Proposition 45:

(i) The estimator of $\mathbf{d}$ is consistent.

(ii) The estimator of the constant term c is not, in general, consistent, and the asymptotic bias is independent of the values assumed by the explanatory variables.

(iii) If the factor of heterogeneity v has mean zero, the asymptotic bias of the constant is positive.

Consequently, we see that in this model the bias only affects one of the parameters. Furthermore, it is an easy matter in this case to correct the bias. Let us examine the residuals of the estimation:

$$\hat{u}_i = \log\left[\Lambda_0\left(y_i\right)\right] - \hat{c}_0 - \mathbf{x}_i^*\hat{\mathbf{d}}_0, \quad i = 1, \ldots, n.$$

When the number of observations is large, we have approximately:

$$\hat{u}_i \approx \log\left[\Lambda_0\left(y_i\right)\right] - \operatorname{plim}_n\left(\hat{c}_0\right) - \mathbf{x}_i^*\mathbf{d},$$

and so:

$$\begin{aligned}\frac{1}{n}\sum_{i=1}^{n}\hat{u}_i &\approx \frac{1}{n}\sum_{i=1}^{n}\log\left[\Lambda_0\left(y_i\right)\right] - \operatorname{plim}_n\left(\hat{c}_0\right) - \frac{1}{n}\sum_{i=1}^{n}\mathbf{x}_i^*\mathbf{d},\\ &\approx c_0 - \operatorname{plim}_n\left(\hat{c}_0\right) - \frac{1}{n}\sum_{i=1}^{n}u_i,\\ &\approx c_0 - \operatorname{plim}_n\left(\hat{c}_0\right) - \mathrm{E}\left(u_i\right).\end{aligned}$$

Thus the estimator of the constant may be adjusted by the difference between the mean of the residual and the theoretical expectation of the error term. This latter is approximated by:

$$\mathrm{E}\left(u\right) \approx -0.57.$$

Notice that this simple method of correcting for the bias does not work if the data is censored.

12.5.3 Parametric Treatment of Heterogeneity

One reasonable way of dealing with heterogeneity is to choose a distribution for the heterogeneity, π, from an appropriate family of parametric distributions. Thus we may select a distribution permitting analytical integration of the basic survival function. This approach was used by Lancaster [Lan79] for certain proportional risk models.

12.5.3.1 Form of the Likelihood

The hazard function is:

$$\lambda_i\left(t\right) = \exp\left(\mathbf{x}_i\boldsymbol{\beta}\right) g\left(t; b\right).$$

After introducing a factor of heterogeneity indicating the omitted variables, we have:

$$\lambda_i\left(t; v\right) = \exp\left(\mathbf{x}_i\boldsymbol{\beta} + v\right) g\left(t, b\right).$$

Integrating, we obtain the survival function:

$$S\left(y_i; \mathbf{x}_i\boldsymbol{\beta} + v, b\right) = \exp\left[-\int_0^{y_i}\lambda_i\left(u; v\right) du\right],$$

$$= \exp\left[-\exp(\mathbf{x}_i\boldsymbol{\beta} + v)\int_0^{y_i} g(u, b)\,du\right],$$

$$= \exp\left[-\exp(\mathbf{x}_i\boldsymbol{\beta} + v)\,G(y_i, b)\right],$$

where G denotes the primitive of g at zero.

At this point it remains to specify the distribution of the error term v, or, equivalently, of $\exp(v)$. Notice that, as an alternative to introducing a constant term on the right-hand side, we can postulate that $\mathrm{E}\left[\exp(v)\right] = 1$.

Furthermore, we have seen that, when $\exp(v)$ follows a gamma distribution, it may be impossible to integrate the survival function analytically. In this case we specify $\mu = \exp(v)$, a gamma distribution with mean one and variance σ^2, for the error term. The density function is:

$$\pi\left(\mu; \sigma^2\right) = \frac{\left(\frac{1}{\sigma^2}\right)^{\frac{1}{\sigma^2}} \exp\left(-\frac{\mu}{\sigma^2}\right)\mu^{\frac{1}{\sigma^2}-1}}{\Gamma\left(\frac{1}{\sigma^2}\right)}. \tag{12.9}$$

After integration, the survival function is:

$$\begin{aligned}
&\tilde{S}\left(y_i \mid \mathbf{x}_i; b, \boldsymbol{\beta}, \sigma^2\right) \\
&\quad= \int_0^{\infty} S\left[y_i, \mathbf{x}_i\boldsymbol{\beta} + \log(\mu), b\right]\pi\left(\mu; \sigma^2\right)d\mu, \\
&\quad= \int_0^{\infty} \exp\left[-\exp(\mathbf{x}_i\boldsymbol{\beta})\,G(y_i; b)\right] \\
&\qquad\times \frac{\left(\frac{1}{\sigma^2}\right)^{\frac{1}{\sigma^2}} \exp\left(-\frac{\mu}{\sigma^2}\right)\mu^{\frac{1}{\sigma^2}-1}}{\Gamma\left(\frac{1}{\sigma^2}\right)}d\mu, \\
&\quad= \frac{\left(\frac{1}{\sigma^2}\right)^{\frac{1}{\sigma^2}}}{\left[\frac{1}{\sigma^2} + \exp(\mathbf{x}_i\boldsymbol{\beta})\,G(y_i; b)\right]^{\frac{1}{\sigma^2}}}, \\
&\quad= \left[1 + \sigma^2\exp(\mathbf{x}_i\boldsymbol{\beta})\,G(y_i; b)\right]^{-\sigma^2}.
\end{aligned}$$

Remark 18: The case of no heterogeneity is obtained by letting σ^2 tend to zero.

$$\begin{aligned}
&\lim_{\sigma^2\to 0}\tilde{S}\left(y_i \mid \mathbf{x}_i; b; \boldsymbol{\beta}, \sigma^2\right) \\
&\quad= \lim_{\sigma^2\to 0}\left[1 + \sigma^2\exp(\mathbf{x}_t\boldsymbol{\beta})\,G(y_i; b)\right]^{-\sigma^{-2}}, \\
&\quad= \lim_{\sigma^2\to 0}\left\{\exp\left(-\frac{1}{\sigma^2}\right)\log\left[1 + \sigma^2\exp(\mathbf{x}_t\boldsymbol{\beta})\,G(y_i; b)\right]\right\}, \\
&\quad= \exp\left[-\exp(\mathbf{x}_i\boldsymbol{\beta})\,G(y_i, b)\right].
\end{aligned}$$

We obtain the density function for this model, accounting for heterogeneity, by partially differentiating the survival function. Thus:

$$\begin{aligned}\tilde{f}\left(y_i | \mathbf{x}_i; b, \beta, \sigma^2\right) &= -\frac{\partial}{\partial y}\tilde{S}\left(y_i | \mathbf{x}_i; b, \beta, \sigma^2\right), \\ &= \exp\left[-\exp\left(\mathbf{x}_i\beta\right)\right] G\left(y_i; b\right) \\ &\quad \times \left[1 + \sigma^2 \exp\left(\mathbf{x}_i\beta\right) G\left(y_i; b\right)\right]^{-\sigma^{-2}-1}.\end{aligned}$$

And the hazard function is:

$$\tilde{\lambda}\left(y_i | \mathbf{x}_i; b, \beta, \sigma^2\right) = \frac{\exp\left(\mathbf{x}_i\beta\right) g\left(y_i, b\right)}{1 + \sigma^2 \exp\left(\mathbf{x}_i\beta\right) G\left(y_i; b\right)}.$$

We see that this function is decreasing in σ^2, which is consistent with the mover-stayer model.

Finally, the log-likelihood is given by:

$$\begin{aligned}\log\left[L\left(b, \beta, \sigma^2\right)\right] &= \sum_{J_1} \mathbf{x}_i\beta + \sum_{J_1} \log\left[g\left(y_i; b\right)\right] \\ &\quad - \sum_{J_1}\left[1 + \sigma^2 \exp\left(\mathbf{x}_i\beta\right) G\left(y_i; b\right)\right] \\ &\quad - \frac{1}{\sigma^2}\sum_{i=1}^{n} \log\left[1 + \sigma^2 \exp\left(\mathbf{x}_i\beta\right) G\left(y_i; b\right)\right].\end{aligned}$$

The parameters may be estimated by means of maximum likelihood.

12.5.3.2 The Assumption of Homogeneity

The estimator of the auxiliary parameter σ^2, which we used in the previous model, provides the opportunity to construct some hypothesis tests. In particular, we may wish to test for homogeneity:

$$H_0 : \sigma^2 = 0.$$

Let us denote, $\hat{b}$, $\hat{\beta}$, and $\hat{\sigma}^2$, the maximum-likelihood estimators of the model calculated without accounting for the constraint that $\alpha = \sigma^2$ must be positive. Note that, even though the constraint has not been explicitly taken into account, the function:

$$S\left(y | \mathbf{x}; b; \beta, \alpha\right) = \left[1 + \alpha \exp\left(\mathbf{x}\beta\right) G\left(y, b\right)\right]^{-\alpha-1} \qquad (12.10)$$

only makes sense if $\alpha \geq 0$. In consequence, the null hypothesis defines a bound on the possible values assumed by α, and so one of the standard regularity conditions of an asymptotically normal distribution is violated. Furthermore, it is not even clear that a solution to the unconstrained likelihood equations exists:

$$0 = \frac{\partial \log [L(\alpha, \beta, b)]}{\partial \left(\hat{\alpha}, \hat{\beta}, \hat{b}\right)'},$$

since a maximum-likelihood solution may, under certain conditions, lie on the boundary of the domain.

While we do not wish to delve too deeply into the theoretical difficulties, it is of some interest to illustrate this problem by evaluating the asymptotic score under the null hypothesis for an uncensored exponential model with heterogeneity. This case corresponds to $g(y, b) = 1$ and $G(y, b) = y$.

The density function is:

$$f\left(y_i | \mathbf{x}_i \beta, \sigma^2\right) = \exp(\mathbf{x}_i \beta) \left[1 + \sigma^2 \exp(\mathbf{x}_i \beta)\, y_i\right]^{-\frac{1}{\sigma^2} - 1},$$

and the log-likelihood for the uncensored case is:

$$\log\left[L_n\left(\beta, \sigma^2\right)\right] = \sum_{i=1}^{n} \mathbf{x}_i \beta,$$

$$= \left(\frac{1}{\sigma^2} + 1\right) \sum_{i=1}^{n} \log\left[1 + \sigma^2 \exp(\mathbf{x}_i \beta)\, y_i\right].$$

Generally, the asymptotic score evaluated under the null hypothesis, given by:

$$\lim_{n \to \infty} \frac{1}{n} \frac{\partial \log [L_n(\beta, 0)]}{\partial \sigma^2},$$

is null. Let us examine its value in this case.

The easiest way to find the score is to perform a limited expansion of the log-likelihood $L_n\left(\beta, \sigma^2\right)$ in the neighbourhood of $\sigma^2 = 0$. We have:

$$\log\left[L_n\left(\beta, \sigma^2\right)\right] \approx \sum_{i=1}^{n} \mathbf{x}_i \beta - \left(\frac{1}{\sigma^2} + 1\right)$$

$$\sum_{i=1}^{n} \left[\sigma^2 \exp(\mathbf{x}_i \beta)\, y_i - \frac{\sigma^2}{2} \exp\left(2\mathbf{x}_i \beta y_i^2\right)\right],$$

$$\approx \sum_{i=1}^{n} \mathbf{x}_i \beta - \sum_{i=1}^{n} \exp(\mathbf{x}_i \beta)\, y_i$$

$$+ \sigma^2 \left[-\sum_{i=1}^{n} \exp(\mathbf{x}_i \beta)\, y_i + \frac{1}{2} \exp\left(2\mathbf{x}_i \beta y_i^2\right)\right],$$

yielding:

$$\frac{\partial \log [L_n(\boldsymbol{\beta}, 0)]}{\partial \sigma^2} = -\sum_{i=1}^{n} \exp(\mathbf{x}_i \boldsymbol{\beta})\, y_i + \frac{1}{n} \sum_{i=1}^{n} \exp(2\mathbf{x}_i \boldsymbol{\beta})\, y_i^2,$$

$$= -\sum_{i=1}^{n} z_i + \frac{1}{2} \sum_{i=1}^{n} z_i^2,$$

where the $\mathbf{z}_i$-s are independent variables with the same exponential distribution parametrized by one.

The asymptotic score is:

$$\lim_n \frac{1}{n} \frac{\partial \log [L_n(\boldsymbol{\beta}, 0)]}{\partial \sigma^2} = \lim_n \left(-\frac{1}{n} \sum_{i=1}^{n} z_i + \frac{1}{2}\frac{1}{n} \sum_{i=1}^{n} z_i^2 \right),$$

$$= -\mathrm{E}(z) + \frac{1}{2} \mathrm{E}\left(z^2\right),$$

$$= -\mathrm{E}(z) + \frac{1}{2} \left\{ \mathrm{var}(z) + [\mathrm{E}(z)]^2 \right\} = 0,$$

since:

$$\mathrm{E}(z) = \mathrm{var}(z) = 1.$$

Observe that the boundary problem we encountered earlier does not affect our ability to apply classical test procedures. In particular, the maximum-score test is founded on the notion of a score which is asymptotically null.

12.6 Renewal Processes

In the preceding sections we focused our attention on the case in which we have a single observation of duration for each individual. This structure is appropriate when we are examining unemployment or life expectancy data. In other types of data, however, we may dispose of information on several durations for each individual. This will be the case, for example, when we examine certain types of purchases by household over a given period of time. Even though we now have several durations for the individual, this situation can be reduced to the preceding one if the durations are independent and have the same distribution. We simply create two indices, one for the agent and the other for the duration. This type of construct is called a *renewal process.*

In this section we shall examine some of the concepts underlying these models, particularly focussing on their relationship to the standard models of duration and to models with discrete dependent variables.

12.6.1 The Processes

We are interested in certain events which may occur at different times. In the following section we shall make the assumption that not more than one of these events may take place at any given point in time.

By convention, observations begin at time $t = 0$, and the timing of the events is denoted:

$$\begin{cases} S_1 & : \text{ time of the first event,} \\ \vdots & \\ S_n & : \text{ time of the } n\text{-th event.} \\ \vdots & \end{cases} \tag{12.11}$$

These dates constitute an increasing series of variables:

$$0 < S_1 < S_2 < \ldots < S_n < S_{n+1} < \ldots$$

Assume that, on average, the duration separating two of these events is strictly positive, implying:

$$\sup_n [S_n] = +\infty. \tag{12.12}$$

The variables $S_n, \ n = 1, 2, \ldots,$ may easily be expressed in terms of the delay between two successive events. Let ζ_n denote the interval separating the $(n-1)$-th and n-th event. We have:

$$\begin{aligned} \zeta_1 &= S_1 > 0, \\ \zeta_2 &= S_2 - S_1 > 0, \\ &\vdots \\ \zeta_n &= S_n - S_{n-1} > 0, \\ &\vdots \\ \Rightarrow S_n &= \zeta_1 + \zeta_2 + \ldots + \zeta_n, \quad \forall n. \end{aligned} \tag{12.13}$$

These concepts can be summarized by the graph in figure 12.15.

Within a bounded interval, a strictly finite number of events may occur. To express this we introduce the set of all positive integers, $\boldsymbol{N}_t$ – reflecting the

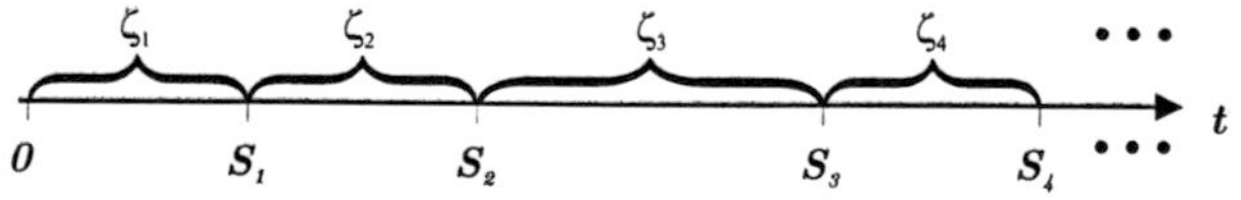

Fig. 12.15. Multiple durations

possible number of occurrences of the event during the interval $[0, t]$, $t \in \mathbb{R}^+$. We thus obtain a family of variables indexed by continuous time $t \in \mathbb{R}^2$. This set of variables contains exactly the same information as the series S_n, $n = 0, 1, \ldots$ reflecting the time of occurrence. We have:

$$\begin{aligned} (N_t = n) &= (S_n \leq t \leq S_{n+1}), \\ (S_n \leq t) &= (N_t \geq n), \end{aligned} \qquad \forall n \in N, \quad \forall t \in R^+. \qquad (12.14)$$

To summarize, we have established that:

Proposition 46: The process underlying the occurrence of these events can equivalently be described by any of the following three rules:

S_n, $n = 1, 2, \ldots$	—	describing the times of the occurrences.
ζ_n, $n = 1, 2, \ldots$	—	describing the interval separating the occurrences.
N_t, $t \in \mathbb{R}^+$	—	describing the number of occurrences occurring before t.

In consequence, when building our probabilistic model, we can choose a distribution to describe any one of the processes.

12.6.2 Definition and Properties of Renewal Processes

Definition 14: The occurrence of events along the lines just described is called a *renewal process* if and only if the durations ζ_n, $n = 1, 2, \ldots$ are independent and follow the same distribution F.

The most intuitive example of this phenomenon is obtained when we choose a shared distribution from the exponential family, which is associated with a constant risk function.

Definition 15: A renewal process is called a *Poisson renewal process* when the duration follows an exponential distribution:

$$F(\zeta) = 1 - \exp(-\lambda\zeta).$$

According to proposition 46, these definitions can be reformulated to reflect the processes (S_n) and (N_t).

12.6.2.1 Definitions Based on (S_n)

We use $*$ to denote the convolution of the probability distributions.

Proposition 47: The occurrences belong to a renewal process if and only if:

(i) The distances $S_n - S_{n-1}$, $n = 1, 2, \ldots$, are independent.
(ii) The distribution of S_n is F^{*n}, $n = 1, 2, \ldots$

The particular case of the Poisson renewal process derives from the products of the convolution of the exponential distributions. Thus S_n follows a gamma distribution with n degrees of freedom after a homothetic transformation. Its density function is:

$$f_n(s) = \frac{\lambda^n s^{n-1} \exp(-\lambda s)}{\Gamma(n)} z_{s \leq 0}.$$

12.6.2.2 Definitions Based on (N_t)

Properties equivalent to those we have just seen are much more difficult to demonstrate in the case of N_t. We shall limit our discussion to providing results for the Poisson process, and then explain how to find the distribution of N_t in the general case.

Proposition 48: The occurrences are described by a Poisson process if and only if:

(i) $t_1 < t_2 < \ldots < t_n$, $\forall n$, the variables $N_{t_1}, N_{t_2} - N_{t_1}, \ldots, N_{t_n} - N_{t_{n-1}}$ are independent (i.e. N_t is a process of independent increments).
(ii) The distribution of $N_t - N_s$ depends only on the distance $t - s$ (the process is stationary).

How can we derive the distribution of N_t from the distribution of the durations? We saw in equation 12.14 that $(N_t \geq n) = (S_n \leq t)$, and conclude that:

$$\begin{aligned}
\Pr(N_t = n) &= \Pr(N_t \geq n) - \Pr(N_t \geq n+1), \\
&= \Pr(S_n \leq t) - \Pr(S_{n+1} \leq t), \\
&= F^{*n}(t) - F^{*(n+1)}(t).
\end{aligned}$$

We now derive the distribution of the variable N_t for a Poisson process. We have:

$$\begin{aligned}
\Pr(N_t = n) &= F^{*n}(t) - F^{*(n+1)}(t), \\
&= \int_0^t \frac{\lambda^n s^{n-1} \exp(-\lambda s)}{(n-1)!} ds - \int_0^t \frac{\lambda^{n+1} s^n \exp(-\lambda s)}{n!} ds, \\
&= \int_0^t \frac{\lambda^n s^{n-1} \exp(-\lambda s)}{(n-1)!} ds - \left\{ \left[\frac{\lambda^n s^n \exp(-\lambda s)}{n!} \right]_0^t \right. \\
&\quad \left. + \int_0^t \frac{\lambda^n s^{n-1}}{(n-1)!} \exp(-\lambda s)\, ds \right\}.
\end{aligned}$$

Applying integration by parts, we obtain:

$$\Pr(N_t = n) = \frac{(\lambda t)^n \exp(-\lambda t)}{n!}.$$

Proposition 49: For a Poisson process, the frequency of occurrences of the event in question before some point in time t follows a Poisson distribution parametrized by λt.

Consequently, we see that postulating a Poisson distribution for discrete values describing the outcome of some event, such as the number of patent applications made by firms, is tantamount to assuming that the distances between the times the applications are made follow an exponential distribution. This assumed distribution in turn justifies the choice of the functional form $\lambda = \exp(\mathbf{x}_i \beta)$ to describe how the parameter is related to the explanatory variables. It also illuminates why the assumption that the modelling error follows a gamma distribution in the case of heterogeneity allows us to integrate the Poisson model as well as the exponential model associated with duration data.

12.6.3 Conserving Duality Properties During Estimation

In conclusion, we shall verify that the "duality" – the equivalence between the representation of durations and counting the number of events in a given period – is maintained at the estimation level when maximum-likelihood methods are applied.

Assume that we have observed events following a Poisson process occurring between time 0 and t. We have N_t, the number of occurrences, and $S_1 \ldots, S_N$, the times of occurrence.

There exist two simple approximations to the parameter λ.

12.6.3.1 Estimation from N_t

We examine the observation N_t. The likelihood is:

$$L(N_t; \lambda) = \frac{(\lambda t) \exp(-\lambda t)}{N_t!},$$

and the maximum-likelihood estimator of λ is:

$$\hat{\lambda}_t = \frac{N_t}{t},$$

the observed frequency of the occurrence of the event over the period in question. This estimator is consistent as t tends toward infinity. Its variance is:

$$\operatorname{var}(\hat{\lambda}) = \frac{\lambda t}{t^2} = \frac{\lambda}{t}.$$

12.6.3.2 Estimation from $S_1 \dots S_{N_t}$

Letting N_t be fixed, we again apply the maximum-likelihood method to a truncated sample of durations $\zeta_1, \dots, \zeta_{N_t}$, omitting the last $t - S_{N_t}$ observations. The likelihood can be approximated by:

$$\tilde{L}(\lambda) = \prod_{j=1}^{N_t} \left[\lambda \exp(-\lambda \zeta_i)\right].$$

The corresponding approximate maximum-likelihood estimator is:

$$\tilde{\lambda}_t = \frac{N_t}{\sum_{j=1}^{N_t} \zeta_j}.$$

Clearly, as t tends to infinity,

$$\frac{1}{t} \sum_{j=1}^{N_t} \zeta_j = \frac{S_{N_t}}{t} \to 1,$$

and the estimators $\hat{\lambda}_t$ and $\tilde{\lambda}_t$ are asymptotically equivalent.

The fact that right-hand side truncation can be ignored here is explained by the fact that the proportion of observations eliminated, as t tends to infinity (given by $\frac{1}{N_t+1}$), tends to zero.

12.7 Optimal Search Strategy

In this section we develop a model of optimal job search. Optimal, in this case, means that the job-seeker attempts to maximize the expected value of his income.

We shall find that his optimal behaviour is to accept the first offer for which the salary ω exceeds a threshold level ξ. This cut-off point can be construed as the reservation wage, and we use this construct to relate models of duration to the Tobit model in chapter 7 and thus to explain the salary the individual finally earns.

Furthermore, this search model will motivate a more detailed analysis of the hazard function, which will appear in composite form – with one aspect corresponding to the supply of jobs and one to the demand for jobs, i.e. the behaviour of the job-seeker.

12.7.1 Solution to the Optimal Search Problem

In order to simplify the presentation we start from a stationary perspective. Assume that the solution exists and is stationary (the existence of the solution is based on the Bellman optimallity principle as well as on several properties of Martingales.)

Consider an individual looking for work who wishes to maximize the expectation of all future incomes over an infinite horizon. Over time she receives a series of randomly distributed job offers. Assume that the occurrence of these job offers is distributed as a Poisson process (cf. section 12.6.2) with frequency μ. In particular, let the duration separating two successive offers follow an exponential distribution with density:

$$\mu \exp(-\mu t).$$

Each job offer is associated with a salary ω. The salaries are assumed random, uncorrelated with the time of occurrence, and share the same distribution F.

The individual responds to each offer in one of the following ways:

(i) She accepts the job offer and (instantaneously) receives the salary ω for all subsequent periods.
(ii) She rejects the offer and (instantaneously) receives some amount b until the next offer, at which point the process repeats.

The sum of money denoted b may represent, for example, the difference between unemployment insurance benefits and the cost of job search.

This (stationary) process can be summarized with a function Ψ, which, for a given wage proposal ω, assumes the values $\Psi(\omega) = 1$ for acceptance and $\Psi(\omega) = 0$ for rejection.

Finally, let us denote Ψ^* the optimal response and I^* the "value of the search" (the expected value of future income corresponding to the optimal search strategy.) Now we wish to examine how Ψ^* and I^* are determined.

Consider a point in time, denoted 0, at which an offer is received. Denote the time of the next offer $\tilde{\xi}$. Incorporating a discounting factor, ρ, and assuming that the individual behaves according to Ψ at time 0 and according to Ψ^* from time ζ on, expected total income is:

$$\begin{aligned} V\left(\Psi, I^*\right) = & \int_0^{\infty} \Psi(\omega) \frac{\omega}{\rho} dF(\omega) \\ & + \mathrm{E}\left[\int_0^{\tilde{\xi}} b \exp(-\rho t)\, dt + I^* \exp\left(-\rho \tilde{\xi}\right)\right] \\ & \times \int_0^{\infty} [1 - \Psi(\omega)]\, dF(\omega). \end{aligned} \tag{12.15}$$

If she accepts the job her cumulative income will be:

$$\frac{\omega}{\rho} = \int_0^{\infty} \omega \exp(-\rho t)\, dt.$$

If she rejects it, this amount is:

$$\mathrm{E}\left[\int_0^{\tilde{\xi}} b\exp(-\rho t)\,dt + I^*\exp\left(-\rho\tilde{\xi}\right)\right].$$

At time zero, it is obviously in the individual's interest to adjust her behaviour, Ψ, so as to maximize the function $V(\Psi, I^*)$. We conclude that the optimal strategy is such that:

$$V\left(\Psi^*, I^*\right) = \max_{\Psi} V\left(\Psi, I^*\right) = I^*. \tag{12.16}$$

These are the equations we now solve to find the expression for Ψ^* and I^*.

Proposition 50:

(i) The optimal function Ψ^* has the form:

$$\Psi^*(\omega) = \begin{cases} 1, & \text{if } \omega \geq \xi, \\ 0, & \text{otherwise.} \end{cases}$$

(ii) The threshold, ξ, representing the reservation wage, is defined by:

$$\xi = b + \frac{\mu}{\rho}\int_{\xi}^{\infty}(\omega - \xi)\,dF(\omega).$$

(iii) The optimal level of human capital is given by:

$$I^* = \int_{\xi}^{\infty}\frac{\omega - \xi}{\rho}\,dF(\omega) + \frac{\xi}{\rho}.$$

Proof:

(i) Notice, to begin with, that it is possible to simplify the expression for the function $V(\Psi, I^*)$. We have:

$$\begin{aligned}
&\mathrm{E}\left[\int_0^{\tilde{\xi}} b\exp(-\rho t) + I^*\exp\left(-\rho\tilde{\xi}\right)\right] \\
&= \mathrm{E}\left\{\frac{b}{\rho}\left[1 - \exp\left(-\rho\tilde{\xi}\right)\right] + I^*\exp\left(-\rho\tilde{\xi}\right)\right\}, \\
&= \frac{b}{\rho} + \left(I^* - \frac{b}{\rho}\right)\mathrm{E}\left[\exp\left(-\rho\tilde{\xi}\right)\right], \\
&= \frac{b}{\rho} + \left(I^* - \frac{b}{\rho}\right)\frac{\mu}{\mu + \rho}, \\
&= \frac{b + I^*\mu}{\mu + \rho}.
\end{aligned}$$

Substituting into expression (12.15) we have:

$$\begin{aligned} V\left(\Psi, I^*\right) &= \int_0^\infty \Psi\left(\omega\right) \frac{\omega}{\rho} dF\left(\omega\right) \\ &\quad + \frac{b + I^*\mu}{\mu+\rho} \int_0^\infty \left[1 - \Psi\left(\omega\right)\right] dF\left(\omega\right), \\ &= \frac{b+I^*\mu}{\mu+\rho} + \int_0^I \Psi\left(\omega\right) \left(\frac{\omega}{\rho} - \frac{b+I^*\mu}{\mu+\rho}\right) dF\left(\omega\right). \end{aligned}$$

The maximum of V over all possible strategies $\Psi = \{0, 1\}$ is clearly obtained at:

$$\Psi^*\left(\omega\right) = \begin{cases} 1, & \text{if } \omega \geq \rho \frac{b+I^*\mu}{\mu+\rho}, \\ 0, & \text{otherwise.} \end{cases}$$

Yielding the threshold:

$$\xi = \rho \frac{b+I^*\mu}{\mu+\rho}.$$

(ii) The optimal value of I^* can now be solved as:

$$\begin{aligned} I^* &= V\left(\Psi^*, I^*\right) \\ &= \frac{b+I^*\mu}{\mu+\rho} + \int_0^\infty \Psi^*\left(\omega\right)\left(\frac{\omega}{\rho} - \frac{b+I^*\mu}{\mu+\rho}\right) dF\left(\omega\right), \\ &= \frac{\xi}{\rho} + \int_0^\infty Z_{\omega \geq \xi} \frac{\omega - \xi}{\rho} dF\left(\omega\right). \end{aligned}$$

(iii) This equation, combined with the definition of the threshold, directly yields the equation for the reservation wage. □

Corollary 6: The reservation wage satisfies the following condition:

$$\xi = b + \frac{\mu}{\rho}\int_\xi^\infty \left[1 - F\left(\omega\right)\right] d\omega. \tag{12.17}$$

Proof: We have:

$$\xi = b - \frac{\mu}{\rho}\int_\xi^\infty \left(\omega - \xi\right) d\left[1 - F\left(\omega\right)\right].$$

Integration by parts yields:

$$\xi = b - \frac{\mu}{\rho}\{(\omega - \xi)[1 - F(\omega)]\}\Big|_{\xi}^{\infty} + \frac{\mu}{\rho}\int_{\xi}^{\infty}[1 - F(\omega)]\,d\omega,$$

$$\xi = b + \frac{\mu}{\rho}\int_{\xi}^{\infty}[1 - F(\omega)]\,d\omega. \qquad \square$$

We see from corollary 6 that ξ is uniquely defined. Furthermore, the function:

$$h(\xi) = \xi - b - \frac{\mu}{\rho}\int_{0}^{\infty}[1 - F(\omega)]\,d\omega,$$

is continuous in ξ, positive as ξ tends to plus infinity, and negative for $\xi = 0$. Clearly it has a solution. In addition:

$$\frac{dh(\xi)}{d\xi} = 1 + \frac{\mu}{\rho}[1 - F(\omega)]\,d\omega > 0.$$

Since h is strictly increasing, the solution is unique.

12.7.2 Distribution of the Duration

The length of unemployment spells in this model depends upon two factors: the supply of work and the behaviour of the job-seeker (who does not accept every proposition).

Denoting the time at which she actually accepts a job ζ, the hazard function associated with ζ is easy to find. We have:

$$\begin{aligned}
\lambda(t) &= \lim_{dt \to 0} \frac{1}{dt}\Pr[t < \zeta \le t + dt \mid \zeta \ge t],\\
&= \lim_{dt \to 0} \frac{1}{dt}\Pr[A \mid B],\\
&= \lim_{dt \to 0} \frac{1}{dt}\Pr[C \mid B]\Pr[D],\\
&= \mu \Pr[\omega > \xi],
\end{aligned}$$

where the propositions are defined by:

A — a suitable job offer received between t and $t + dt$,
B — unemployed at time t,

C — a job offer received between t and $t + dt$,
D — the job offer accepted.

$$\lambda = \mu [1 - F(\xi)] \tag{12.18}$$

The instantaneous frequency is independent of time, which reflects our assumption of a stationary process.

Equation (12.18) reflects a decomposition of the duration of unemployment into an involuntary aspect, associated with μ, and a voluntary aspect $[1 - F(\xi)]$.

Obviously, in our stationary-process framework we cannot distinguish between these two aspects on the basis of simple observations on the duration ξ. This distinction becomes possible, however, if we have data, not only on the duration, but also on the salary (cf. section 12.7.4).

12.7.3 Calculating Elasticities (Chesher-Lancaster [CL83])

If we desire to use the model of optimal job search in the context of policy analysis, our interest will focus on how certain exogenous variables which impact on search behaviour (i.e. on μ and F) and on the cost of job search (i.e. on b) affect the wage rate and duration of unemployment. In order to pursue this we shall calculate several elasticities.

12.7.3.1 Elasticities with Respect to b

Differentiating equation (12.17), for the reservation wage with respect to b, we obtain:

$$\begin{aligned}\frac{\partial \xi}{\partial b} &= 1 - \frac{\mu}{\rho}[1 - F(\xi)]\frac{\partial \xi}{\partial b},\\ &= \frac{1}{1 + \frac{\mu}{\rho}[1 - F(\xi)]},\\ &= \frac{1}{1 + \frac{\lambda}{\rho}}.\end{aligned}$$

Thus, the elasticity of the reservation wage with respect to b is:

$$\frac{\partial \log(\xi)}{\partial \log(b)} = \frac{b}{\xi}\frac{1}{1 + \frac{\lambda}{\rho}}. \tag{12.19}$$

From corollary 6 we see that the reservation wage must be strictly greater that b, implying that:

$$0 \leq \frac{\partial \log(\xi)}{\partial \log(b)} \leq 1. \tag{12.20}$$

For example, an increase in unemployment insurance will have a positive effect on b, and in consequence on the reservation wage. Under the optimal strategy, the job-seeker will tend to refuse a greater number of jobs. This can be observed directly if we calculate the rate of re-employment λ :

$$\frac{\partial \log(\lambda)}{\partial \log(\beta)} = -\frac{\partial \log\{\mu[1-F(\xi)]\}}{\partial \log(b)},$$

$$\frac{\partial \log(\lambda)}{\partial \log(b)} = -\frac{f(\xi)}{1-F(\xi)}\frac{1}{1+\frac{\lambda}{\rho}}. \tag{12.21}$$

The hazard function for the distribution of salary offers, $\frac{f}{1-f}$, appears explicitly in this equation.

12.7.3.2 *Elasticities with Respect to μ*

Reasoning in the same vein, we derive the equation for the reservation wage:

$$\begin{aligned}\frac{\partial \xi}{\partial \mu} &= \frac{1}{\rho}\int_{\xi}^{\infty}[1-F(\xi)]\frac{\partial \xi}{\partial \mu},\\ &= \frac{1}{\rho}\int_{\xi}^{\infty}[1-F(\omega)]\,d\omega\,\frac{1}{1+\frac{\lambda}{\rho}},\\ &= \frac{\xi-b}{\mu\left(1+\frac{\lambda}{\rho}\right)},\end{aligned}$$

$$\frac{\partial \log(\xi)}{\partial \log(\mu)} = \frac{\xi-b}{\xi}\frac{1}{1+\frac{\lambda}{\rho}}. \tag{12.22}$$

This elasticity is also bounded by zero and one. The elasticity for the rate of re-employment is:

$$\frac{\partial \log(\lambda)}{\partial \log(\mu)} = 1-\frac{f(\xi)}{1-F(\xi)}\frac{\xi-b}{1+\frac{\lambda}{\rho}}. \tag{12.23}$$

12.7.3.3 *Expressing Elasticities in Terms of the Salary Received*

When the job-seeker accepts a job, her average salary is given by:

$$\bar{\omega} = \mathrm{E}[\omega|\,\omega > \xi] = \frac{\int_{\xi}^{\infty}\omega dF(\omega)}{1-F(\xi)}.$$

Integrating by parts:

$$\bar{\omega} = \xi + \frac{\int_{\xi}^{\infty} [1 - F(\omega)]\, d\omega}{1 - F(\xi)},$$

$$= \xi + \frac{\xi - b}{\frac{\mu}{\rho}[1 - F(\xi)]},$$

and so:

$$\frac{\bar{\omega} - \xi}{\xi - b} = \frac{\rho}{\lambda}. \tag{12.24}$$

Consequently, we see that some elasticities can be expressed as functions of only the "salaries", $b,\ \xi,\ \bar{\omega}$, for which data may be available in some surveys. We have:

$$\begin{aligned} \frac{\partial \log(\xi)}{\partial \log(b)} &= \frac{b}{\xi}\frac{\bar{\omega} - \xi}{\bar{\omega} - b}, \\ \frac{\partial \log(\xi)}{\partial \log(\mu)} &= \frac{\xi - b}{\xi}\frac{\bar{\omega} - \xi}{\bar{\omega} - b}. \end{aligned} \tag{12.25}$$

12.7.4 Estimating Structural Models

Optimal job search models may form the basis for the simultaneous estimation of dependencies between explanatory variables and the supply function (μ, F), and the relationship between these variables and the reservation wage. Retaining the framework of a stationary process, we shall limit our examination to individual explanatory variables $\mathbf{x}_i$. These may appear in μ and F so that, for the i-th individual, we shall adopt the notation:

$$\mu(\mathbf{x}_i; \boldsymbol{\beta}) \quad \text{and} \quad \mathrm{F}(\omega; \mathbf{x}_i, \alpha).$$

The reservation wage for the i-th individual is defined by:

$$\xi_i = b + \frac{\mu(\mathbf{x}_i; \boldsymbol{\beta})}{\rho} \int_{\xi_i}^{\infty} [1 - F(\omega; \mathbf{x}_i, \alpha)]\, d\omega. \tag{12.26}$$

We see that this value depends upon $\mathbf{x}_i$, and that the specification is complete when we have the parameters $b,\ \alpha,\ \boldsymbol{\beta}$, and ρ. We write this function

$$\xi(\mathbf{x}_i; b, \alpha, \boldsymbol{\beta}, \rho).$$

Notice at this point that the assumption of optimal behaviour, which underlies equation (12.26), yields a specification which can be solved for the wage offer. This is an important difference between this model and the reservation wage analysis in the Tobit model (cf. chapter 7), where the specifications where selected independently.

Assume that the individual observations are independent and contain data on both the duration and the salary received. In light of the fact that some data may be truncated on the right-hand side, we can distinguish between two types of observations:

(i) uncensored observations ($i \in J_1$), for which we have both the duration and the actual salary, and

(ii) censored observations ($i \in J_2$), for which we have a truncated duration and the "salary" b, (which, to simplify, we assume fixed and identical across individuals).

Denoting $y_i = \min\left(\zeta_i, \bar{\zeta}_i\right)$ the observed duration, $\tilde{\omega}_i = \min(\omega_i, b)$ the observed wage, and d_i an index for truncated variables, the likelihood of the observations is given by:

$$L(y, d, \tilde{\omega}; b, \boldsymbol{\beta}, \alpha, \rho) = \prod_{i:d_i=1} \left[f_i(\omega_i \mid \omega_i > \xi_i)\, \tilde{f}_i(y_i)\right] \times \prod_{i:d_i=0} \left[1 - \tilde{F}_i(y_i)\right],$$

where $\tilde{f}_i$, and $\tilde{F}_i$ represent the distribution of the duration and where $f_i(\omega_i \mid \omega_i > \xi_i)$ designates the conditional density of ω_i given that $\omega_i > \xi_i$.

Since:

$$\begin{aligned}
1 - \tilde{F}_i(y_i) &= \exp(-\mu(\mathbf{x}_i; \boldsymbol{\beta}) \\
&\quad \times \{1 - F[\xi(\mathbf{x}_i; b, \boldsymbol{\beta}, \alpha, \rho), \mathbf{x}_i, \alpha]\}\, y_i), \\
\tilde{f}_i(y_i) &= \mu(\mathbf{x}_i; \boldsymbol{\beta}) \{1 - F[\xi(\mathbf{x}_i; b, \boldsymbol{\beta}, \alpha, \rho), \mathbf{x}_i, \alpha]\} \\
&\quad \times [1 - F_i(y_i)], \\
f_i(\omega_i \mid \omega_i > \xi_i) &= \frac{f(\omega_i; \mathbf{x}_i, \alpha)}{1 - F[\xi(\mathbf{x}_i; b, \boldsymbol{\beta}, \alpha, \rho)\, \mathbf{x}_i, \alpha]},
\end{aligned}$$

we finally arrive at the likelihood:

$$L(y, d, \tilde{\omega}; b, \boldsymbol{\beta}, \alpha, \rho) = \prod_{i=1}^{n} \left[1 - \tilde{F}_i(y_i)\right] \times \prod_{i \in J_1} \{\mu(\mathbf{x}_i; \boldsymbol{\beta})\, f(\omega_i; \mathbf{x}_i, \alpha)\}.$$

The parameters can now be estimated using maximum-likelihood procedures. Unfortunately, this will not necessarily be simple, as the reservation wage ξ_i, defined by the implicit equation (12.26), must be recalculated at each iteration.

It is not possible to solve this equation analytically, even for simple distributions of the wage offers (cf. exercise 9).

12.8 Non-Parametric and Semi-Parametric Approaches

In the preceding sections, we examined models of duration which were adapted to the data. To do this we specified distributions from the family of parametric distributions. This approach is only appropriate if the selected specification is correct or, at least, if the specification error has little impact on the results.

During our analysis of these models three key notions emerged in the context of the hazard function:

(i) how does it depend on time?
(ii) what impact do the exogenous variables have on the duration? and
(iii) what is the effect of heterogeneity?

In the simple case, when these effects are multiplicative, we obtained a function of the type:

$$\lambda(\mathbf{x}; t; v) = \lambda_0(t)\, g(\mathbf{x})\, v,$$

in which the base hazard, the effect over g of the exogenous variables, and the distribution of heterogeneity v are assigned a parametric form. Now we shall look at how robust the estimation methods are when applied to the principal parameters (i.e. those appearing in g) and to errors in the distribution and in v. From a practical perspective, it appears that the results are very sensitive to errors in the distribution of heterogeneity π, and a little less so to errors in the base hazard λ_0. We give an example of this sensitivity in the first section.

One way to deal with this lack of robustness is to avoid specifying a functional form for the distributions of λ_0 and/or π. This leads us to introduce models which are only partially parametric (semi-parametric) and joint estimation procedures for the parameters of interest and the unknown functions. We shall now examine these methods more closely for the cases of:

(i) non-parametric estimation of the hazard function in the absence of explanatory variables and of heterogeneity,
(ii) estimation of the effect of the explanatory variables when the base hazard is not specified, and
(iii) estimation of the distribution of heterogeneity and of the relevant parameters when only the functions λ and g are parametric.

In order to keep the presentation simple, we shall restrict our discussion to the main principles underlying these methods, and not delve into their asymptotic properties.

12.8.1 Non-Robustness with Respect to the Distribution of Heterogeneity

This particular form of lack of robustness is easily tested – we simply estimate the data under several specifications of the distribution π while keeping everything else constant. We reproduce the results of a study conducted by Kiefer and Neumann [KN81] using data on unemployment. The hazard function is:

$$\log\left[\lambda\left(\mathbf{x};\,t;\,v\right)\right] = \mathbf{x}\boldsymbol{\beta} + \mathbf{b}\log\left(\mathbf{t}\right) + \mathbf{v}.$$

The heterogeneity is modelled using normal, log-normal, and gamma distributions. Clearly, the estimates of the relevant parameters, b and β, differ significantly under the various assumptions.

Variables	Normal	Log-normal	Gamma
Constant	−3.92 (2.8)	−13.2 (4.7)	5.90 (3.4)
log(t)	−0.066 (0.15)	−0.708 (0.17)	−0.576 (0.17)
Age	0.0036 (0.048)	−0.106 (0.03)	−0.202 (0.06)
Education	0.0679 (0.233)	−0.322 (0.14)	−0.981 (0.301)
Previous level of Employment	−0.0512 (0.0149)	0.0042 (0.023)	−0.034 (0.016)
Amount of Unemployment Insurance	−0.0172 (0.0036)	0.0061 (0.0051)	−0.003 (0.004)
Married (0,1)	0.833 (0.362)	0.159 (0.30)	−0.607 (0.496)
Unemployment Rate	−26.12 (9.5)	25.8 (10.3)	−17.9 (11.2)
Education - Age	−0.0028 (0.0044)	0.0062 (0.034)	−0.0152 (0.0053)

Sample size 456; standard error in parenthesis

12.8.2 The Kaplan-Meier Estimator

The estimator most used for models of duration is the *Kaplan-Meier estimator*. It is used for duration data which is uncorrelated and identically distributed, and hence contains no explanatory variables and no heterogeneity. The data may be censored.

The hazard function λ_0 is not specified – it corresponds to a base survival function S_0. The underlying idea involves constructing an estimator of the survival rate which is based on a discrete model of duration. Denoting p_i^0 the probability of exit from the population during period i, and $P_i^0 = \prod_{j \leq i} \left(1 - p_j^0\right)$ the probability of not having exited at the beginning of $i + 1$, we can approximate the probability of leaving by replacing the theoretical quantities with their estimates. This procedure has two problems, however:

(i) The model is in discrete time, while the times of exit are random and hence not equi-distant.

(ii) The data may be censored.

To account for this latter issue, we must inspect each data point $y_i = \min(\zeta_i, \xi_i)$ and ascertain whether or not it is a censored value. Denote:

$$d_i = \begin{cases} 1, & \text{if } y_i < \xi_i, \\ 0, & \text{otherwise}, \end{cases}$$

to denote uncensored data.

In the case of complete data, the probability of exit is determined for the data of how many individuals left the population at this date. The value is:

$$N(y_i) = \sum_{j=1}^{n} I_{i,j},$$

where:

$$I_{ij} = \begin{cases} 1, & \text{if } y_j < y_i, \\ 0, & \text{otherwise}. \end{cases}$$

The corresponding probability is:

$$\Pr(y_i) = \frac{1}{n - N(y_i)}.$$

Applying this to our original idea, we obtain the following estimator.

Definition 16: The Kaplan-Meier estimator of the survival function is:

$$\hat{S}_0(t) = \prod_{i: y_i < t, d_i = 1} \left[1 - \frac{1}{n - N(y_i)}\right].$$

This estimator is very simple to calculate, requiring only a reordering of the variables. Denoting the ordered variables $y_{(i)} < \ldots < y_{(2)} < \ldots < y_{(n)}$, we distinguish between those which are, and those which are not, censored:

$$d_{(i)} = \begin{cases} 1, & \text{if complete,} \\ 0, & \text{otherwise.} \end{cases}$$

The estimator is:

$$\hat{S}_0(t) = \prod_{i:y_{(i)}<t} \left(1 - \frac{1}{n-i+1}\right)^{d_{(i)}}. \tag{12.27}$$

For example, if the observations are:

$$\begin{bmatrix} 5^+ & 2 & 1^+ & 3 & 6 & 7^+ & 8 \end{bmatrix},$$

(where the superscript + indicates that the data is censored), the ordered values are:

$$\begin{bmatrix} 1^+ & 2 & 3 & 5^+ & 6 & 7^+ & 8 \end{bmatrix}.$$

The Kaplan-Meier estimator of the survival function is:

$$\begin{aligned}
&\hat{S}(t) = 1 && \text{if } t \in [0, 2], \\
&\hat{S}(t) = \left(1 - \tfrac{1}{6}\right) && \text{if } t \in (2, 3], \\
&\hat{S}(t) = \left(1 - \tfrac{1}{6}\right)\left(1 - \tfrac{1}{5}\right) && \text{if } t \in (3, 6], \\
&\hat{S}(t) = \left(1 - \tfrac{1}{6}\right)\left(1 - \tfrac{1}{5}\right)\left(1 - \tfrac{1}{3}\right) && \text{if } t \in (6, 8], \\
&\hat{S}(t) = 0 && \text{if } t \in (8, \infty).
\end{aligned}$$

Remark 19: Clearly, the approximation to the survival function which we propose here is in the form of a step-wise function, while the true function is continuous. It is possible to smooth the estimator $\hat{S}$ in order to obtain a continuous function.

It can be shown that the Kaplan-Meier estimator is consistent and asymptotically normal. Or, more precisely:

Proposition 51: Assume that the duration data and the censoring (ξ_i), are stochastic and independent, with survival functions S_0 and S_1 respectively, for all values $t_1, \ldots, t_p$ we have:

$$\sqrt{n}\left[\hat{S}_0(t_1) - S_0(t_1), \ldots, \hat{S}_0(t_p) - S_0(t_p)\right] \sim \mathrm{N}(0, \Sigma).$$

The general form for Σ is:

$$\Sigma_{ij} = -S_0(t_1)\, S_0(t_j) \int_0^{\min(t_i, t_j)} \frac{dS_0(u)}{S_0(u)^2\, S_1(u)}.$$

Example 24: When the censoring and the duration follow the exponential distribution with parameters μ and λ respectively, we have:

$$
\begin{aligned}
S_0(u) &= \exp(-\lambda u), \\
S_1(u) &= \exp(-\mu u), \\
\Sigma_{ij} &= \exp\left[-\lambda\left(t_i + t_j\right)\right] \int_0^{\min\left(t_i, t_j\right)} \frac{\lambda \exp(-\lambda u)\, du}{\exp(-\mu - 2\lambda)\, u}, \\
&= \frac{\lambda}{\lambda + \mu} \exp\left[-\lambda\left(t_i + t_j\right)\right]\left[\exp(\lambda + \mu)\min\left(t_i, t_j\right) - 1\right].
\end{aligned}
$$

The variance is given by:

$$
\begin{aligned}
\operatorname{var}\left\{\sqrt{n}\left[\hat{S}_0(t) - S_0(t)\right]\right\} \approx\ & \frac{\lambda}{\lambda + \mu} \exp(-\lambda t) \\
& \times \left[\exp(\mu t) - \exp(-\lambda t)\right].
\end{aligned}
$$

As μ increases, censoring becomes more dominant and fewer uncensored observations remain, explaining why the variance is an increasing function of μ. At the limit, $\mu = +\infty$, the variance is infinite (except when $t = 0$).

In the other limiting case, $\mu = 0$, there is no censoring and the variance is $\exp(-\lambda t)\left[1 - \exp(-\lambda t)\right]$. This is minimized at the extremes $t = 0$ and $t = +\infty$.

Remark 20: If we calculate the estimator without considering the existence of censoring, we obtain the following approximation:

$$
\tilde{S}_0(t) = \prod_{i:y_i<t}\left[1 - \frac{1}{n - N(y_i)}\right].
$$

This is always less than $\hat{S}_0(t)$. It constitutes a consistent approximation to the survival function of Y and hence underestimates the survival of ζ.

12.8.3 Cox's Partial Likelihood

In the previous subsection we examined a non-parametric formulation. In general, the model comprises parameters and unknown functions simultaneously, so we need to develop tools which account for this duality. These methods are called semi-parametric. One of the first approaches to this problem to appear in the literature was *Cox's partial likelihood,* which applies to proportional hazard models. This model corresponds to a hazard function of the form:

$$
\lambda(t; \beta; \lambda_0) = \exp(x\beta)\, \lambda_0(t).
$$

The underlying idea is that we consider the base hazard function λ_0 as a nuisance parameter to be eliminated. Working with notation similar to that in the preceding paragraphs, we denote $y_{(1)} \leq \ldots \leq y_{(n)}$ the ordered, and perhaps censored, data; $d_{(i)}$ the variable indicating whether or not the observation $y_{(i)}$ is complete; and $\Re_{y_{(i)}} = \left\{ j : y_{(j)} \geq y_{(i)} \right\}$ the set of individuals remaining in the population at the point in time in which the one represented by $y_{(i)}$ exits.

Given that we know which individuals remain in the population, the probability that the next one to leave is the one associated with $y_{(i)}$ is:

$$\frac{\lambda\left(y_{(i)}; \beta, \lambda_0\right)}{\sum_{j \in \Re_{y_{(i)}}} \lambda\left(y_j; , \beta, \lambda_0\right)},$$

assuming, of course, that the observation $y_{(i)}$ is complete.

The expression for this probability can be simplified to:

$$\frac{\exp\left(\mathbf{x}_{(i)}\beta\right)}{\sum_{j \in \Re_{y_{(i)}}} \exp\left(\mathbf{x}_j \beta\right)},$$

where $\mathbf{x}_{(i)}$ denotes the values of the explanatory variables associated with $y_{(i)}$. Notice that the unknown function λ_0 has disappeared.

The partial likelihood is found by multiplying over the complete and the censored observations:

$$L_p(\beta) = \prod_{i=1}^{n} \left[\frac{\exp\left({}_i\beta\right)}{\sum_{j \in \Re_{y_{(i)}}} \exp\left(\mathbf{x}_j \beta\right)} \right]^{d_i} \tag{12.28}$$

Cox's partial maximum-likelihood estimator is thus defined as a solution, $\tilde{\beta}$, to the problem:

$$\max_{\beta} \left\{ \log\left[L_p(\beta) \right] \right\} = \sum_{i=1}^{n} d_i \log \left[\frac{\exp\left(\mathbf{x}_{(i)}\beta\right)}{\sum_{j \in \Re_{\left(y_{(i)}\right)}} \exp\left(\mathbf{x}_j \beta\right)} \right].$$

Remark 21: One advantage of this approach is numeric. Notice that the formulation of the partial likelihood is similar to the expression for the likelihood in a polychotomous logit model. The techniques we learned for the latter are hence directly applicable to the former.

It can be shown that the function $L_p(\beta)$ has an interpretation in terms of marginal likelihood. This interpretation hinges on the rank of the observations (at least in the uncensored case). This is why the estimator which we have just defined is consistent, asymptotically normal and with asymptotic precision which can be approximated by:

$$-\frac{\partial^2 \log\left[L_p\left(\tilde{\beta}\right)\right]}{\partial\beta\partial\beta'}.$$

12.8.4 Semi-Parametric Estimation when the Specification of the Base Hazard Function and of the Effect of the Exogenous Variables is Non-Parametric

Operational estimation methods may also be applied when the model includes exogenous variables and incorporates the effect of heterogeneity. We shall consider a model in which the observed variable, y – a possibly censored duration – is distributed $\ell\,(y|\,\mathbf{x}_i;\, v;\, \boldsymbol{\theta})$, parametrized by $\boldsymbol{\theta}$ and conditional on the exogenous variables $\mathbf{x}_i$ and on a measure of heterogeneity v.

The distribution of the duration, conditional only on the exogenous variables, is obtained by integrating with respect to the distribution of heterogeneity π. It is:

$$\ell\,(y|\,\mathbf{x}_i\boldsymbol{\theta};\,\pi) = \int \ell\,(y|\,\mathbf{x}_i;\, v;\, \boldsymbol{\theta})\,\pi\, dv.$$

This function depends upon two types of parameters: $\boldsymbol{\theta}$, which is a vector of real numbers, and π, which is a function.

By analogy with the usual parametric case, we may decide to develop a maximum-likelihood approach. The estimator is then defined as a solution $(\boldsymbol{\theta}, \pi)$ to the optimization problem:

$$\max_{\theta,\pi}\left\{\left(\sum_{i=1}^{n} \log\left[\ell\,(y_i|\,\mathbf{x}_i;\, \boldsymbol{\theta};\, \pi)\right]\right)\right\}$$
$$= \sum_{i=1}^{n} \log\left[\int \ell\,(y_i|\,\mathbf{x}_i;\, v;\, \boldsymbol{\theta})\,\pi\, dv\right].$$

A priori, this is a difficult optimization to perform, as it is simultaneously over a vector $\boldsymbol{\theta}$ and a distribution π. In fact, however, making use of our knowledge that distribution functions are increasing, we can establish that the solution, $\hat{\pi}$, must be a step-wise function.

Proposition 52: For a given $\boldsymbol{\theta}$ and a fixed sample size n, the maximum-likelihood estimator of the distribution π is a discrete distribution assuming at most n values.

Introducing the values v_j, $j = 1, \ldots, n$, which may be assigned weights π_j, $j = 1, \ldots, n$, our optimization is over a finite number of values:

$$\max_{\theta} \max_{v_1,\ldots,v_n} \max_{\substack{\pi_i,\pi_j \geq 0 \\ \sum_j \pi_j = 1}} \sum_{i=1}^{n} \log \left[\sum_{i=1}^{n} \ell \left(y_i | \mathbf{x}_i; v_j; \boldsymbol{\theta} \right) \pi_j \right].$$

Using simulation methods, the performance of this approach was analysed by Heckman-Singer [HS84] . They used a hazard function from the Weibull family of distributions:

$$\ell \left(y | \mathbf{x}; v; \boldsymbol{\theta} \right) = \boldsymbol{\theta}_1 y^{\boldsymbol{\theta}_1 - 1} \exp \left[\boldsymbol{\theta}_2 + v - y^{\boldsymbol{\theta}_1} \exp \left(\boldsymbol{\theta}_2 + v \right) \right],$$

without censoring and under several different distributions of heterogeneity.

This study revealed that:

(i) the estimates of $\boldsymbol{\theta}_1, \boldsymbol{\theta}_2$ are quite precise,

(ii) the estimate π of the distribution of heterogeneity is not very close to the actual distribution, even for large sample sizes.

Exercises

12.1 (a) Verify that $\frac{dr(t)}{dt} = -1 + \lambda(t) r(t)$.

(b) Find the case for which: $r(t) = \frac{1}{\lambda(t)}$, $\forall t$.

Considering that:

$$\begin{aligned} dr(t) &= -dt + \lambda(t) dtr(t), \\ &\approx -dt [1 - \lambda(t) dt] + r(t) [\lambda(t) dt], \end{aligned}$$

interpret the equality in part (ii)(a)

12.2 Consider the hazard function defined:

$$f(t) = \exp \left(a_0 + a_1 \frac{t^{b_1 - 1}}{b_1} + a_2 \frac{t^{b_2 - 1}}{b_2} \right).$$

(the Box-Cox formulation)

(a) Show that for $a_1 = 0$ and $a_2 = 0$ we have the distribution associated with exponential models.

(b) When $a_1 = 0$ and $b_2 \to 0$ it corresponds to the Weibull distribution.

(c) Which distribution is reflected by $a_1 = 0$ and $b_2 = 0$?

12.3 What constraints are imposed on the hazard function by the fact that the corresponding survival function must by downward sloping and that $S(0) = 1$ and $S(+\infty) = 0$?

12.4 Let x_1 and x_2 be independent and identically distributed variables, and let g be an increasing function.

(a) Show that $E\{[g(x_1) - g(x_2)](x_1 - x_2)\}$ is always positive.
(b) Express $E\{[g(x_1) - g(x_2)](x_1 - x_2)\}$ as a function of $\text{cov}[x_1, g(x_1)]$, and derive the positiveness of this covariance.

12.5 The following interpretation of the residuals in survival models has been proposed. Let the model be specified as: $S(\zeta_i, x_1, \theta)$, and let the maximum-likelihood estimator of θ be $\hat{\theta}$. The residual is defined as:

$$R_i = -\log\left[S\left(\zeta_i, x_1, \hat{\theta}\right)\right].$$

(a) What is the distribution of $S(\zeta_i, x_1, \theta)$? and of $-\log[S(\zeta_i, x_1, \theta)]$?
(b) Derive the distribution of $-\log\left[S\left(\zeta_i, x_1, \hat{\theta}\right)\right]$.
(c) What happens when the data are truncated and ζ_i is replaced with y_i?
(d) Does this conception of the residual seem appropriate to you?

12.6 Duration Model based on the Gamma Distribution
Consider n independent observations, $y_i, \ldots, y_n$, drawn from the distribution:

$$f(y) = \frac{a^{\nu} y^{\nu-1}}{\Gamma(\nu)} \exp(-ay).$$

(a) Verify that the model is exponential and that the canonical statistics are $\sum_{i=1}^{n} y_i$ and $\sum_{i=1}^{n} log(y_i)$.
(b) Write the likelihood equations for $\hat{a}$ (for a) and $\hat{\nu}$ (for ν). (Denote Ψ the derivative of the function Γ).
(c) Perform the change of parameters $(a, \nu) \rightarrow \left(b = \frac{\nu}{a}, \nu\right)$, and derive:

$$\hat{b} = \sum_{i=1}^{n} \frac{y_1}{n}.$$

Show that $\hat{\nu}$ satisfies an implicit function to be determined.
(d) Demonstrate that $\hat{b}$ and $\hat{\nu}$ are asymptotically uncorrelated, and that:

$$\text{var}\left(\hat{b}\right) \approx \frac{b^2}{n\nu},$$
$$\text{var}(\hat{\nu}) \approx \frac{1}{n}.$$

12.7 Consider the proportional risk model:

$$\lambda_i(t) = \exp\left[\sum_{k=1}^{K} \beta_k \log(x_{ik})\right] g(t).$$

Interpret the parameter β as the elasticity of the hazard with respect to the explanatory variable x_k.

12.8 Referring to section 12.7.3:
(a) Calculate:

$$\frac{\partial \log(\xi)}{\partial \log(b)} + \frac{\partial \log(\xi)}{\partial \log(\mu)}.$$

(b) Use this result to show that these two elasticities may not both be greater that $\frac{1}{2}$.

(c) Suggest a simple test which will allow us to reject the assumption of optimal search under some conditions.

12.9 Explain the equation for the reservation wage [cf. equation (12.26)] when the distribution function F is: exponential, Weibull, and Pareto.

12.10 Assume that the factor of heterogeneity is scalar, and that the partial mapping $v \rightarrow \lambda(t; v)$ is increasing:

(a) Show that the partial mapping: $v \rightarrow r(t; v)$ is decreasing. Interpret this result.

(b) Use the equality $r(t) = E_t r(t; v)$ and lemma 6 to establish that:

$$-\frac{dr(t)}{dt} + E_t \frac{\partial}{\partial t} r(t; v) = \text{cov}_t \left[r(t; v), \lambda(t; v) \right].$$

(c) Derive the sign of the heterogeneity bias (recall that the correlation between two increasing functions of the same random variable is always positive).

Appendix 12.1 Asymptotic Properties of ML under Ignored Heterogeneity

The study of the convergence of estimators and their limit values rests upon the search for the pseudo true values. We begin by finding these in the case of sampling, then use our result to deal with models with explanatory variables.

A12.1 The Case of Sampling ($d = 0$)

Denoting the density of the error term g_0, the (pseudo) log-likelihood is:

$$\sigma_{i=1}^{n} \log\left(g_0 \{\log[\Lambda_0(Y_i)] - c\}\right).$$

The (pseudo) maximum likelihood of c converges to a value $\bar{c}_0$ defined as:

$$\begin{aligned} &\mathrm{E}_0 \{\log[g_0(u + v + c_0 - \bar{c}_0)]\} \\ &\qquad \geq \mathrm{E}_0 \{\log[g_0(u + v + c_0 - c)]\}, \quad \forall c, \end{aligned}$$

where E_0 designates expectation with respect to the joint distribution of (u, v).

A12.2 The Case with Explanatory Variables ($d \neq 0$)

In the general case, the (pseudo) log-likelihood is:

$$\sum_{i=1}^{n} \log\left(g_0 \left\{\log\left[\Lambda_0(y_i) - c - x_i^* d\right]\right\}\right).$$

So the (pseudo) maximum-likelihood estimator of (c, d) converges to a value $\left(c_0^*, d_0^*\right)$, solution to:

$$\max_{c,d} \left[\mathrm{E}_{x^*}\left(\mathrm{E}_0 \left\{\log\left[g_0\left(u + v + c_0 - c - x^* d_0 - x^* d\right)\right]\right\}\right)\right].$$

Now, from the definition of $\bar{c}$ we have:

$$\mathrm{E}_0 \{\log[g_0(u + v + c_0 - \bar{c}_0)]\} \geq \mathrm{E}_0 \{\log[g_0(u + v + a)]\}.$$

From which we derive that, for all values (c, d):

$$\begin{aligned} &\mathrm{E}_0 \{\log [g_0 (u + v + c_0 - \bar{c}_0)]\} \\ &\qquad \geq \mathrm{E}_0 \left\{\log \left[g_0 \left(u + v + c_0 - c - x^* d_0 - x^* d\right)\right]\right\}, \end{aligned}$$

and that:

$$\begin{aligned} &\mathrm{E}_{x^*} (\mathrm{E}_0 \{\log [g_0 (u + v + c_0 - \bar{c}_0)]\}) \\ &\qquad \geq \mathrm{E}_{x^*} \left(\mathrm{E}_0 \left\{\log \left[g_0 \left(u + v + c_0 - c - x^* d_0 - x^* d\right)\right]\right\}\right). \end{aligned}$$

Assuming the uniqueness of the pseudo true value, this implies that $c_0^* = \bar{c}_0$ and $d_0^* = d_0$. In particular, we conclude that the estimator $\hat{d}_0$ converges to the true value d_0.

A12.3 Direction of the Bias of the Constant Term

The true pseudo-value $\bar{c}_0$ solves:

$$\max_{0} (\mathrm{E}_0 \{\log [g_0 (u + v + c_0 - c)]\}),$$

where $g_0 (u) = \exp (u) \exp \left[- \exp (u)\right]$. The solution $\bar{c}_0$ satisfies the first-order condition:

$$\begin{aligned} 0 = \mathrm{E} &\left[\frac{d \log [g_0 (u + v + c_0 - \bar{c}_0)]}{du}\right], \\ &= \mathrm{E}_0 \left[1 - \exp (u + v + c_0 - \bar{c}_0)\right], \\ &= 1 - \mathrm{E}_0 \left[\exp (u)\right] \mathrm{E}_0 \left[\exp (v)\right] \exp (c_0 - \bar{c}_0), \\ &= 1 - \mathrm{E}_0 \left[\exp (v)\right] \exp (c_0 - \bar{c}_0), \\ &\quad \text{since} \quad \mathrm{E}_0 \left[\exp (u)\right] = 1 \end{aligned}$$

$$\mathrm{E}_0 \left[\exp (v)\right] = \exp (\bar{c}_0 - c_0).$$

Because of convexity, $\exp (\bar{c}_0 - c_0) \geq \exp [\mathrm{E}_0 (v)] = 1$, since the mean of v is zero.

Bibliography

[AB74] T. Amemiya and M. Boskin. Regression analysis when the dependent variable is truncated lognormal, with an application to the determination of the duration of welfare dependency. *International Economic Review*, 15:485, 1974.

[AG57] T. W. Anderson and L. Goodman. Statistical inference about markov chains. *Journal of the American Mathematical Society*, 28:89, 1957.

[Aki74] M. Ben Akiva. Multidimensional choice models: Alternative structures of travel demand models. *Transportation Research Record*, page 568, 1974.

[Ame76] T. Amemiya. The m.l., the minimum chi-square and the non-linear weighted least squares estimator in the general qualitative response model. *Journal of the American Statistical Association*, 71:347, 1976.

[Ame77] T. Amemiya. The modified second round estimator in the general qualitative response model. *Journal of Econometrics*, 5:295, 1977.

[Ame78] T. Amemiya. On a two step estimation of a multivariate logit model. *Journal of Econometrics*, 8:13, 1978.

[And84] J. A. Anderson. Regression and ordered categorical variables. *Journal: Royal Statistical Society - Series B.*, page 1, 1984.

[AS70] J. Ashford and R. Sowden. Multivariate probit analysis. *Biometrics*, 26:535, 1970.

[Ber44] J. Berkson. Application of the logistic function to bio-assay. *Journal of the American Statistical Association*, 39:357, 1944.

[Ber51] J. Berkson. Why I prefer logit to probit. *Biometrics*, 7:327, 1951.

[BHM86] R. Blundell, J. C. Ham, and C. Meghir. Unemployment and female labour supply. *Economic Journal, The*, 1986.

[BLV86] M. Bouissou, J. J. Laffont, and Q. Vuong. Disequilibrium econometrics on microdata. *Review of Economic Studies*, 172:113, 1986.

[Boy73] R. Boyles. On the convergence of the e.m. algorithm. *Journal: Royal Statistical Society - Series B.*, 45:47, 1973.

[CI87] A. D. Chesher and A. Irish. Residual analysis in the grouped and censored normal linear model. *Annals of Econometrics*, 1987.

[CL83] A. D. Chesher and T. Lancaster. An econometric analysis of reservation wages. *Econometrica*, 51:1661, 1983.

[Cos81] S. Cosslett. Maximum likelihood estimator for choice based samples. *Econometrica*, 49:1289, 1981.

[Cra46] Harald Cramer. *Mathematical Methods of Statistics*. Princeton University Press, 1946.

[DLR77] A. Dempster, N. Laird, and D. Rubin. Maximum likelihood from incomplete data via the e.m. algorithm. *Journal: Royal Statistical Society - Series B.*, 39:1, 1977.

[DM81] R. Davidson and J. MacKinnon. Several tests for model specification in the presence of alternative hypothesis. *Econometrica*, 49:781, 1981.

[FJ72] R. Fair and D. M. Jaffee. Methods of estimation for markets in disequilibrium. *Econometrica*, 40:497, 1972.

[GHH84] Z. Griliches, B. Hall, and J. Hausman. Econometric methods for counting data with an application to the patents, r&d relationship. *Econometrica*, 1984.

[Gil79] C. Gilbert. Econometric models for discrete economic processes, 1979.

[GL85] Christian Gourieroux and G. Laroque. The aggregation of commodities in quantity rationing models. *International Economic Review*, 26:681, 1985.

[GLM80] Christian Gourieroux, J. J. Laffont, and A. Monfort. Test of the equlibrium vs. disequilibrium hypothesis, a comment. *International Economic Review*, 1980.

[GM81] Christian Gourieroux and A. Monfort. Asymptotic properties of the maximum likelihood estimator in dichotomous logit models. *Journal of Econometrics*, 17:83, 1981.

[GMRT86] Christian Gourieroux, A. Monfort, E. Renault, and A. Trognon. Generalized residuals. *Annals of Econometrics*, 1986.

[GMT80] Christian Gourieroux, A. Monfort, and A. Trognon. Pseudo maximum likelihood methods: Application to poisson models. *Econometrica*, 1980.

[GMT85] Christian Gourieroux, A. Monfort, and A. Trognon. (1985), "Moindres Carrés Asymptotiques", *Annales de l'INSEE*, 58, 91–122.

[Hab74] S. Haberman. *The Analysis of Frequency Data*. University of Chicago Press, 1974.

[Hec76] J. Heckman. The common structure of statistical models of truncation, sample selection and limited dependent variables and a simple estimator for such models. *Annals of Economic and Social Measurement*, 5:475, 1976.

[Hec78] J. Heckman. Simple statistical models for discrete panel data. *Annales de l'INSEE*, 30-31:227, 1978.

[HM84] J. Hausman and Daniel McFadden. A specification test for the multinomial logit model. *Econometrica*, 52:1219, 1984.

[HS84] J. Heckman and B. Singer. The identifiability of the proportional hazard model. *Review of Economic Studies*, page 231, 1984.

[Jen69] R. Jennrich. Asymptotic properties of nonlinear least squares estimators. *Journal of the American Mathematical Society*, 40:633, 1969.

[Joh84] John Johnston. *Econometric Methods*. McGraw-Hill, Inc., 1984.

[KMM76] M. Kohn, Charles F. Manski, and D. Mundel. An empirical investigation of factors which influence college going behavior. *Annals of Economic and Social Measurement*, 5:391, 1976.

[KMZ83] S. Kawasaki, J. McMillan, and K. Zimmerman. Inventories and price inflexibility. *Econometrica*, 154, 1983.

[KN81] N. Kiefer and G. Neumann. Individual effects in a nonlinear model: Explicit treatment of heterogeneity in the empirical job-search model. *Econometrica*, 49:965, 1981.

[KS86] R. Klein and R. Spady. Semiparametric estimation of the binary outcome model, 1986.

[KNO81] H. König, M. Nerlove, and G. Oudiz. On the formation of price expectations: an analysis of business test data by log-linear probability models. *European Economic Review*, 16:103, 1981.

[Lan76] T. Lancaster. Prediction of poisson values, 1976.

[Lan79] T. Lancaster. Econometric methods for the duration of unemployment. *Econometrica*, 47:939, 1979.

[Man75] Charles F. Manski. Maximum score estimation of the stochastic utility model of choice. *Journal of Econometrics*, 3:205, 1975.

[Man85] Charles F. Manski. Semi-parametric analysis of discrete response: Asymptotic properties of the maximum score estimator. *Journal of Econometrics*, 27:313, 1985.

[McF74] Daniel McFadden. Conditional logit analysis of qualitative choice behavior. In Paul Zarembka, editor, *Frontiers in Econometrics*, page 105. American Elsevier Publishing Company, Inc., 1974.

[McF76] Daniel McFadden. Quantal choice analysis: a survey. *Annals of Economic and Social Measurement*, 5:363, 1976.

[McR77] E. McRae. Estimation of time varying markov processes with aggregate data. *Econometrica*, 45:183, 1977.

[MN75] G. S. Maddala and F. Nelson. Specification errors in limited dependent variables models, 1975.

[Mor79] K. Morimune. Comparisons of normal and logistic models in the bivariate dichotomous analysis. *Econometrica*, 47:957, 1979.

[MR70] L. Miller and R. Radner. Demand and supply in u.s. higher education: A progress report. *American Economic Review*, 60, 1970.

[Ner83] M. Nerlove. Expectations, plans and realizations in theory and practice. *Econometrica*, 51:1251, 1983.

[NN86] W. Narendranathan and S. Nickell. In R. Blundell and Walker, editors, *Unemployment Search and Labour Supply*. American Elsevier Publishing Company, Inc., 1986.

[Poi77] Dale Poirier. A curious relationship between probit and logit models, 1977.

[Poi80] Dale Poirier. A lagrange multiplier test for skewness in binary logit models. *Economic Letters*, 5:141, 1980.

[Rob82] P. Robinson. On the asymptotic properties of estimators of models containing limited dependent variables. *Econometrica*, 50:27, 1982.

[Ron86] G. Ronning. The informational content of responses from business surveys. Toulouse University, 1986. from: Conference on Applied Microeconometrics.

[Ruu83] P. Ruud. Sufficient conditions for the consistency of maximum likelihood estimation despite mispecification of distribution in multinomial discrete choice models. *Econometrica*, 51:225, 1983.

[Say73] G. M. El Sayad. Bayesian and classical analysis of poisson regression. *Journal: Royal Statistical Society - Series B.*, page 445, 1973.

[Sch78] P. Schmidt. Constraints on the parameters in simultaneous tobit and probit models, 1978.

[SY81] D. Stapelton and D. Young. Censored normal regression with measurement error on the dependent variable, 1981.

[The71] Henri Theil. *Principles of econometrics*. John Wiley & Sons, 1971.

[Tob58] J. Tobin. Estimation of relationships for limited dependent variables. *Econometrica*, 26:24, 1958.

[Tve72a] A. Tversky. Choice by elimination. *Journal of Mathematical Psychology*, 9:341, 1972.

[Tve72b] A. Tversky. Elimination by aspects: A theory of choice. *Psychology Review*, 79:281, 1972.

[Tve77] A. Tversky. Features of similarity. *Psychology Review*, 84:327, 1977.

Index

CPSIA information can be obtained at www.ICGtesting.com
Printed in the USA
LVOW10s0648300514

387915LV00005B/49/P